First World War
and Army of Occupation
War Diary
France, Belgium and Germany

19 DIVISION
Divisional Troops
Royal Army Medical Corps
57 Field Ambulance
14 August 1915 - 21 May 1919

WO95/2072/1

The Naval & Military Press Ltd
www.nmarchive.com
Published in association with The National Archives

Published by

The Naval & Military Press Ltd

Unit 10 Ridgewood Industrial Park,

Uckfield, East Sussex,

TN22 5QE England

Tel: +44 (0) 1825 749494

www.naval-military-press.com

www.nmarchive.com

This diary has been reprinted in facsimile from the original. Any imperfections are inevitably reproduced and the quality may fall short of modern type and cartographic standards.

Contents

Document type	Place/Title	Date From	Date To
Heading	19 Divn 57 Field Ambulance 1915 July-1919 May		
Heading	19th Division 57th Field Ambnce Jly 1915-1919 May		
Heading	19th. Division 57th. Field Ambulance Vol: I 14th-31st July 15		
Miscellaneous	O.C. Bn 57 Field Ambulance 19 E Division.		
Heading	19th. Division 57th Field Ambulance Vol: II From 1-31.8.15		
Miscellaneous	Sunday August 1st 1915.		
War Diary	Robermetz	14/08/1915	30/08/1915
War Diary	Bois De Pacaut	31/08/1915	31/08/1915
Heading	19th Division 57th Field Ambulance Vol III Sept 15.		
War Diary	Bois De Pacaut	01/09/1915	30/09/1915
Heading	19th Division 57th Field Ambulance Vol 4 Oct 15		
War Diary	Bois De Pacaut	01/10/1915	02/10/1915
War Diary	Zelobes	03/10/1915	19/10/1915
War Diary	Locon	20/10/1915	30/10/1915
War Diary	Aveluy Post	27/10/1916	30/10/1916
War Diary	Locon	31/10/1915	31/10/1915
Heading	19th Division 57th. F.A. Vol: 5 Nov 1915		
War Diary	Locon	01/11/1915	24/11/1915
War Diary	Robecq	25/11/1915	30/11/1915
Heading	19th Div 57th. F.A. Vol: 6 December 1915 No. 57 F.A.		
War Diary	Robecq	01/12/1915	04/12/1915
War Diary	Vielle Chapelle	05/12/1915	31/12/1915
Heading	19th Div F/157/2 57th. F.A. Vol: Jan 1916		
War Diary	Vieille Chapelle	01/01/1916	21/01/1916
War Diary	Robecq	22/01/1916	31/01/1916
Heading	Feb 1916. 57th Fld. Anbulance		
Heading	57th F.A. 19th Div Vol 8		
War Diary	Robecq	01/02/1916	15/02/1916
War Diary	Merville	16/02/1916	29/02/1916
Heading	March 1916 57. F. Amb Vol 9		
War Diary	Merville	01/03/1916	31/03/1916
Heading	April 1916 19th Div No. 57 F. Amb.	09/06/1916	09/06/1916
War Diary	Merville	01/04/1916	17/04/1916
War Diary	Busnes	18/04/1916	18/04/1916
War Diary	Cottes T.11602	19/04/1916	20/04/1916
War Diary	Cottes	21/04/1916	30/04/1916
Heading	19th Div. No. 57 F. Amb. May 1916	26/06/1916	26/06/1916
War Diary	Cottes	01/05/1916	07/05/1916
War Diary	La Chaussee	08/05/1916	31/05/1916
Heading	June 1916. No. 57 F.A.	05/08/1916	05/08/1916
War Diary	La Chaussee	01/06/1916	14/06/1916
War Diary	Rainneville	15/06/1916	15/06/1916
War Diary	Lavieville	16/06/1916	30/06/1916
Heading	19th. Division No. 57. Field Ambulance July. 1916		
Miscellaneous	A.D.M.S. 19 Div.	01/08/1916	01/08/1916
War Diary	Lavieville	01/07/1916	03/07/1916
War Diary	Albert	04/07/1916	09/07/1916
War Diary	Henencourt Wood	10/07/1916	19/07/1916

War Diary	Albert	20/07/1916	30/07/1916
War Diary	Behencourt	31/07/1916	31/07/1916
Heading	19th Div. Of 57 Field Ambulance R.A.M.C. From 1.8.16 To 31.8.16 (Volume No. 14)	09/10/1916	09/10/1916
War Diary	Behencourt	01/08/1916	02/08/1916
War Diary	Ailly Le Haut Clocher	03/08/1916	06/08/1916
War Diary	Schaeschen	07/08/1916	07/08/1916
War Diary	Locre	08/08/1916	31/08/1916
Heading	19th. Div. 57th. Field Ambulance Sept. 1916		
Miscellaneous	A.D.M.S. 19th Division	01/10/1916	01/10/1916
Heading	War Diary Of 57th Field Ambulance R.A.M.C. From 1.9.16 To 30.9.16 (Volume No. 15)		
War Diary	Locre	01/09/1916	06/09/1916
War Diary	Pont Nieppe	07/09/1916	20/09/1916
War Diary	Strazeele	21/09/1916	30/09/1916
Heading	19th Div 57th. Field Ambulance Oct. 1916		
Heading	War Diary Of 57th Field Ambulance R.A.M.C. For Period 1st. October 1916 To 31st October 1916 (Volume No 16)		
War Diary	Strazeele	01/10/1916	04/10/1916
War Diary	Doullens	05/10/1916	05/10/1916
War Diary	Couin	06/10/1916	16/10/1916
War Diary	Warloy	17/10/1916	31/10/1916
Heading	19th Div 57th Field Ambulance From 1.11.16 To 30.11.16 (Volume No. 17)		
Miscellaneous	A.D.M.S 19th Division	01/12/1916	01/12/1916
War Diary	Warloy	01/11/1916	24/11/1916
War Diary	Candas	25/11/1916	25/11/1916
War Diary	Vacquerie	26/11/1916	30/11/1916
Heading	18th Div. 57th. Field Ambulance. Dec. 1916	31/01/1917	31/01/1917
Heading	War Diary Of 57th Field Ambulance R.A.M.C. For Period 1st December 1916 To 31st December 1916.		
Miscellaneous	A.D.M.S. 19th December	01/01/1917	01/01/1917
War Diary	Vacquerie	01/12/1916	31/12/1916
Heading	19th Div. 57th. Field Ambulance. Jan 1917		
Heading	War Diary Of 57th Field Ambulance R.A.M.C. For Period 1st January 1917 To 31st January 1917. (Vol 19)		
War Diary	Vacquerie	01/01/1917	08/01/1917
War Diary	Beauquesne	09/01/1917	09/01/1917
War Diary	Coigneaux	10/01/1917	31/01/1917
Heading	19th. Div. 57th. Field Ambulance. Feb. 1917	04/04/1917	04/04/1917
War Diary	Coigneaux	01/02/1917	20/02/1917
War Diary	Louvencourt	21/02/1917	28/02/1917
Heading	19th. Div. 57th Field Ambulance. Mar. 1917.	11/05/1917	11/05/1917
War Diary	Louvencourt	01/03/1917	08/03/1917
War Diary	Bretel	09/03/1917	09/03/1917
War Diary	Ligny Sur Canche	10/03/1917	11/03/1917
War Diary	Siracourt	12/03/1917	12/03/1917
War Diary	Sains Les Pernes	13/03/1917	14/03/1917
War Diary	Livossart	15/03/1917	15/03/1917
War Diary	Kivossart	16/03/1917	17/03/1917
War Diary	Isbergues	18/03/1917	18/03/1917
War Diary	Lynde	19/03/1917	19/03/1917
War Diary	Recques	20/03/1917	31/03/1917
Heading	19th. Div. No. 57. F.A. April. 1917.	06/06/1917	06/06/1917
War Diary	Recques	01/04/1917	01/04/1917

War Diary	Wizernes	02/04/1917	03/04/1917
War Diary	La Wattine	04/04/1917	16/04/1917
War Diary	Hallines	17/04/1917	17/04/1917
War Diary	Le Cinq Rues	18/04/1917	18/04/1917
War Diary	Berthen	19/04/1917	30/04/1917
Heading	19th. Div. No 57 F.A. May. 1917	10/07/1917	10/07/1917
Heading	War Diary No 57 Field Ambulance 19th Division Vol XXIII May 1st To 31st 1917		
War Diary	Vlamertinghe	01/05/1917	10/05/1917
War Diary	Berthen	11/05/1917	21/05/1917
War Diary	Westoutre	22/05/1917	31/05/1917
Heading	War Diary No 57 Fd Amb Vol XXIV June 1st-30th. (Volume)		
War Diary	Westoutre	01/06/1917	12/06/1917
War Diary	Locre	13/06/1917	18/06/1917
War Diary	Mt Kokereele	19/06/1917	30/06/1917
Heading	No. 57 F.A. July. 1917	10/09/1917	10/09/1917
Heading	War Diary No 57 Fd Amb Vol XXV July 1917		
War Diary	Mt Kokereele	01/07/1917	01/07/1917
War Diary	Locre	02/07/1917	31/07/1917
Heading	No. 57. F.A. Aug. 1917	01/10/1917	01/10/1917
War Diary	Locre	01/08/1917	07/08/1917
War Diary	Mont Kokerele	08/08/1917	09/08/1917
War Diary	Quesques	10/08/1917	10/08/1917
War Diary	Alincthun Chateau	11/08/1917	27/08/1917
War Diary	Ey Houck	28/08/1917	28/08/1917
War Diary	Strazeele	29/08/1917	31/08/1917
Heading	No. 57. F.A. Sept. 1917.	05/11/1917	05/11/1917
War Diary	Strazeele	01/09/1917	05/09/1917
War Diary	Tyrone Farm S of M36 A. 9.4 Sheet 2.8	06/09/1917	07/09/1917
War Diary	Tyrone Farm Dranoutre	08/09/1917	11/09/1917
War Diary	Locre	12/09/1917	30/09/1917
Heading	No. 57. F.A. Oct. 1917.	08/12/1917	08/12/1917
Heading	War Diary Of No. 57 Field Ambulance. From. 1.10.17 To 31.10.17 Volume. No 28.		
War Diary	Locre	01/10/1917	31/10/1917
Heading	War Diary Of 57th. Field Ambulance R.A.M.C. From 1-11-17 To 30-11-17. Volume 28. Nov. 1917	17/01/1918	17/01/1918
War Diary	Locre	01/11/1917	09/11/1917
War Diary	Strazeele	10/11/1917	10/11/1917
War Diary	Ebblingham	11/11/1917	30/11/1917
Heading	War Diary Of 57th Field Ambulance. R.A.M.C. From 1-12-17 To 31-12-17. Volume 30. Dec 1917		
War Diary	Eblinghem	01/12/1917	06/12/1917
War Diary	Arques	07/12/1917	07/12/1917
War Diary	Gomiecourt	08/12/1917	08/12/1917
War Diary	Etricourt	09/12/1917	09/12/1917
War Diary	Metz-En-Couture	10/12/1917	15/12/1917
War Diary	Bus	16/12/1917	31/12/1917
Heading	War Diary Of 57th Field Ambulance. R.A.M.C. From 1-1-18 To 31-1-18 Volume 31 Jan. 1918		
War Diary	Bus	01/01/1918	31/01/1918
Heading	War Diary Of 57 Field Ambulance. R.A.M.C. From-1-2-18 To 28-2-18 Volume 32. Feb. 1918		
War Diary	Bus	01/02/1918	28/02/1918

Heading	War Diary. Of 57 Field Ambulance. R.A.M.C. From 1-3-18 To 31-3-18 Volume 32 Mar. 1918		
War Diary	Bus	01/03/1918	05/03/1918
War Diary	Sanders Camp (Haplincourt)	06/03/1918	20/03/1918
War Diary	Map Sheet 57 C Sq I35 B 8-3	21/03/1918	22/03/1918
War Diary	Loch Camp Fremicourt	22/03/1918	23/03/1918
War Diary	H 35 D Bancourt		
War Diary	Brickfields Sq No 29	23/03/1918	24/03/1918
War Diary	Grevillers	25/03/1918	25/03/1918
War Diary	Miramount Goods Stn	25/03/1918	25/03/1918
War Diary	Bucquoy	25/03/1918	25/03/1918
War Diary	Hebuterne	26/03/1918	26/03/1918
War Diary	Couterelle	26/03/1918	28/03/1918
War Diary	Candas	29/03/1918	29/03/1918
War Diary	Dranoutre	30/03/1918	31/03/1918
Heading	War Diary Of 57 Field Ambulance. R.A.M.C. From 1-4-18 To 30-4-18 Volume 34 Confidential April 1918.		
War Diary	Dranoutre	01/04/1918	01/04/1918
War Diary	Ravelsberg Camp	02/04/1918	07/04/1918
War Diary	Ravelsberg	08/04/1918	10/04/1918
War Diary	Hagedorne	11/04/1918	11/04/1918
War Diary	Berthen	12/04/1918	14/04/1918
War Diary	Remy Siding	15/04/1918	30/04/1918
Heading	No. 57 F.A. May 1918.		
Heading	War Diary Of 57 Field Ambulance. R.A.M.C. From 1-5-18 To 31-5-18 Volume 35.		
War Diary	Remy Siding	01/05/1918	01/05/1918
War Diary	Waratah Camp	02/05/1918	02/05/1918
War Diary	Waratah	03/05/1918	05/05/1918
War Diary	Waratah Camp	06/05/1918	12/05/1918
War Diary	Mendinghem	13/05/1918	18/05/1918
War Diary	Aulnay L'Aitre	19/05/1918	28/05/1918
War Diary	Chaumuzy	29/05/1918	31/05/1918
Heading	War Diary Of 57th Field Ambulance R.A.M.C. From 1-6-18 To 30-6-18 Volume 36. June 1918.	07/08/1918	07/08/1918
War Diary	Bours Ault	01/06/1918	03/06/1918
War Diary	Disc-Magenta	04/06/1918	20/06/1918
War Diary	La Mesnil	21/06/1918	21/06/1918
War Diary	Reuves	22/06/1918	30/06/1918
Heading	War Diary Of 57th Field Ambulance. R.A.M.C. From 1-9-18 To 31-9-18 Volume 37 July 1918.		
War Diary	Broussy Le Grand	01/07/1918	03/07/1918
War Diary	Rumilly	04/07/1916	06/07/1916
War Diary	Amettes	13/06/1918	31/07/1918
Heading	War Diary Of 57th Field Ambulance. R.A.M.C. From 1-8-18 To 31-8-18 Volume. 38. Aug. 1918.		
War Diary	Amettes	01/08/1918	06/08/1918
War Diary	Bois Des Dames	07/08/1918	26/08/1918
War Diary	Pont De Reville	27/08/1918	31/08/1918
Heading	War Diary Of 57 Field Ambulance.R.A.M.C. From 1-9-18 To 30-9-18 Volume 39 Sept. 1918		
War Diary	Pont De Reville	01/09/1918	04/09/1918
War Diary	Ammezin	05/09/1918	30/09/1918
Heading	War Diary. Of. 57 Field Ambulance From 1-10-18 To 31-10-18 Volume. 40 Oct 1918		
War Diary	Ammezin	01/10/1918	03/10/1918

War Diary	Anchel	04/10/1918	04/10/1918
War Diary	Saulty	05/10/1918	07/10/1918
War Diary	Bapauiee Camplain	08/10/1918	09/10/1918
War Diary	Rumilly	10/10/1918	12/10/1918
War Diary	Caum des	13/10/1918	16/10/1918
War Diary	Avesues	17/10/1918	28/10/1918
War Diary	Cayn on des	29/10/1918	31/10/1918
Heading	War Diary Of 57th Field Ambulance. R.A.M.C. From 1-11-18 To 30-11-18 Volume 41. Nov. 1918		
War Diary	Cayn on des	01/11/1918	01/11/1918
War Diary	Vendegies	02/11/1918	03/11/1918
War Diary	Preseau	04/11/1918	04/11/1918
War Diary	Jenlain	05/11/1918	05/11/1918
War Diary	Bray	06/11/1918	07/11/1918
War Diary	St Vaast	08/11/1918	08/11/1918
War Diary	Faronieres	09/11/1918	12/11/1918
War Diary	Major laer Le Pehit	13/11/1918	16/11/1918
War Diary	Rieux	17/11/1918	30/11/1918
Heading	War Diary of 57 Field Ambulance For December 1918. Volume 41		
War Diary	Cambrai	01/12/1918	01/12/1918
War Diary	Favrel	02/12/1918	02/12/1918
War Diary	Havernas	03/12/1918	09/12/1918
War Diary	Noeux	17/12/1918	31/12/1918
Miscellaneous	Sanitary Report Of A.D.M.S. 19th Division For Month Of December. 1918.		
Miscellaneous	Os.C. Field Ambulance. M.Cs. i/c Units.	27/12/1918	27/12/1918
Heading	19 Div Box 1795 War Diary Of J57 Field Ambulance. R.A.M.C. From 1-1-19 To 31-1-19 Volume 43. Jan 1919		
War Diary	Noeux	01/01/1919	30/01/1919
Heading	War. Diary. Of 57 Field Ambulance RAMC From 1-2-19 To 28-2-19 Volume. 44. Feb. 1919		
War Diary	Noeux	01/02/1919	28/02/1919
Heading	War Diary. Of 57 Field Ambulance From 1-3-19 To 31-3-19 Volume. 45. Feb. 1919		
War Diary	Noeux	01/03/1919	24/03/1919
War Diary	Villers L'Hopital	25/03/1919	31/03/1919
Heading	No Diary For April 1919		
Heading	War Diary Of Field Ambulance. From 1-5-19 To 21-5-19 Volume 47. Completed		
War Diary	Villers Hopital	01/05/1919	21/05/1919

19 DIVN

57 FIELD AMBULANCE

1915 JULY – 1919 MAY

19TH DIVISION

57TH FIELD AMBNCE

JLY 1915-~~DEC 1918~~ 1919 MAY

19th Division

121/6243

57th Field Ambulance

Vol: I

14th - 31st July '15

Dec '18

Confidential.

War Diary. By
O.C.
57th Field Ambulance
19th Division.

Sling Camp Bulford July 14th 1915.

Received orders at 7 p.m. for embarkation of the Unit on Friday the 16th inst. Also time table & details of entrainment in two trains from Amesbury Station. Issued orders for final inspection and completion of men's overseas kits, to-morrow, also the packing of the Wagons. Worked out the details of the Personnel & transport for entrainment in the two trains.

J.E. Powell Major
R.A.M.C.

July 15th 1915. Packed all wagons ready for to-morrow. Issued remainder of overseas kit to men, also active Service Pay books. Closed all accounts and returned cash books to Regimental Paymaster.
Sent cheques for Bank balances to Cashier Southern Command.

J.E.P.

July 16th 1915. Southampton Docks.

The whole Ambulance marched out from Sling Camp at 6·15 a.m. entrained at Amesburg and arrived here at 10·20 a.m. The Personnel and transport of the ambulance were divided up into three parties and embarked in the following ships

"City of Dunkirk"
"Architect"
+ "Duchess of Argyle"

The two former ships sailed at 6·30 p.m. but the latter ship has been detained until to-morrow as the weather is too rough for such a small ship. — J.E.P.

July 17th 1915.

We sailed from Southampton at 5·15 p.m. and arrived at Havre at 12 Midnight after a good voyage No carnalthies occurred on the voyage. J.E.P.

July 18th 1915. Havre

We disembarked at Havre at 7 a.m. and marched to Camp 5 having first joined up with the one Officer and 19 men of the A.S.C, 9 Waggons, one Cycle and 27 horses from the S.S. "City of Dunkirk" — On arrival at Camp 5 we found the remainder of the ambulance had arrived the previous day — The Unit is now complete. J.E.P.

July 19th '15. We entrained at Havre at 15 o'clock at Point No 1 Gare marchandises in addition to the Field Ambulance a detachment of the 5th South Wales Borderers also entrained in the same train. We left Havre at 18.59 o'clock and the R.T.O. handed me a movement order and Time Table as far as Les Fontenettes. J.E.P.

July 20th '15. The train arrived at Audruicq at 1 p.m. which was the Regulating Station. At this Station I received orders to detrain the Field Ambulance at St. Omer, also the situation of my billetting area. – The train arrived at St. Omer at 2.30 p.m. & the whole Field Ambulance detrained in one hour. – The unit then marched out 7½ miles to its billetting areas at Barlinghem and MORINGHEM arriving at 6 p.m. The unit is now attached to the 57th Brigade. J.E.P.

July 21st '15. – The A.D.M.S. 19th Division visited the Ambulance this morning and issued orders for the evacuation of the Sick to No. 10 Stationary Hospital St. Omer. Arrangements with regard to Water Supply & Latrine accommodation were completed. J.E.P.

Wednesday July 21st 1915. (continued). The G.O.C. 57th Brigade, visited the ambulance and ordered a cycle orderly to be attached permanently to his Headquarters to carry all orders from the Brigade to the Ambulance.
J.E.P.

Thursday July 22nd 1915. MORINGHEM
The Field ambulance is still resting here. I received orders at 5.45 a.m. from the Brigade Major 57th Brigade to have my Field Ambulance ready for an early move to-morrow morning. – I therefore took measures accordingly.
J.E.P.

Friday July 23rd 1915.
I received orders at 3.30 a.m. that the 57th Brigade group which includes the 57th Field ambulance would march to-day to RENESCURE the head of the column to pass the starting point at 10 a.m. – The 57th Field Ambulance reached RENESCURE at 6.30 p.m. where we were billeted for the night. Received Brigade orders at 11.55 p.m. to march to-morrow ~~at~~ to the neighbourhood of AIRE. Head of the column to pass the starting point at 8 a.m.
J.E.P.

Saturday July 24th 1915. The Ambulance marched out from RENESCURE at 8 a.m. this morning There was a Mid-day halt from 11 a.m. to 12·30 p.m. The Field Ambulance arrived in its Billet at 2 p.m. The Billet is a large farm to the West of AIRE, distant about 2 miles from the town. J.E.P.

Sunday July 25th 1915. The Field Ambulance is resting in its billet to-day. – No orders have yet been received with regard to our next march. A few cases of Sickness from the 57th Brigade units have been to-day evacuated to the Lucknow Casualty Clearing Station at AIRE. J.E.P.

Monday July 26th 1915. The Ambulance is still resting here, the 57th Brigade has not yet moved out from their billets – We continue to receive small numbers of Sick from the Brigade units, most of whom we evacuate to the Lucknow Casualty Clearing Station. General Sir Douglas Haig visited the Ambulance this evening! J.E.P.

Tuesday July 27th 15. The Tent Subdivisions of each Section were practised this morning in preparing to deal with urgent Surgical cases requiring operation. The A.D.M.S. 19th Division visited the Ambulance this morning and stated he would inspect the Ambulance at work at 3 p.m. on Thursday the 29th inst.
7 Motor Ambulances and one Motor cycle arrived last night. – Our Transport is now complete. J.E.P.

Wednesday July 28th 15. The Unit still remains in the same billets, the men are sleeping in large barns full of straw. The weather continues fine with a few showers and rather a high wind. – No orders of importance have been received to-day. – There is a plentiful supply of water here but I have it all sterilized by boiling or by the bleaching powders in the Water Carts. J.E.P.

Thursday July 29th 15. The A.D.M.S. 19th Division inspected the Ambulance at Field work and preparing to deal with urgent Surgical cases. At the end of the inspection he said it was very satisfactory! – Received orders at 6.40 p.m. from the 19th Division to be out of these billets by 8 a.m. to-morrow to make room for the R.F. Corps who are coming in. J.E.P.

Friday July 30th '15. Received orders from Headquarters 57th Brigade to march to HARTEVENTE to pass the Starting point at 9·30 a.m. arrived in our billets at 1 p.m.
Received Brigade orders to march to-morrow to billets at ROBERMETZ East of MERVILLE, head of the column to pass the starting point at 1·15 p.m. The weather has been fine & warm, the roads dusty. The men are billeted in Farm barns. J.E.P.

Saturday July 31st '15. The Field Ambulance marched from HARTEVENT at 12·30 p.m and arrived in their billets at 4 p.m. The accommodation for Officers and men is insufficient and nearly all the Officers are sleeping out. The water also is some distance away. The weather continues fine. The roads are rough and dusty. The Position of our billets is Square L 25 A 7 7 On Map Sheet 36 A.

J.E. Powell
Major RAMC
O.C. 57th Field Ambulance

19th Division

121/8607

Aug '15

57th Field Ambulance

Vol: II.

From 1-31. 8. 15

Sunday August 1st 1915. The Ambulance was visited by Colonel Pike D.S.O. DDMS Indian Army Corps & Colonel Birt ADMS 19th Division to-day. – I was ordered to pitch tents & open out to receive the Sick from the Brigade. – The Billets are not considered satisfactory, the accommodation is too limited & the water supply is some distance away and not good. J.E.P.

Monday August 2nd 1915. Lieutenant General Sir James Willcocks inspected the Ambulance drawn up in Column of Route on the road this morning at 12.30 p.m. – I sent two Ambulance Waggons to collect the sick of the Brigade this morning & have had all the Circular tents pitched. J.E.P.

Tuesday August 3rd 1915. The 57th Infantry Brigade marched to Estaire this morning. I received orders to remove 82 men to Estaire who were unable to march. I sent all my ambulance transport to Brigade Headquarters by 10 a.m. for this purpose. – I am also receiving the sick from the Brigade. J.E.P.

Wednesday August 4th 1915. The Unit still remains halted in the same billets and we continue to collect the sick of the 57th Brigade group. It rained heavily last night, but is fine this morning and the ground is drying rapidly. Received orders to take the Bearer Division Officers with me and to attach ourselves to No 7 British Field Ambulance, Lahore Division at 9.30 a.m. to-morrow for 24 hours. J.E.P.

Thursday August 5th 1915. I reported with my three Bearer Division Officers at No. 7 British Field Ambulance La Gorgue at 9.30 a.m. and we were shewn the normal working of the Ambulance dealing with Sick & Wounded – Also the system of Sanitation in force. – In the afternoon we visited their advanced Dressing Station and at night went into the trenches to establish communication with the Regimental Aid Posts. Their Advanced Dressing Station is about one mile behind the trenches. – In my absence the D.D.M.S. Indian Army Corps inspected the 57th Field Ambulance encampment.

J.E.P.

Friday August 6th 1915. I returned with the three Bearer Division Officers to the 57th Field Ambulance this morning. The 57th Field Ambulance has from to-day been detached from the 57th Infantry Brigade and attached to the 56th Infantry Brigade. The weather is wet, heavy heavy showers of rain falling. I paid out to the men this evening. J.E.P.

Saturday August 7th 1915. The weather is dull and cloudy. We are still in the same billets and collecting sick from both the 57th Brigade + a part of the 56th Brigade. I went in to the Maire of MERVILLE this afternoon and rendered billeting certificates for the week. J.E.P.

Sunday August 8th 1915. The weather continues dull and showery. A voluntary church service for all denominations in the Unit was held this morning in one of the Barns of our Billeting area. - Circulars were received from the D.D.M.S. of the Corps with regard to the destruction of flies + also the situation, construction + working of Aid Posts + Advanced Dressing Stations. J.E.P.

Monday August 9th 1915. The weather was hot & oppressive in the morning, ending in rain in the afternoon. Flies are becoming very prevalent now, measures have been taken as far as possible to destroy their breeding places, & all refuse & manure is being burnt in incinerators. J.E.P.

Tuesday August 10th 1915. The weather continues hot and oppressive. Sent Lieutenant ADRIAN St. JOHNSTON R.A.M.C. of this Ambulance to No 2 London Casualty Clearing Station last evening with Pyrexia U.O. probably Influenza. Also sent to the same Casualty Clearing Station Captain J A RITSON of the 7th South Lancashire Regt suffering from acute appendicitis. J.E.P.

Wednesday August 11th 1915. The Ambulance has cleared a large number of sick from both the 56th and 57th Infantry Brigades throughout the day. The weather continues fine and warm. Flies are very prevalent, all food and provisions are protected with gauze. – All manure and refuse is being burnt, and "tangle-foot" papers are being used for the destruction of flies. J.E.P.

Thursday August 12th 1915. The weather continues fine. – amongst the sick evacuated yesterday was one case of a dislocated hip & one case of fractured radius – The prevailing disease was diarrhoea. The Ambulance ceases to collect sick from the 57th Brigade from to-morrow, and collect only from the 56th Brigade to-morrow. J.E.P.

Friday August 13th 1915. One Officer Captain E. M. JAMES of the 10th Royal Warwickshire Regt. suffering from diarrhoea was collected last night and sent in to the No. 2 London Casualty Clearing Station. The weather is showery to-day. – Two heavy draught horses and one mule have been struck off the strength from to-day, having been evacuated to the Base from the Mobile Veterinary Section. J.E.P.

J.E. Powell
Major RAMC
O.C. 57th Field Ambulance

Army Form C. 2118

Instructions regarding War Diaries and Intelligence Summaries are contained in F. S. Regs., Part II. and the Staff Manual respectively. Title Pages will be prepared in manuscript.

WAR DIARY
or
INTELLIGENCE SUMMARY

(Erase heading not required.)

Place	Date	Hour	Summary of Events and Information	Remarks and references to Appendices
ROBERMETZ	14/8/15	9 p.m.	There were only two admissions to the Field Ambulance during the day both of these cases were evacuated to No. 7 Casualty Clearing Station. – Four other cases were returned to duty, leaving only four cases remaining. Billeting certificates were handed to the Maire of MERVILLE and sent to the Branch Requisition Office for the previous week. – The weather has been fine and cool.	J.E.P.
"	15/8/15	9 p.m.	There was only one admission to the Field Ambulance during the day – a case of Fractured Radius in a Driver of the Army Service Corps attached to this Field Ambulance. – He was evacuated to the No. 2 London Casualty Clearing Station. Three other cases were evacuated to duty, leaving only one case remaining. There were heavy thunder showers in the morning, but the afternoon and evening were fine. – There was a Voluntary Church Service for all denominations at 11 a.m.	J.E.P.
"	16/8/15	9 p.m.	There were four cases admitted to the Field Ambulance during the day, three cases were evacuated to the No. 2 London Casualty Clearing Station leaving two cases remaining. All available officers of the Ambulance attended during the morning a demonstration by expert Entomologists of the breeding places of flies, their life history and the best methods for their destruction. There was a very heavy thunderstorm in the afternoon, with heavy rain.	J.E.P.

1875 Wt. W593/826 1,000,000 4/15 J.B.C. & A. A.D.S.S./Forms/C. 2118.

Instructions regarding War Diaries and Intelligence Summaries are contained in F. S. Regs., Part II. and the Staff Manual respectively. Title Pages will be prepared in manuscript.

WAR DIARY
or
INTELLIGENCE SUMMARY
(Erase heading not required.)

Army Form C. 2118.

Place	Date	Hour	Summary of Events and Information	Remarks and references to Appendices
ROBERMETZ	17/8/15	9 p.m.	There were three patients admitted to the Field Ambulance during the day and two evacuated to No. 7 Casualty Clearing Station, leaving three remaining. A dose of Anti-tetanic serum 1500 units was given to one case as a prophylactic. There were heavy thunder showers again during the day, which has made the camp very wet & muddy. All the circular bell tents have been treated with Cutch and copper Sulphate to render them less visible.	J.E.P.
"	18/8/15	9 p.m.	The weather has been fine and the ground has dried considerably, but the nights are becoming cold. – The health of the Unit continues good. – There were three cases admitted to the Field Ambulance yesterday, none evacuated leaving six remaining. — All available officers of the Unit attended a demonstration on the means of combating gas this morning. All officers passed through a trench full of gas, wearing smoke helmets, there was no appreciable effect of the gas felt.	J.E.P.
"	19/8/15	9 p.m.	The weather has continued fine and the ground is drying satisfactorily. There were two admissions during the day and four cases evacuated, leaving three remaining. – One of the cases admitted was that of an officer viz 2nd LIEUT. WILLIAM ROBERT BRANDT 7th Loyal North Lancashire Regt – He was admitted with severe diarrhoea and was evacuated to the No. 2 London Casualty Clearing Station.	J.E.P.

1875 Wt. W593/826 1,000,000 4/15 J.B.C. & A. A.D.S.S./Forms/C. 2118.

Army Form C. 2118

Instructions regarding War Diaries and Intelligence Summaries are contained in F. S. Regs., Part II. and the Staff Manual respectively. Title Pages will be prepared in manuscript.

WAR DIARY
or
INTELLIGENCE SUMMARY

(Erase heading not required.)

Place	Date	Hour	Summary of Events and Information	Remarks and references to Appendices
ROBERMETZ	20/8/15	9 p.m.	One Officer LIEUT. JOHN DOUGLAS WILKINSON R.A.M.C. 57th Field Ambulance was admitted during the day, and also two other cases were admitted. Three cases were evacuated leaving one Officer and two men remaining. — 1475 francs were paid out to the men of the Unit during the afternoon. Chaplain The Rev G.W. HARTE reported his departure for the 58th Field Ambulance. Chaplain The REV MIDDLETON reported his arrival to be attached to this unit. Chaplain The REV. WIMBUSH reported his arrival to be attached to this unit. Captain D.F. MACKENZIE R.A.M.C. reported his arrival for duty with this unit and has been posted to A. Section. Temporary LIEUT. J.R. FORDE R.A.M.C. reported his departure for duty with the 19th British Field Ambulance.	XIX Divisional Order No 114 dated 18/8/15 J.E.P.
"	21/8/15	9 p.m.	Billeting certificates for the week were rendered to the Maire of MERVILLE to-day & the duplicate sent to the Branch Requisition Office G.H.Q. There were ten cases admitted to the Field Ambulance during the day and four cases evacuated to No. 7 Casualty Clearing Station, leaving one Officer and eight other cases remaining. — The weather has been moderately fine with a few light showers in the morning.	J.E.P.

1875 Wt. W593/826 1,000,000 4/15 J.B.C. & A. A.D.S.S./Forms/C. 2118.

Army Form C. 2118.

Instructions regarding War Diaries and Intelligence Summaries are contained in F. S. Regs., Part II. and the Staff Manual respectively. Title Pages will be prepared in manuscript.

WAR DIARY
or
INTELLIGENCE SUMMARY
(Erase heading not required.)

Place	Date	Hour	Summary of Events and Information	Remarks and references to Appendices
ROBERMETZ	22/8/15	9 p.m.	Three cases were admitted to the Field Ambulance during the day and one case evacuated back to duty, leaving one Officer and eleven men remaining. Parade church service was held in the open at 9·30 a.m. both for C. of E. and Nonconformists. – Roman Catholics attended service in MERVILLE church. The weather has been fine and sunny.	J.E.P.
"	23/8/15	9 p.m.	There were 14 cases admitted to the Field Ambulance during the day and 8 cases evacuated, leaving one Officer and 17 Men remaining in the Ambulance. Received an order from the A.D.M.S. XIX Division at 11·45 a.m. to take over the Baths at MERVILLE. I detailed temporary LIEUT ANGLIN R.A.M.C. for this duty. – The weather has been fine and clear.	J.E.P.
"	24/8/15	9 p.m.	Only one case was admitted to the Field Ambulance during the day and one Officer LIEUT J.D. WILKINSON R.A.M.C. and ten other cases were evacuated, leaving eight cases remaining in the Ambulance. – The weather has been fine and much warmer than for some days previously.	J.E.P.
"	25/8/15	9 p.m.	Five cases were admitted to the Field Ambulance during the day and five cases evacuated, leaving eight cases remaining. – The weather continues fine and warm. – All excreta from the latrines is now being burnt, ~~[illegible]~~ a special incinerator for this purpose is being built. – Trench Latrines are being given up.	J.E.P.

1875 Wt. W593/826 1,000,000 4/15 J.B.C. & A. A.D.S.S./Forms/C. 2118.

Instructions regarding War Diaries and Intelligence Summaries are contained in F. S. Regs., Part II. and the Staff Manual respectively. Title Pages will be prepared in manuscript.

WAR DIARY
or
INTELLIGENCE SUMMARY
(Erase heading not required.)

Army Form C. 2118

Place	Date	Hour	Summary of Events and Information	Remarks and references to Appendices
ROBERMETZ	26/8/15	9 p.m.	Nine cases were admitted to the Field Ambulance during the day and nine cases evacuated leaving eight cases remaining. – The weather continues bright and warm and the health of the unit remains good. – The O.C. Sanitary Section XIX Division visited the unit to-day and made various practical suggestions with regard to the details of sanitation.	J.E.P.
"	27/8/15	9 p.m.	One Officer, LIEUT. BREWSTER J.S. North Lanc. Regt. and seven cases were admitted to the Field Ambulance during the day, and one officer and eight cases were evacuated, leaving seven cases remaining. I received during the day R.A.M.C. order No. 1. by Col Birt A.M.S. commanding RAMC XIX Division The 57th Field Ambulance will march from its present billet at 1 p.m. on the 31st. 8. 15 proceeding via MERVILLE – PACAUT to the BOIS DE PACAUT (Sq Q 33 b 7.4.)	J.E.P.
"	28/8/15	9 p.m.	One Officer, MAJOR OPPENHEIMER A. East Lanc Regt. and 20 cases were admitted to the ambulance during the day, and 10 cases were evacuated leaving 17 cases remaining. The prevailing disease was scabies. Two Officers and one man of the 5th S.W. Borderers were accidentally injured by a Bomb explosion and evacuated to No. 2. London Casualty Clearing Station. One of the officers CAPTAIN LEWIS died before admission to the Field Ambulance the other Officer who was admitted to the Field Ambulance and evacuated was LIEUT. JONES B.O.	J.E.P.

1875 Wt. W593/826 1,000,000 4/15 J.B.C. & A. A.D.S.S./Forms/C. 2118.

Instructions regarding War Diaries and Intelligence Summaries are contained in F. S. Regs., Part II. and the Staff Manual respectively. Title Pages will be prepared in manuscript.

WAR DIARY
or
INTELLIGENCE SUMMARY
(Erase heading not required.)

Army Form C. 2118

Place	Date	Hour	Summary of Events and Information	Remarks and references to Appendices
ROBERMETZ	29-8-15	9 p.m.	There were four cases admitted to the Field Ambulance during the day and sixteen cases evacuated, leaving five cases remaining. I despatched an advanced Party of 15 N.C.Os and men at 2 p.m. to take over our new Billet at BOIS de PACAUT from the 22nd Field Ambulance. Church Parade was held at 9·30 a.m. – The weather has become cold and wet this evening.	J.E.P.
"	30-8-15	9 p.m.	Six cases were admitted to the Field Ambulance during the day and eight cases were evacuated leaving three cases remaining. – Made all arrangements for marching out of these billets to-morrow. – The weather has been dry but much colder.	J.E.P.
BOIS DE PACAUT	31-8-15	9 p.m.	One Officer 2nd LIEUT N. HALFHIDE 1st East Lancashire Regt. was admitted to the Field Ambulance with Bronchitis and evacuated to No. 2 London Casualty Clearing Station. Four other cases were admitted during the day and 10 cases evacuated. – One transfer was also received from No. 22 Field Ambulance (Gunshot wound of Right chest) and evacuated. There were no cases remaining. – The Field Ambulance marched out from ROBERMETZ at 1 p.m. and arrived in our present billet at 3 p.m. The farm buildings have been taken over entirely for use as a hospital all the Personnel are billeted in an orchard near. The weather is dry but cold.	J.E.P.

J.E. Powell
Major RAMC
O.C. 57th Field Ambulance

1875 Wt. W593/826 1,000,000 4/15 J.B.C. & A. A.D.S.S./Forms/C. 2118.

19th Division

Sept '15

121

0971

57th Field Ambulance

Vol III

Sept 15.

Instructions regarding War Diaries and Intelligence Summaries are contained in F. S. Regs., Part II. and the Staff Manual respectively. Title Pages will be prepared in manuscript.

WAR DIARY
or
INTELLIGENCE SUMMARY
(Erase heading not required.)

Army Form C. 2118

Place	Date	Hour	Summary of Events and Information	Remarks and references to Appendices
BOIS de PACAUT	1/9/15	9 p.m.	Four cases were admitted to the Field Ambulance during the day and four cases evacuated by No. 8 Motor Ambulance Convoy to LILLERS, leaving no cases remaining. During the day the Barns and rooms of the Farm were scrubbed out and the walls whitewashed preparatory to the reception of Patients. Tents were erected for the treatment of Scabies and other infectious cases. Incinerators were built and other conservancy arrangements developed. Rain fell throughout the afternoon and made the roads and paths very muddy.	J.E.P.
"	2/9/15	9 p.m.	Six cases were admitted to the Field Ambulance during the day and one case evacuated by No. 8. Motor Ambulance Convoy, leaving 5 cases remaining. The Road in front of the hospital needs repair, and this has been taken in hand by the Unit. another Incinerator has been built and a large closed urine pit dug. Heavy rain fell again throughout the evening making the condition of the ground very bad especially in the Horse lines. Trenches have been dug here to lead the water off. Temp. Lieut. G.C. ANGLIN R.A.M.C. left this unit to-day under instructions from the A.D.M.S. XIX Division, for temporary duty as Medical Officer i/c 10th Worcester Regt.	J.E.P.
"	3/9/15	9 p.m.	Heavy rain fell throughout last night and almost continuously during the day, rendering the ground, roads and paths into a quagmire. Four cases were evacuated by No. 8 Motor Ambulance Convoy and four cases admitted leaving 5 cases remaining. Two surgical operations were performed during the day. The condition of the weather prevented any improvements being carried out.	J.E.P.

1875 Wt. W593/826 1,000,000 4/15 J.B.C. & A. A.D.S.S./Forms/C. 2118.

Instructions regarding War Diaries and Intelligence Summaries are contained in F. S. Regs., Part II. and the Staff Manual respectively. Title Pages will be prepared in manuscript.

WAR DIARY
or
INTELLIGENCE SUMMARY
(Erase heading not required.)

Army Form C. 2118

Place	Date	Hour	Summary of Events and Information	Remarks and references to Appendices
BOIS DE PACAUT	4/9/15	9 p.m.	There were five cases admitted to the Field Ambulance to-day and two cases were evacuated, leaving eight cases remaining. Prevailing disease Nil. The weather has continued very showery and the condition of the ground bad but the roads and paths have been scraped and paved where possible with brick and other material. – The Horse lines have also been drained to a certain extent.	J.E.P.
"	5/9/15	9 p.m.	There were six cases admitted to the Field Ambulance during the day and seven cases evacuated by No. 8 Motor Ambulance Convoy, leaving seven cases remaining. Church Parade was held in the open air at 9.30 a.m. – Billeting certificates were rendered for the past week. – The weather has been dry and the condition of the ground is improving.	J.E.P.
"	6/9/15	9 p.m.	Seven cases were admitted to the Field Ambulance and four cases were evacuated during the day, leaving ten cases remaining. – The Men of the unit were paid during the afternoon, a total of 1680 francs. – The weather continues fine and the ground is drying rapidly. – Further improvements in sanitation were carried out	J.E.P.
"	7/9/15	9 p.m.	Two Officers both of the 9th South Lancashire Regt. namely 2nd Lieut T. G. PERCY and 2nd Lieut R. TAYLOR were both admitted to the Field Ambulance during the day and evacuated to the 2nd London Casualty Clearing Station. – Four other cases were admitted and four evacuated, leaving ten cases remaining. The weather continues fine.	J.E.P.

1875 Wt W593/826 1,000,000 4/15 J.B.C. & A. A.D.S.S./Forms/C. 2118.

Instructions regarding War Diaries and Intelligence Summaries are contained in F. S. Regs., Part II. and the Staff Manual respectively. Title Pages will be prepared in manuscript.

WAR DIARY
or
INTELLIGENCE SUMMARY
(Erase heading not required.)

Army Form C. 2118

Place	Date	Hour	Summary of Events and Information	Remarks and references to Appendices
BOIS DE PACAUT	8/9/15	9 p.m.	Seven cases were admitted to the Field Ambulance during the day and seven cases evacuated, leaving ten cases remaining. – The weather continues fine and dry. Further improvements to the roads and paths have been carried out by filling in the uneven portions with broken brick etc.	J.E.P.
"	9/9/15	9 p.m.	Eight cases were admitted to the Field Ambulance during the day and six cases evacuated leaving twelve cases remaining. – No Officers were admitted. ~~and~~ The ~~m~~ prevailing disease is Scabies. Received a notification from the O.C. XIX Divisional Train that he would inspect the A.S.C. personnel, horses and transport of this unit at 2.30 p.m. to-morrow in accordance with K.R. Para 1221. – Made arrangements for this inspection. – The weather continues fine and dry.	J.E.P.
"	10/9/15	9 p.m.	Seven cases were admitted during the day to the Field Ambulance and two cases evacuated, leaving seventeen cases remaining. The weather continues fine. The O.C. XIX Divisional Train inspected all the horses and transport of the unit at 2.30 p.m. and made various suggestions which will be carried out.	J.E.P.
"	11/9/15	9 p.m.	One Officer LIEUT C.S. HUNT 7th K.O. Royal LANCASTER Regt. was admitted during the day and evacuated to No. 2. London Casualty Clearing Station. Three other cases were admitted and five cases evacuated leaving fifteen cases remaining. – Billeting certificates for the week were rendered to the Maire of the Commune. – Orders were received from the A.D.M.S. for 1 Officer 3 N.C.O.s and 15 men to KING's Road Advanced Dressing Station and 1 Officer 1 N.C.O. and 8 men to the MARAIS Advanced Dressing to proceed to-morrow for 48 hours instruction in the evacuation of wounded at those stations.	J.E.P.

1875 Wt W593/826 1,000,000 4/15 J.B.C. & A. A.D.S.S./Forms/C. 2118.

Army Form C. 2118

WAR DIARY
or
INTELLIGENCE SUMMARY
(Erase heading not required.)

Instructions regarding War Diaries and Intelligence Summaries are contained in F. S. Regs., Part II. and the Staff Manual respectively. Title Pages will be prepared in manuscript.

Place	Date	Hour	Summary of Events and Information	Remarks and references to Appendices
BOIS DE PACAUT	12/9/15	9 p.m.	There were nine cases admitted during the day and six evacuated leaving eighteen cases remaining. One Officer, 3 N.C.Os and 15 men left for the KINGS ROAD advanced dressing station and one Officer 1 NCO & 8 men left for the MARAIS advanced dressing station at 2 p.m. Church Parade was held at 9.30 a.m. The weather continues fine & dry.	J.E.P.
"	13/9/15	9 p.m.	Eleven cases were admitted to the Field Ambulance during the day and six cases evacuated leaving 23 cases remaining. – I visited the advanced dressing stations at KING'S ROAD and MARAIS during the evening. I made arrangements with the O.C. 58th Field Ambulance to relieve the detachments at the advanced dressing stations to-morrow afternoon. – The weather has continued fine.	J.E.P.
"	14/9/15	9 p.m.	Two cases were admitted to the Field Ambulance during the day and ten cases evacuated leaving fifteen cases remaining. Light showers of rain fell in the morning but the weather has cleared up since then. Went in to the Field Cashier and drew some pay for the men. Called at the office of the A.D.M.S. and met the D.M.S. of the 1st Army. The detachments at the two Advanced Dressing Stations were relieved during the afternoon.	J.E.P.
"	15/9/15	9 p.m.	Six cases were admitted to the Field Ambulance during the day and five cases evacuated leaving sixteen cases remaining. I visited the two advanced dressing stations during the evening, ~~take~~ at MARAIS and KING'S ROAD. Received an order from the A.D.M.S. during the evening to supply chlorinated drinking water to the Headquarters 57th Inf. Brigade.	J.E.P.

1875 Wt W593/826 1,000,000 4/15 J.B.C. & A. A.D.S.S./Forms/C. 2118.

Instructions regarding War Diaries and Intelligence Summaries are contained in F. S. Regs., Part II. and the Staff Manual respectively. Title Pages will be prepared in manuscript.

WAR DIARY
or
INTELLIGENCE SUMMARY
(Erase heading not required.)

Army Form C. 2118.

Place	Date	Hour	Summary of Events and Information	Remarks and references to Appendices
BOIS DE PACAUT	16/9/15	9 p.m.	Twelve cases were admitted to the Field Ambulance during the day and ~~t~~ four cases evacuated leaving twentyfour cases remaining. The weather has been dry and warm. I visited MARAIS advanced dressing station and the Regimental Aid posts of the 58th Inf. Brigade during the afternoon and evening.	J.E.P.
"	17/9/15	9 p.m.	Twelve cases were ~~again~~ admitted during the day and eleven cases evacuated leaving twentyfive cases remaining. The health of the unit remains good. The weather continues fine and dry.	J.E.P.
"	18/9/15	9 p.m.	There were eight cases admitted to the Field Ambulance during the day and eleven cases evacuated leaving 22 cases remaining. – Billeting certificates for the week were rendered to the Maire. – The D.D.M.S. Indian Army Corps inspected the Field Ambulance during the morning, including all the books and records. The last detachments returned during the afternoon from KING'S ROAD and MARAIS advanced dressing stations.	J.E.P.
"	19/9/15	9 p.m.	There were nine admissions during the day and eleven cases evacuated leaving twenty cases remaining. The A.D.M.S. XIX Division inspected the Field ambulance during the afternoon. The weather continues fine and dry	J.E.P.
"	20/9/15	9 p.m.	Sixteen cases were admitted during the day, eighteen cases evacuated leaving eighteen cases remaining. Went out at 10 a.m. with the A.D.M.S. to select a site for a new Advanced Dressing Station. – The A.D.M.S. selected a site in a house on the RUE DE BOIS in Square X 17 d 6/6 Ref. Map Sheet 36a 36b combined Sheet. Received verbal orders from the A.D.M.S. at 12.45 p.m. to send out a section to this advanced Dressing Station during the afternoon. B Section left Headquarters at 4.30 and arrived at 6.30 p.m. at the dressing station.	J.E.P.

1875 Wt W593/826 1,000,000 4/15 J.B.C. & A. A.D.S.S./Forms/C. 2118.

Instructions regarding War Diaries and Intelligence Summaries are contained in F. S. Regs., Part II. and the Staff Manual respectively. Title Pages will be prepared in manuscript.

WAR DIARY
or
INTELLIGENCE SUMMARY
(Erase heading not required.)

Army Form C. 2118

Place	Date	Hour	Summary of Events and Information	Remarks and references to Appendices
BOIS DE PACAUT	21/9/15	9 p.m.	Six cases were admitted during the day and eighteen cases were evacuated leaving six remaining. The Personnel of the Unit were moved out of Bivouacs during the day into billets in the Barns of a neighbouring Farm. — Received R.A.M.C Operation Order No. 2 by Colonel BIRT A.M.S. dated 21/9/15 at 1·30 p.m. covering the verbal orders issued to me yesterday re the establishment of an advanced Dressing Station and the Aid Posts with which to establish communication. Visited the Advanced Dressing Station in the evening, the personnel are digging a "Dug-out" for the reception of wounded.	J.E.P.
"	22/9/15	9 p.m.	One Officer sick was ~~evacuated~~ admitted and evacuated during the day, one Officer wounded was admitted and is remaining. Two wounded men were admitted and are remaining. Thirteen sick were admitted and evacuated, leaving six remaining. — Colonel HINGE A.D.M.S. visited the Field Ambulance during the morning and the Advanced Dressing Station in the afternoon. The weather continues fine	J.E.P.
"	23/9/15	9 p.m.	One Officer wounded accidentally and one Officer sick were admitted during the day 15 Sick and 3 wounded were admitted during the day. Two wounded Officers were evacuated and 11 sick and 2 wounded other ranks were evacuated. All the tents of the unit were pitched and equipped with straw and blankets for the reception of sick and wounded. Total accommodation of the Field Ambulance is now 250. — Visited the advanced Dressing Station during the evening.	J.E.P.

1875 Wt W593/826 1,000,000 4/15 J.B.C. & A. A.D.S.S./Forms/C. 2118.

Army Form C. 2118

WAR DIARY
or
INTELLIGENCE SUMMARY
(Erase heading not required.)

Instructions regarding War Diaries and Intelligence Summaries are contained in F. S. Regs., Part II. and the Staff Manual respectively. Title Pages will be prepared in manuscript.

Place	Date	Hour	Summary of Events and Information	Remarks and references to Appendices
BOIS DE PACAUT	24/9/15	9 p.m.	Forty five sick were admitted and transferred to this Field Ambulance during the day. Fifteen sick and two wounded were evacuated, leaving one Officer sick, 40 other ranks sick and one wounded remaining. – Received Operation order No. 4 dated 23/9/15 by Colonel HINGE O.C. R.A.M.C. XIX Division containing medical arrangements for collection and evacuation of sick and wounded during the impending action. This Field Ambulance is to collect and receive the sick of the whole division. – Made arrangements accordingly. Visited the advanced dressing station during the evening. Rain fell during the evening.	J.E.P.
"	25/9/15	9 p.m.	One Officer sick, was admitted and two sick Officers evacuated, leaving none remaining. Fifteen other ranks sick were admitted and five evacuated, leaving 51 remaining. – Heavy rain fell throughout the day making the roads very muddy and difficult for motor transport. I visited the Advanced Dressing Station morning and evening, they received 58 wounded during the day and evacuated them to the 59th Field Ambulance at MESPLAUX FARM. The Officer i/c the Advanced Dressing Station reported that the Bearer Division of the Ambulance had worked very well and creditably.	J.E.P.
"	26/9/15	11 a.m. 3 p.m. 5 p.m. 9 p.m. 10 p.m.	Rendered Billeting certificates for the previous eight days to the Maire of the Commune. Called at Office of A.D.M.S. Visited the Advanced Dressing Station – No wounded are coming in at present. One Officer was admitted sick and evacuated during the day. 29 other ranks sick were admitted and 9 sick and 1 wounded were evacuated, leaving 68 remaining. Received orders from A.D.M.S. to send one Medical Officer and five large ambulance cars together with 5 large cars from the 58th Field Ambulance, as one convoy to evacuate wounded cases from LILLERS to ARQUES. – The Convoy left at 11.15 p.m.	J.E.P.

Instructions regarding War Diaries and Intelligence Summaries are contained in F. S. Regs., Part II. and the Staff Manual respectively. Title Pages will be prepared in manuscript.

WAR DIARY
or
INTELLIGENCE SUMMARY

(Erase heading not required.)

Army Form C. 2118

Place	Date	Hour	Summary of Events and Information	Remarks and references to Appendices
BOIS DE PACAUT	27/9/15	4.15 a.m.	Received orders from the A.D.M.S. to have two Officers and the Personnel of 1 Tent-Subdivision and one Officer and the Personnel of 1 Bearer Subdivision, ready to move at once when ambulance motor cars called for them. – To be attached to the 4th Army Corps for temporary duty. – Issued the necessary orders.	
		11 a.m.	The A.D.M.S. visited the Field Ambulance and inspected all the wards.	
		12 Noon	I visited the Advanced Dressing Station and withdrew one Officer and 36 Bearers to Headquarters. One Medical Officer with 5 Sunbeam ambulance Cars returned from Convoy duty.	J.E.P.
		2.35 p.m.	A motor ambulance Convoy of 8 cars (from No. 2 M.A. Convoy MERVILLE) arrived and left at once with 2 Officers and 19 men Tent Subdivision and 1 Officer and 36 men Bearer Subdivision for temporary duty with the 4th Army Corps. Reported their departure to A.D.M.S. Heavy rain has again fallen, rendering the roads very muddy and difficult for transport.	
		9 p.m.	3 Officers sick were admitted and none evacuated. 22 other ranks sick were admitted and 23 evacuated leaving 3 Officers and 67 men remaining.	
"	28/9/15	2 p.m.	Received message from the Officer i/c the Advanced Dressing Station, that numerous German shells had fallen in close proximity and that several casualties had occurred amongst the R.F.A. near. – Visited the Advanced Dressing Station and found that the shelling had ceased. There are good "dug-outs" for the Personnel and Patients there.	
		9 p.m.	Three sick Officers were evacuated, 28 other ranks sick were admitted and 27 evacuated leaving 68 remaining. – Heavy rain continues to fall. Three Officers and 55 men returned at 7.30 p.m. from temporary duty with the 4th Army Corps. – Reported their arrival to the A.D.M.S.	J.E.P.

1875 Wt. W593/826 1,000,000 4/15 J.B.C. & A. A.D.S.S./Forms/C. 2118.

Instructions regarding War Diaries and Intelligence Summaries are contained in F. S. Regs., Part II. and the Staff Manual respectively. Title Pages will be prepared in manuscript.

WAR DIARY
or
INTELLIGENCE SUMMARY
(Erase heading not required.)

Army Form C. 2118.

Place	Date	Hour	Summary of Events and Information	Remarks and references to Appendices
BOIS DE PACAUT	29/9/15	9 p.m.	One Officer sick, was admitted and evacuated during the day. 31 other ranks sick were admitted and twelve evacuated leaving 88 cases remaining. — I visited the advanced Dressing Station during the afternoon. — The weather continues very wet and cold and the condition of the roads + surrounding ground is bad.	J.E.P.
"	30/9/15	9 p.m.	One Officer sick, was admitted and evacuated during the day, 39 other ranks sick were admitted and 27 cases evacuated, leaving 100 cases remaining. Visited the Advanced Dressing Station in the afternoon and met the D.D.M.S. Indian Corps there. — Made arrangements to relieve the Officer in charge of the advanced dressing station for a few days rest, also to reinforce the Bearers out there by 18 men. Received Operation Order No. 7 by Colonel H.A. HINGE A.M.S. rearranging the duties of the three Divisional Field Ambulances. — The 57th Field Ambulance will continue to collect the sick from the area west of the Canal DE LA LAWE. Heavy rain fell again this evening and the temperature is low making the conditions bad for the men in the trenches and increasing the sick rate.	J.E.P.

J.E. Powell
Major R.A.M.C.
Commanding 57th Field Ambulance

1875 Wt. W593/826 1,000,000 4/15 J.B.C. & A. A.D.S.S./Forms/C. 2118.

Oct 1915

19th Division

121/7437

~~H.Q. 19th Division~~

57th Field Ambulance

Vol 4

Col 15

Army Form C. 2118

Instructions regarding War Diaries and Intelligence Summaries are contained in F. S. Regs., Part II. and the Staff Manual respectively. Title Pages will be prepared in manuscript.

WAR DIARY
or
INTELLIGENCE SUMMARY
(Erase heading not required.)

Place	Date	Hour	Summary of Events and Information	Remarks and references to Appendices
BOIS DE PACAUT	1/10/15	9 p.m.	Relieved one officer, one N.C.O. and ten men from the Advanced Dressing station and in addition to their reliefs, sent up a reinforcement of 1 N.C.O. and 18 Bearers. — Visited the Advanced Dressing Station in the afternoon and paid the men of the detachment there. The weather has been fine & dry but very cold. One Officer sick was admitted during the day. 30 other ranks sick, including 12 transfers from the 58th Field Ambulance were admitted during the day and sixteen were evacuated, leaving 1 Officer and 114 men remaining.	J.E.P.
"	2/10/15	11 a.m.	Rendered billeting certificates for the week to the Maire of the Commune.	
		3 p.m.	The A.D.M.S. visited the Field Ambulance.	
		5 p.m.	I visited the Advanced Dressing Station, & found that the "dug-outs" had been improved considerably — a layer of bricks & sand bags have been added to the roof, and the dug-out has also been deepened somewhat.	
		8 p.m.	Received Operation order No. 10 dated 2/10/15 from the ADMS. — This Field Ambulance is to hold itself in readiness to move at short notice to ZELOBES.	
		9 p.m.	One Sick Officer remaining. 4 other ranks admitted and 41 evacuated, leaving 77 cases remaining	J.E.P.

1875 Wt. W593/826 1,000,000 4/15 J.B.C. & A. A.D.S.S./Forms/C. 2118.

Army Form C. 2118

Instructions regarding War Diaries and Intelligence Summaries are contained in F. S. Regs., Part II. and the Staff Manual respectively. Title Pages will be prepared in manuscript.

WAR DIARY
or
INTELLIGENCE SUMMARY
(Erase heading not required.)

Place	Date	Hour	Summary of Events and Information	Remarks and references to Appendices
ZELOBES	3/10/15	9 p.m.	Visited ZELOBES in the morning to inspect our prospective New billets. at 3·45 p.m. The A.D.M.S. visited the Field Ambulance and ordered the unit to move to ZELOBES as soon as possible. – I sent forward an advance party at once to take over the billets at ZELOBES. – The remainder of the unit packed up and marched off at 6 p.m. arriving at ZELOBES at 9.20 p.m. – I left 1 Officer an N.C.O. & ten men to clear up our old billets & come on later in the evening. Only 2 cases were admitted to Hospital to-day. – One Officer was evacuated to duty 36 men were evacuated to the Casualty Clearing Station ST. VENANT. 10 men were transferred to the 58th Field Ambulance and 8 men to duty, leaving 25 cases remaining which were brought with the unit. – The weather has been cold but fine.	J.E.P.
"	4/10/15	9 a.m.	Office – and arranging accommodation in the Hospital and making sanitary arrangements.	
		12 Noon	Visited the A.D.M.S.	
		2 p.m.	Visited the advanced dressing station. Weather is cold & showery.	
		6 p.m.	attended a conference with the A.D.M.S. & the other C.Os. of Field Ambulances on the reorganisation of the Field Ambulance into a Bearer Division, 2 Tent-Subdivisions & Headquarters.	J.E.P.
		9 p.m.	15 Sick were admitted and 28 sick evacuated, leaving 12 sick remaining. 12 wounded were admitted and 8 wounded evacuated leaving 4 wounded remaining.	

1875 Wt. W593/826 1,000,000 4/15 J.B.C. & A. A.D.S.S./Forms/C. 2118.

WAR DIARY
or
INTELLIGENCE SUMMARY
(Erase heading not required.)

Army Form C. 2118

Instructions regarding War Diaries and Intelligence Summaries are contained in F. S. Regs., Part II. and the Staff Manual respectively. Title Pages will be prepared in manuscript.

Place	Date	Hour	Summary of Events and Information	Remarks and references to Appendices
ZELOBES	5/10/15	9 p.m.	The weather has been wet and cold throughout the day, raining all day. – I visited the advanced dressing station in the afternoon. – 25 sick and two wounded were admitted during the day and 13 sick and 3 wounded were evacuated, leaving 24 sick and 3 wounded remaining.	J.E.P.
"	6/10/15	9 p.m.	The weather has been damp, cold and misty throughout the day. – I visited the advanced dressing station in the afternoon – The Royal Engineers have now laid the tramway all the way down to the advanced dressing station, this will facilitate the evacuation of the wounded considerably. – One wounded Officer was admitted and evacuated. sixteen other ranks, sick and 3 wounded were admitted, ~~leaving~~ 11 sick and 3 wounded were evacuated, leaving 29 sick and 3 wounded remaining.	J.E.P.
"	7/10/15	9 p.m.	The A.D.M.S. of the Division and also the D.D.M.S. of the Corps inspected the ambulance at different times during the morning. – The day has been cold and foggy but otherwise dry. – One Officer wounded was admitted and evacuated. 12 other ranks wounded were admitted and eleven evacuated. 19 other ranks sick were admitted and 23 evacuated leaving 25 sick and 4 wounded remaining.	J.E.P.
"	8/10/15	9 p.m.	There were 23 sick admitted during the day and one wounded admitted – 13 sick and and 2 wounded were evacuated, leaving 35 sick and 3 wounded remaining. – I visited the advanced dressing station during the ~~morning~~ afternoon, there are two very good dug-outs there now capable of accommodating wounded & personnel. The weather has been dry and there has been considerable shelling on both sides	J.E.P.

1875 Wt. W593/826 1,000,000 4/15 J.B.C. & A. A.D.S.S./Forms/C. 2118.

Instructions regarding War Diaries and Intelligence Summaries are contained in F. S. Regs., Part II. and the Staff Manual respectively. Title Pages will be prepared in manuscript.

WAR DIARY
or
INTELLIGENCE SUMMARY
(Erase heading not required.)

Army Form C. 2118

Place	Date	Hour	Summary of Events and Information	Remarks and references to Appendices
ZELOBES	9/10/15	9 p.m.	Seventeen sick and seven wounded were admitted during the day, 22 sick and five wounded were evacuated, leaving 30 sick remaining and 5 wounded remaining. The weather has continued dry but cold and foggy. Visited the advanced dressing station in the afternoon.	J.E.P.
"	10/10/15	9 p.m.	The weather has continued fine. 7 sick and two wounded were admitted during the day. 20 sick and 3 wounded were evacuated leaving 17 sick and 4 wounded remaining. – I visited the advanced dressing station in the afternoon, also the Regimental aid posts. – We have now given up the Regt. Aid Post of the 57th Brigade Battalion and are now only serving two Aid Posts, those of the 58th Brigade Battalion. In my absence the A.D.M.S. visited the Field Ambulance.	J.E.P.
"	11/10/15	9 p.m.	Twenty sick and seven wounded were admitted during the day, eight sick and eight wounded were evacuated leaving 29 sick and 3 wounded remaining. – The A.D.M.S. visited the Field Ambulance in the morning. – Paid the men of the unit at Headquarters in the afternoon. – The weather has continued fine.	J.E.P.
"	12/10/15	9 p.m.	One Officer wounded was admitted and evacuated during the day. 19 other ranks sick and six wounded were admitted. 21 sick and 4 wounded were evacuated, leaving 27 sick and five wounded remaining. – The weather has continued fine. Visited the advanced Dressing Station in the afternoon.	J.E.P.
"	13/10/15	9 p.m.	The weather has continued fine. Two Officers sick and one Officer wounded were admitted and all three evacuated during the day. 21 other ranks sick and 11 wounded were admitted, 20 sick and 5 wounded were evacuated, leaving 28 sick remaining and 11 wounded remaining. I visited the advanced Dressing Station in the afternoon.	J.E.P.

1875 Wt. W593/826 1,000,000 4/15 J.B.C. & A. A.D.S.S./Forms/C. 2118.

Instructions regarding War Diaries and Intelligence Summaries are contained in F. S. Regs., Part II. and the Staff Manual respectively. Title Pages will be prepared in manuscript.

WAR DIARY
or
INTELLIGENCE SUMMARY
(Erase heading not required.)

Army Form C. 2118

Place	Date	Hour	Summary of Events and Information	Remarks and references to Appendices
ZELOBES	14/10/15	9 a.m.	Office	
		11 a.m.	The D.D.M.S. Indian Corps and the A.D.M.S. XIX Division visited the Field Ambulance	
		2 p.m.	I visited the Advanced Dressing Station.	
		9 p.m.	One Officer sick was admitted and evacuated. One Officer wounded was admitted and is remaining. Six other ranks sick and four wounded were admitted, seven sick and nine wounded were evacuated, leaving 27 sick and six wounded remaining. – The weather has been fine.	J.E.P.
"	15/10/15	9 a.m.	Office	
		10 a.m.	The A.D.M.S. XIX Division inspected the Field Ambulance.	
		2 p.m.	Visited the advanced Dressing Station and paid the men of the unit out there.	
		3 p.m.	The D.D.M.S. Indian Corps visited the advanced Dressing Station	
		9 p.m.	One wounded Officer was evacuated during the day. 13 other ranks sick and 4 wounded were admitted during the day – 12 sick and 5 wounded were evacuated leaving 28 sick and 5 wounded remaining.	J.E.P.
"	16/10/15	9 p.m.	The weather has been cold and misty. 12 other ranks sick and 3 wounded were admitted during the day, 18 sick and 4 wounded were evacuated, leaving 22 sick and 4 wounded remaining.	J.E.P.
"	17/10/15	9 p.m.	The weather continues cold and misty but there has been no rain. – I visited the advanced dressing Station in the afternoon. 10 other ranks sick and 10 wounded were admitted during the day. 11 sick and 9 wounded were evacuated, leaving 21 sick and 5 wounded remaining. The prevailing disease is Scabies	J.E.P.
"	18/10/15	9 p.m.	14 sick and one wounded were admitted during the day, eight sick and 2 wounded were evacuated, leaving 27 sick and 4 wounded remaining. – The prevailing disease continues to be Scabies. – The weather is still dry and cold.	J.E.P.

Instructions regarding War Diaries and Intelligence Summaries are contained in F. S. Regs., Part II. and the Staff Manual respectively. Title Pages will be prepared in manuscript.

WAR DIARY
or
INTELLIGENCE SUMMARY
(Erase heading not required.)

Army Form C. 2118

Place	Date	Hour	Summary of Events and Information	Remarks and references to Appendices
ZELOBES	19/10/15	9 p.m.	Received orders from the A.D.M.S. XIX Division for the Field Ambulance (less the Bearer Division at Sq X 17 d Map sheet 36 A) to move to-morrow to LOCON and to open there for the reception of sick and wounded at 2 p.m. Surgeon-General Macpherson D.M.S. 1st Army visited the Field Ambulance to-day. 8 sick and eleven wounded were admitted during the day, 13 sick and 12 wounded were evacuated leaving 22 sick and 3 wounded remaining.	J.E.P.
LOCON	20/10/15	9 p.m.	The Field Ambulance moved this morning from ZELOBES to LOCON and opened up for the reception of casualties by 1 p.m. — Reported arrival here to A.D.M.S. One Officer sick was admitted and evacuated, 19 other ranks sick and 1 wounded were admitted during the day and 8 sick and 2 wounded were evacuated, leaving 33 sick and 2 wounded remaining.	J.E.P.
"	21/10/15	9 p.m.	The A.D.M.S. XIX Division inspected the Field Ambulance during the morning. 13 sick and 4 wounded were admitted during the day. 22 sick and 4 wounded were evacuated, leaving 24 sick and 2 wounded remaining. Rain has fallen during the evening.	J.E.P.
"	22/10/15	9 p.m.	One wounded Officer was admitted and evacuated during the day. 23 sick and 7 wounded other ranks were admitted during the day and 14 sick and 5 wounded were evacuated leaving 33 sick and 3 wounded remaining. — Received R.A.M.C. Routine orders ordering the 57th Field Ambulance to be prepared to evacuate the School at short notice. The advanced dressing station is to evacuate all cases to MESPLAUX.	J.E.P.

1875 Wt. W593/826 1,000,000 4/15 J.B.C. & A. A.D.S.S./Forms/C. 2118.

Instructions regarding War Diaries and Intelligence Summaries are contained in F. S. Regs., Part II. and the Staff Manual respectively. Title Pages will be prepared in manuscript.

WAR DIARY
or
INTELLIGENCE SUMMARY
(Erase heading not required.)

Army Form C. 2118

Place	Date	Hour	Summary of Events and Information	Remarks and references to Appendices
LOCON	23/10/15	9 p.m.	Six sick and one wounded were admitted and sixteen sick and two wounded were evacuated leaving 23 sick and two wounded remaining. – Arranged with the O.C. 58th Field Ambulance to collect the sick from two of the Regiments of the Brigade in Reserve and for the 58th Field Ambulance to collect the sick from the other two Regiments & also from Brigade Headquarters. – The weather continues cold and foggy.	J.E.P.
"	24/10/15	9 p.m.	Sixteen sick were admitted during the day, eleven sick and one wounded were evacuated leaving 28 sick and one wounded remaining. – I visited the advanced dressing station in the afternoon the new "Omnibus dug-out" is now very nearly completed. – Rain began to fall this afternoon making the roads very slippery.	J.E.P.
"	25/10/15	9 p.m.	There has been a continuous downpour of rain all day, making the condition of the roads very bad. There were seven cases sick admitted and 9 sick and one wounded evacuated leaving 26 cases sick and no wounded remaining. Indented to-day on the Royal Engineers for material to provide shelter and standing room for the horses of the unit.	J.E.P.
"	26/10/15	9 p.m.	7 cases sick and one wounded were admitted during the day, 9 cases sick and one wounded were evacuated leaving 24 sick remaining. – The one wounded case died at the advanced Dressing Station. – I visited the advanced dressing station in the afternoon Enemy shells were falling in close proximity between 2 & 3 p.m. but no damage was done – Work on the "dug-out" had to be abandoned in consequence of this shelling. – The ~~day~~ weather has been fine to-day.	J.E.P.

1875 Wt. W593/826 1,000,000 4/15 J.B.C. & A. A.D.S.S./Forms/C. 2118.

Army Form C. 2118

Instructions regarding War Diaries and Intelligence Summaries are contained in F. S. Regs., Part II. and the Staff Manual respectively. Title Pages will be prepared in manuscript.

WAR DIARY
or
INTELLIGENCE SUMMARY
(Erase heading not required.)

Place	Date	Hour	Summary of Events and Information	Remarks and references to Appendices
LOCON	27/10/15	9 p.m.	Major Powell proceeded to-day on 7 days leave to England. 8 cases sick admitted to-day, 7 cases sick evacuated leaving 25 cases sick remaining. LIEUT. C. W. S. DAVIES-JONES R.A.M.C. (T.C.) reported for duty with this Ambulance under orders of A.D.M.S. and was taken on the strength. Weather today has been bad, return of rain.	[illegible] Capt RAMC
"	28/10/15	9 p.m.	15 cases sick admitted, 10 cases sick evacuated, leaving 30 cases sick remaining. Lieut St Johnstone R.A.M.C. detailed as member of board at CALONNE to condemn a supply of Condensed Milk. Weather remains wet + foggy.	[illegible]
"	29/10/15	9 p.m.	11 cases sick admitted, 8 cases sick evacuated, leaving 33 cases sick remaining. 2nd LIEUT: D. A. EDLIN. No 4 Trench Mortar Battery admitted and evacuated - disease Gonorrhoea. Received 5 permanent Passes from A.P.M. for Ambulance cars on RUE DU BOIS proceeding to and returning from Advanced Dressing Station. Paid out personnel at Headquarters. Total Fr. 1810.	[illegible]
"	30/10/15	9 p.m.	13 cases sick admitted, 14 cases sick evacuated, leaving 32 cases sick remaining. D.D.M.S. Indian Corps, Colonel Kirkpatrick, visited the Ambulance and Advanced Dressing Station. No 51152 Pte NORRIS. C. H. of this unit admitted to 59 Field Ambulance suffering from bullet wound right side of chest, received on returning from duty at Regimental Aid Post. One wounded officer - 7th L. N. Lancs - admitted and evacuated; result of bomb accident at Brigade Headquarters. Weather cold and fine.	[illegible]

1875 Wt. W593/826 1,000,000 4/15 J.B.C. & A. A.D.S.S./Forms/C. 2118.

Instructions regarding War Diaries and Intelligence Summaries are contained in F. S. Regs., Part II. and the Staff Manual respectively. Title Pages will be prepared in manuscript.

WAR DIARY

~~or INTELLIGENCE SUMMARY~~

(Erase heading not required.)

Army Form C. 2118

Place	Date	Hour	Summary of Events and Information	Remarks and references to Appendices
AVELUY. POST.	27/10/16.	9am	OC to Bureau DIVN & Cyclist POST.	
		3PM	on NORTH to report to R.T.O PROUVILLERS. for transfer to OC 13 F.A.	
		7PM.	Two cases viz NO 4655 Cpl MILLS. T.V } treated for S.I.W Rt hand & NO 3665. Pte COX J } " " S.I.W Lt Hand. As both these cases looked suspicious of being self inflicted & the evidence of both the NCO & man unsatisfactory I sent them to 57 F.A. & wrote OC of their unit. 17th K.R.R.C as to whether they were self inflicted wounds or not.	
			EO	
AVELUY POST.	28/10/16	6am.	Received wire from O.C. 5 D.S.C stating that I was to send all Daimler & Talbot cars to him by 8am. Having received no intimation from ADMS 19th Divn I sent urgent message to the latter & informed him I was awaiting instructions from him on the matter.	
		7am	Orders received from ADMS 19th DIVN to despatch all Daimler & Sunbeam cars to OC 5.D.S.C	
		7.45am	Cars despatched to OC 5 D.S.C	
		8.30	Three M.A.C cars arrived for duty (temp^y) in place of those sent to D.S.C	

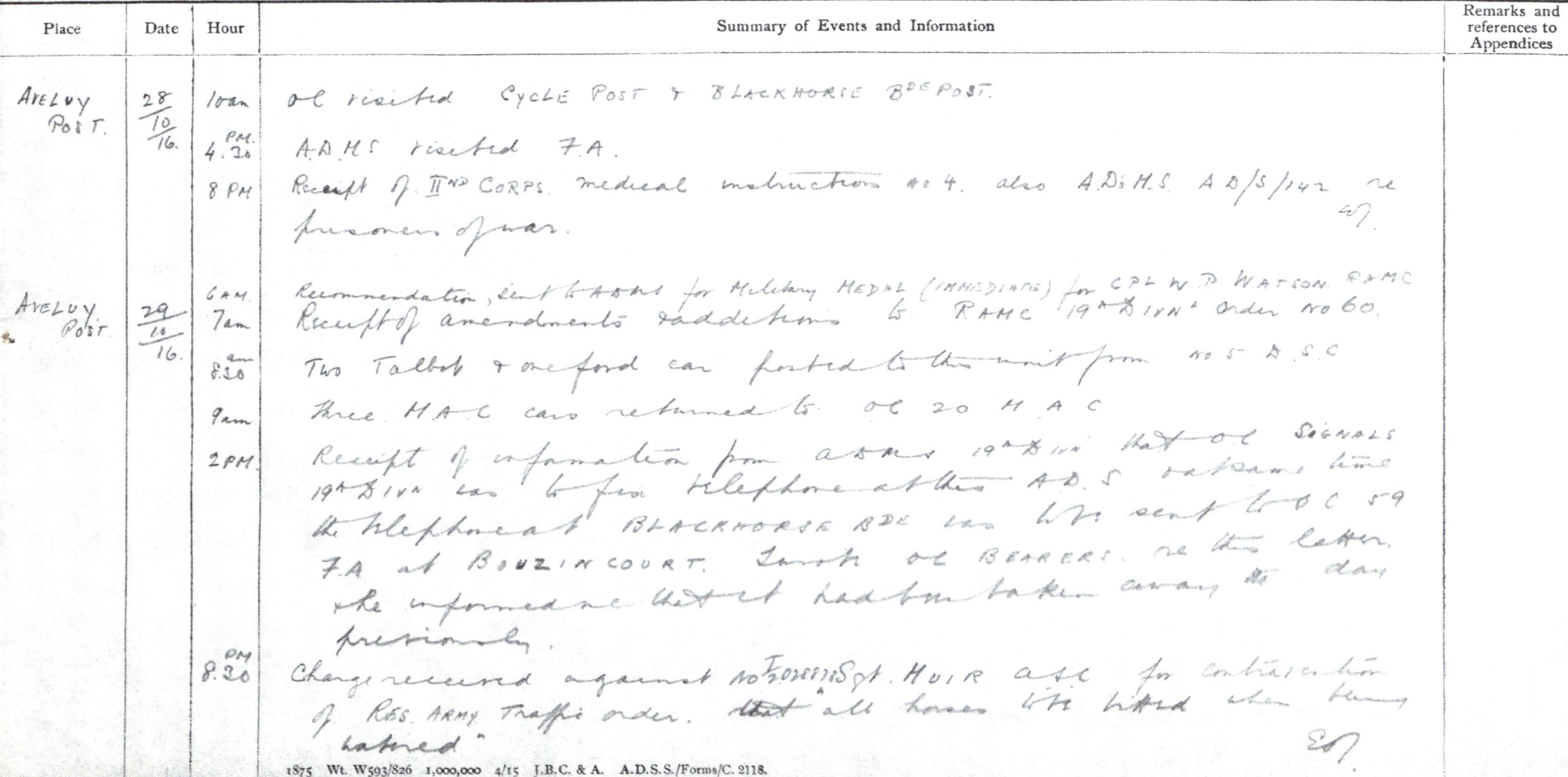

Instructions regarding War Diaries and Intelligence Summaries are contained in F. S. Regs., Part II. and the Staff Manual respectively. Title Pages will be prepared in manuscript.

WAR DIARY

~~or~~

~~INTELLIGENCE SUMMARY~~

(Erase heading not required.)

Army Form C. 2118

Place	Date	Hour	Summary of Events and Information	Remarks and references to Appendices
AVELUY POST.	28/10/16.	10am	OC visited CYCLE POST & BLACKHORSE BDE POST.	
		PM. 4.30	A.D.M.S visited F.A.	
		8 PM	Receipt of II ND CORPS. medical instructions No 4. also A.D.M.S. AD/S/142 re prisoners of war. [illegible]	
AVELUY. POST.	29/10/16.	6AM.	Recommendation, sent to ADMS for Military MEDAL (IMMEDIATE) for CPL W.D. WATSON. RAMC	
		7am	Receipt of amendments & additions to RAMC 19th DIVN Order No 60.	
		am 8.30	Two Talbot & one ford car posted to this unit from No 5 D.S.C	
		9am	Three M.A.C cars returned to OC 20 M.A.C	
		2PM.	Receipt of information from ADMS 19th DIVN that OC SIGNALS 19th DIVN has to fix telephone at this A.D.S & at same time the telephone at BLACKHORSE BDE has to be sent to OC 59 F.A at BOUZINCOURT. I asked OC BEARERS re this latter & he informed me that it had been taken away the day previously.	
		PM 8.30	Charge received against No T/[illegible] Sgt. MUIR ASC for contravention of RES. ARMY Traffic order. ~~that~~ "all horses to be led when being watered" [illegible]	

1875 Wt. W593/826 1,000,000 4/15 J.B.C. & A. A.D.S.S./Forms/C. 2118.

Instructions regarding War Diaries and Intelligence Summaries are contained in F. S. Regs., Part II. and the Staff Manual respectively. Title Pages will be prepared in manuscript.

WAR DIARY

~~or~~

~~INTELLIGENCE SUMMARY~~

(Erase heading not required.)

Army Form C. 2118.

Place	Date	Hour	Summary of Events and Information	Remarks and references to Appendices
AVELUY POST.	30/10/16.	7am	Receipt of A.D.M.S [illegible]/4A/94. that 8 men (T.Us) would be detailed when required at AVELUY POST for temp. duty to load & unload motor ambulances. these men to come from OC SANITY SECT. 19th DIVN.	
		9am	SgtMUIR'S CASE taken by OC. case dismissed as no RESERVE ARMY Traffic orders received by me. S.S.M DORMAN A.S.C informed that in future all mules must be bitted when taken to water.	
		12 Noon	Recommendation for promotion of L/CPL. WOOD. P.G & Pte FOULSHAM. to Rank of CPL & L/CPL respectively vice CPL SALISBURY struck off strength & posted to WIRELESS COY. [illegible]	
			PTE TIMMONS, attd with Supply waggon to 19 DIVNL TRAIN, met with an accident & Pte McDERMID. SENT to replace him.	
		2PM.	OC wrote O/C. 19th DIVNL BATHS. to inform him that Pte MOY at present attd 19th DIVNL BATHS was to return to duty with the BEARER DIVN of this unit.	
		6PM.	Two Talbot cars arrived from 5 [illegible]	

[illegible signature]

2449 Wt. W14957/M90 750,000 1/16 J.B.C. & A. Forms/C.2118/12.

Instructions regarding War Diaries and Intelligence Summaries are contained in F. S. Regs., Part II. and the Staff Manual respectively. Title Pages will be prepared in manuscript.

WAR DIARY
or
INTELLIGENCE SUMMARY
(Erase heading not required.)

Army Form C. 2118

Place	Date	Hour	Summary of Events and Information	Remarks and references to Appendices
LOCON	31/10/15	9pm	9 cases sick admitted and one case wounded, 10 cases sick evacuated and one wounded, leaving 31 cases sick remaining. No 40029 L/Cpl Fraser returned from India Corps H.Q. where he has been assisting the A.P.M. D.M.S 1st Army, Surg: General Macpherson circulated a farewell letter on handing over his duties to Colonel Pike. Weather cold and showery.	D F Mackenzie Capt RAMC

D F Mackenzie
Capt RAMC
57th Field Ambulance.

1875 Wt. W593/826 1,000,000 4/15 J.B.C. & A. A.D.S.S./Forms/C. 2118.

19th Division

57th Fa.
Vol: 5

121
7693

Nov 1915

Nov 15.

Instructions regarding War Diaries and Intelligence Summaries are contained in F. S. Regs., Part II. and the Staff Manual respectively. Title Pages will be prepared in manuscript.

WAR DIARY
or
INTELLIGENCE SUMMARY
(Erase heading not required.)

Army Form C. 2118

Place	Date	Hour	Summary of Events and Information	Remarks and references to Appendices
LOCON	1/11/15	9 p.m.	8 cases sick admitted, 6 cases sick evacuated, leaving 33 cases sick remaining. Prevailing disease continues to be Scabies. Four reinforcements R.A.M.C. arrived from the Base for duty & taken on the strength. War Diary for October forwarded to A.G. Base and Duplicate Copy for September to O/c R.A.M.C. Records. Weather very wet and muddy.	D.F.M.
"	2/11/15	9 p.m.	18 cases sick admitted, 11 cases sick evacuated, leaving 40 cases sick remaining. Paid Personnel at Advanced Dressing Station.	D.F.M.
"	3/11/15	9 p.m.	5 cases admitted sick + one wounded, 15 cases sick evacuated + one wounded, leaving 30 cases sick remaining. Weather wet + misty.	D.F.M.
"	4/11/15	9 p.m.	7 cases sick admitted, 8 cases sick evacuated, leaving 29 cases sick remaining. Lieut: Davies-Jones R.A.M.C. detailed to report for duty to A.D.M.S Meerut Division + struck off strength accordingly. Lieut: Dew. R.A.M.C re-called from Advanced Dressing Station + detailed to take over charge of Baths from Indian Corps. Notification received from Casualty Clearing Station that No: 14285 Pte AIREY. R. 7/R. Lancs. Regt. evacuated on 2-11-15, suspicious case of Diphtheria, has given a positive result on bacteriological exam: A.D.M.S. has been notified and also M.O. of the Regt. concerned. Weather fine but cold.	D.F.M.

1875 Wt. W593/826 1,000,000 4/15 J.B.C. & A. A.D.S.S./Forms/C. 2118.

Army Form C. 2118

Instructions regarding War Diaries and Intelligence Summaries are contained in F. S. Regs., Part II. and the Staff Manual respectively. Title Pages will be prepared in manuscript.

WAR DIARY
or
INTELLIGENCE SUMMARY

(Erase heading not required.)

Place	Date	Hour	Summary of Events and Information	Remarks and references to Appendices
LOCON	5/11/15	9 p.m.	10 cases sick were admitted during the day and six cases evacuated leaving 33 cases remaining. – Weather cold and showery and the roads exceedingly muddy. – The order detailing Lieut. DEW for charge of the Corps Baths has been cancelled. Lieut. DEW has now under instructions from the A.D.M.S. XIX Division been detailed for ~~duty~~ temporary duty with the LAHORE Division Indian Corps. I reported my arrival for duty and resumed command of the Field Ambulance on return from seven days leave of absence in England. J.E. Powell Major R.A.M.C.	J.E.P.
"	6/11/15	9 p.m.	One Officer sick was ~~evacuated~~ admitted and evacuated during the day. Eight other ranks sick were admitted and twelve evacuated leaving 29 remaining. – I visited the advanced Dressing Station in the RUE DU BOIS at Square X 17 d Ref. Map Sheet BETHUNE 36 A / 36 B. The road leading to the advanced Dressing station has been partially repaired but still needs further repair at LE TOURET. The weather continues damp and very cold.	combined sheet. J.E.P.
"	7/11/15	9 p.m.	Seven sick and one wounded were admitted during the day. Ten sick and one wounded were evacuated, leaving 26 sick remaining. – The weather has been fine and cold, but the mud on the roads and in the trenches is not drying up owing to the dampness of the atmosphere. Two Privates joined the unit as Reinforcements to-day.	J.E.P.
"	8/11/15	9 p.m.	Eighteen sick were admitted during the day and eight sick evacuated leaving 36 remaining. All Officers attended a lecture at 2.30 p.m. given by Major Grant R.A.M.C. D.A.D.M.S. XIX Division, on the various forms of suffocating gas used and the best means of combating them. – The weather has been fine and not so cold.	J.E.P.

1875 Wt. W593/826 1,000,000 4/15 J.B.C. & A. A.D.S.S./Forms/C. 2118.

Army Form C. 2118

WAR DIARY
or
INTELLIGENCE SUMMARY
(Erase heading not required.)

Instructions regarding War Diaries and Intelligence Summaries are contained in F. S. Regs., Part II. and the Staff Manual respectively. Title Pages will be prepared in manuscript.

Place	Date	Hour	Summary of Events and Information	Remarks and references to Appendices
LOCON	9/11/15	9 p.m.	Nine sick were admitted during the day and eleven were evacuated leaving thirty four sick remaining. I visited the Advanced Dressing Station during the afternoon. LIEUT. RHODES R.A.M.C. reported his arrival for duty this evening as a Reinforcement. Heavy rain is falling and there is a high wind this evening.	J.E.P.
"	10/11/15	9 p.m.	Seven sick were admitted during the day and six were evacuated leaving thirty five remaining. Heavy showers of rain fell in the morning but the remainder of the day has been fine. LIEUT. RHODES R.A.M.C. reported his departure this day having been detailed for duty by the A.D.M.S. XIX Division as Medical Officer in charge the 88th Brigade R.F.A. From to-day the XIX Division becomes attached to the XI Army Corps in place of the Indian Army Corps. – Major General FASKEN G.O.C. XIX Division inspected the 57th Field Ambulance to-day at 12·10 p.m.	J.E.P.
"	11/11/15	9 p.m.	Three sick were admitted during the day and nine sick evacuated leaving twenty nine remaining. The A.D.M.S. XIX Division inspected the Field Ambulance to-day. Heavy rain is again falling this evening.	J.E.P.
"	12/11/15	9 p.m.	Fourteen sick were admitted and nineteen evacuated leaving twenty four cases remaining. Heavy showers of rain have fallen throughout the day and there is also a high wind. Captain G.P. KIDD R.A.M.C. reported his departure this day on ten days leave of absence to ENGLAND. – This morning I visited the Advanced Dressing Station, the RUE L'EPINETTE and the RUE DE CAILLOUX and the Ruined Brewery in the latter road, to see if it is possible to send Ambulance Cars further forward to facilitate the evacuation of the wounded from the trenches. – Sent a report on the subject to the A.D.M.S.	J.E.P.

1875 Wt. W593/826 1,000,000 4/15 J.B.C. & A. A.D.S.S./Forms/C. 2118.

Instructions regarding War Diaries and Intelligence Summaries are contained in F. S. Regs., Part II. and the Staff Manual respectively. Title Pages will be prepared in manuscript.

WAR DIARY
or
INTELLIGENCE SUMMARY
(Erase heading not required.)

Army Form C. 2118

Place	Date	Hour	Summary of Events and Information	Remarks and references to Appendices
LOCON	13/11/15	9 p.m.	Four cases were ~~[illegible]~~ admitted during the day and eight evacuated, leaving twenty cases remaining. – Billeting certificates for the week were rendered to the Maire. The weather has continued wet & stormy.	J.E.P.
"	14/11/15	9 p.m.	Four cases were admitted during the day and twelve cases evacuated leaving twelve cases sick remaining. The Field Ambulance is still collecting all the Scabies cases of the Division but the numbers have diminished considerably recently. – The weather is now fine and cold with frost at night and the mud is beginning to dry up a little.	J.E.P.
"	15/11/15	9 p.m.	Twelve cases were admitted during the day and eight evacuated, leaving sixteen remaining. The A.D.M.S. XIX Division visited the Field Ambulance during the morning. I visited the Advanced Dressing Station in the afternoon. – The weather continues dry and cold with hard frost at night.	J.E.P.
"	16/11/15	9 p.m.	Thirteen cases sick were admitted and nine cases evacuated leaving twenty cases remaining. The Field Ambulance is now collecting sick from the whole of the Reserve Brigade, in accordance with XIX Division R.A.M.C. Routine Orders issued to-day. ~~[illegible]~~ I issued pay to all the men at the Headquarters of the Unit this afternoon. A thaw has set in and heavy rain is falling this evening.	J.E.P.
"	17/11/15	9 p.m.	52 sick and one wounded were admitted during the day, seventeen sick were evacuated leaving 55 sick and one wounded remaining. The prevailing disease is "chilled feet". – Some of these men had not been issued with Trench boots or Whale oil – Reported this to the A.D.M.S. LIEUT. WILKINSON R.A.M.C. reported his departure this day for temporary duty as M.O. i/c XIX Divisional R.E. – The weather has been cold and wet with frequent showers of sleet.	J.E.P.

1875 Wt. W593/826 1,000,000 4/15 J.B.C. & A. A.D.S.S./Forms/C. 2118.

Instructions regarding War Diaries and Intelligence Summaries are contained in F. S. Regs., Part II. and the Staff Manual respectively. Title Pages will be prepared in manuscript.

WAR DIARY
or
INTELLIGENCE SUMMARY

(Erase heading not required.)

Army Form C. 2118

Place	Date	Hour	Summary of Events and Information	Remarks and references to Appendices
LOCON	18/11/15	9 p.m.	Twentyone sick were admitted during the day, of which eight were chilled feet, twentyfour sick and one wounded were evacuated, leaving 52 cases remaining. LIEUT. H.R. DEW R.A.M.C. reported his arrival for duty this day in connection of temporary duty with the LAHORE DIVISION, Indian Corps. There was a hard frost in the night, but a thaw set in this morning.	J.E.P.
"	19/11/15	9 p.m.	Twentyfive sick were admitted to the Field Ambulance during the day and twentyseven cases evacuated leaving 49 cases remaining. – Visited the advanced dressing station in the afternoon and took up 610 francs with me for the pay of the detachment there. There was a hard frost again last night but thawed during the day.	J.E.P.
"	20/11/15	9 p.m.	Twentyone sick were admitted during the day and thirtytwo evacuated, leaving thirtyeight cases remaining. A court of Enquiry was assembled to-day ~~to~~ at the 57th Field Ambulance to enquire into the circumstances under which No. 41621 Pte Carpenter G. R.A.M.C. of this unit was accidentally shot in both legs on the 7th inst. There has been no change in the weather	J.E.P.
"	21/11/15	9 p.m.	Two officers sick were admitted during the day and evacuated. 17 other ranks sick were admitted during the day and 15 were evacuated, leaving 40 cases remaining. There has been no change in the weather. Received R.A.M.C. Operation Orders by A.D.M.S. XIX Division, ordering 1 Section of the Field Ambulance to move to ROBECQ on the 23/11/15 and open out for the reception of sick. The advanced dressing station to be closed on the 24th inst. and the Bearers to rejoin Headquarters of the Unit on the evening of the 24th inst. and the whole Unit less one section to march to ROBECQ on the morning of the 25th inst.	J.E.P.

Instructions regarding War Diaries and Intelligence Summaries are contained in F. S. Regs., Part II. and the Staff Manual respectively. Title Pages will be prepared in manuscript.

WAR DIARY
or
INTELLIGENCE SUMMARY
(Erase heading not required.)

Army Form C. 2118

Place	Date	Hour	Summary of Events and Information	Remarks and references to Appendices
LOCON	22/11/15	9 p.m.	There were twentysix cases sick and one wounded admitted to the Field Ambulance during the day – Forty sick and one wounded were evacuated leaving twentysix cases remaining. – I went to ROBECQ in the afternoon to see about the billeting of the men and the accommodation for Patients in the Mill at ROBECQ. Detailed LIEUT. H.R. DEW in charge of the Section to march to ROBECQ to-morrow.	J.E.P.
"	23/11/15	9 p.m.	One Officer accidentally wounded was admitted and evacuated during the day, ten cases accidentally wounded were ~~evacu~~ admitted and nine wounded evacuated. Thirteen sick were admitted; 28 sick evacuated, leaving eleven sick and one wounded remaining. LIEUT. DEW in charge of one section marched off at 12·45 p.m. for the Mill ROBECQ and opened for the reception of sick. LIEUT. THOMSON recalled from the advanced Dressing Station reported his arrival at Headquarters. Rendered Billeting Certificates to the Maire of LACOUTURE for the advanced Dressing Station Party up to and including 24/11/15	J.E.P.
"	24/11/15	9 p.m.	Twenty sick were admitted and twenty evacuated during the day, leaving eleven sick and one wounded remaining. Rendered billeting certificates to the Maire of LOCON up to and including the 25/11/15. Handed over the advanced Dressing Station to the 46th Division and withdrew Captain SMALLEY and the Bearer Division at 3·30 p.m. The weather is milder but damp, some rain fell.	J.E.P.
ROBECQ	25/11/15	9 p.m.	Eight sick were admitted and eight ~~evacu~~ evacuated during the day, leaving 11 sick and one wounded remaining. The Field Ambulance marched at 1 p.m. from LOCON and arrived at the MILL, ROBECQ at 3·30 p.m. Reported arrival to A.D.M.S. XIX Division. The weather was dry but cold.	J.E.P.

1875 Wt. W593/826 1,000,000 4/15 J.B.C. & A. A.D.S.S./Forms/C. 2118.

Instructions regarding War Diaries and Intelligence Summaries are contained in F. S. Regs., Part II. and the Staff Manual respectively. Title Pages will be prepared in manuscript.

WAR DIARY
or
INTELLIGENCE SUMMARY
(Erase heading not required.)

Army Form C. 2118

Place	Date	Hour	Summary of Events and Information	Remarks and references to Appendices
ROBECQ	26/11/15	9 p.m.	Seventeen sick were admitted and seven evacuated leaving 21 sick and 1 wounded remaining. The Mill used as a hospital is exceedingly cold and heating by means of Braziers is very unsatisfactory owing to the smoke and fumes given off. Saw the D.A.D.M.S. about it who went to Divisional Headquarters and have been promised three stoves for the Hospital, also that the first floor will be roofed in with boards.	J.E.P.
"	27/11/15	9 p.m.	One Officer was admitted sick and evacuated during the day. Eleven other ranks [illegible] were admitted and fifteen were evacuated, leaving 17 sick and one wounded remaining. Lieut. Colonel Dorich [illegible] A.A. & Q.M.G. inspected the Hospital building this morning with a view to improvements and warming of the building by the Royal Engineers. An R.E. Officer came in the afternoon [illegible] the necessary [illegible] arrangements. I have indented for Coke for the Braziers [illegible] smokes so much. – The weather continues dry but very cold with hard frost.	
"	28/11/15	9 p.m.	Ten sick and one wounded were admitted during the day and nine sick and one wounded evacuated, leaving 18 sick and one wounded remaining. Further arrangements were made with the R.E. with regard to warming the mill & the work should commence tomorrow. A certain amount of coke was obtained from Béthune during the day. The weather continues dry and cold with hard frost.	G.M. Lt. [illegible]

1875 Wt. W593/826 1,000,000 4/15 J.B.C. & A. A.D.S.S./Forms/C. 2118.

Instructions regarding War Diaries and Intelligence Summaries are contained in F. S. Regs., Part II. and the Staff Manual respectively. Title Pages will be prepared in manuscript.

WAR DIARY
or
~~INTELLIGENCE SUMMARY~~
(Erase heading not required.)

Army Form C. 2118

Place	Date	Hour	Summary of Events and Information	Remarks and references to Appendices
Robecq	29/11/15	9.0 pm	Fourteen sick were admitted during the day and nine sick and one wounded evacuated, leaving 23. sick remaining. The C.O. being on the sick list this morning, command was taken over by Capt. G.P. Kidd during the temporary absence of Capt. D.J. Mackenzie on leave. Scheme of training as recommended by the A.D.M.S. was commenced this morning, the men being sent for a short route march. The weather turned wet again and there was much rain during the day.	GPK
"	30/11/15	"	Eleven sick were admitted during the day and fifteen evacuated leaving nineteen remaining Col. H.A. Hinge, A.D.M.S., inspected the hospital this morning and made various suggestions with regard to improvements. The work of improving and warming the mill is being continued by the R.E. The weather was warmer but fine & bright.	GPK
~~ROBECQ~~	~~1/12/15~~	~~9 pm~~	~~Fourteen sick were admitted during~~	

J.E. Powell
Major R.A.M.C.
O.C. 57th Field Ambulance

1875 Wt. W593/826 1,000,000 4/15 J.B.C. & A. A.D.S.S./Forms/C. 2118.

19th [illegible]

F/154/1

December 191[illegible]

57th F.A.
Vol: 6

121
7935.

No. 57 F.A.

Army Form C. 2118

Instructions regarding War Diaries and Intelligence Summaries are contained in F. S. Regs., Part II. and the Staff Manual respectively. Title Pages will be prepared in manuscript.

WAR DIARY
or
INTELLIGENCE SUMMARY
(Erase heading not required.)

Place	Date	Hour	Summary of Events and Information	Remarks and references to Appendices
ROBECQ	1/12/15	9 p.m.	14 sick were admitted during the day and 8 evacuated leaving 25 remaining. The weather is now very much milder. – The Royal Engineers are continuing the work of improving the hospital structurally. The D.D.M.S. 11th Corps inspected the Field Ambulance during the afternoon. All ranks that could be spared from duty were sent on a Route march during the morning.	J.E.P.
"	2/12/15	9 p.m.	One Officer wounded accidentally was admitted and evacuated during the day, 15 other ranks sick were admitted and 13 evacuated, leaving 27 cases remaining. The men were taken on a Route march during the morning and a lecture on Nursing duties given in the afternoon to the Tent Division. – The weather continues mild.	J.E.P.
"	3/12/15	9 p.m.	10 sick were admitted and 15 cases evacuated during the day, leaving 22 cases remaining. – The improvements in the Hospital have now been completed by the Royal Engineers and they have also put in two stoves. – The weather continues mild but it has rained all day.	J.E.P.
"	4/12/15	9 p.m.	Received orders at 11 a.m. from the A.D.M.S. to send the Bearer Division to take over forthwith the Advanced Dressing Station at ST. VAAST Sq M 32 d. The Bearer division moved off at 12 Noon under Captain KIDD and LIEUT. ST. JOHNSTON. There were 12 cases admitted and 31 cases evacuated leaving 3 cases remaining.	J.E.P.
VIELLE CHAPELLE	5/12/15	9 p.m.	Received orders from the A.D.M.S. at 10 p.m. last night for the remainder of the unit to march at 9 a.m. to-day to the school at VIELLE CHAPELLE Sq R/28 c and open there for the reception of casualties. This move was completed by 1 p.m. – One horse ambulance wagon ~~was~~ fell into a deep ditch last night and has broken in two. Reported it to the Ordnance Corps for salvage as our efforts to do so were unavailing. One mule strayed from the Advanced Dressing Station last night and is lost. Reported this to A.P.M.	J.E.P.

1875 Wt. W593/826 1,000,000 4/15 J.B.C. & A. A.D.S.S./Forms/C. 2118.

Army Form C. 2118

Instructions regarding War Diaries and Intelligence Summaries are contained in F. S. Regs., Part II. and the Staff Manual respectively. Title Pages will be prepared in manuscript.

WAR DIARY
or
INTELLIGENCE SUMMARY
(Erase heading not required.)

Place	Date	Hour	Summary of Events and Information	Remarks and references to Appendices
VIELLE CHAPELLE	6/12/15	9 p.m.	One Officer sick, namely the G.O.C. XIX Division was admitted and evacuated during the day. 31 sick and 6 wounded were admitted and 19 sick and 4 wounded were evacuated, leaving 44 sick and 2 wounded remaining. – The A.D.M.S. inspected the Field Ambulance in the morning. I inspected the Advanced Dressing Station ~~in~~ at ST. VAAST in the afternoon.	J.E.P.
"	7/12/15	9 p.m.	Two Officers sick were ~~admitted~~ admitted and evacuated during the day, 37 sick were admitted and ~~the~~ 34 sick and 2 wounded were evacuated, leaving 47 sick remaining. The A.D.M.S. XIX Division visited the Field Ambulance and also the Advanced dressing station in the morning. I paid the men at Headquarters in the afternoon.	J.E.P.
"	8/12/15	9 p.m.	Two Officers sick were admitted and evacuated during the day. 26 sick and one wounded other ranks were admitted and one wounded and 22 sick were evacuated during the day leaving 51 cases remaining. – Visited the advanced dressing station in the afternoon and paid the men of the Bearer division. –	J.E.P.
"	9/12/15	9 p.m.	One Officer wounded was admitted and evacuated during the day. One other rank wounded and 20 sick were admitted, and one wounded and 22 sick evacuated, leaving 49 sick remaining. LIEUT. R.O.C. THOMSON reported his arrival on completion of temporary duty as M.O. i/c 8th Gloucestershire Regt. The weather continues very wet, it has rained all day	J.E.P.
"	10/12/15	9 p.m.	Captain A.A. SMALLEY reported his arrival on return from 10 days leave of absence to England. 27 sick and one wounded were admitted during the day and 23 cases evacuated leaving 54 cases remaining. – Heavy showers of rain have fallen throughout the day. The A.D.M.S. visited the Ambulance during the afternoon.	J.E.P.

1875 Wt. W593/826 1,000,000 4/15 J.B.C. & A. A.D.S.S./Forms/C. 2118.

Army Form C. 2118

Instructions regarding War Diaries and Intelligence Summaries are contained in F. S. Regs., Part II. and the Staff Manual respectively. Title Pages will be prepared in manuscript.

WAR DIARY
or
INTELLIGENCE SUMMARY
(Erase heading not required.)

Place	Date	Hour	Summary of Events and Information	Remarks and references to Appendices
VIEILLE CHAPELLE	11/12/15	9 p.m.	Two Officers sick and one wounded were admitted and evacuated during the day. 39 sick and 18 wounded other ranks were admitted and 42 were evacuated, leaving 69 remaining. I visited the Advanced Dressing Station in the afternoon. The weather continues very wet.	J.E.P.
"	12/12/15	9 p.m.	~~[illegible]~~ 18 sick and 13 wounded were admitted during the day, 44 cases were evacuated, leaving 56 cases remaining. — I withdrew 20 Bearers from the Advanced Dressing Station to-day as they are not required there and they are more usefully employed at Headquarters. — I have now only one Section of Bearers at the Advanced Dressing Station namely 36.	J.E.P.
"	13/12/15	9 p.m.	One wounded Officer, 8 wounded men and 20 sick were admitted and one Officer and 40 other ranks were evacuated, leaving 44 cases remaining. Under instructions from the A.D.M.S. I have detailed 12 Privates to proceed to-morrow morning at 8 a.m. to join the 46th Division. — The Field Ambulance is now two Officers and 25 men under establishment. — The weather is dry but much colder	J.E.P.
"	14/12/15	9 p.m.	One sick Officer & one wounded Officer, 25 sick and 9 wounded other ranks were admitted during the day. 1 Officer and 19 other ranks were evacuated, leaving 59 cases remaining. The A.D.M.S. XIX Division & the D.A.D.M.S. XI Corps visited the Field Ambulance & the Advanced Dressing Station this morning. — I visited the Advanced Dressing Station in the afternoon. — The A.S.C. personnel, horses, mules and vehicles were inspected to-day by the O.C. XIX Divisional Train. The weather is dry but very cold.	J.E.P.

1875 Wt. W593/826 1,000,000 4/15 J.B.C. & A. A.D.S.S./Forms/C. 2118.

Instructions regarding War Diaries and Intelligence Summaries are contained in F. S. Regs., Part II. and the Staff Manual respectively. Title Pages will be prepared in manuscript.

WAR DIARY
or
INTELLIGENCE SUMMARY
(Erase heading not required.)

Army Form C. 2118

Place	Date	Hour	Summary of Events and Information	Remarks and references to Appendices
VIEILLE CHAPELLE	15/12/15	9 p.m.	One sick Officer was admitted and two Officers evacuated during the day, 2 other ranks wounded and 22 sick were admitted and 35 cases evacuated, leaving 48 cases remaining. The weather continues cold and dry.	J.E.P.
"	16/12/15	9 p.m.	40 sick and three wounded were admitted during the day to the Field Ambulance ~~[illegible]~~ 32 cases were evacuated, leaving 59 cases remaining. A Section of the 131st Field Ambulance, consisting of 4 Officers and 62 men arrived at 5 p.m. to be attached to this unit for instruction for 7 days.	J.E.P.
"	17/12/15	9 p.m.	Two Officers were admitted and one evacuated during the day, 25 other ranks were admitted and 30 evacuated, leaving 1 Officer and 54 other ranks remaining. – It has rained steadily throughout the day. – Made arrangements for the instruction of the Officers, N.C.O.s & men of the Section of the 131st Field Ambulance in the duties of the various Sections, Nursing, Clerical general duty etc. I sent one Officer & 19 Bearers to the advanced Dressing Station for instruction in the morning for 3 days – I visited them in the afternoon.	J.E.P.
"	18/12/15	9 p.m.	One Officer was admitted and two Officers evacuated during the day. 31 other ranks were admitted and 23 evacuated, leaving 62 cases remaining. Major General Bridges C.M.G. Commanding the XIX Division visited the Field Ambulance during the morning. The A.D.M.S. XIX Division also visited the Field Ambulance during the day. The weather continues cold & damp.	J.E.P.

1875 Wt. W593/826 1,000,000 4/15 J.B.C. & A. A.D.S.S./Forms/C. 2118.

Instructions regarding War Diaries and Intelligence Summaries are contained in F. S. Regs., Part II. and the Staff Manual respectively. Title Pages will be prepared in manuscript.

WAR DIARY
or
INTELLIGENCE SUMMARY
(Erase heading not required.)

Army Form C. 2118

Place	Date	Hour	Summary of Events and Information	Remarks and references to Appendices
VIEILLE CHAPELLE	19/12/15	9 p.m.	Brigadier General Lewis commanding 56th Infantry Brigade was admitted ~~r evacuated~~ suffering from gout. One sick Officer was admitted and evacuated & one wounded Officer was admitted & died in the Field Ambulance. 37 other ranks were admitted during the day and 28 cases evacuated leaving 71 cases remaining. – The weather is damp & cold.	J.E.P.
"	20/12/15	9 p.m.	One Officer sick was admitted during the day. – One case of Infectious disease, Scarlet Fever was admitted from the 187th Coy. R.E. and evacuated during the day. 28 other ranks sick & wounded were admitted and 56 cases evacuated, leaving 44 cases remaining.	J.E.P.
"	21/12/15	9 p.m.	One sick Officer was evacuated during the day. 40 other ranks were admitted during the day and 36 evacuated leaving 48 remaining. – I visited the Advanced dressing Station in the afternoon. Rain has fallen continuously during the day. – Lieut. & Quartermaster A. Bennett reported his departure this day on 10 days leave of absence in England.	J.E.P.
"	22/12/15	9 p.m.	One Officer died of wounds in the Field Ambulance to-day, notification by wire was sent to the A.G. G.H.Q. A.A.G. 1st Army & D.A.G. Base. – One sick Officer was admitted & evacuated during the day. There were 31 other ranks admitted and 25 evacuated leaving 54 remaining. – I paid the personnel at Headquarters during the afternoon	J.E.P.
"	23/12/15	9 p.m.	3 sick Officers were admitted to the Field Ambulance during the day and two were evacuated. There were 57 other ranks sick admitted during the day and 39 cases evacuated leaving One Officer and 72 men remaining. – The A.D.M.S. visited the Field Ambulance in the morning. – Also the Officer i/c the Canadian Mobile Laboratory with regard to the investigation into the nature of the cases of diarrhoea which are becoming rather prevalent during the last week. – I visited the Advanced Dressing Station in the afternoon & paid the personnel there.	J.E.P.

1875 Wt. W593/826 1,000,000 4/15 J.B.C. & A. A.D.S.S./Forms/C. 2118.

Army Form C. 2118

Instructions regarding War Diaries and Intelligence Summaries are contained in F. S. Regs., Part II. and the Staff Manual respectively. Title Pages will be prepared in manuscript.

WAR DIARY
or
INTELLIGENCE SUMMARY
(Erase heading not required.)

Place	Date	Hour	Summary of Events and Information	Remarks and references to Appendices
VIEILLE CHAPELLE	24/12/15	9 p.m.	Two cases of Sick Officers were evacuated during the day, and one Officer sick was admitted. ~~+~~ 17 other ranks were admitted and 23 evacuated leaving 66 cases remaining. Heavy rain again fell to-day and consequently the condition of the ground at the Advanced Dressing Station is becoming very bad for the ambulance cars.	J.E.P.
"	25/12/15	9 p.m.	29 sick and 8 wounded were admitted during the day and 43 cases were evacuated, leaving 56 sick and 4 wounded remaining. – Visited the Advanced Dressing Station during the morning and made arrangements for the disposal of the ambulance cars in better positions and for the carrying of the wounded to the cars. ~~[illegible]~~ Billeting certificates & distribution lists for the week were rendered to-day	J.E.P.
"	26/12/15	9 p.m.	Three sick Officers were admitted to the Field Ambulance during the day and are remaining. – Thirty three sick and 8 wounded other ranks were admitted and 32 cases were evacuated leaving ~~[illegible]~~ 3 Officers, 65 sick and 4 wounded remaining. – B Section of 130th Field Ambulance arrived during the afternoon to be attached to this Unit for seven days instruction. – Heavy rain showers continue to fall and many of the roads are under water.	J.E.P.
"	27/12/15	9 p.m.	One wounded Officer and two sick Officers were admitted during the day, two Officers were evacuated leaving 4 remaining. 48 other ranks were admitted and 45 were evacuated, leaving 72 cases remaining. – One Officer and a party of Bearers of the 130th Field Ambulance left for the Advanced Dressing Station ~~[illegible]~~ at 10 a.m. for instruction. – The remainder of the Section is being instructed in the duties at the Main Dressing Station.	J.E.P.

1875 Wt. W593/826 1,000,000 4/15 J.B.C. & A. A.D.S.S./Forms/C. 2118.

Army Form C. 2118

WAR DIARY
or
INTELLIGENCE SUMMARY
(Erase heading not required.)

Instructions regarding War Diaries and Intelligence Summaries are contained in F. S. Regs., Part II. and the Staff Manual respectively. Title Pages will be prepared in manuscript.

Place	Date	Hour	Summary of Events and Information	Remarks and references to Appendices
VIEILLE CHAPELLE	28/12/15	9 p.m.	One wounded Officer was admitted during the day and four Officers sick and wounded were evacuated. 36 other ranks sick and 13 wounded were admitted and 46 cases evacuated, leaving 66 sick and 9 wounded remaining. The Field Ambulance Personnel, including the Army Service Corps attached, the horses & transport and also the main dressing station were all inspected by the G.O.C. the XIX Division in the afternoon. The G.O.C. expressed his satisfaction with all he had seen. Lieut. D.T. O'FLYNN R.A.M.C. (T.C.) reported his arrival for duty with the Field Ambulance this day. — Captain Smalley and Captain OWENS relieved Captain KIDD and Lieut. St JOHNSTONE at the advanced Dressing station, the two latter returning to Headquarters of the Unit.	J.E.P.
"	29/12/15	9 p.m.	Two Officers were admitted to the Field Ambulance during the day and 3 Officers evacuated. 33 other ranks were admitted and 39 cases evacuated, leaving 69 cases remaining. I visited the advanced Dressing Station in the morning. — The D.D.M.S. 11th Corps and the A.D.M.S. XIX Division visited the Field Ambulance in the afternoon. The weather has been fine and clear to-day.	J.E.P.
"	30/12/15	9 p.m.	23 sick and 4 wounded were admitted during the day and 33 cases were evacuated leaving 59 cases sick and 4 wounded remaining. The weather has again been fine but colder. — Lieut. A. St. Johnston reported his departure this day for duty as M.O. i/c the 9th Bn. Welsh Regiment.	J.E.P.

1875 Wt. W593/826 1,000,000 4/15 J.B.C. & A. A.D.S.S./Forms/C. 2118.

Army Form C. 2118

WAR DIARY
or
INTELLIGENCE SUMMARY
(Erase heading not required.)

Instructions regarding War Diaries and Intelligence Summaries are contained in F. S. Regs., Part II. and the Staff Manual respectively. Title Pages will be prepared in manuscript.

Place	Date	Hour	Summary of Events and Information	Remarks and references to Appendices
VIEILLE CHAPELLE	31/12/15	9 p.m.	Four sick Officers were admitted during the day and none were evacuated. 35 other ranks sick and 4 wounded were admitted during the day and 33 cases were evacuated, leaving 65 cases sick and four wounded remaining. Lieut. WILKINSON R.A.M.C. (T.C.) reported his arrival for duty with the Field Ambulance on completion of temporary duty as M.O. i/c 9th South Lancashire Regt. The weather has been fine but the roads continue to be soft and muddy.	J.E.P.

J. E. Powell
Major R.A.M.C.
O.C. 57th Field Ambulance

1875 Wt. W593/826 1,000,000 4/15 J.B.C. & A. A.D.S.S./Forms/C. 2118.

19th Dw

F/154/2

57th F. A.
Vol: 7

Jan 1916

Army Form C. 2118

Instructions regarding War Diaries and Intelligence Summaries are contained in F. S. Regs., Part II. and the Staff Manual respectively. Title Pages will be prepared in manuscript.

WAR DIARY
or
INTELLIGENCE SUMMARY
(Erase heading not required.)

Place	Date	Hour	Summary of Events and Information	Remarks and references to Appendices
VIEILLE CHAPELLE	1/1/16	9 p.m.	Two Officers sick were admitted during the day and 5 Officers were evacuated leaving one Officer remaining. – 46 other ranks were admitted during the day and 42 cases were evacuated, leaving 73 cases remaining. Lieut & Quartermaster BENNET reported his arrival on return from 10 days leave. Captain D.F. MACKENZIE reported his departure on 7 days special leave to England. – The weather is very stormy to-day.	J.E.P.
"	2/1/16	9 p.m.	One Officer sick was admitted and two were evacuated during the day. 35 other ranks sick and wounded were admitted and 49 were evacuated during the day leaving 56 sick and 3 wounded remaining. The weather continues very wet and stormy. I visited the advanced dressing station in the morning. The A.D.M.S. visited the Field Ambulance in the morning. Lieut H.R. DEW RAME reported his arrival this evening on completion of temporary duty with the 8th North Staffords Regt.	J.E.P.
"	3/1/16	9 p.m.	38 sick and 7 wounded were admitted during the day, 46 cases were evacuated leaving 55 sick and 3 wounded remaining. – One case of German measles and one case of Mumps were admitted and transferred to the No. 7 General Hospital MALASSISE. – All precautions with regard to isolation and disinfection were taken and the Special Infectious Report forwarded in each case. C. Section 131st Field Ambulance arrived in the afternoon for 7 days instruction. – The weather continues stormy	J.E.P.

1875 Wt. W593/826 1,000,000 4/15 J.B.C. & A. A.D.S.S./Forms/C. 2118.

Instructions regarding War Diaries and Intelligence Summaries are contained in F. S. Regs., Part II. and the Staff Manual respectively. Title Pages will be prepared in manuscript.

WAR DIARY
or
INTELLIGENCE SUMMARY
(Erase heading not required.)

Army Form C. 2118

Place	Date	Hour	Summary of Events and Information	Remarks and references to Appendices
VIEILLE CHAPELLE	4/1/16	9 p.m.	3 sick Officers were admitted during the day and one was evacuated leaving 2 remaining. There were 62 other ranks sick and 5 wounded admitted and 50 evacuated, leaving 71 sick and 4 wounded remaining. The weather has been mild and damp.	J.E.P.
"	5/1/16	9 p.m.	Two sick Officers were evacuated during the day and none admitted. 39 other ranks sick and wounded were admitted during the day. 54 cases were evacuated, leaving 60 cases remaining. – I visited the advanced dressing station during the morning, the condition of the ground there is still very damp and muddy.	J.E.P.
"	6/1/16	9 p.m.	One sick Officer was admitted during the day, 27 other ranks sick were admitted and 23 cases were evacuated, leaving 64 cases remaining. Lieut. WILKINSON reported his departure on 10 days leave of absence to England. Lieut. O'FLYNN reported his departure for temporary duty as M.O. i/c 9th Cheshire Regt.	J.E.P.
"	7/1/16	9 p.m.	One wounded and two sick Officers were admitted during the day, 3 Officers were evacuated leaving one Officer remaining. 18 sick and 4 wounded were admitted and 42 were evacuated leaving 44 cases remaining. – The A.D.M.S. visited the Field Ambulance in the morning. I paid the men at Headquarters in the afternoon	J.E.P.
"	8/1/16	9 p.m.	Two sick and one wounded Officers were admitted to the Field Ambulance and also evacuated during the day, leaving 1 sick Officer remaining. 36 sick and 18 wounded other ranks were admitted during the day and 24 sick and 18 wounded were evacuated leaving 54 sick and 2 wounded remaining. – I visited the advanced Dressing Station during the afternoon and paid the men there. – The weather has become considerably colder to-day. – Billeting certificates for the week were rendered to-day.	J.E.P.

1875 Wt. W593/826 1,000,000 4/15 J.B.C. & A. A.D.S.S./Forms/C. 2118.

Army Form C. 2118

Instructions regarding War Diaries and Intelligence Summaries are contained in F. S. Regs., Part II. and the Staff Manual respectively. Title Pages will be prepared in manuscript.

WAR DIARY
or
INTELLIGENCE SUMMARY
(Erase heading not required.)

Place	Date	Hour	Summary of Events and Information	Remarks and references to Appendices
VIEILLE CHAPELLE	9/1/16	9 p.m.	29 sick and 6 wounded were admitted to the Field Ambulance during the day and 36 cases were evacuated leaving 51 sick and 4 wounded cases remaining. – No Officers were admitted during the day, there is still one sick Officer remaining. – The weather continues damp, but no rain has fallen during the day.	J.E.P.
"	10/1/16	9 p.m.	One sick Officer was admitted to the Field Ambulance and one evacuated during the day leaving one Officer remaining. 26 other ranks sick and 20 wounded were admitted and 50 cases were evacuated, leaving 46 sick and 5 wounded remaining. The A.D.M.S. visited the Field Ambulance during the morning. Lieut. J.F. MacLeod R.A.M.C. (T.C.) reported his arrival for duty this day. – There has been no change in the weather.	J.E.P.
"	11/1/16	9 p.m.	One sick Officer was admitted during the day and two were evacuated, leaving no Officers remaining. – 28 sick other ranks and 10 wounded were admitted and 42 cases were evacuated, leaving 40 sick and 7 wounded remaining. – I visited the advanced dressing station in the afternoon, the ground is drying there a little and there is less water in the dugouts.	J.E.P.
"	12/1/16	9 p.m.	One sick Officer was admitted and evacuated during the day. 23 sick and 5 wounded other ranks were admitted and 24 sick and 9 wounded were evacuated, leaving 39 cases sick and 3 wounded remaining. – The erection of a new shed for a cookhouse for the hospital was completed to-day. – All the tents were pitched to-day to be cleaned and dryed. – Captain MACKENZIE returned from special leave this evening.	J.E.P.

1875 Wt. W593/826 1,000,000 4/15 J.B.C. & A. A.D.S.S./Forms/C. 2118.

Instructions regarding War Diaries and Intelligence Summaries are contained in F. S. Regs., Part II. and the Staff Manual respectively. Title Pages will be prepared in manuscript.

WAR DIARY
or
INTELLIGENCE SUMMARY
(Erase heading not required.)

Army Form C. 2118

Place	Date	Hour	Summary of Events and Information	Remarks and references to Appendices
VIEILLE CHAPELLE	13/1/16	9 p.m.	20 sick and 5 wounded were admitted during the day, 25 sick and 8 wounded were evacuated leaving 34 cases remaining. One case of measles was evacuated to No. 7 General Hospital Malassise during the day. An instructional Tube-Helmet parade was held both morning and afternoon and the men practised in the use of these helmets. – The weather continues stormy.	J.E.P.
"	14/1/16	9 p.m.	20 sick and 2 wounded were admitted during the day, 15 sick were evacuated and one wounded died, leaving 39 sick and 1 wounded remaining. The D.A.D.M.S. visited the Field Ambulance during the morning. The weather has been dry but cold.	J.E.P.
"	15/1/16	9 p.m.	One sick Officer was transferred from the 59th Field Ambulance to this unit today. 14 sick and 5 wounded were admitted during the day, 17 sick and 5 wounded were evacuated, leaving 36 sick and one wounded remaining. – Surgeon-General Pike D.M.S. 1st Army visited the Field Ambulance in the morning – & visited the advanced Dressing Station in the afternoon. The weather continues dry.	J.E.P.
"	16/1/16	9 p.m.	Two sick Officers were admitted during the day and 3 were evacuated, leaving no Officers remaining. 16 sick and 7 wounded other ranks were admitted, 26 sick and 5 wounded were evacuated, leaving 26 sick and 3 wounded remaining. Lieut. WILKINSON R.A.M.C. reported his arrival to-day on return from 10 days leave to England.	J.E.P.
"	17/1/16	9 p.m.	One sick Officer was admitted and evacuated during the day. 10 other ranks sick and 7 wounded were admitted, 15 sick and 7 wounded were evacuated, leaving 21 sick and 3 wounded remaining. One case of suspected Cerebro-Spinal Meningitis was transferred to-day to No. 7 General Hospital MALASSISE. All precautions were taken. – The A.D.M.S. XIX Division visited the Field Ambulance during the morning. – It has rained during the afternoon and evening.	J.E.P.

1875 Wt. W593/826 1,000,000 4/15 J.B.C. & A. A.D.S.S./Forms/C. 2118.

Instructions regarding War Diaries and Intelligence Summaries are contained in F. S. Regs., Part II. and the Staff Manual respectively. Title Pages will be prepared in manuscript.

WAR DIARY
or
INTELLIGENCE SUMMARY
(Erase heading not required.)

Army Form C. 2118

Place	Date	Hour	Summary of Events and Information	Remarks and references to Appendices
VIEILLE CHAPELLE	18/1/16	9 p.m.	One sick Officer was admitted and evacuated during the day. 26 other ranks sick and 9 wounded were admitted, 23 sick and 9 wounded were evacuated leaving 24 sick and 3 wounded remaining. Received R.A.M.C. Operation Order No. 21. dated 18/1/16 ordering the Field Ambulance to move to ROBECQ on the 22/1/16 handing over these buildings to No. 131 Field Ambulance 38th Division.	J.E.P.
"	19/1/16	9 p.m.	One sick Officer was transferred from the 59th Field Ambulance and is remaining. 20 other ranks sick and 5 wounded were admitted, 24 sick and 3 wounded were evacuated leaving 20 sick and 5 wounded remaining. – One case of measles was admitted during the day and evacuated to No. 7 General Hospital MALASSISE. – I visited the ~~[illegible]~~ Advanced Dressing Station in the afternoon.	J.E.P.
"	20/1/16	9 p.m.	One sick and one wounded Officer were admitted to the Field Ambulance during the day and one wounded Officer was evacuated leaving 2 Officers remaining. – 19 sick and 8 wounded other ranks were admitted and 20 sick and 8 wounded were evacuated leaving 19 sick and 5 wounded remaining. – Received XIX Division R.A.M.C. Operation Order No. 21, directing me to hand over the Advanced Dressing Station on the 21st inst. and the Main Dressing Station on the 22nd inst. to the 131st Field Ambulance 38th Division and for this unit to move to ROBECQ on the 22nd inst. Lieut. A. P. FRY R.A.M.C. (T.C.) reported his arrival for duty with this unit.	J.E.P.
"	21/1/16	9 p.m.	One sick Officer was admitted during the day and 2 Officers evacuated to Casualty Clearing Station and one Officer discharged to duty, leaving none remaining. 5 sick and 5 wounded other ranks were admitted, 10 sick and 7 wounded were evacuated leaving 14 sick and 3 wounded remaining. The Bearer Division handed over the Advanced Dressing Station at 12 Noon to-day to the 131st Field Ambulance and returned to Headquarters.	J.E.P.

1875 Wt. W593/826 1,000,000 4/15 J.B.C. & A. A.D.S.S./Forms/C. 2118.

Army Form C. 2118

Instructions regarding War Diaries and Intelligence Summaries are contained in F. S. Regs., Part II. and the Staff Manual respectively. Title Pages will be prepared in manuscript.

WAR DIARY
or
INTELLIGENCE SUMMARY
(Erase heading not required.)

Place	Date	Hour	Summary of Events and Information	Remarks and references to Appendices
ROBECQ	22/1/16	9 p.m.	4 sick and 3 wounded other ranks were admitted during the day, 8 sick and 3 wounded were evacuated and 8 sick and 3 wounded were transferred to the 131st Field Ambulance leaving 2 sick remaining. The Field Ambulance marched at 10 a.m. to ROBECQ in Divisional reserve and opened for the reception of sick at the Mill in that village. Lieut. R.W. SUTHERLAND R.A.M.C. (T.C.) reported his arrival for duty this day in relief of Captain Mackenzie R.A.M.C. — The weather has been fine and dry.	J.E.P.
"	23/1/16	9 p.m.	Seven sick other ranks were admitted during the day to the Field Ambulance and 5 cases evacuated leaving 4 cases remaining. Captain D.F. Mackenzie R.A.M.C. reported his departure this day for duty with No. 33 Casualty Clearing Station in accordance with instructions received from D.M.S. 1st Army. The weather has been fine and dry. The A.D.M.S.	J.E.P.
"	24/1/16	9 p.m.	Eight sick were admitted to the Field Ambulance during the day, five cases were evacuated leaving seven cases remaining. The weather has been fine and dry but cold. Medical stores and equipment are being sorted and checked and the panniers are being replenished. — Sanitary improvements are also being carried out.	J.E.P.
"	25/1/16	9 p.m.	Nine sick were admitted to the Field Ambulance during the day, six were evacuated leaving ten cases remaining. The weather continues fine and dry. The transport both horse and mechanical are being washed and overhauled. — The checking of equipment is being continued.	J.E.P.
"	26/1/16	9 p.m.	One sick Officer was admitted and evacuated during the day. 20 other ranks were admitted and 14 cases evacuated, leaving 16 cases remaining. The tents are now being pitched to have the ropes and pegs repaired. The weather continues dry.	J.E.P.

1875 Wt. W593/826 1,000,000 4/15 J.B.C. & A. A.D.S.S./Forms/C. 2118.

Instructions regarding War Diaries and Intelligence Summaries are contained in F. S. Regs., Part II. and the Staff Manual respectively. Title Pages will be prepared in manuscript.

WAR DIARY
or
INTELLIGENCE SUMMARY
(Erase heading not required.)

Army Form C. 2118

Place	Date	Hour	Summary of Events and Information	Remarks and references to Appendices
ROBECQ	27/1/16	9 p.m.	One sick Officer was admitted and evacuated during the day. Twenty two other ranks were admitted and 17 cases evacuated, leaving 21 cases remaining. The checking of equipment and stores is still being carried on. The weather is dull and misty.	J.E.P.
"	28/1/16	9 p.m.	One sick Officer was admitted and evacuated during the day. Ten other ranks sick were admitted and 14 were evacuated leaving 17 cases remaining. Two cases of Mumps were admitted from the XIX Divisional Train and evacuated to No. 7 General Hospital MALASSISE. The weather is damp and misty.	J.E.P.
"	29/1/16	9 p.m.	One sick Officer was admitted and evacuated during the day. Thirteen other ranks sick were admitted and fourteen were evacuated leaving sixteen cases remaining. The checking of equipment and stores is being continued. The weather is dull and misty but mild. Billeting certificates for the week were rendered.	J.E.P.
"	30/1/16	9 p.m.	No Officers were admitted during the day. Six other ranks sick were admitted and seven cases evacuated leaving 15 cases remaining. – The weather has become much colder and there is a thick mist to-day. Lieut. D. O'Flynn R.A.M.C. (T.C.) reported his departure for duty as Regimental M.O.	J.E.P.
"	31/1/16	9 p.m.	Thirteen other ranks sick were admitted during the day, 7 cases were evacuated to a Casualty Clearing Station, 3 cases to Corps Rest Station and one case to duty, leaving 17 cases remaining. The equipment of the Personnel was inspected this morning and all available ranks subsequently taken for a Route march. The weather is misty and cold. The ambulance equipment is being carefully checked and overhauled.	J.E.P.

J.E. Powell
Lieut Col. R.A.M.C.
O.C. 57th Field Ambulance

1875 Wt. W593/826 1,000,000 4/15 J.B.C. & A. A.D.S.S./Forms/C. 2118.

Feb 1916.

57th Fld Amb

57th F.A.
19th Div.
Vol 8.

Instructions regarding War Diaries and Intelligence Summaries are contained in F. S. Regs., Part II. and the Staff Manual respectively. Title Pages will be prepared in manuscript.

WAR DIARY
or
INTELLIGENCE SUMMARY
(Erase heading not required.)

54th F.A.

Army Form C. 2118

Place	Date	Hour	Summary of Events and Information	Remarks and references to Appendices
ROBECQ	Feb 1st 16 1/2/16	9 p.m.	No Officers were admitted during the day to the Field Ambulance. Twelve other ranks sick were admitted and thirteen cases evacuated leaving sixteen cases remaining. During the morning all available ranks were exercised in Squad drill and Physical drill. – In the afternoon the Tent Division were given a lecture on Nursing duties. The weather continues very cold.	J.E.P.
"	2/2/16	9 p.m.	Three Officers sick were admitted to the Field Ambulance during the day and all three were evacuated to a Casualty Clearing Station. – Thirteen other ranks sick were admitted and eleven were evacuated leaving 18 cases remaining. During the morning all available ranks were exercised in Stretcher Drill and in the afternoon the Bearer Division were instructed in First aid. – The weather continues dry and cold.	J.E.P.
"	3/2/16	9 p.m.	One Officer was admitted sick during the day and evacuated to a Casualty Clearing Station. Nine other ranks sick were admitted and seven evacuated, leaving 20 cases remaining. All available ranks were sent on a Route march in the morning and in the afternoon the Nursing Division received a lecture on Nursing duties. – The weather continues cold and dry with a strong North-Westerly wind.	J.E.P.
"	4/2/16	9 p.m.	~~One~~ Two sick officers ~~were~~ admitted & detained in officers ward. Fourteen other ranks sick were admitted, nine evacuated, leaving twenty five remaining. Prevailing disease at present is Influenza. In morning all ranks not on duty were exercised in Squad & Physical Drill. In afternoon bearers were lectured on first aid & use of Rogers trench stretcher, of which 36 have been supplied to unit.	[illegible]

1875 Wt. W593/826 1,000,000 4/15 J.B.C. & A. A.D.S.S./Forms/C. 2118.

Instructions regarding War Diaries and Intelligence Summaries are contained in F. S. Regs., Part II. and the Staff Manual respectively. Title Pages will be prepared in manuscript.

WAR DIARY
or
INTELLIGENCE SUMMARY
(Erase heading not required.)

Army Form C. 2118

Place	Date	Hour	Summary of Events and Information	Remarks and references to Appendices
ROBECQ	Feb 5/2/16	9 p.m.	Two sick officers remain in hospital. Sixteen other ranks admitted, fourteen evacuated leaving twenty-seven in hospital sick. One slightly wounded – result of bomb accident – admitted & detained. Kit inspection of personnel held in morning. Lt.Col J.E. Powell RAMC. left this day on ten days leave in England. Capt A.A. Smalley RAMC took over temporary charge in his absence	AAS
"	6/2/16	9 p.m.	One sick officer admitted & detained – making three in Hospital. Eleven other ranks sick admitted, fourteen evacuated leaving twenty-four in hospital. Lt. Drew returned from leave in England while Lt McLeod and 1 N.C.O. proceeded on leave. Weather continues fine. Voluntary church parade this morning.	AAS
"	7/2/16	9 p.m.	One sick officer admitted, two evacuated to C.C.S. Two remaining. Eleven other ranks sick admitted, nineteen evacuated leaving 16 in hospital. All personel not on duty were taken a route march in the morning. Nursing section were lectured to in the afternoon.	AAS
"	8/2/16	9 p.m.	One sick officer evacuated leaving one in hospital. Fifteen other ranks admitted nine evacuated leaving twenty-two in hospital. Short route march in morning, after which personel were paid. Tent subdivision were lectured in afternoon. A.D.M.S. inspected the hospital in afternoon. Criticism was that there was not sufficient "eyewash" about.	AAS

1875 Wt. W593/826 1,000,000 4/15 J.B.C. & A. A.D.S.S./Forms/C. 2118.

Instructions regarding War Diaries and Intelligence Summaries are contained in F. S. Regs., Part II. and the Staff Manual respectively. Title Pages will be prepared in manuscript.

WAR DIARY
or
INTELLIGENCE SUMMARY
(Erase heading not required.)

Army Form C. 2118

Place	Date	Hour	Summary of Events and Information	Remarks and references to Appendices
ROBECQ	9/2/16	9 p.m	One sick officer remaining. Seventeen other ranks sick admitted twenty-three evacuated leaving sixteen in hospital. All available ranks exercised in physical drill in morning. Lecture to bearers on first aid in afternoon. Weather fine with fairly sharp frost at night.	A.W.S.
"	10/2/16	9 p.m	One sick officer remaining. Fifteen other ranks sick were admitted, six were evacuated leaving twenty-six in hospital. All ranks not on duty were exercised in a route march in the morning. In the afternoon reinocculations were commenced. The A.D.M.S. inspected the hospital in the afternoon.	A.W.S.
"	11/2/16	9 p.m	One sick officer remaining. Eight other ranks sick were admitted, twelve were evacuated, leaving twenty-two remaining in hospital. Prevailing diseases are Influenza & Septic Throats. Personnel were exercised in physical drill in the morning, and bearers were lectured on first aid in the afternoon.	A.W.S.
"	12/2/16	9 p.m	Officer still remaining. Nineteen other ranks sick admitted; fourteen evacuated leaving twenty-seven in hospital. Prevailing disease Influenza. Personnel were taken a route march in the morning. Capt H.B. Owens RAMC left the unit to take up temporary duty as M.O. 1/c 8th Gloucesters.	A.W.S.

1875 Wt. W593/826 1,000,000 4/15 J.B.C. & A. A.D.S.S./Forms/C. 2118.

Instructions regarding War Diaries and Intelligence Summaries are contained in F. S. Regs., Part II. and the Staff Manual respectively. Title Pages will be prepared in manuscript.

WAR DIARY
or
INTELLIGENCE SUMMARY
(Erase heading not required.)

Army Form C. 2118

Place	Date	Hour	Summary of Events and Information	Remarks and references to Appendices
ROBECQ	13/2/16	9 p.m.	One sick officer remaining. Eleven other ranks sick admitted, seventeen evacuated leaving twenty in hospital. Nonconformist & C of E Church parades in morning. In morning I rode over to inspect new billets at Regnier le Clerc which B & C Sections are going to take over on the 19th. Billets appear very good	A.A.S.
"	14/2/16	9 p.m.	Sick officer evacuated to duty. Nineteen other ranks sick admitted, sixteen evacuated leaving twenty-three in hospital. Prevailing disease still Influenza. I went to Merville to make enquiries about Corps Rest Camp which A Section is taking over on the 15th. also saw Town Major there about billets.	A.A.S.
"	15/2/16	9 p.m.	I returned to duty from ten days leave of absence in England and took over command of the Ambulance from Captain A. A. Smalley R.A.M.C. — arranged to leave for MERVILLE at 8 a.m. tomorrow with A Section of the Field Ambulance to take over the Corps Rest Station. Leaving B & C Sections open at ROBECQ for the reception of sick until the 19th inst. Heavy rain is falling tonight. J. E. Powell Lieut Col. R.A.M.C.	J.E.P.
MERVILLE	16/2/16	9 p.m.	I left ROBECQ at 8 a.m. with A Section and took over the XI Corps Rest Station at MERVILLE from the 58th Field Ambulance, having completed the taking over I reported personally at the Office of the D.D.M.S. XI Corps. — During the day the Field Ambulance Detachment at ROBECQ, admitted one officer and discharged one officer to Duty, leaving two sick officers remaining. Ten other ranks were admitted and fifteen evacuated leaving 21 cases remaining. Heavy rain fell during the morning but it cleared in the afternoon.	J.E.P.

1875 Wt. W593/826 1,000,000 4/15 J.B.C. & A. A.D.S.S./Forms/C. 2118.

Instructions regarding War Diaries and Intelligence Summaries are contained in F. S. Regs., Part II. and the Staff Manual respectively. Title Pages will be prepared in manuscript.

WAR DIARY
or
INTELLIGENCE SUMMARY
(Erase heading not required.)

Army Form C. 2118

Place	Date	Hour	Summary of Events and Information	Remarks and references to Appendices
MERVILLE	17/2/16	9 p.m.	Thirtyone cases were admitted to the Corps Rest Station during the day and 20 cases were evacuated to duty and 4 cases to a Casualty Clearing Station leaving 142 cases remaining. Twentyone cases were admitted to the Field Ambulance and 21 cases evacuated leaving ~~21~~ 2 Officers and 21 cases remaining. The weather has been fine but cold.	J.E.P.
"	18/2/16	9 p.m.	Twentynine cases were admitted to the Corps Rest Station during the day and 8 cases were evacuated to duty and 7 cases to a Casualty Clearing Station leaving 156 cases remaining. One Officer was admitted to the Field Ambulance and evacuated during the day, sixteen other ranks were admitted and 21 cases were evacuated and 10 cases transferred, leaving 2 Officers and one other rank remaining. The weather has been very wet raining all day.	J.E.P.
"	19/2/16	9 p.m.	Thirtytwo cases were admitted to the Corps Rest Station during the day, 19 cases were returned to duty and 11 cases sent to a Casualty Clearing Station, leaving 158 cases remaining. There were no admissions to the Field Ambulance during the day, two Officers and one man were returned to duty, leaving no cases remaining. – Captain Kidd rejoined the Unit for duty from the A.D.M.S.'s Office. The Detachment of the Field Ambulance consisting of B & C Sections handed over the Hospital buildings etc at ROBECQ to the 106th Field Ambulance and moved into billets at REGNIER LE CLERC Sq K34 d 8-7. – Billeting certificates were rendered to day up to the 18th not inclusive. – The weather has been cold and damp.	J.E.P.

1875 Wt. W593/826 1,000,000 4/15 J.B.C. & A. A.D.S.S./Forms/C. 2118.

Instructions regarding War Diaries and Intelligence Summaries are contained in F. S. Regs., Part II. and the Staff Manual respectively. Title Pages will be prepared in manuscript.

WAR DIARY
or
INTELLIGENCE SUMMARY
(Erase heading not required.)

Army Form C. 2118

Place	Date	Hour	Summary of Events and Information	Remarks and references to Appendices
MERVILLE	20/2/16	9 p.m.	Fourteen cases were admitted to the Corps Rest Station during the day, 18 cases were returned to duty and 14 cases sent to a Casualty Clearing Station, leaving 140 cases remaining. There were four cases admitted to the Field Ambulance and 4 cases evacuated to a Casualty Clearing Station during the day, leaving no cases remaining. Lieut. A.P. FRY R.A.M.C. reported his arrival for duty this day on return from a course of Instruction in mining. The weather is fine and cold.	J.E.P.
"	21/2/16	9 p.m.	Thirtyfour cases were admitted to the Corps Rest Station during the day, 8 cases were returned to duty and 10 cases were sent to a Casualty Clearing Station, leaving 156 cases remaining. – No cases were admitted to the Field Ambulance during the day. The weather has been dry and cold.	J.E.P.
"	22/2/16	9 p.m.	Thirtyfour cases were admitted to the Corps Rest Station during the day, 7 cases were returned to duty and 8 cases were sent to a Casualty Clearing Station, leaving 175 cases. – Twelve cases were admitted to the Field Ambulance during the day, 4 cases were evacuated to a Casualty Clearing Station and 8 cases were transferred to the Corps Rest Station, leaving no cases remaining. Heavy snow fell throughout the morning and it is freezing to-night. I paid the men of the Unit to-day.	J.E.P.
"	23/2/16	9 p.m.	Eighteen cases were admitted to the Corps Rest Station during the day, 17 cases were returned to Duty and 13 cases were sent to a Casualty Clearing Station, leaving 163 cases remaining. – Two cases were admitted to the Field Ambulance and two cases evacuated to a Casualty Clearing Station leaving no cases remaining. – Captain A.A. Smalley R.A.M.C. reported his departure this day for temporary duty as M.O. i/c 8th North Stafford Regt.	J.E.P.

-1875 -Wt. W593/826 1,000,000 4/15 J.B.C. & A. A.D.S.S./Forms/C. 2118.

WAR DIARY
or
INTELLIGENCE SUMMARY
(Erase heading not required.)

Army Form C. 2118

Instructions regarding War Diaries and Intelligence Summaries are contained in F. S. Regs., Part II. and the Staff Manual respectively. Title Pages will be prepared in manuscript.

Place	Date	Hour	Summary of Events and Information	Remarks and references to Appendices
MERVILLE	24/2/16	9 p.m.	Fourteen cases were admitted to the Corps Rest Station during the day, 12 cases were returned to duty and 12 cases were sent to the Casualty Clearing Station, leaving 153 cases remaining. Three cases were admitted to the Field Ambulance, 1 case was evacuated to a Casualty Clearing Station and two cases sent to the Corps Rest Station. – I visited the billets of the Field Ambulance detachment in the morning with the D.A.D.M.S. – Hard frost continues	J.E.P.
"	25/2/16	9 p.m.	Eighteen cases were admitted to the Corps Rest Station during the day, 21 cases were returned to duty and ten cases sent to a Casualty Clearing Station, leaving 140 cases remaining. Three cases were admitted to the Field Ambulance, 2 cases were sent to a Casualty Clearing Station and one case was transferred to the Corps Rest Station, leaving no cases remaining. Captain H.B. OWENS R.A.M.C. reported his arrival for duty this day on completion of temporary duty with the 8th Bn. Gloucester Regt. – Lieut. J.F. MACLEOD R.A.M.C. also reported his arrival this day on return from leave in England. – Snow is falling this evening and the frost continues	J.E.P.
"	26/2/16	9 p.m.	34 cases were admitted to the Corps Rest Station during the day, 17 cases were evacuated, leaving 157 cases remaining. – Six cases were admitted to the Field Ambulance, 2 cases were sent to a Casualty Clearing Station and 4 cases transferred to the Corps Rest Station, leaving no cases remaining. – Billeting certificates were rendered both for the Detachment and for the Headquarters at the Corps Rest Station. – The frost has broken up, a rapid thaw having set in to-day.	J.E.P.

Army Form C. 2118

Instructions regarding War Diaries and Intelligence Summaries are contained in F. S. Regs., Part II. and the Staff Manual respectively. Title Pages will be prepared in manuscript.

WAR DIARY
or
INTELLIGENCE SUMMARY
(Erase heading not required.)

Place	Date	Hour	Summary of Events and Information	Remarks and references to Appendices
MERVILLE	27/2/16	9 p.m.	Thirty cases were admitted to the Corps Rest Station, 17 cases were returned to duty and 7 cases sent to a Casualty Clearing Station leaving 163 cases remaining. One case was admitted to the Field Ambulance and transferred to the Corps Rest Station, leaving no cases remaining. – Orders were received from the A.D.M.S. 19th Division, for the Detachment to open up for the reception of all cases of Scabies from the Division. – Some snow and sleet fell during the day. Orders were also received from the ADMS. 19th Division for the Bearer Division of the Field Ambulance to remain ready to move at 2 hours notice	J.E.P.
"	28/2/16	9 p.m.	Twenty six cases were admitted to the Corps Rest Station during the day, 19 cases were returned to duty and 5 cases sent to a Casualty Clearing Station, leaving 165 cases remaining. Five cases were admitted to the Field Ambulance and two cases transferred from the 59th Field Ambulance, 4 cases were evacuated to a Casualty Clearing Station, leaving 3 cases of Scabies remaining. – The Bearer Division paraded in their new equipment at 2 p.m. under Captain KIDD R.A.M.C. and were taken for a 5 mile route march, at the end of which, they were carefully inspected by the D.D.M.S. 11th Corps. The men almost without exception expressed a preference for this new equipment.	J.E.P.
"	29/2/16	9 p.m.	29 cases were admitted to the Corps Rest Station during the day, 15 cases were returned to duty and 5 cases sent to a Casualty Clearing Station, leaving 174 cases remaining. – There were 9 cases admitted to the Field Ambulance, 2 cases were transferred to the Corps Rest Station leaving 10 cases remaining. The weather is finer and milder now.	

J.E. Powell
Lieut. Colonel RAMC

1875 Wt. W593/826 1,000,000 4/15 J.B.C. & A. A.D.S.S./Forms/C. 2118.

March 1916

57. F. Amb

Vol 9

Army Form C. 2118

Instructions regarding War Diaries and Intelligence Summaries are contained in F. S. Regs., Part II. and the Staff Manual respectively. Title Pages will be prepared in manuscript.

WAR DIARY
or
INTELLIGENCE SUMMARY
(Erase heading not required.)

Place	Date	Hour	Summary of Events and Information	Remarks and references to Appendices
MERVILLE	1/3/16	9 p.m.	Twentynine cases were admitted to the Corps Rest Station during the day and thirty cases were discharged leaving 173 cases remaining. — Five cases were admitted to the Field Ambulance suffering from Scabies, none were discharged leaving 15 cases remaining. — Supplied a fatigue party of 40 men from the R.A.M.C. personnel from 2 to 5 p.m. to unload a coal barge at La Gorgue. — The weather is dry but cold.	J.E.P.
"	2/3/16	9 p.m.	Twentynine cases were admitted to the Corps Rest Station during the day, 23 cases were returned to duty and 3 cases were sent to a Casualty Clearing Station, leaving 176 cases remaining. Seven cases were admitted to the Field Ambulance, 3 cases were transferred to the Corps Rest Station, leaving 19 cases of Scabies remaining. — a fatigue party of 40 men was again supplied from 2 to 5 p.m. for the unloading of a coal barge. — Some rain fell this afternoon.	J.E.P.
"	3/3/16	9 p.m.	I inspected the Detachment Scabies hospital this morning and found it working satisfactorily. Twentyseven cases were admitted to the Corps Rest Station during the day, 21 cases were returned to duty and seven cases sent to a Casualty Clearing Station, leaving 175 cases remaining. — Eleven cases were admitted to the Field Ambulance during the day three cases were sent to a Casualty Clearing Station and 4 cases transferred to the Corps Rest Station, leaving 23 cases of Scabies remaining. — a fatigue party of 40 men was again supplied from 2–5 p.m. for unloading a coal barge at La Gorgue. — Heavy rain has fallen during the afternoon & evening.	J.E.P.

1875 Wt. W593/826 1,000,000 4/15 J.B.C. & A. A.D.S.S./Forms/C. 2118.

Army Form C. 2118

Instructions regarding War Diaries and Intelligence Summaries are contained in F. S. Regs., Part II. and the Staff Manual respectively. Title Pages will be prepared in manuscript.

WAR DIARY
or
INTELLIGENCE SUMMARY
(Erase heading not required.)

Place	Date	Hour	Summary of Events and Information	Remarks and references to Appendices
MERVILLE	4/3/16	9 p.m.	There were twenty five cases admitted to the Corps Rest Station during the day, 19 cases were returned to duty and 4 cases sent to a Casualty Clearing Station, leaving 177 cases remaining. — Six cases were admitted to the Field Ambulance during the day, 1 case was sent to a Casualty Clearing Station, 2 cases were transferred to the Corps Rest Station and 5 cases were returned to duty, leaving 21 cases Scabies remaining. Billeting certificates for the week were rendered to-day. Snow fell throughout the morning	J.E.P.
"	5/3/16	9 p.m.	There were twenty three cases admitted to the Corps Rest Station during the day, 23 cases were returned to duty and 3 cases sent to a Casualty Clearing Station, leaving 174 cases remaining. — Ten cases were admitted to the Field Ambulance, 1 case was sent to a Casualty Clearing Station, 5 cases transferred to the Corps Rest Station and 4 cases returned to duty, leaving 21 cases of Scabies remaining. — Showers of snow & rain fell during the day.	J.E.P.
"	6/3/16	9 p.m.	Thirteen cases were admitted to the Corps Rest Station during the day, 24 cases were returned to duty and 7 cases sent to a Casualty Clearing Station, leaving 156 cases remaining. — Eleven cases were admitted to the Field Ambulance, one case was transferred to the Corps Rest Station and six cases were returned to duty, leaving 25 cases of Scabies remaining. Showers of snow and rain again fell during the morning and it remains cold & wet. The new Infantry equipment was issued to the remainder of the personnel to-day — all the men are now equipped.	J.E.P.

1875 Wt. W593/826 1,000,000 4/15 J.B.C. & A. A.D.S.S./Forms/C. 2118.

Instructions regarding War Diaries and Intelligence Summaries are contained in F. S. Regs., Part II. and the Staff Manual respectively. Title Pages will be prepared in manuscript.

WAR DIARY
or
INTELLIGENCE SUMMARY
(Erase heading not required.)

Army Form C. 2118

Place	Date	Hour	Summary of Events and Information	Remarks and references to Appendices
MERVILLE	7/3/16	9 p.m.	One hundred and twelve cases were admitted to the Corps Rest Station during the day, the increase in sick is probably accounted for by the recent severe weather we have been having. 36 cases were returned to duty and 10 cases sent to a Casualty Clearing Station leaving 222 cases remaining. — Five cases were admitted to the Field Ambulance 5 cases were transferred to the Corps Rest Station and two cases returned to duty, leaving 23 cases of scabies remaining.	J.E.P.
"	8/3/16	9 p.m.	Thirtyone cases were admitted to the Corps Rest Station during the day. 46 cases were returned to duty and 17 cases were sent to a Casualty Clearing Station, leaving 190 cases remaining. — Six cases were admitted to the Field Ambulance one case was sent to a Casualty Clearing Station 7 cases were transferred to the Corps Rest Station & 4 cases were returned to duty, leaving 17 cases of Scabies remaining. Three inches of snow fell during last night. — Captain A.A. SMALLEY RAMC reported his arrival for duty on completion of temporary duty as M.O. i/c 8th North Stafford Regt.	J.E.P.
"	9/3/16	9 p.m.	Forty three cases were admitted to the Corps Rest Station during the day, 7 cases were sent to a Casualty Clearing station and 21 cases were returned to duty, leaving 205 cases remaining. One officer and 4 men were admitted to the Field Ambulance during, one officer was transferred to a Casualty Clearing Station, 3 cases to the Corps Rest Station, 4 cases were returned to duty, leaving 13 cases of Scabies remaining. — The weather has been dry but cold to-day. — The A.D.M.S. XIX Division visited the Corps Rest Station, also inspected the Detachment Hospital for Scabies at REGNIER LE CLERC, this morning.	J.E.P.

1875 Wt. W593/826 1,000,000 4/15 J.B.C. & A. A.D.S.S./Forms/C. 2118.

Instructions regarding War Diaries and Intelligence Summaries are contained in F. S. Regs., Part II. and the Staff Manual respectively. Title Pages will be prepared in manuscript.

WAR DIARY
or
INTELLIGENCE SUMMARY

(Erase heading not required.)

Army Form C. 2118

Place	Date	Hour	Summary of Events and Information	Remarks and references to Appendices
MERVILLE	10/3/16	9 p.m.	Twentyfour cases were admitted to the Corps Rest Station during the day, 22 cases were returned to duty and 10 cases sent to a Casualty Clearing Station, leaving 197 cases remaining. Two Officers were admitted to the Field Ambulance during the day and evacuated to a Casualty Clearing Station. – Thirteen other ranks were admitted to the Field Ambulance, one case was sent to a Casualty Clearing Station, 4 cases were transferred to the Corps Rest Station and one case was sent to duty, leaving 20 cases of Scabies remaining. – Showers of snow and sleet fell during the morning. – Billeting Certificates for the week were rendered.	J.E.P.
"	11/3/16	9 p.m.	Fifty cases were admitted to the Corps Rest Station during the day, 29 cases were returned to duty and 6 cases were sent to a Casualty Clearing Station, leaving 212 cases remaining. One Officer was admitted to the Field Ambulance and evacuated to a Casualty Clearing Station during the day. 11 other ranks were admitted to the Field Ambulance one case was sent to a Casualty Clearing Station, 5 cases were transferred to the Corps Rest Station and 3 cases were returned to duty, leaving 22 cases of Scabies remaining. – The weather has been damp with some rain but it has been a little milder.	J.E.P.
"	12/3/16	9 p.m.	Thirtyseven cases were admitted to the Corps Rest Station during the day, 38 cases were returned to duty and 8 cases sent to a Casualty Clearing Station, leaving 203 cases remaining. Four cases were admitted to the Field Ambulance, 2 cases were transferred to the Corps Rest Station, leaving 24 cases of Scabies remaining. – The weather has been fine and dry to-day.	J.E.P.

Instructions regarding War Diaries and Intelligence Summaries are contained in F. S. Regs., Part II. and the Staff Manual respectively. Title Pages will be prepared in manuscript.

WAR DIARY
or
INTELLIGENCE SUMMARY

(Erase heading not required.)

Army Form C. 2118

Place	Date	Hour	Summary of Events and Information	Remarks and references to Appendices
MERVILLE	13/3/16	9 p.m.	Twentysix cases were admitted to the Corps Rest station during the day, 26 cases were returned to duty and 6 cases sent to a Casualty Clearing Station, leaving 199 cases remaining. – Six cases were admitted to the Field Ambulance, one case was evacuated to a Casualty Clearing Station, 3 cases were transferred to the Corps Rest Station and 5 cases were returned to duty, leaving 21 cases of Scabies remaining. – a fatigue party of 40 men from this unit were employed unloading a coal barge during the afternoon. The weather has been fine and warm during the day.	J.E.P.
"	14/3/16	9 p.m.	Forty two cases were admitted to the Corps Rest Station during the day, 26 cases were sent to duty and 5 cases were sent to a Casualty Clearing Station, leaving 208 cases remaining. Eight cases were admitted to the Field Ambulance, 3 cases were transferred to the Corps Rest Station and 6 cases were returned to duty, leaving 20 cases of Scabies remaining. Lieut. J.F. MACLEOD R.A.M.C. reported his departure this day for temporary duty as M.O. i/c 9th Bn. Welsh Regiment. – I inspected the Field Ambulance detachment this morning.	J.E.P.
"	15/3/16	9 p.m.	Thirty five cases were admitted to the Corps Rest Station during the day, 34 cases were returned to duty, and 8 cases sent to a Casualty Clearing Station, leaving 201 cases remaining. – Five cases were admitted to the Field Ambulance, 1 case was transferred to the Corps Rest Station and 4 cases were returned to duty, leaving 20 cases of Scabies remaining. The weather continues fine and warm.	J.E.P.
"	16/3/16	9 p.m.	Thirtynine cases were admitted to the Corps Rest Station, 33 cases were returned to duty and 8 cases were sent to a Casualty Clearing Station, leaving 199 cases remaining. – Seven cases were admitted to the Field Ambulance, 2 cases were transferred to the Corps Rest Station and one case was returned to duty, leaving 24 cases of Scabies remaining. – The weather continues fine and dry.	J.E.P.

1875 Wt. W593/826 1,000,000 4/15 J.B.C. & A. A.D.S.S./Forms/C. 2118.

Instructions regarding War Diaries and Intelligence Summaries are contained in F. S. Regs., Part II. and the Staff Manual respectively. Title Pages will be prepared in manuscript.

WAR DIARY
or
INTELLIGENCE SUMMARY
(Erase heading not required.)

Army Form C. 2118

Place	Date	Hour	Summary of Events and Information	Remarks and references to Appendices
MERVILLE	17/3/16	9 p.m.	Forty four cases were admitted to the Corps Rest Station, 30 cases were returned to duty and six cases were sent to a Casualty Clearing Station, leaving 207 cases remaining. – Three cases were admitted to the Field Ambulance during the day ~~during~~ leaving 27 cases of Scabies remaining. – The A.D.M.S. 33rd Division visited the Corps Rest Station during the afternoon. The weather continues fine and dry.	J.E.P.
"	18/3/16	9 p.m.	Thirty four cases were admitted to the Corps Rest Station, 35 cases were returned to duty and 8 cases were sent to a Casualty Clearing Station, leaving 198 cases remaining. – Four cases were admitted to the Field Ambulance during the day and 4 cases were returned to duty leaving 27 cases of Scabies remaining. – Billeting certificates for the week were rendered. The weather continues fine and dry.	J.E.P.
"	19/3/16	9 p.m.	Thirty three cases were admitted to the Corps Rest Station, 25 cases were returned to duty and 7 cases sent to a Casualty Clearing Station, leaving 199 cases remaining. Two cases were admitted to the Field Ambulance, and one case was sent to duty leaving 28 cases of Scabies remaining. – Under instructions from the A.D.M.S. 19th Division, six wheeled stretchers were sent to the 59th Field Ambulance to-day on loan. – The weather continues fine and dry.	J.E.P.
"	20/3/16	9 p.m.	Thirty cases were admitted to the Corps Rest Station, 32 cases were returned to duty and 5 cases were sent to a Casualty Clearing Station, leaving 192 cases remaining. Five cases were admitted to the Field Ambulance, one case was sent to a Casualty Clearing Station, one case was sent to duty and 5 cases were sent to the Corps Rest Station, leaving 26 cases of Scabies remaining. I visited the detachment hospital this morning. The weather continues fine and dry.	J.E.P.

Instructions regarding War Diaries and Intelligence Summaries are contained in F. S. Regs., Part II. and the Staff Manual respectively. Title Pages will be prepared in manuscript.

WAR DIARY
or
INTELLIGENCE SUMMARY
(Erase heading not required.)

Army Form C. 2118

Place	Date	Hour	Summary of Events and Information	Remarks and references to Appendices
MERVILLE	21/3/16	9 p.m.	Thirty two cases were admitted to the Corps Rest Station, 31 cases were returned to duty and 4 cases sent to a Casualty Clearing Station, leaving 189 cases remaining. Four cases were admitted to the Field Ambulance, 4 cases were returned to duty and 4 cases were transferred to the Corps Rest Station, leaving 22 cases of Scabies remaining. The Ordnance equipment of the ambulance is being checked to-day by the Quartermaster. – The weather is colder to-day and some rain has fallen.	J.E.P.
"	22/3/16	9 p.m.	Fifty two cases were admitted to the Corps Rest Station during the day, 32 cases were returned to duty and one case was sent to a Casualty Clearing Station, leaving 208 cases remaining. Six cases were admitted to the Field Ambulance during the day, one case was sent to a Casualty Clearing Station, 3 cases were transferred to the Corps Rest Station and 3 cases were sent back to duty, leaving 21 cases of Scabies remaining. The checking of the Ordnance equipment was completed to-day. Rain has fallen throughout the day.	J.E.P.
"	23/3/16	9 p.m.	Thirty one cases were admitted to the Corps Rest Station, 43 cases were returned to duty, 10 cases were evacuated to a Casualty Clearing Station and one case was transferred to the 129th Field Ambulance with Scabies, leaving 185 cases remaining. I paid the personnel of the unit to-day. The weather has been dry but cold.	J.E.P.
"	24/3/16	9 p.m.	Thirty eight cases were admitted to the Corps Rest Station during the day, 35 cases were returned to duty and 10 cases sent to a Casualty Clearing Station, leaving 178 cases remaining. Eight cases were admitted to the ~~Corps Rest Station~~ Field Ambulance, 4 cases were transferred to the Corps Rest Station and 2 cases were returned to duty, leaving 25 cases remaining. Lieut. J.D. WILKINSON R.A.M.C. reported his departure this day for temporary duty as M.O. i/c 86th Brigade R.F.A. Snow and sleet fell nearly all day.	J.E.P.

1875 Wt. W593/826 1,000,000 4/15 J.B.C. & A. A.D.S.S./Forms/C. 2118.

Army Form C. 2118

Instructions regarding War Diaries and Intelligence Summaries are contained in F. S. Regs., Part II. and the Staff Manual respectively. Title Pages will be prepared in manuscript.

WAR DIARY
or
INTELLIGENCE SUMMARY
(Erase heading not required.)

Place	Date	Hour	Summary of Events and Information	Remarks and references to Appendices
MERVILLE	25/3/16	9 p.m.	Thirty four cases were admitted to the Corps Rest Station during the day, 28 cases were returned to duty and six cases were sent to a Casualty Clearing Station, leaving 178 cases remaining. – Two cases were admitted to the Field Ambulance, one case was sent to the Corps Rest Station and 7 cases were returned to duty, leaving 18 cases of Scabies remaining. – The weather is still cold and showers of rain fell during the afternoon and evening.	J.E.P.
"	26/3/16	9 p.m.	Twenty nine cases were admitted to the Corps Rest Station, 23 cases were returned to duty and 3 cases were sent to a Casualty Clearing Station, leaving 181 cases remaining. – Five cases were admitted to the Field Ambulance, one case was sent to a Casualty Clearing Station, one case to the Corps Rest Station and 3 cases were returned to duty, leaving 19 cases remaining. – One Nursing Orderly with a Field Medical Companion & Water bottle was attached to-day for duty until further orders to the Forrest Control Depôt at LA MOTTE – Captain SMALLEY R.A.M.C. was detailed to visit this Depôt daily.	J.E.P.
"	27/3/16	9 p.m.	Thirty six cases were admitted to the Corps Rest Station, 31 cases were sent to duty and 4 cases were sent to a Casualty Clearing Station, leaving 182 cases remaining. – Two cases were admitted to the Field Ambulance, 4 cases were transferred to the Corps Rest Station, leaving 19 cases remaining. – Heavy rain has fallen throughout the afternoon and evening. – I took over the duties of A.D.M.S. the Division to-day during the absence of Colonel HINGE A.M.S. on leave.	J.E.P.

1875 Wt. W593/826 1,000,000 4/15 J.B.C. & A. A.D.S.S./Forms/C. 2118.

Instructions regarding War Diaries and Intelligence Summaries are contained in F. S. Regs., Part II. and the Staff Manual respectively. Title Pages will be prepared in manuscript.

WAR DIARY
or
INTELLIGENCE SUMMARY
(Erase heading not required.)

Army Form C. 2118

Place	Date	Hour	Summary of Events and Information	Remarks and references to Appendices
MERVILLE	28/3/16	9 p.m.	Thirty three cases were admitted to the Rest Station. – Seventy three to duty and twelve to CCS leaving 180 remaining. New Motor Transport Officer Sec Lt Martin has reported to the Division for Duty. The Detachment reports seven cases of Scabies admitted & 7 evacuated. Weather changeable but generally fine.	H.R.D.
"	29.3.16	9 pm	Thirty four cases were admitted to the Rest Station – thirty one were evacuated to duty and CCS. – leaving 183 in the Station. Following order [illegible] 35th division will no longer send cases here – their place [illegible] being taken by 34th Division. The detachment report 4 cases of Scabies admitted – three to duty. leaving 13 remaining.	H.R.D.
"	30.3.16	9 pm	Admissions today totalled 26. while 35 went to duty & 5 to CCS. leaving 168 only in the Rest Station. 34th Division availed themselves of the Station for the first time. Detachment report shows 14 Scabies cases under treatment. Leave is coming in regularly – for the whole unit.	H.R.D.
"	31.3.16	9 pm	Twenty three cases were admitted today – 16 were sent to duty & seven to CCS. Rather a large proportion of wounded and shell shock cases. The remaining total was 170. – Lieut Sutherland went on leave tonight. His position as O/c XI corps Baths temporarily falls on Lieut McLeod on his arrival back from temporary duty with a regiment.	H.R.D.

H R Dew [illegible] RAMC for Lieut Col. RAMC
OC 57th F Ambulance.

1875 Wt. W593/826 1,000,000 4/15 J.B.C. & A. A.D.S.S./Forms/C. 2118.

April 1916 19th Div

No. 57 F. Amb.

57
F.AMB
Vol 10

Army Form C. 2118

Instructions regarding War Diaries and Intelligence Summaries are contained in F. S. Regs., Part II. and the Staff Manual respectively. Title Pages will be prepared in manuscript.

WAR DIARY
or
INTELLIGENCE SUMMARY

(Erase heading not required.)

Place	Date	Hour	Summary of Events and Information	Remarks and references to Appendices
Merville	1.4.16	9pm	Twenty two cases were admitted to the Rest Station twenty five to duty and three sent to CCS. – 164 only remaining. The Detachment report 13 Scabies cases remaining, after two were discharged to duty. Lieut McLeod has not yet returned from temporary duty. Lieut Fry in the meantime is in charge of the XI Corps baths.	
"	2.4.16	9pm	Today twenty four cases were admitted to the Rest Station – twenty two were sent to duty and four to CCS leaving 162 remaining. The Detachment admitted three cases of Scabies and discharged three to duty and one to CCS	
"	3.4.16	9pm	Thirty five cases were admitted today. nineteen sent to duty and three to CCS. The Detachment report from Repair that six cases were admitted – three cases sent to the Rest Station and two to CCS leaving eleven still being under treatment for Scabies. The weather lately has been very fine and sickness is apparently diminishing	
"	4.4.16	9pm	Today 39 cases were admitted to the Rest Station – twenty were sent to duty and three evacuated to CCS leaving 186 cases in the Station [illegible]. The Detachment one was discharged leaving 15 still under treatment. The sick of the 38th Division has increased and now they have only 16 vacancies here. New confidential orders re collecting wounded & their evacuation were received today. also instruction concerning rocket signals	

1875 Wt. W593/826 1,000,000 4/15 J.B.C. & A. A.D.S.S./Forms/C. 2118.

Instructions regarding War Diaries and Intelligence Summaries are contained in F. S. Regs., Part II. and the Staff Manual respectively. Title Pages will be prepared in manuscript.

WAR DIARY
or
INTELLIGENCE SUMMARY
(Erase heading not required.)

Army Form C. 2118

Place	Date	Hour	Summary of Events and Information	Remarks and references to Appendices
Merville	6.4.16	9 pm	Numbers in the Rest camps have increased to 196. ~~Forty two were admitted~~ & twenty sent to duty and three to CCS. The Detachment report 15 cases of Scabies being treated – four being admitted and four being discharged. Lieut. McLeod has just returned from temporary duty and has taken over control of the XI Corps baths	[illegible initials]
"	6.4.16	9 pm	Today. Thirty two cases were admitted to the Rest Station – thirty one were sent to duty while four were evacuated to Casualty Clearing Station. The total now in the Rest Station is 184. The Detachment admitted four cases – evacuated five – sent one to duty and now have under treatment thirteen cases of scabies	[illegible initials]
"	7/4/16	9 p.m.	Forty one cases were admitted to the Corps Rest Station during the day, 29 cases were returned to duty, 5 cases were sent to a Casualty Clearing Station, leaving 191 cases remaining. Seven cases were admitted to the Field Ambulance, two cases were transferred to the Corps Rest Station, leaving 18 cases remaining. – The Personnel at Headquarters were paid during the afternoon. – On the return of Colonel HINGE A.D.M.S. from leave I returned to my Unit this evening on the completion of my temporary duty as A.D.M.S. The weather has been cold and dull during the day. – J.E. Powell Lt. Col. R.A.M.C.	J.E.P.
"	8/4/16	9 p.m.	Thirty one cases were admitted to the Corps Rest Station during the day, 22 cases were returned to duty and 8 cases were sent to a Casualty Clearing Station, leaving 192 cases remaining. – Five cases were admitted to the Field Ambulance, 2 cases were sent to a Casualty Clearing Station, one case was sent to the Corps Rest Station and two cases were returned to duty, leaving 18 cases remaining. – There has been a cold East wind to-day.	J.E.P.

1875 Wt. W593/826 1,000,000 4/15 J.B.C. & A. A.D.S.S./Forms/C.2118.

Army Form C. 2118

Instructions regarding War Diaries and Intelligence Summaries are contained in F. S. Regs., Part II. and the Staff Manual respectively. Title Pages will be prepared in manuscript.

WAR DIARY
or
INTELLIGENCE SUMMARY
(Erase heading not required.)

Place	Date	Hour	Summary of Events and Information	Remarks and references to Appendices
MERVILLE	9/4/16	9 p.m.	Fifteen cases were admitted to the Corps Rest Station during the day, 32 cases were returned to duty and 3 cases were sent to a Casualty Clearing Station, leaving 172 cases remaining. Six cases were admitted to the Field Ambulance, one case was transferred to the Corps Rest Station and three cases were returned to duty leaving 20 cases remaining. The weather continues fine and dry. Lieut. J.D. WILKINSON R.A.M.C. reported his arrival to-day for duty, on completion of temporary duty as M.O. i/c 33rd Brigade R.F.A.	J.E.P.
"	10/4/16	9 p.m.	Twenty two cases were admitted to the Corps Rest Station during the day, 34 cases were returned to duty and 5 cases were sent to a Casualty Clearing Station, leaving 155 cases remaining. — Three cases were admitted to the Field Ambulance, one case was sent to the Casualty Clearing Station, one case to the Corps Rest Station and two cases were returned to duty, leaving 19 cases remaining. The weather has been fine and warm. I detailed Captain A.A. SMALLEY and Lieut. J.D. WILKINSON to attend Lectures & Demonstrations by the Chemical Adviser 1st Army at AIRE on the 11th and 12th April.	J.E.P.
"	11/4/16	9 p.m.	Eighteen cases were admitted to the Corps Rest Station during the day, 22 cases were returned to duty, leaving 151 cases remaining. — Three cases were admitted to the Field Ambulance, 2 cases were sent to the Corps Rest Station and one case was sent to duty, leaving 19 cases remaining. Rain fell during the night and [illegible] all the morning.	J.E.P.
"	12/4/16	9 p.m.	Thirty cases were admitted to the Corps Rest Station, 25 cases were sent to duty and 3 cases were sent to a Casualty Clearing Station, leaving 153 cases remaining. — No cases were admitted to the Field Ambulance, 7 cases were returned to duty, leaving 12 cases remaining. LIEUT. A.P. FRY reported his departure this day for temporary duty as M.O. i/c 5th South Lancashire Regt. — Rain fell again all day to-day.	J.E.P.

Army Form C. 2118

Instructions regarding War Diaries and Intelligence Summaries are contained in F. S. Regs., Part II. and the Staff Manual respectively. Title Pages will be prepared in manuscript.

WAR DIARY
or
INTELLIGENCE SUMMARY
(Erase heading not required.)

Place	Date	Hour	Summary of Events and Information	Remarks and references to Appendices
MERVILLE	13/4/16	9 p.m.	Twenty five cases were admitted to the Corps Rest Station during the day, 33 cases were returned to duty and two cases were sent to a Casualty Clearing station, leaving 143 cases remaining. – Four cases were admitted to the Field Ambulance and two cases were returned to duty, leaving 14 cases remaining. – The day has been fine but with a strong North Westerly wind.	J.E.P.
"	14/4/16	9 p.m.	Thirty nine cases were admitted to the Corps Rest Station during the day; 24 cases were evacuated to duty and 3 cases to a Casualty Clearing Station, leaving 155 cases remaining. One Officer and 5 other ranks were admitted to the Field Ambulance, one officer was sent to a Casualty Clearing Station and one man transferred to the Corps Rest Station leaving 18 cases remaining in the Field Ambulance. – Billeting certificates were rendered for the week. – Lieut. R.W. SUTHERLAND R.A.M.C. was evacuated to No 2 London Casualty Clearing Station suffering from Nephritis. – The weather is cold.	J.E.P.
"	15/4/16	9 p.m.	Forty six cases were admitted to the Corps Rest Station during the day, 26 cases were returned to duty, leaving 175 cases remaining. Four cases were admitted to the Field Ambulance to-day and 4 cases were returned to duty leaving 18 cases remaining. – Lieut. A.P. FRY R.A.M.C. reported his arrival for duty on completion of temporary duty with 9th South Lancashire Regt. – 1 Officer and 8 other ranks arrived as an advance party from the 131st Field Ambulance to take over the Corps Rest Station. The weather has been fine.	J.E.P.
"	16/4/16	9 p.m.	Thirty nine cases were admitted to the Corps Rest Station, 34 cases were returned to duty and 5 cases were sent to a C.C. Station, leaving 175 cases remaining. – Five cases were admitted to the Field Ambulance, 3 cases were sent to a C.C. Station, one case to the Corps Rest Stn, and two cases to duty, leaving 17 cases remaining. – Captain G.P. KIDD R.A.M.C. reported his arrival for duty on return from 10 days leave. – LIEUT. J.L. COCHRANE R.A.M.C. reported his arrival for duty on first posting to a unit. The weather has been fine.	J.E.P.

Instructions regarding War Diaries and Intelligence Summaries are contained in F. S. Regs., Part II. and the Staff Manual respectively. Title Pages will be prepared in manuscript.

WAR DIARY
or
INTELLIGENCE SUMMARY

(Erase heading not required.)

Army Form C. 2118

Place	Date	Hour	Summary of Events and Information	Remarks and references to Appendices
MERVILLE	17/4/16	9 p.m.	Handed over the XI Corps Rest Station to the 131st Field Ambulance at 11 a.m. and transferred 175 cases in the Rest Station to them. – Also handed over the Detachment Scabies Hospital to the 131st Field Ambulance and transferred 17 cases of Scabies to them. – The duties of Officer i/c Corps Baths, Officer i/c Sanitation of MERVILLE and M.O. i/c Forest Ba[illegible] Depot LA MOTTE were also handed over to the 131st Field Ambulance. – The whole of the Ambulance personnel then moved into billets at MERVILLE. Received orders from the A.D.M.S. to march to BUSNES at 10 a.m. tomorrow.	J.E.P.
BUSNES	18/4/16	9 p.m.	The Field Ambulance with all its transport marched at 10 a.m. from MERVILLE to BUSNES and went into billets there, arriving 1.15 p.m. The weather was very showery and windy. I went into St. VENANT at 6 p.m. to see the A.D.M.S. and received orders to march with the 56th Infantry Brigade tomorrow morning to COTES and open out there for the reception of casualties.	J.E.P.
COTES T. 11 b 0 2	19/4/16	9 p.m.	The Field Ambulance marched with the 56th Infantry Brigade from BUSNES at 11 a.m. and arrived at COTES at 1.30 p.m. and opened up for the reception of sick in that area. Two cases were admitted to the Field Ambulance and none were evacuated. The weather has been wet and cold.	J.E.P.
"	20/4/16	9 p.m.	One Officer was admitted and evacuated to No 2 Canadian C.C.S. – Two other ranks were transferred from No 59 Field Ambulance, to be seen by the A.D.M.S. – Four cases are remaining in the Field Ambulance. – The A.D.M.S. visited the Field Ambulance and inspected all the arrangements made. – Rain fell in the morning, but the afternoon has been fine. Billet-de-Logements were given to the inhabitants.	J.E.P.

1875 Wt. W593/826 1,000,000 4/15 J.B.C. & A. A.D.S.S./Forms/C. 2118.

Army Form C. 2118

WAR DIARY
or
INTELLIGENCE SUMMARY
(Erase heading not required.)

Instructions regarding War Diaries and Intelligence Summaries are contained in F. S. Regs., Part II. and the Staff Manual respectively. Title Pages will be prepared in manuscript.

Place	Date	Hour	Summary of Events and Information	Remarks and references to Appendices
COTTES	21/4/16	9 p.m.	Seven cases were admitted to the Field Ambulance and two cases evacuated to a Casualty Clearing Station, leaving 9 cases remaining. Lieut. J.D. WILKINSON R.A.M.C. reported his departure this day for permanent duty as M.O. i/c 26th Brigade R.F.A. All the personnel have been busily employed all day on fatigue duties, the Tent Division in cleaning, whitewashing & preparing the hospital generally; the Bearer division building latrines and incinerators, cleaning up the village and cleaning out the drains. – The Soldiers Institute provides music and games for the men in the evening. The morning was fine, but the afternoon and evening was very wet.	J.E.P.
COTTES	22/4/16	9 p.m.	Eleven cases were admitted to the Field Ambulance during the day, two cases were evacuated to a Casualty Clearing Station, and two cases ~~[illegible]~~ were returned to duty, leaving 16 cases remaining. – There has been a persistent downpour of rain throughout the day ~~which~~ has limited the amount of outdoor work. – Billeting Certificates for the week ~~were~~ rendered to-day.	J.E.P.
"	23/4/16	9 p.m.	Two Officers were admitted to the Field Ambulance and evacuated during the day, four other ranks were admitted, 5 cases were evacuated to a C.C.S. and one case was returned to duty, leaving 14 cases remaining. – Lieut. J.L. COCHRANE RAMC reported his departure for duty as temporary M.O. i/c 9th Cheshire Regt. Lieut & QMR. A. BENNETT reported his arrival for duty on completion of ten days leave in England. – All the personnel of the Unit were paid this morning. The day has been fine throughout.	J.E.P.
"	24/4/16	9 p.m.	Eight cases were admitted to the Field Ambulance during the day, nine cases were evacuated to a Casualty Clearing Station and two cases were returned to duty, leaving eleven cases remaining. In the morning the men were taken for a nine mile route march. – In the afternoon Captain SMALLEY R.A.M.C. gave a lecture on gas poisoning and the measures of prevention. The weather has been fine.	J.E.P.

Instructions regarding War Diaries and Intelligence Summaries are contained in F. S. Regs., Part II. and the Staff Manual respectively. Title Pages will be prepared in manuscript.

WAR DIARY
or
INTELLIGENCE SUMMARY
(Erase heading not required.)

Army Form C. 2118

Place	Date	Hour	Summary of Events and Information	Remarks and references to Appendices
COTTES	25/4/16	9 p.m.	Thirteen cases were admitted to the Field Ambulance during the day, and nine cases were evacuated to a C.C.S. and two cases were returned to duty, leaving 13 cases remaining. Lieut. J.F. MACLEOD R.A.M.C. reported his departure this day for permanent duty as M.O. i/c 19th Divisional Ammunition Column. Captain C.F. BURTON R.A.M.C. reported his arrival for duty with the Field Ambulance. Sergt. Major PRIEST was evacuated to a C.C.S. to-day suffering from P.U.O. – The Personnel were exercised in Physical Drill in the morning. Lectures were given in the afternoon. The weather continues fine and warm.	J.E.P.
"	26/4/16	9 p.m.	One Officer was admitted and evacuated during the day to C.C.S. 18 other ranks were admitted to the Field Ambulance during the day, 7 cases were evacuated to a C.C.S. and two cases were sent to duty leaving 22 cases remaining. – The Personnel were exercised in Squad and Company Drill during the morning & lectures were given during the afternoon. The weather continues fine and warm.	J.E.P.
"	27/4/16	9 p.m.	Twelve cases were admitted to the Field Ambulance during the day, 2 cases were evacuated to a Casualty Clearing Station and 2 cases were returned to duty leaving 30 cases remaining. The A.D.M.S. 19th Division inspected the Field Ambulance this morning, the whole of the Personnel Horses, and transport. – Lectures to the Personnel were given in the afternoon. The weather continues fine and warm.	J.E.P.
"	28/4/16	9 p.m.	One Officer was admitted and evacuated to a C.C.S. five ~~[illegible]~~ other ranks sick were admitted to the Field Ambulance, 15 cases were evacuated to a C.C.S. and 4 cases were returned to duty, leaving 16 cases remaining. – C Section complete left at 7 a.m. this morning for Field training with the 56th Infantry Brigade, they returned at 5.30 p.m. – I visited them in the Field during the operations. The weather continues fine and warm.	J.E.P.

1875 Wt. W593/826 1,000,000 4/15 J.B.C. & A. A.D.S.S./Forms/C. 2118.

Army Form C. 2118

WAR DIARY
or
INTELLIGENCE SUMMARY
(Erase heading not required.)

Instructions regarding War Diaries and Intelligence Summaries are contained in F. S. Regs., Part II. and the Staff Manual respectively. Title Pages will be prepared in manuscript.

Place	Date	Hour	Summary of Events and Information	Remarks and references to Appendices
COTTES	29/4/16	9 p.m.	Seven cases were admitted to the Field Ambulance, 5 cases were evacuated to a Casualty Clearing Station and 4 cases were returned to duty, leaving 14 cases remaining. – B Section marched out at 9 a.m. for Field training with the 56th Infantry Brigade returning at 7 p.m. Billeting Certificates for the week were rendered. – Lectures were given in the afternoon. The weather continues fine and warm.	J.E.P.
"	30/4/16	9 p.m.	Eleven cases were admitted to the Field Ambulance, 4 cases were evacuated to a Casualty Clearing Station, and three cases were returned to duty, leaving 18 cases remaining. Captain F. C. BURTON R.A.M.C. reported his departure this day on permanent transfer to No. 59 Field Ambulance. The weather continues fine and warm.	J.E.P.
"	~~[illegible]~~	~~[illegible]~~		

J. E. Powell
Lieut. Colonel R.A.M.C.
O.C. 57th Field Ambulance

1875 Wt. W593/826 1,000,000 4/15 J.B.C. & A. A.D.S.S./Forms/C. 2118.

19th Div.

May 1916.

No. 57 F. Amb.

Instructions regarding War Diaries and Intelligence Summaries are contained in F. S. Regs., Part II. and the Staff Manual respectively. Title Pages will be prepared in manuscript.

WAR DIARY
or
INTELLIGENCE SUMMARY
(Erase heading not required.)

Army Form C. 2118

57 F. Amb

Vol 11

Place	Date	Hour	Summary of Events and Information	Remarks and references to Appendices
COTTES	1/5/16	9 p.m.	Eleven cases were admitted to the Field Ambulance during the day, 13 cases were evacuated including two cases of German measles to No. 7 General Hospital MALASSISE. – Sixteen cases are remaining. – The Personnel were exercised in Stretcher drill and in carrying Patients during the morning – Lectures were given in the afternoon. The weather continues fine.	J.E.P.
"	2/5/16	9 p.m.	Eight cases were admitted to the Field Ambulance during the day, six cases were evacuated to a C.C.S. and one case was returned to duty, leaving 17 cases remaining. – The A.D.M.S. visited the Field Ambulance in the morning. The Personnel were taken for a route march in the morning. There was a thunderstorm in the afternoon. – The G.O.C. Division visited the Field Ambulance this evening.	J.E.P.
"	3/5/16	9 p.m.	Nine cases were admitted to the Field Ambulance during the day, 10 cases were evacuated to a Casualty Clearing Station, including one case of German measles to No. 7 General Hospital. Sixteen cases were left remaining. – The Personnel were exercised in Squad and Company Drill in the morning & lectures were given in the afternoon. The weather has been fine & warm.	J.E.P.
"	4/5/16	9 p.m.	Nine cases were admitted to the Field Ambulance during the day, 15 cases were evacuated to a Casualty Clearing Station including one case of German measles to No. 7 General Hospital. Four cases were returned to duty, leaving six cases remaining. The Personnel were exercised in Stretcher Drill and collecting and carrying Patients in the morning and lectures were given in the afternoon. The weather continues fine & warm.	J.E.P.
"	5/5/16	9 p.m.	Eleven cases were admitted to the Field Ambulance during the day, eleven cases were evacuated to a Casualty Clearing Station and two cases were returned to duty, leaving 4 cases remaining. The Personnel were taken for a Route March in the morning – Lectures were given in the afternoon. The weather is cloudy and hot.	J.E.P.

1875 Wt. W593/826 1,000,000 4/15 J.B.C. & A. A.D.S.S./Forms/C. 2118.

Instructions regarding War Diaries and Intelligence Summaries are contained in F. S. Regs., Part II. and the Staff Manual respectively. Title Pages will be prepared in manuscript.

WAR DIARY
or
INTELLIGENCE SUMMARY
(Erase heading not required.)

Army Form C. 2118

Place	Date	Hour	Summary of Events and Information	Remarks and references to Appendices
COTTES	6/5/16	9 p.m.	Ten cases were admitted to the Field Ambulance during the day, eleven cases were evacuated to a Casualty Clearing Station including one case of German measles to No. 7 General Hospital MALASSISE. Three cases were returned to duty leaving no cases remaining. The A.D.M.S. visited the Field Ambulance in the afternoon. Made all arrangements for entraining the Unit on Monday the 8th inst. – The weather continues fine. – The personnel were paid in the afternoon.	J.E.P.
"	7/5/16	9 p.m.	One officer and 14 men were admitted to the Field Ambulance during the day and one officer and 14 men were evacuated to a Casualty Clearing Station leaving no cases remaining. – The Field Ambulance was closed at 6 p.m. this evening under instructions from the A.D.M.S. – Captain OWENS R.A.M.C. and one man left at 7.30 a.m. this morning for the new area as a billeting party. Lieut. COCHRANE R.A.M.C. rejoined the Unit for duty on completion of temporary duty as M.O. i/c 9th Cheshire Regt. All the equipment and kit was packed in the Wagons this evening. – The weather has been showery. Billeting certificates were rendered and certificates obtained from the Inhabitants that no damage had been done by the men of the Unit.	J.E.P.
LA CHAUSSÉE	8/5/16	9 p.m.	The dismounted personnel marched off at 4 p.m. under Captain KIDD RAMC for entrainment at LILLERS at 6.21 a.m. The Transport and mounted personnel under Captain SMALLEY marched off at 7 a.m. for entrainment at LILLERS at 11.11 a.m. and the motor convoy left at 9 a.m. arriving here at 3.30 p.m. – The Dismounted personnel arrived here from their detraining station at 6 p.m. – The transport has not yet arrived. – The Unit is now in the 3rd Corps of the 4th Army. – I visited the A.D.M.S. this evening. The weather has been colder and windy with heavy showers.	J.E.P.

1875 Wt. W593/826 1,000,000 4/15 J.B.C. & A. A.D.S.S./Forms/C. 2118.

Army Form C. 2118

Instructions regarding War Diaries and Intelligence Summaries are contained in F. S. Regs., Part II. and the Staff Manual respectively. Title Pages will be prepared in manuscript.

WAR DIARY
or
INTELLIGENCE SUMMARY
(Erase heading not required.)

Place	Date	Hour	Summary of Events and Information	Remarks and references to Appendices
LA CHAUSSÉE	9/5/16	9 p.m.	The morning and afternoon have been occupied in cleaning out and preparing the building which we are occupying for use as a hospital. This building was deserted and exceedingly dirty. We are now ready to receive the sick of the Brigade of Infantry and also all the artillery of the Division and other small units in this area. Lieut. E.C. LINDSEY (T.C.) R.A.M.C. reported his arrival for duty this day as a Reinforcement. – The weather is cold and light showers have fallen.	J.E.P.
"	10/5/16	9 p.m.	Eight cases were admitted to the Field Ambulance during the day, four cases were evacuated to a Casualty Clearing Station leaving four cases remaining. – The Personnel were employed in general fatigues, building incinerators, latrines, refuse pits etc. and removing manure and rubbish from the vicinity of the hospital and billets. – The weather continues cold but dry	J.E.P.
"	11/5/16	9 p.m.	Thirteen cases were admitted to the Field Ambulance during the day including one case of German measles, one case was evacuated to a Casualty Clearing Station and 4 cases were transferred to the Corps Scabies Section, leaving 12 cases remaining. – The A.D.M.S. visited the Hospital to-day. The Personnel were employed in making sanitary improvements in connection with the hospital. The weather has been dry but still continues cold.	J.E.P.
"	12/5/16	9 p.m.	Twenty three cases were admitted to the Field Ambulance, 12 cases were evacuated to a Casualty Clearing Station and 3 cases were evacuated to the Corps Scabies Section leaving 20 cases remaining. The Personnel were taken for a short route march with their packs on this morning. The weather has been fine and warm to-day.	J.E.P.
"	13/5/16	9 p.m.	Eight cases were admitted to the Field Ambulance during the day, 7 cases were evacuated to a Casualty Clearing Station, leaving 21 cases remaining. – Lieut. E.C. LINDSEY R.A.M.C. under instructions from the A.D.M.S. 19th Division reported his departure this day for temporary duty as M.O. i/c 7th East Lancashire Regt. – Billeting certificates for the ~~[illegible]~~ week were rendered to-day. – Heavy rain fell during the night and it has been showering throughout the day.	J.E.P.

1875 Wt. W593/826 1,000,000 4/15 J.B.C. & A. A.D.S.S./Forms/C. 2118.

Instructions regarding War Diaries and Intelligence Summaries are contained in F. S. Regs., Part II. and the Staff Manual respectively. Title Pages will be prepared in manuscript.

WAR DIARY
or
INTELLIGENCE SUMMARY
(Erase heading not required.)

Army Form C. 2118

Place	Date	Hour	Summary of Events and Information	Remarks and references to Appendices
LACHAUSSÉE	14/5/16	9 p.m.	Two Officers and eleven other ranks were admitted to the Field Ambulance. Two officers and eight other ranks were evacuated to a Casualty Clearing Station, one case was transferred to the Corps Scabies Section and two cases were returned to duty, leaving 21 cases remaining. – The weather has been fine to-day. Church Parade was held in the morning.	J.E.P.
"	15/5/16	9 p.m.	Seven other ranks were admitted to the Field Ambulance during the day. Two cases were evacuated to a Casualty Clearing Station, six cases to the Divisional Rest Station and one case was sent to Duty leaving 19 cases remaining. Heavy rain fell last night and also this morning. – A Patient in the Field Ambulance attempted to commit suicide this morning by cutting his throat with a razor – the wound is not of a very serious nature. – All the evidence in the case has been taken and forwarded to the man's Commanding Officer and the man has been placed in arrest. The A.D.M.S. has also been notified. Lieut E Doherty RAMC reported his arrival as a reinforcement.	J.E.P.
"	16/5/16	9 p.m.	Two Officers and 13 other ranks were admitted to the Field Ambulance during the day and two Officers and 5 other ranks were evacuated to a Casualty Clearing Station one case was sent to the Divisional Rest Station, one case to the Corps Scabies Section, and two cases were returned to duty, leaving 23 cases remaining. The Bearer Division under Captain SMALLEY went out at 10 a.m. for Field Training. The weather has been fine and dry.	J.E.P.
"	17/5/16	9 p.m.	Admitted – One Officer + 7 other ranks. To CCS – One Officer + 4 other ranks. To Div. Rest Station – 4. Corps Scabies Sect – 2. To Duty. 3 Lieut Col. J.E. Powell reported his departure on 10 days leave to England – command assumed by Capt. G.P. Kidd RAMC. Lieut Doherty, under instructions from ADMS reported his departure for temp. duty with 7th S. Lancs Reg. Weather fine today.	GPK

1875 Wt. W593/826 1,000,000 4/15 J.B.C. & A. A.D.S.S./Forms/C. 2118.

Instructions regarding War Diaries and Intelligence Summaries are contained in F. S. Regs., Part II. and the Staff Manual respectively. Title Pages will be prepared in manuscript.

WAR DIARY
or
INTELLIGENCE SUMMARY
(Erase heading not required.)

Army Form C. 2118

Place	Date	Hour	Summary of Events and Information	Remarks and references to Appendices
LA CHAUSSEE	~~9.0pm~~ 18.5.16	9.0pm	Admitted - 17 (O.R). To Rest Camp - 3. To Scabies Sect. 3. Trans. to 19 FA 2. Remaining 26. ADMS called during the morning and inspected the Hospital. Inspector of Remounts called in afternoon & cast one H.D. horse Sections carried out night scheme from 9.0 pm - 12.0 midnight - each section marching by a different route to a fixed rendezvous to give NCOs practice in map reading. Result quite satisfactory. Weather fine & very hot.	GBR
"	19.5.16	9.0pm	Admitted - 15. To CCS - 1. To Rest Camp - 4. To Duty - 2. Remaining - 27 Weather remains fine and very hot.	GBR
"	20.5.16	"	Admitted - 8. To Rest Camp. 11. To Corps Scabies Sect - 4. To Duty - 1. Remaining - 19. Bearer Division under Capt SMALLEY departed for two days field training under unit arrangement in the vicinity of PICQUIGNY. Full bearer division transport and equipment was taken & the party will bivouac for two nights	GBR
"	21.5.16	"	Admitted - 13. To Rest Camp - 5. To Corps Scabies Sect - 2. Remaining - 25. D.D.M.S. IIIrd Corps visited and inspected the hospital and billets during the afternoon and expressed himself as quite satisfied with all arrangements. Weather remains fine and warm and the men are being given every opportunity of bathing in the pools near the river.	GBR
"	22.5.16	"	Admitted - 6. To C.C.S - 4. (one case of German measles - developed since admission). To Rest Camp - 6. To Duty - 3. Remaining - 18. Bearer Division returned from two days training. A complete kit inspection was held during the morning & the last blanket withdrawn from the personnel today. ADMS held a conference at the ambulance this afternoon & visited the hospital and billets afterwards. Weather rather cooler but still fine.	GBR

1875 Wt. W593/826 1,000,000 4/15 J.B.C. & A. A.D.S.S./Forms/C. 2118.

Instructions regarding War Diaries and Intelligence Summaries are contained in F. S. Regs., Part II. and the Staff Manual respectively. Title Pages will be prepared in manuscript.

WAR DIARY
or
~~INTELLIGENCE SUMMARY~~
(Erase heading not required.)

Army Form C. 2118

Place	Date	Hour	Summary of Events and Information	Remarks and references to Appendices
LA CHAUSSÉE	23.5.16	9.0 pm	Admissions - 9. To Corps Scabies Sect. - 3. Remaining 24. The weather still being fine & warm, the mornings are still being chiefly occupied in bathing the men and in short marches & physical drill	GPK
"	24.5.16	"	Admissions - 12. To C.C.S - 4. To Divisional Rest Camp - 6. To Scabies Sect. - 1 Dental cases transferred to 59 F.A. - 3. To Duty - 2. Remaining 20. A good deal of rain fell during the day & the weather is cooler.	GPK
"	25.5.16	"	Admitted - Officers - 2. O.R. - 8. To C.C.S. Officers. 1 O.R. 3. To Rest Camp. Off. 1. O.R. 1. To Duty - 3. Remaining - 21. Arrangements have been made to obtain green fodder for horses once or twice per week as required. Weather remains fine.	GPK
"	26.5.16	"	Admitted - 9. To C.C.S. 3. To Rest Camp. 1. To Duty. 1. Remaining - 25. Orders received that 2000 extra rations & other comforts for patients are being held for us by 59. F.A. for use in the event of an engagement. Weather remains fine & warm.	GPK
"	27.5.16	"	Admitted - 7. To C.C.S. - 4. To Duty - 3. Remaining - 25. One case of ? Cerebro-Spinal Meningitis admitted from 19. D.A.C. & evacuated to No 39. C.C.S. Weather still fine & warm.	GPK
"	28.5.16	10.0 AM	Lieut Col. J. E. Powell Rowe reported his arrival from ten days leave in England and assumed command of the unit today. Lieut A. P. Ing Rowe, under orders from A.D.M.S. reported his departure to take over sanitary duty on H.Q. 4th, 10 R. War. Reg.	J.E.P.
		9 p.m.	Admitted 11 other ranks, To Div. Rest. Stn. 1. To Corps Scabies Section 2. To Duty 4. Remaining 29.	

1875 Wt. W593/826 1,000,000 4/15 J.B.C. & A. A.D.S.S./Forms/C. 2118.

Instructions regarding War Diaries and Intelligence Summaries are contained in F. S. Regs., Part II. and the Staff Manual respectively. Title Pages will be prepared in manuscript.

WAR DIARY
or
INTELLIGENCE SUMMARY
(Erase heading not required.)

Army Form C. 2118

Place	Date	Hour	Summary of Events and Information	Remarks and references to Appendices
LA CHAUSSÉE	29/5/16	9 p.m.	14 other ranks were admitted to the Field Ambulance, 4 cases were sent to a Casualty Clearing Station, 4 cases to the Divisional Rest Station, 5 cases to the Corps Scabies Section and 4 cases to Duty. Leaving 26 cases remaining. – The prevailing disease is Scabies. – Lieut. Lindsey R.A.M.C. reported his arrival for duty on completion of temporary duty as M.O. i/c 7th East Lancs Regt. – The weather is fine & dry.	J.E.P.
"	30/5/16	9 p.m.	Twelve other ranks were admitted to the Field Ambulance, 4 cases were sent to a Casualty Clearing Station, 3 cases to the Corps Scabies Section and 4 cases were returned to duty leaving 27 cases remaining. – A working party of 40 men under an Officer is being sent daily to No. 39 Casualty Clearing Station to assist in making a Camp. – The remainder of the personnel were occupied in hospital duties, general fatigues, physical drill and a bathing parade. – Lieut DOHERTY R.A.M.C. reported his arrival for duty on completion of temporary duty as M.O. i/c 7th South Lancs. Regt. – The weather is fine and dry.	J.E.P.
"	31/5/16	9 p.m.	A working party under an Officer was again sent to No. 39 Casualty Clearing Station to assist in making a Camp. – The remainder of the personnel were occupied in a short route march and a bathing parade. – Captain A.A. SMALLEY R.A.M.C. reported his departure to-day on ten days leave of absence to England. Nine cases were admitted to the Field Ambulance during the day, two cases were sent to a Casualty Clearing Station, five cases to the Divisional Rest Stn. and 7 cases were returned to duty, leaving 22 cases remaining. – The weather continues fine and dry.	J.E.P.

J. E. Powell
Lieut. Colonel R.A.M.C.
O.C. No. 57 Field Ambulance.

1875 Wt. W593/826 1,000,000 4/15 J.B.C. & A. A.D.S.S./Forms/C. 2118.

June 1916.

S

No. 57 F.A.

Instructions regarding War Diaries and Intelligence Summaries are contained in F. S. Regs., Part II. and the Staff Manual respectively. Title Pages will be prepared in manuscript.

WAR DIARY
or
INTELLIGENCE SUMMARY
(Erase heading not required.)

57 Fd Amb

Army Form C. 2118

June

Vol 12

Place	Date	Hour	Summary of Events and Information	Remarks and references to Appendices
LA CHAUSSÉE	1/6/16	9 p.m.	A working party under an Officer was again sent to No. 39 Casualty Clearing Station to assist in forming a camp. The remainder of the personnel not on duty were taken for a route march followed by a bathing parade. The weather continues fine & dry. Seven cases were admitted to the Field Ambulance, five cases were sent to a Casualty Clearing Station and 5 cases to the Divisional Rest Station, two cases were transferred to the Corps Scabies Section and one case was sent to duty, leaving sixteen cases remaining.	J.E.P.
"	2/6/16	9 p.m.	Working party as usual proceeded to No. 39 Casualty Clearing Station under an Officer. The weather continues fine and dry. Twelve cases were admitted to the Field Ambulance during the day, one case was sent to a Casualty Clearing Station, one case was sent to the Divisional Rest Stn. and four cases were sent to the Corps Scabies Section and 5 cases were returned to duty leaving 17 cases remaining.	J.E.P.
"	3/6/16	9 p.m.	Working party proceeded as usual to No. 39 Casualty Clearing Station. The remainder of the Personnel not on duty were exercised in physical drill. – The Personnel were paid this morning. The weather is colder and also showery. LIEUT. A.P. FRY R.A.M.C. reported his arrival to-day on completion of temporary duty as M.O. i/c 10th Royal Warwick Regt. Three cases were admitted to the Field Ambulance during the day, one case was sent to the Divisional Rest Station and two cases were returned to duty leaving 17 cases remaining.	J.E.P.

1875 Wt. W593/826 1,000,000 4/15 J.B.C. & A. A.D.S.S./Forms/C. 2118.

Instructions regarding War Diaries and Intelligence Summaries are contained in F. S. Regs., Part II. and the Staff Manual respectively. Title Pages will be prepared in manuscript.

WAR DIARY
or
INTELLIGENCE SUMMARY

(Erase heading not required.)

Army Form C. 2118

Place	Date	Hour	Summary of Events and Information	Remarks and references to Appendices
LA CHAUSSÉE	4/6/16	9 p.m.	Four cases were admitted to the Field Ambulance during the day, 4 cases were sent to a Casualty Clearing Station and 3 cases were returned to duty, leaving 14 cases remaining. The weather has been cold and showery. – A working party proceeded to No. 39 Casualty Clearing Station as usual.	J.E.P.
"	5/6/16	9 p.m.	Lieut. J.L. COCHRANE R.A.M.C. reported his departure this day for temporary duty as M.O. i/c 10th Worcestershire Regt. The A.D.M.S. 19th Division together with the Sanitary Officer 4th Army visited the Field Ambulance this morning and inspected the sanitary arrangements and expressed their satisfaction. – The usual working party proceeded to No. 39 Casualty Clearing Station. Four cases were admitted to the Field Ambulance during the day, 3 cases were sent to a Casualty Clearing Stn. and 2 cases were returned to duty, leaving 13 cases remaining. – The weather continues cold and showery.	J.E.P.
"	6/6/16	9 p.m.	Captain H.B. OWENS R.A.M.C. reported his departure this day for temporary duty as M.O. i/c 88th Brigade R.F.A. – The usual working party proceeded to No. 39 Casualty Clearing Stn. Heavy rain fell throughout the morning and afternoon. Eight cases were admitted to the Field Ambulance during the day. 5 cases were sent to the Divisional Rest Station, leaving 16 cases remaining.	J.E.P.
"	7/6/16	9 p.m.	Captain H.R. DEW R.A.M.C. reported his arrival for duty this day on return from 14 days leave of absence in England. Heavy showers of rain have again fallen to-day. Seven sick and 10 cases of accidental bomb wounds were admitted during the day. 9 cases were sent to a Casualty Clearing Station, two cases to the Divisional Rest and one case was returned to duty, leaving 21 cases remaining.	J.E.P.

1875 Wt. W593/826 1,000,000 4/15 J.B.C. & A. A.D.S.S./Forms/C. 2118.

Instructions regarding War Diaries and Intelligence Summaries are contained in F. S. Regs., Part II. and the Staff Manual respectively. Title Pages will be prepared in manuscript.

WAR DIARY
or
INTELLIGENCE SUMMARY
(Erase heading not required.)

Army Form C. 2118

Place	Date	Hour	Summary of Events and Information	Remarks and references to Appendices
LACHAUSSÉE	8/6/16	9 p.m.	Four cases were admitted to the Field Ambulance during the day and four cases were sent to a Casualty Clearing Station, leaving 21 cases remaining. The usual working party was sent to No. 39 Casualty Clearing Station, the remainder of the personnel not on duty were taken for a Route march. – The weather continues cold and showery – heavy rain fell during the day.	J.E.P.
"	9/6/16	9 p.m.	One case was admitted to the Field Ambulance during the day, five cases were sent to the Divisional Rest Station and two cases were returned to duty leaving 15 cases remaining. – During the afternoon I went with the A.D.M.S. 19th Division to LAVIÉVILLE to inspect a proposed site for this Field Ambulance at some future date. The weather continues cold and showery.	J.E.P.
"	10/6/16	9 p.m.	One case only was admitted to the Field Ambulance during the day, three cases were sent to the Divisional Rest Station and three cases were returned to duty, leaving 10 cases remaining. – Billeting certificates for the week were rendered to-day. A Board on unserviceable clothing was held to-day. – The Personnel not on duty were exercised in Physical drill during the morning. – The weather continues cold & showery	J.E.P.
"	11/6/16	9 p.m.	Nine cases were admitted to the Field Ambulance during the day, one case was sent to a Casualty Clearing Station and one case to the Divisional Rest Station, leaving 17 cases remaining. The weather still continues cold and showery. – The working party proceeded as usual to No. 39 Casualty Clearing Station. – Captain A. A. SMALLEY R.A.M.C. reported his arrival for duty on return from 10 days leave in England.	J.E.P.

1875 Wt. W593/826 1,000,000 4/15 J.B.C. & A. A.D.S.S./Forms/C. 2118.

Army Form C. 2118

Instructions regarding War Diaries and Intelligence Summaries are contained in F. S. Regs., Part II. and the Staff Manual respectively. Title Pages will be prepared in manuscript.

WAR DIARY
or
INTELLIGENCE SUMMARY

(Erase heading not required.)

Place	Date	Hour	Summary of Events and Information	Remarks and references to Appendices
LA CHAUSSÉE	12/6/16	9 p.m.	Thirteen cases were admitted to the Field Ambulance during the day, five cases were evacuated to a Casualty Clearing Station, five cases were sent to the Divisional Rest Station, one case was sent to the Corps Scabies Section and one case was returned to duty, leaving 18 cases remaining. – The working party proceeded as usual to No 39 Casualty Clearing Station. – The weather continues cold and showery.	J.E.P.
"	13/6/16	9 p.m.	Fourteen cases were admitted to the Field Ambulance during the day, one case was evacuated to a Casualty Clearing Station one case was returned to duty, and 7 cases were sent to the Divisional Rest Station, leaving 23 cases remaining. – The working party completed their work at No. 39 Casualty Clearing Station to-day & will not be further required. – Weather still cold and showery.	J.E.P.
"	14/6/16	9 p.m.	Two Officers and three other ranks were admitted during the day, one Officer and 16 men were evacuated to a Casualty Clearing Station, one Officer and 8 men were sent to the Divisional Rest Station and one case to the Corps Scabies Section, leaving one case remaining. – During the afternoon orders were received from the A.D.M.S. 19th Division for the Field Ambulance to move at 10 a.m. to-morrow to RAINNEVILLE and on the following day to march to LAVIEVILLE and open there for the reception of casualties. The evening was spent in packing equipment and stores.	J.E.P.
RAINNEVILLE	15/6/16	9 p.m.	Billeting certificates were rendered at LA CHAUSSEE prior to departure and certificates obtained from the inhabitants. – The unit marched out at 10 a.m. and arrived at RAINNEVILLE at 4 p.m. where we moved into billets. The weather was cold but dry, no rain falling. – One case still remains in the Field Ambulance – no cases were admitted during the day.	J.E.P.

1875 Wt. W593/826 1,000,000 4/15 J.B.C. & A. A.D.S.S./Forms/C. 2118.

Instructions regarding War Diaries and Intelligence Summaries are contained in F. S. Regs., Part II. and the Staff Manual respectively. Title Pages will be prepared in manuscript.

WAR DIARY
or
INTELLIGENCE SUMMARY
(Erase heading not required.)

Army Form C. 2118

Place	Date	Hour	Summary of Events and Information	Remarks and references to Appendices
LAVIEVILLE	16/6/16	10 p.m.	Having rendered billeting certificates for the night, the Unit marched out of RAINNEVILLE at 11.30 a.m. and halted at FRANKVILLERS at 2.30 p.m. – From there a small advance party was sent on to LAVIEVILLE to take over the hospital & billets from No. 24 Field Ambulance. – The remainder of the Unit arrived here at 10 p.m. and opened for the reception of casualties. The day has been fine and warm. Two cases were admitted to the Field Ambulance and two cases were transferred to the Field Ambulance from No. 24 Field Ambulance, leaving 5 cases remaining.	J.E.P.
"	17/6/16	9 p.m.	The Unit has been occupied in cleaning up the surroundings of the Hospital and billets today also in making new latrines, urine pits and incinerator. Four G.S. Wagons in charge of the Quartermaster were sent to No. 59 Field Ambulance to draw the surplus stores which had been stored there. – The weather has been fine and warm again. – Six cases were admitted to the Field Ambulance during the day, 3 cases were evacuated to a Casualty Clearing Station by No 21 M.A.C. 2 cases were sent to the Divisional Rest Station, one case was transferred to No. 24 Field Ambulance & one case was sent to Duty, leaving 4 cases remaining.	J.E.P.
"	18/6/16	9 p.m.	Seven cases were admitted to the Field Ambulance during the day, including one case of Scarlet Fever and one case of Diphtheria evacuated to No 39 Casualty Clearing Stn. Two other cases were evacuated to No. 36 Casualty Clearing Stn. and one case to the Divisional Rest Stn. leaving six cases remaining. – The weather has been fine and warm. Four G.S. Wagons were again sent to complete the collection of surplus stores from No. 59 Field Ambulance. – The remainder of the Personnel were all busy on general fatigues, cleaning out yards & wards and preparing barns for the reception of casualties.	J.E.P.

1875 Wt. W593/826 1,000,000 4/15 J.B.C. & A. A.D.S.S./Forms/C. 2118.

Instructions regarding War Diaries and Intelligence Summaries are contained in F. S. Regs., Part II. and the Staff Manual respectively. Title Pages will be prepared in manuscript.

WAR DIARY
or
INTELLIGENCE SUMMARY
(Erase heading not required.)

Army Form C. 2118

Place	Date	Hour	Summary of Events and Information	Remarks and references to Appendices
LAVIEVILLE	19/6/16	9 p.m.	Two Officers and seven other ranks sick were admitted to the Field Ambulance during the day one Officer and 3 men were evacuated to a Casualty Clearing station and one Officer and 2 men were sent to the Divisional Rest Station and one case was returned to Duty, leaving 4 cases remaining. – Two tons of straw were obtained to-day for the use of Patients. The Personnel were employed in various fatigues. The weather has been fine	J.E.P.
"	20/6/16	9 p.m.	Six cases were admitted to the Field Ambulance, two cases were evacuated to a Casualty clearing station and two cases to the Divisional Rest Station and one case was sent to duty, leaving eight cases remaining. The weather is now warm and fine. – The Personnel were employed in general fatigues, white washing and the general preparation of the billets as wards.	J.E.P.
"	21/6/16	9 p.m.	Eight cases were admitted to the Field Ambulance, and one case evacuated to a Casualty Clearing Station, leaving 15 cases remaining. – The weather continues fine and warm. In the morning I went with the D.A.D.M.S. 34th Division, taking Captain SMALLEY R.A.M.C. my Bearer Division Officer with me, to see the Advanced Dressing Station of the 103rd Field Ambulance and their arrangements for the evacuation of casualties In the afternoon the A.D.M.S. 19th Division visited the Field Ambulance, inspecting the accommodation and the arrangements made.	J.E.P.
"	22/6/16	9 p.m.	Eight cases were admitted to the Field Ambulance, 2 cases were sent to Casualty Clearing Stn. 5 cases were sent to the Divisional Rest Stn. one case to the Corps Scabies Section and three cases were sent to duty, leaving 12 cases remaining. The weather continues fine and warm. The Personnel were all bivouaced out to-day vacating all billets. The D.D.M.S. IIIrd Corps visited the Field Ambulance this morning and appeared satisfied with the arrangements.	J.E.P.

1875 Wt. W593/826 1,000,000 4/15 J.B.C. & A. A.D.S.S./Forms/C. 2118.

Instructions regarding War Diaries and Intelligence Summaries are contained in F. S. Regs., Part II. and the Staff Manual respectively. Title Pages will be prepared in manuscript.

WAR DIARY
or
INTELLIGENCE SUMMARY
(Erase heading not required.)

Army Form C. 2118

Place	Date	Hour	Summary of Events and Information	Remarks and references to Appendices
LAVIEVILLE	23/6/16	9 p.m.	During the day nine cases were admitted to the Field Ambulance, 3 cases were ~~admitted~~ evacuated to a Casualty Clearing Stn., four cases were sent to the Divisional Rest Stn. and one case was returned to duty, leaving 13 cases remaining. – a heavy thunderstorm ~~burst~~ came on this afternoon, with very heavy rain. – Medical arrangements for the 19th Division during Operations were received this evening.	J.E.P.
"	24/6/16	9 p.m.	Eight cases were admitted during the day, one case was evacuated to a Casualty Clearing Stn. 5 cases were sent to the Divisional Rest Stn. and one case to the Corps Scabies Section and one case was returned to duty, leaving 13 cases remaining. – Captain H.B. OWENS R.A.M.C. reported his arrival for duty on completion of temporary duty as M.O. i/c 88th Brigade R.F.A. – Billeting certificates for the week were rendered to-day. The weather is fine & warm.	J.E.P.
"	25/6/16	9 p.m.	One case of self-inflicted wound was admitted during the day and evacuated to No. 39 Casualty Clearing Station ST. OUEN. – Three cases were transferred to the Divisional Rest Station, one case to the 59th Field Ambulance and 4 cases were sent to duty, leaving 5 cases remaining. – 3 Motor ambulance cars from No. 21 M.A.C. and 2 Motor ambulance cars from No. 59 Field Ambulance arrived to-day to be attached for duty. Received a Priority telegram at 11 a.m. from A.D.M.S. that Medical arrangements 3rd Corps No 2. come into force forthwith. The weather continues fine & warm.	J.E.P.
"	26/6/16	9 p.m.	One wounded German prisoner was admitted to the Field Ambulance during the day and transferred to No. 59 Field Ambulance under instructions from headquarters 25th Inf. Brigade. R.A.M.C. Order No. 39 by A.D.M.S. 19th Division was received this evening, giving proposed medical movements during the forthcoming operations. – A thunderstorm ~~[illegible]~~ came on during the afternoon with very heavy rain.	J.E.P.

1875 Wt. W593/826 1,000,000 4/15 J.B.C. & A. A.D.S.S./Forms/C. 2118.

Army Form C. 2118

Instructions regarding War Diaries and Intelligence Summaries are contained in F. S. Regs., Part II. and the Staff Manual respectively. Title Pages will be prepared in manuscript.

WAR DIARY
or
INTELLIGENCE SUMMARY
(Erase heading not required.)

Place	Date	Hour	Summary of Events and Information	Remarks and references to Appendices
LAVIEVILLE	27/6/16	9 p.m.	Seven cases were transferred from the 26th Field Ambulance, 2 cases were admitted one case was transferred to a Casualty Clearing Station, one case was transferred to No 59 Field Ambulance and 9 cases were transferred to the Divisional Rest Station leaving 5 cases remaining. – The D.D.M.S. 3rd Corps & also the A.D.M.S. 19th Division visited the Field Ambulance this morning. – Five wounded were detained and evacuated in motor lorries to FRECHENCOURT for C.C.S VECQUEMONT. – Heavy showers of rain fell during the day.	J.E.P.
"	28/6/16	9 p.m.	No cases were admitted to the Field Ambulance during the day, 4 cases were transferred to the Divisional Rest Station and one case was transferred to No. 59 Field Ambulance leaving no cases remaining. – Twelve wounded were detained during the day and sent in Motor lorries to FRECHENCOURT Rest Camp for C.C.S. VECQUEMONT. – Heavy rain has again fallen during the day making the condition of the roads & trenches very bad.	J.E.P.
"	29/6/16	9 p.m.	One case of measles was admitted during the day and evacuated to No 39 Casualty Clearing Station There are no cases remaining. Four cases of wounded were detained and sent in Motor lorries to FRECHENCOURT Rest Camp for C.C.S. VECQUEMONT. – The A.D.M.S. visited the Field Ambulance during the evening. The weather has been dull and cloudy but no rain fell to-day.	J.E.P.
"	30/6/16	9 p.m.	One officer and one other rank were admitted to the Field Ambulance, and both were evacuated to a Casualty Clearing station. Ten cases ~~xxx~~ wounded were ~~xxx~~ detained and sent in Motor Lorries to FRECHENCOURT Rest Camp for C.C.S. Vecquemont An alternative scheme for the Bearer division was received to-day from the A.D.M.S. – The weather has been dry but cloudy.	J.E.P.

J.E. Powell, Lieut Colonel RAMC
O.C. No 57 Field Ambulance

1875 Wt. W593/826 1,000,000 4/15 J.B.C. & A. A.D.S.S./Forms/C. 2118.

19th Division

No 57. Field Ambulance

July 1916

5
July 1916

1911

18/6

To – A D M S

17 Div

I forward you herewith copy of my War Diary for the month of July. For transmission to D.A.G. for their disposal.

J. E. Powell Lt Col

No 57 Fd Amb

19

Army Form C. 2118

- 57 F Amb

Vol 13

Instructions regarding War Diaries and Intelligence Summaries are contained in F. S. Regs., Part II. and the Staff Manual respectively. Title Pages will be prepared in manuscript.

WAR DIARY
or
~~INTELLIGENCE SUMMARY~~

(Erase heading not required.)

Place	Date	Hour	Summary of Events and Information	Remarks and references to Appendices
LAVIEVILLE	1/7/16	9 p.m.	Operations commenced at 7.30 a.m. 462 cases have been admitted and 350 cases have been detained during the day. 397 cases have been evacuated, leaving 415 cases remaining (262 cases admitted + 153 detained) Surgeon General Macpherson A.M.S. + D.D.M.S. 3rd Corps visited the Ambulance at 11 a.m. – The D.D.M.S. again visited at 3 p.m. – The A.D.M.S. visited the ambulance at 1 p.m. 3.30 p.m. and 3 p.m. – Very few lorries have passed during the day and much of the evacuation has been done in our own cars and 3 M.A.C. cars. – At 1 p.m. I received orders from ADMS for our own cars to collect from 8th Division Collecting Station + Crucifix Corner Dressing Station to 24th Field Ambulance HENENCOURT. – At 6.30 p.m. I received orders from A.D.M.S. to send my Bearer Division under Captain A.A. SMALLEY to Crucifix Corner to assist and relieve Bearers of 8th Division. – They left at 7.30 p.m. – The weather has been fine and warm.	J.E.P.
"	2/7/16	9 p.m.	The day has been fine and warm. – At 2 a.m. received telegram from A.D.M.S. that Bearer Division would be required to proceed to assembly trenches S.W. of ALBERT during the day. – At 6.30 a.m. I proceeded to CRUCIFIX Corner and directed Captain SMALLEY to withdraw all his Bearers from the trenches and AID POSTS where they had been working continuously all night and to await further orders at Crucifix Corner. – At 9.45 a.m. I received telegram from A.D.M.S. for the Bearer Division to move forthwith to assembly trenches S.W. of ALBERT with the 56th Brigade, they arrived there at 3 p.m. + I reported their arrival to the A.D.M.S. – The A.D.M.S. visited the ambulance at 12.30 p.m. + the D.D.M.S. visited the ambulance at 5 p.m. 466 cases have been admitted to the Field Ambulance up to Noon to-day and have all been evacuated by this evening by Lorries, M.A.C. cars and the unit cars. – In addition to the above 700 cases have been detained and evacuated by lorries. Total 1166. The ambulance at present being clear of all cases.	J.E.P.

1875 Wt. W593/826 1,000,000 4/15 J.B.C. & A. A.D.S.S./Forms/C. 2118.

Army Form C. 2118

Instructions regarding War Diaries and Intelligence Summaries are contained in F. S. Regs., Part II. and the Staff Manual respectively. Title Pages will be prepared in manuscript.

WAR DIARY
or
INTELLIGENCE SUMMARY
(Erase heading not required.)

Place	Date	Hour	Summary of Events and Information	Remarks and references to Appendices
LAVIEVILLE	3/7/16	9 p.m.	The day has been fine and warm. 15 cases wounded were admitted and 744 wounded were detained, 729 cases were evacuated leaving 35 remaining. – The evacuation has worked satisfactorily to-day. – At 2 p.m. I visited the Bearer Division in the assembly trenches S.W. of ALBERT. – at 3 p.m. I received orders to send a Bearer Division Officer for duty to the 10th Royal Warwick Regt. I detailed Lieut. E.C. DOHERTY R.A.M.C. who proceeded forthwith. at 5 p.m. Brigadier General HAMBRO Q branch 3rd Corps visited the Ambulance. at 6 p.m. I received orders for the Bearer Division to proceed forthwith to BAPAUME POST to take over from the 58th Field Ambulance Bearers. They reported their arrival there at 7.45 p.m. at 10 p.m. I visited the A.D.M.S. in his Office.	J.E.P.
ALBERT	4/7/16	9 p.m.	Five cases only were admitted during the day and 83 cases were detained, and 90 cases were evacuated leaving no cases remaining. A total of 2028 cases have been cleared during the past four days. – Received orders at 9.30 a.m. to hand over the Main Dressing Stn. and collecting Stn to No. 104 Field Ambulance and to proceed to the Civil Hospital ALBERT and there open a Main Dressing Station. The Unit on relief by No 104 Field Ambulance marched out from LAVIEVILLE at 4 p.m. arriving at the Civil Hospital ALBERT at 5.40 p.m. I visited the Bearer Division at BAPAUME POST at 7.30 p.m. and arranged for their relief by 58th Fd. Ambulance bearers at 10 a.m. to-morrow. – Heavy rain has fallen throughout the afternoon. Billeting certificates were rendered prior to departure.	J.E.P.

1875 Wt. W593/826 1,000,000 4/15 J.B.C. & A. A.D.S.S./Forms/C. 2118.

Instructions regarding War Diaries and Intelligence Summaries are contained in F. S. Regs., Part II. and the Staff Manual respectively. Title Pages will be prepared in manuscript.

WAR DIARY
or
INTELLIGENCE SUMMARY
(Erase heading not required.)

Army Form C. 2118

Place	Date	Hour	Summary of Events and Information	Remarks and references to Appendices
ALBERT	5/7/16	9 p.m.	The A.D.M.S. visited the Field Ambulance at 11 a.m. and at 10 p.m. – I reported the Unit open for the reception of casualties at 10 a.m. – I visited BAPAUME POST at 10.30 a.m. when the Bearer Division was relieved by the Bearer Division of No. 58 Field Ambulance. at 2 p.m. I visited the A.D.S. 90th Field Ambulance at BECOURT Chateau & arranged with the Officer i/c there to evacuate all 19th Division casualties in my own ambulance cars – I detailed two cars for this purpose. One Officer wounded in the abdomen was admitted and evacuated No 9/2 Field Ambulance WARLOY and two other lying cases were admitted and evacuated by No 21 M.A.C. – The day has been fine	J.E.P.
"	6/7/16	9 p.m.	The Bearer Division relieved the Bearer Division of the 58th Field Ambulance at BAPAUME POST at 10 a.m. – During the day the Bearer Division personnel suffered the following casualties from shell fire – 1 man killed and 1 Sergeant and 7 men wounded. The D.D.M.S. Corps and the A.D.M.S. Division visited the Field Ambulance at 10.30 a.m. Brigadier General HAMBRO Q. Branch 3rd Corps visited the Field Ambulance at 3.30 p.m. The day has been fine. Nine wounded Officers were admitted during the night, one Officer died and the remainder were evacuated. 47 other ranks wounded were admitted, nearly all very serious cases. – One man died 39 were evacuated and 7 cases are remaining. – I visited BAPAUME POST at 5.30 p.m. and under instructions from the A.D.M.S. arranged to withdraw one Bearer Subdivision this evening.	J.E.P.

1875 Wt. W593/826 1,000,000 4/15 J.B.C. & A. A.D.S.S./Forms/C. 2118.

Army Form C. 2118

Instructions regarding War Diaries and Intelligence Summaries are contained in F. S. Regs., Part II. and the Staff Manual respectively. Title Pages will be prepared in manuscript.

WAR DIARY
or
INTELLIGENCE SUMMARY
(Erase heading not required.)

Place	Date	Hour	Summary of Events and Information	Remarks and references to Appendices
ALBERT	7/7/16	9 p.m.	Heavy rain has fallen throughout the day. I visited BAPAUME POST at 12 Noon and relieved my Bearer Sub-division with two Officers & Bearer Sub-division from the 59th Field Ambulance who had just arrived to be temporarily attached to this Unit. — I sent Captain OWENS and C Section Bearer Subdivision at 11 a.m. to work along BECOURT avenue to this Main dressing station. — at 4 p.m. I visited BECOURT Chateau A.D.S. and withdrew Captain OWEN's Bearer Subdivision as they were not further required. The A.D.M.S. visited the Field Ambulance at 4.30 p.m. — I again visited BAPAUME POST at 5.40 p.m. to ascertain if casualties from the 9th K.O. R. Lancs Regt., and 13th Royal Fusiliers were being evacuated satisfactorily and was informed that they were now coming through satisfactorily. Two Officers and 78 other ranks were admitted up till 12 Noon, including one French soldier and ~~3~~ German Prisoners wounded. — Two Officers and 81 other ranks were evacuated, one man died leaving 3 men remaining.	J.E.P.
"	8/7/16	9 p.m.	The weather has been fine to-day. — The A.D.M.S. visited the Ambulance at 10.30 a.m. and at 1 p.m. — I visited BAPAUME POST at 11 a.m. and 4 p.m. and made arrangements for the evacuation of seriously wounded German Prisoners from the 13th Royal Fusiliers Regimental aid Post. — Captain Owens and a Bearer Subdivision proceeded to BAPAUME POST at 10 a.m. and relieved the 59th Field Ambulance Bearers. — at 4.30 p.m. Captain SMALLEY and Lieut. FRY with another Bearer subdivision proceeded to reinforce Captain OWENS the difficulty of evacuation has proved very great, owing to the great carrying distance & the mud & water in the trenches. — Ten Officers and 140 other ranks wounded have been admitted during the day and 9 Officers and 140 men were evacuated, leaving one Officer and 3 men remaining. One Officer German Prisoner and 6 German Private soldiers were admitted wounded and evacuated.	J.E.P.

1875 Wt. W593/826 1,000,000 4/15 J.B.C. & A. A.D.S.S./Forms/C. 2118.

Instructions regarding War Diaries and Intelligence Summaries are contained in F. S. Regs., Part II. and the Staff Manual respectively. Title Pages will be prepared in manuscript.

WAR DIARY
or
INTELLIGENCE SUMMARY
(Erase heading not required.)

Army Form C. 2118

Place	Date	Hour	Summary of Events and Information	Remarks and references to Appendices
ALBERT	9/7/16	9 p.m.	Received orders from A.D.M.S. to withdraw Bearer Division from BAPAUME POST on relief by Bearer Division No. 104 Field Ambulance, this was done at 11·30 a.m. The A.D.M.S. visited the Field Ambulance at 10·30 a.m. – The A.D.M.S. 34th Division also visited the Field Ambulance at 11·30 a.m. – Orders from the A.D.M.S. were also received to close the Field Ambulance here at 8 a.m. To-morrow the 10th inst and transfer any casualties to No. 103 Field Ambulance who are taking over here and on relief to move into Billets at HENENCOURT WOOD and remain closed. The day has been fine and warm. – Four wounded Officers and 63 wounded men were admitted to-day and 5 Officers and 64 men were evacuated leaving two men remaining. Two wounded German Officers are included in the above figures.	J.E.P.
HENENCOURT WOOD	10/7/16	9 p.m.	Handed over the Main Dressing Station at the Civil Hospital ALBERT to No. 103 Field Ambulance at 8 a.m. and marched off at 8·30 a.m. by sections at 500 yards interval arriving at HENENCOURT WOOD at 11 a.m. where the Unit is accommodated in huts and remains closed. The day has been fine and warm. The D.D.M.S. 3rd Corps visited the Ambulance at 5 p.m. – Since Noon yesterday up to 8 A.M. to-day, Four wounded Officers and 60 wounded men were admitted to the Field Ambulance, 4 Officers and 61 men were evacuated and one man transferred to No 103 Field Ambulance, leaving no cases remaining.	J.E.P.
"	11/7/16	9 p.m.	The Field Ambulance remains closed and no cases are admitted. The sick of the 56th and 58th Brigades are collected daily and conveyed to the 58th Field Ambulance. – The morning was spent in checking and repacking equipment. – In the afternoon the personnel were all paid, and a Court of Enquiry was held to enquire into the loss of wheeled stretcher carriers in the Field. – The day has been fine.	J.E.P.

1875 Wt. W593/826 1,000,000 4/15 J.B.C. & A. A.D.S.S./Forms/C. 2118.

Army Form C. 2118

Instructions regarding War Diaries and Intelligence Summaries are contained in F. S. Regs., Part II. and the Staff Manual respectively. Title Pages will be prepared in manuscript.

WAR DIARY
or
INTELLIGENCE SUMMARY

(Erase heading not required.)

Place	Date	Hour	Summary of Events and Information	Remarks and references to Appendices
HENENCOURT WOOD	12/7/16	9 p.m.	The day has been fine but cold. The A.D.M.S. visited the Field ambulance this morning. A board was held on unserviceable clothing this morning. The checking of equipment and stores has continued.	J.E.P.
"	13/7/16	9 p.m.	The day has been fine but cold, one heavy shower of rain fell early this morning. A parade and inspection of all personnel was held this morning. Made arrangements for bathing the men to-morrow at HENENCOURT. Rev. Captain R. WIMBUSH C.F. left to-night for England on leave, on the termination of his contract.	J.E.P.
"	14/7/16	9 p.m.	Some rain fell this morning early, but the remainder of the day has been dry but dull and cold. – The Personnel have proceeded in small parties throughout the day to the Baths at HENENCOURT. – The A.D.M.S. held a conference at 2.30 p.m. to-day with the Os.C. Bearer Divisions and the M.Os i/c Regiments with regard to the evacuation of wounded from the Regimental Aid Posts.	J.E.P.
"	15/7/16	9 p.m.	Received orders from the A.D.M.S. this morning for the Bearer Division to hold itself in readiness to move at an hour's notice with the 56th Infantry Brigade. Held a Medical Board in the morning on a candidate from the 10th Royal Warwick Regt. for a commission in the Regular Army. – The Personnel were employed in large fatigue parties in cleaning up the wood. The weather has been dry but cold.	J.E.P.
"	16/7/16	9 p.m.	The Personnel were again employed in large fatigue parties in cleaning up the wood and its surroundings. – The Bearer Division continue to "stand to" ready to move at an hour's notice. – Steady rain began falling during the evening.	J.E.P.

Instructions regarding War Diaries and Intelligence Summaries are contained in F. S. Regs., Part II. and the Staff Manual respectively. Title Pages will be prepared in manuscript.

WAR DIARY
or
INTELLIGENCE SUMMARY
(Erase heading not required.)

Army Form C. 2118

Place	Date	Hour	Summary of Events and Information	Remarks and references to Appendices
HENENCOURT WOOD	17/7/16	9 p.m.	Heavy showers of rain fell during the day, rendering the conditions in the wood very damp and muddy. – The Bearer Division was inspected by Captain SMALLEY O.C. Bearer Division. – The order holding the Bearer Division ready to start at an hour's notice has been cancelled. The Rev WILLIS C.F. (C of E) reported his arrival for duty this morning.	J.E.P.
"	18/7/16	9 p.m.	The weather continues damp and cold – some rain fell in the morning. The Field Ambulance remains closed, merely collecting cases from the 58th and 56th Infantry Brigades and conveying them to the 58th Field Ambulance. I attended with the O.C. Bearer Division a conference at the A.D.M.S.' Office at 6 p.m.	J.E.P.
"	19/7/16	9 p.m.	The day has been fine and warm. – During the morning I went to BECOURT CHATEAU and went over the ground of SAUSAGE VALLEY with my O.C. Bearer Division with a view to taking over the Chateau as an advanced Dressing Station and evacuating wounded from the front line to the Chateau. – at 7 p.m. urgent orders were received from the ~~[illegible]~~ A.D.M.S. for the Bearer Division to march off at once following the 56th Infantry Brigade to Sq S 14 c ALBERT Map Sheet – the Bearer Division proceeded in rear of the Brigade at 8 p.m.	J.E.P.
ALBERT	20/7/16	9 p.m.	at 10 p.m. last night orders from the A.D.M.S. to proceed forthwith to the Civil Hospital ALBERT were received, there to take over from No. 103 Field Ambulance and form a Corps Main Dressing Station. Two Tent subdivisions of 103 Field Ambulance are to be attached to this Unit and assist in forming the Corps Dressing Station. The Unit marched off at 12.20 a.m. and arrived at ALBERT Civil Hospital at 2.30 a.m. The taking over of the Main Dressing was not completed until 12 Noon. The A.D.M.S. visited the Ambulance at 11 a.m. 3 p.m. and 6 p.m. – I visited the Advanced Dressing Station at ~~[illegible]~~ Sq S 14 c at 6 a.m.	J.E.P.

T1836 Wt. W593/826 1,000,000 4/15 J.B.C. & A. A.D.S.S./Forms/C. 2118.

Instructions regarding War Diaries and Intelligence Summaries are contained in F. S. Regs., Part II. and the Staff Manual respectively. Title Pages will be prepared in manuscript.

WAR DIARY
or
INTELLIGENCE SUMMARY

(Erase heading not required.)

Army Form C. 2118

Place	Date	Hour	Summary of Events and Information	Remarks and references to Appendices
ALBERT	21/7/16	9 p.m.	The day has been fine and warm. 13 wounded Officers and 125 wounded men have been admitted during the day. 13 Officers and 139 men have been evacuated and one man has died leaving 5 cases remaining. The D.D.M.S. Corps visited the Field Ambulance at 11 a.m. and the A.D.M.S. Division at 12 Noon. The Personnel have been employed throughout the day pitching Hospital Marquees cleaning out all the wards vacated by Infantry, also the grounds and equipping all the Marquees and wards ready for the reception of casualties. The Bearer Division arrived at 9 p.m. having been withdrawn to Headquarters on relief by Bearer Division 58th Field Ambulance.	J.E.P.
"	22/7/16	9 p.m.	The day has been fine and warm. The A.D.M.S. visited the ambulance at 10.30 a.m. and 1 p.m. – Received orders from the A.D.M.S. this evening to send two Operating tents 50 stretchers 100 Blankets and 50 ground Sheets, also three Horse Ambulance Wagons to the Advanced Dressing Station, this was carried out. Seven Officers and 101 other ranks were admitted during the day, 5 Officers and 97 other ranks were evacuated and 4 other ranks died, leaving 2 Officers and 5 men remaining.	J.E.P.
"	23/7/16	9 p.m.	The day has again been fine and warm. The A.D.M.S. visited the ambulance at 10.30 a.m. and 7 p.m. The D.D.M.S. Corps visited the ambulance at 11 a.m. – Sixteen Officers and 199 other ranks wounded were admitted up till 11 a.m. and a total of 25 Officers and 335 other ranks up to 6 p.m. were admitted. – The evacuation of these cases worked well and the main Dressing Station was practically clear by 7 p.m.	J.E.P.

1875 Wt. W593/826 1,000,000 4/15 J.B.C. & A. A.D.S.S./Forms/C. 2118.

Army Form C. 2118

WAR DIARY
or
INTELLIGENCE SUMMARY
(Erase heading not required.)

Instructions regarding War Diaries and Intelligence Summaries are contained in F. S. Regs., Part II. and the Staff Manual respectively. Title Pages will be prepared in manuscript.

Place	Date	Hour	Summary of Events and Information	Remarks and references to Appendices
ALBERT	24/7/16	9 p.m.	The day has been fine but cooler than yesterday. 17 Wounded Officers and 288 other ranks were admitted during the day and 17 Officers and 314 other ranks were evacuated, there were five deaths leaving four cases remaining. No Inspecting Officers visited the Dressing Station to-day.	J.E.P.
"	25/7/16	9 p.m.	The weather has been fine and warm. The D.D.M.S. 3rd Corps visited the Field Ambulance at 11 a.m. and interviewed all Medical Officers. The A.D.M.S. visited the Field Ambulance at 11.30 a.m. and 7 p.m. 13 Officers and 89 other ranks wounded were admitted. 13 Officers and 87 other ranks were evacuated, 2 men died of their wounds and 4 cases were left remaining.	J.E.P.
"	26/7/16	9 p.m.	The weather has continued fine and warm. Three Officers and complete Personnel of two Tent Subdivisions of the 71st Field Ambulance arrived this morning to be attached to this Field Ambulance for duty. also one Motor Ambulance Convoy Medical Officer to superintend evacuations. Captain A. B. JONES R.A.M.C. (T.C.) has reported his arrival for duty this day. – 13 Officers and 221 other ranks were admitted during the day 13 Officers and 205 other ranks were evacuated, 10 other ranks died of their wounds leaving 10 cases remaining.	J.E.P.
"	27/7/16	9 p.m.	The weather has been fine and warm. The A.D.M.S. visited the ambulance at 10.30 a.m. and 7 p.m. Orders were received at 4 p.m. for the two Tent Subdivisions of the 103rd Field Ambulance to rejoin their Headquarters to-day and they left at 6 p.m. – Orders were received from the D.D.M.S. Corps to expand and prepare the accommodation here for 1000 patients. – Indents for the necessary Marquees and Stores were made out and sent in. Four Officers and 117 wounded men were admitted, 3 Officers and 110 men were evacuated 5 men died, leaving 1 Officer and 12 men remaining.	J.E.P.

1875 Wt. W593/826 1,000,000 4/15 J.B.C. & A. A.D.S.S./Forms/C. 2118.

Instructions regarding War Diaries and Intelligence Summaries are contained in F. S. Regs., Part II. and the Staff Manual respectively. Title Pages will be prepared in manuscript.

WAR DIARY
or
INTELLIGENCE SUMMARY
(Erase heading not required.)

Army Form C. 2118

Place	Date	Hour	Summary of Events and Information	Remarks and references to Appendices
ALBERT	28/7/16	9 p.m.	The weather has been fine and warm to-day, but the dust is increasing. — One Officer and 73 other ranks were admitted during the day, two Officers and 71 other ranks were evacuated, Ten men died from their wounds leaving 4 cases remaining. Four operations were performed and several saline transfusion given.	J.E.P.
"	29/7/16	9 p.m.	The day has been exceptionally hot. — 300 Bolsters, 300 Pyjama suits, 192 Pailliasses and 40 trestles were received from the Medical Rest Camp FRECHENCOURT. — I drew 3 loads of straw from LAVIEVILLE for stuffing the Pailliasses and Bolsters. I visited the A.D.M.S. at 10.30 a.m. Ten Officers and 93 other ranks wounded were admitted during the day, 8 Officers and 87 other ranks were evacuated, 3 men died of their wounds, leaving two Officers and 7 other ranks remaining.	J.E.P.
"	30/7/16	9 p.m.	The weather continues fine and hot. The A.D.M.S. visited the Field Ambulance to-day at 11.30 a.m. Five Officers and 84 other ranks wounded were admitted during the day 5 Officers and 76 other ranks were evacuated, one Officer and one other rank died leaving one Officer and 14 men remaining. Received orders at 6 p.m. this evening to hand over the Corps Main Dressing Stn. to No. 2 Field Ambulance at 12 Noon to-morrow and march to BEHENCOURT and go into Bivouacs there the Unit remaining closed.	J.E.P.

1875 Wt. W593/826 1,000,000 4/15 J.B.C. & A. A.D.S.S./Forms/C. 2118.

Army Form C. 2118

Instructions regarding War Diaries and Intelligence Summaries are contained in F. S. Regs., Part II. and the Staff Manual respectively. Title Pages will be prepared in manuscript.

WAR DIARY
or
INTELLIGENCE SUMMARY
(Erase heading not required.)

Place	Date	Hour	Summary of Events and Information	Remarks and references to Appendices
BEHENCOURT	31/7/16	9 p.m.	The day been exceptionally hot. I handed over the Corps Main Dressing Station at 12 Noon to O.C. No 2 Field Ambulance and the Unit marched off at 1 p.m and halted at 3.30 p.m. for two hours for dinner arriving there at 7.30 p.m. to go into Bivouacs. Lieut. Cochrane RAMC reported his departure this day for temporary duty as M.O. i/c 7th South Lancs Regt. – Up to 12 Noon 7 Officers and 147 other ranks wounded were admitted, 8 Officers and 136 other ranks were evacuated, 10 other ranks died and 18 were transferred to No. 2 Field Ambulance, leaving no cases remaining.	J.E.P.

J. E. Powell
Lieut Colonel R.A.M.C
O.C. 57th Field Ambulance

1875 Wt. W593/826 1,000,000 4/15 J.B.C. & A. A.D.S.S./Forms/C. 2118.

Confidential

Army Form C. 2118

Instructions regarding War Diaries and Intelligence Summaries are contained in F. S. Regs., Part II. and the Staff Manual respectively. Title Pages will be prepared in manuscript.

WAR DIARY

~~or~~

~~INTELLIGENCE SUMMARY~~

~~(Erase heading not required.)~~

Place	Date	Hour	Summary of Events ~~and Information~~	Remarks and references to Appendices
August 1916			19th Div of 57 Field Ambulance R.A.M.C from 1.8.16 to 31.8.16 (Volume No. 14)	

1875 Wt. W593/826 1,000,000 4/15 J.B.C. & A. A.D.S.S./Forms/C. 2118.

Army Form C. 2118

Instructions regarding War Diaries and Intelligence Summaries are contained in F. S. Regs., Part II. and the Staff Manual respectively. Title Pages will be prepared in manuscript.

WAR DIARY
or
~~INTELLIGENCE SUMMARY~~
(Erase heading not required.)

Place	Date	Hour	Summary of Events and Information	Remarks and references to Appendices
BEHENCOURT	1/8/16	9 p.m.	The day has again been very hot. – The morning was occupied in pitching tents, unloading wagons and checking equipment and contents of panniers. – The afternoon was occupied in bathing. – Orders were received from the A.D.M.S. at 8 p.m. for the mounted portion of the Field Ambulance including all transport to march to Billets at CARDONETTE to-morrow the 2nd inst. and on the 3rd inst. to a concentration area around LONGPRE and FLIXECOURT. – The Dismounted portion of the Unit will march from here on the 3rd inst. and entrain at MERICOURT.	J.E.P.
"	2/8/16	9 p.m.	The weather has been fine and warm. The mounted portion of the Field Ambulance under Captain SMALLEY marched off at 5 p.m. for CARDONETTE. – The morning was spent in striking tents and packing all the wagons. – Lieut. A.D. FRY R.A.M.C. reported his arrival for duty on return from the Divisional Rest Station. Lieut J.L. COCHRANE R.A.M.C. reported his arrival for duty this day on completion of duty as temporary M.O. i/c 9th South Lancs Regt.	J.E.P.
AILLY LE HAUT CLOCHER	3/8/16	9 p.m.	The weather has continued fine and warm. The dismounted portion of the Field Ambulance entrained at 6 p.m. at FRECHENCOURT for LONGPRE and will march here (6 miles) to-night. The mounted portion including all transport arrived here at 5 p.m. I travelled here with the convoy of motor ambulance cars, leaving BEHENCOURT at 2 p.m. and arriving here at 5 p.m. There are excellent billets here.	J.E.P.

1875 Wt. W593/826 1,000,000 4/15 J.B.C. & A. A.D.S.S./Forms/C. 2118.

Army Form C. 2118

Instructions regarding War Diaries and Intelligence Summaries are contained in F. S. Regs., Part II. and the Staff Manual respectively. Title Pages will be prepared in manuscript.

WAR DIARY
or
~~INTELLIGENCE SUMMARY~~
(Erase heading not required.)

Place	Date	Hour	Summary of Events and Information	Remarks and references to Appendices
AILLY LE HAUTCLOCHER	4/8/16	9 p.m.	The day has been fine but cooler than for some days past. – The dismounted portion of the Field Ambulance arrived here at 5 a.m. this morning. – The morning was spent in preparing and equipping an empty house for the reception of sick. The A.D.M.S. visited the Field Ambulance at 11 a.m.	J.E.P.
"	5/8/16	9 p.m.	The weather has continued fine and cool. – One Sick Officer and 10 other ranks were admitted during the day. 10 other ranks were evacuated to No. 2 Stationary Hospital ABBEVILLE leaving one officer remaining. – Sick are being collected from all the units of the 56th Infantry Brigade.	J.E.P.
"	6/8/16	9 p.m.	One Officer and 16 other ranks were admitted to the Field Ambulance "sick" to-day – Two officers and 16 other ranks were evacuated to No. 5 Stationary Hospital ABBEVILLE leaving no cases remaining. The day has been fine and warm. – Orders were received this morning for the Unit to entrain at PONT REMY at 9.58 a.m. to-morrow the 7th inst. – The Unit to be at the station 3 hours before departure of train. – The ~~19th~~ Division is proceeding to join the V Corps Second Army.	J.E.P.
SCHAESCHEN	7/8/16	10 p.m.	Six other ranks sick were admitted to the Field Ambulance since Noon yesterday and evacuated to No 5 Stationary Hospital. The day has been fine but cloudy. The Unit marched off from AILLY LE HAUTCLOCHER at 4.15 a.m. arriving at PONT REMY at 9 a.m. and entrained forthwith leaving by train at 9.58 a.m. and arriving at ~~[illegible]~~ BAILLEUL at 8 p.m. where the Unit detrained and marched into Billets here at 10 p.m.	J.E.P.

1875 Wt. W593/826 1,000,000 4/15 J.B.C. & A. A.D.S.S./Forms/C. 2118.

Instructions regarding War Diaries and Intelligence Summaries are contained in F. S. Regs., Part II. and the Staff Manual respectively. Title Pages will be prepared in manuscript.

WAR DIARY
or
~~INTELLIGENCE SUMMARY~~
(Erase heading not required.)

Army Form C. 2118

Place	Date	Hour	Summary of Events and Information	Remarks and references to Appendices
LOCRE	8/8/16	9 p.m.	Received orders from the A.D.M.S. at 11 p.m. last night to send advance parties at 8.30 a.m. to-day to take over from the 2nd/2nd Northumbrian Field Ambulance, the Advanced Dressing Station at LINDENHOEK the Main Dressing Station at the Hospice at LOCRE and also a sectional Hospital at WESTOUTRE – these orders were carried out and the Field Ambulance arrived at the Hospice LOCRE at 2 p.m. and opened up for the reception of casualties, also opened a Divisional Rest Station for the reception of 200 sick. – I visited the Advanced Dressing Station at 4 p.m. – The A.D.M.S. visited the Ambulance at 4.30 p.m. The weather continues fine and warm.	J.E.P.
"	9/8/16	9 p.m.	The weather continues fine and warm. – 2 Officers and 27 other ranks sick and 9 other ranks wounded were admitted during the day. – 2 Officers and 11 other ranks were evacuated to a Casualty Clearing Station. – The personnel have been employed erecting kitchens, bath houses and latrines etc. also clearing out drains, Walls and barns for the reception of sick and wounded.	J.E.P.
"	10/8/16	9 p.m.	To-day has been cloudy and a little rain has fallen. The A.D.M.S. made a long ~~tour~~ of inspection at 11 a.m. – Sent in a long indent for articles required for the Officers Hospital. 13 other ranks sick were admitted to the Field Ambulance ~~Three~~ cases was transferred to a Casualty Clearing Station and 13 cases were transferred to the Divisional Rest Station, leaving 15 cases remaining in the Field Ambulance. 24 sick and 2 wounded were admitted to the Divisional Rest Station during the day.	J.E.P.

1875 Wt. W593/826 1,000,000 4/15 J.B.C. & A. A.D.S.S./Forms/C. 2118.

Instructions regarding War Diaries and Intelligence Summaries are contained in F. S. Regs., Part II. and the Staff Manual respectively. Title Pages will be prepared in manuscript.

WAR DIARY
or
INTELLIGENCE SUMMARY
(Erase heading not required.)

Army Form C. 2118

Place	Date	Hour	Summary of Events and Information	Remarks and references to Appendices
LOCRE	11/8/16	9 p.m.	The weather continues fine and warm. The Personnel of the Unit were paid in the morning. I visited the Advanced Dressing Station at 2 p.m. – 27 cases were admitted to the Field Ambulance during the day, 9 cases were evacuated to a Casualty Clearing Station, and 10 cases were transferred to the Divisional Rest Station, leaving 23 cases remaining in the Field Ambulance. – 43 cases were admitted to the Rest Station, 4 cases were evacuated to a Casualty Clearing Stn. leaving 65 cases remaining in the Rest Station.	J.E.P.
"	12/8/16	9 p.m.	Two Officers and 19 other ranks were admitted to the Field Ambulance during the day. Two officers and 8 other ranks were evacuated to a Casualty Clearing Stn., 3 cases were transferred to the Divisional Rest Stn. leaving 31 cases remaining in the Field Ambulance. 22 cases were admitted to the Divisional Rest Stn. 2 cases were evacuated to a Casualty Clearing Stn. and 3 cases were returned to duty, leaving 82 cases remaining in the Divisional Rest Stn. – The weather continues fine and warm.	J.E.P.
"	13/8/16	9 p.m.	One Officer and 15 other ranks were admitted to the Field Ambulance during the day one officer and 11 other ranks were evacuated to a Casualty Clearing Stn. 8 cases were transferred to the Rest Station leaving 27 cases remaining in the Field Amb. 24 cases were admitted to the Rest Station during the day, 3 cases were evacuated to a Casualty Clearing Stn. and 8 cases were returned to duty, leaving 95 cases remaining in the Rest Station. – The weather has been hot and sultry.	J.E.P.

1875 Wt. W593/826 1,000,000 4/15 J.B.C. & A. A.D.S.S./Forms/C. 2118.

Instructions regarding War Diaries and Intelligence Summaries are contained in F. S. Regs., Part II. and the Staff Manual respectively. Title Pages will be prepared in manuscript.

WAR DIARY
or
~~INTELLIGENCE SUMMARY~~
(Erase heading not required.)

Army Form C. 2118

Place	Date	Hour	Summary of Events and Information	Remarks and references to Appendices
LOCRE	14/8/16	9 p.m.	Some slight showers of rain fell during the day and the sky is cloudy. One Officer and 28 other ranks were admitted to the Field Ambulance during the day, 3 cases were evacuated to a Casualty Clearing Station and 7 cases were transferred to the Divisional Rest Station, leaving One Officer and 45 other ranks remaining in the Field Ambulance. — 19 cases were admitted to the Divisional Rest Station 4 cases were evacuated to a Casualty Clearing Stn. and 11 cases were returned to duty, leaving 99 cases remaining in the Divisional Rest Stn.	J.E.P.
"	15/8/16	9 p.m.	Some sharp showers of rain fell again to-day but the weather still remains fine on the whole. One Officer and 15 other ranks were admitted to the Field Ambulance, one Officer and 6 other ranks were evacuated to a Casualty Clearing Stn. 11 cases were transferred to the Divisional Rest Stn. leaving One Officer and 43 other ranks remaining in the Field Ambulance. — 26 cases were admitted to the Divisional Rest Stn. 2 cases were evacuated to a Casualty Clearing Stn. and 12 cases were returned to duty, leaving 111 cases remaining in the Divisional Rest Stn.	J.E.P.
"	16/8/16	9 p.m.	The weather continues fine and cool with a few showers. 3 Officers and 5 other ranks were admitted to the Field Ambulance during the day, One Officer and 4 other ranks were evacuated to a Casualty Clearing Station and 14 cases were transferred to the Divisional Rest Station, 2 cases were returned to duty, leaving 3 Officers and 28 other ranks remaining in the Field Ambulance. — 33 cases were admitted to the Divisional Rest Stn. one case was evacuated to a Casualty Clearing Stn. 9 cases were returned to duty, leaving 134 cases remaining in the Divisional Rest Stn. There was a Bathing Parade for the Personnel at LOCRE Baths to-day.	J.E.P.

1875 Wt. W593/826 1,000,000 4/15 J.B.C. & A. A.D.S.S./Forms/C. 2118.

Instructions regarding War Diaries and Intelligence Summaries are contained in F. S. Regs., Part II. and the Staff Manual respectively. Title Pages will be prepared in manuscript.

WAR DIARY
or
INTELLIGENCE SUMMARY
(Erase heading not required.)

Army Form C. 2118

Place	Date	Hour	Summary of Events and Information	Remarks and references to Appendices
LOCRE	17/8/16	9 p.m.	Heavy showers of rain fell during the day. The A.D.M.S. visited and inspected the Field Ambulance at 10.30 a.m. – 2 Officers and 11 other ranks were admitted to the Field Ambulance, one Officer and one man were evacuated to a Casualty Clearing Stn. 7 cases were transferred to the Divisional Rest Stn. leaving 4 Officers and 31 other ranks remaining in the Field Ambulance. – 23 cases were admitted to the Divisional Rest Stn. 2 cases were evacuated to a Casualty Clearing Stn. and 13 cases were returned to duty, leaving 142 cases remaining in the Rest Stn.	J.E.P.
"	18/8/16	9 p.m.	Heavy showers of rain fell again to-day. There was a bathing parade for the Personnel at LOCRE Baths to-day. Four Officers and 14 other ranks were admitted to the Field Ambulance, 4 Officers and 6 other ranks were evacuated to a Casualty Clearing Stn. – 4 cases were transferred to the Divisional Rest Stn., leaving 4 Officers and 35 other ranks remaining in the Field Ambulance. – 21 cases were admitted to the Divisional Rest Stn. 6 cases were evacuated to a Casualty Clearing Stn. 19 cases were returned to duty, leaving 138 cases remaining in the Divisional Rest Stn.	J.E.P.
"	19/8/16	9 p.m.	Heavy rain fell throughout the day, but this evening it has ceased and become quite fine. 14 cases were admitted to the Field Ambulance, 3 cases were evacuated to a Casualty Clearing Stn. 7 cases were transferred to the Divisional Rest Stn. leaving 4 Officers and 39 other ranks remaining in the Field Ambulance. – 26 cases were admitted to the Divisional Rest Stn. 7 cases were evacuated to a Casualty Clearing Stn. and 15 cases were returned to duty, leaving 142 cases remaining in the Divisional Rest Stn.	J.E.P.

1875 Wt. W593/826 1,000,000 4/15 J.B.C. & A. A.D.S.S./Forms/C. 2118.

Army Form C. 2118

Instructions regarding War Diaries and Intelligence Summaries are contained in F. S. Regs., Part II. and the Staff Manual respectively. Title Pages will be prepared in manuscript.

WAR DIARY
or
INTELLIGENCE SUMMARY
(Erase heading not required.)

Place	Date	Hour	Summary of Events and Information	Remarks and references to Appendices
LOCRE	20/8/16	9 p.m.	Some heavy showers of rain fell during the day. – One Officer and 13 other ranks were admitted to the Field Ambulance, 5 cases were evacuated to a Casualty Clearing Station, 21 cases were transferred to the Divisional Rest Stn, and one Officer and one other rank were returned to duty, leaving 4 Officers and 25 other ranks remaining in the Field Ambulance. – 25 cases were admitted to the Divisional Rest Stn, 7 cases were evacuated to a Casualty Clearing Stn. and 18 cases were returned to duty, leaving 142 cases remaining in the Divisional Rest Stn	J.E.P.
"	21/8/16	9 p.m.	The day has been fine and cool. – One Officer and 12 other ranks were admitted to the Field Ambulance during the day, 2 cases were transferred to a Casualty Clearing Stn. and 4 cases were transferred to the Divisional Rest Stn. and one case was returned to duty, leaving 5 Officers and 30 other ranks remaining in the Field Ambulance. — 17 cases were admitted to the Divisional Rest Stn, 7 cases were evacuated to a Casualty Clearing Stn. and 23 cases were returned to duty leaving 129 cases remaining in the Divisional Rest Station. I visited the A.D.S. in the afternoon.	J.E.P.
"	22/8/16	9 p.m.	The weather continues fine and cool. The D.D.M.S. IX Corps visited and inspected the Field Ambulance, the Divisional Rest Stn. and Officer's Wards this afternoon at 2.30 p.m. – One Officer and 22 other ranks were admitted to the Field Ambulance, 14 cases were evacuated to a Casualty Clearing Stn, 6 cases were transferred to the Divisional Rest Stn. leaving 6 Officers and 32 other ranks remaining in the Field Ambulance. – 21 cases were admitted to the Divisional Rest Stn. 5 cases were evacuated to a Casualty Clearing Stn. and 17 cases were returned to duty, leaving 128 cases remaining in the Divisional Rest Stn.	J.E.P.

1875 Wt. W593/826 1,000,000 4/15 J.B.C. & A. A.D.S.S./Forms/C. 2118.

Instructions regarding War Diaries and Intelligence Summaries are contained in F. S. Regs., Part II. and the Staff Manual respectively. Title Pages will be prepared in manuscript.

WAR DIARY
or
~~INTELLIGENCE SUMMARY~~
(Erase heading not required.)

Army Form C. 2118

Place	Date	Hour	Summary of Events and Information	Remarks and references to Appendices
LOCRE	23/8/16	9 p.m.	The weather has continued fine and cool. I visited the Advanced Dressing Stn. at 6 p.m. this evening. The "Gas Alert" was in force from 12 Midnight last night to 2 p.m. to-day, made arrangements for all Personnel and Patients to be aroused at night if necessary. Had all gas helmets inspected and Instructions read out on parade. — 21 cases were admitted to the Field Ambulance during the day, 2 Officers and 9 other ranks were evacuated to a Casualty Clearing Stn. 7 cases were transferred to the Divisional Rest Stn. 2 cases were returned to duty, leaving 4 Officers and 35 other ranks remaining in the Field Ambulance. 22 cases were admitted to the Divisional Rest Stn, 3 cases were evacuated to a Casualty Clearing Stn. and 12 cases were returned to duty, leaving 135 cases remaining.	J.E.P.
"	24/8/16	9 p.m.	The weather continues fine and cool. 16 cases were admitted to the Field Ambulance during the day, 8 cases were evacuated to a Casualty Clearing Stn. 12 cases were transferred to the Divisional Rest Stn. and 2 cases were returned to duty, leaving 4 Officers and 29 other ranks remaining in the Field Ambulance. — 36 cases were admitted to the Divisional Rest Station, 11 cases were evacuated to a Casualty Clearing Stn. and 21 cases were returned to duty, leaving 139 cases remaining in the Divisional Rest Stn.	J.E.P.
"	25/8/16	9 p.m.	The weather has been cloudy and some showers of rain have fallen. — 3 Officers and 25 other ranks were admitted to the Field Ambulance, 3 Officers and 12 other ranks were evacuated to a Casualty Clearing Stn, 7 cases were transferred to the Divisional Rest Stn. and one case was sent to duty, leaving 4 Officers and 34 other ranks remaining in the Field Ambulance. — 29 cases were admitted to the Divisional Rest Stn. 3 cases were evacuated to a Casualty Clearing Stn. 19 cases were returned to duty and 10 cases were sent to a Convalescent Camp, leaving 136 cases remaining in the Divisional Rest Stn.	J.E.P.

1875 Wt. W593/826 1,000,000 4/15 J.B.C. & A. A.D.S.S./Forms/C. 2118.

Instructions regarding War Diaries and Intelligence Summaries are contained in F. S. Regs., Part II. and the Staff Manual respectively. Title Pages will be prepared in manuscript.

WAR DIARY
or
INTELLIGENCE SUMMARY
(Erase heading not required.)

Army Form C. 2118

Place	Date	Hour	Summary of Events and Information	Remarks and references to Appendices
LOCRE	26/8/16	9 p.m.	Showers of rain have fallen during the day. 22 cases were admitted to the Field Ambulance 17 cases were evacuated to a Casualty Clearing Stn. and 11 cases were transferred to the Divisional Rest Stn. one wounded case died, leaving 4 Officers and 27 other ranks remaining in the Field Ambulance. – The Prevailing Disease is Pyrexia N.Y.D. 29 cases were admitted to the Divisional Rest Stn. 2 cases were evacuated to a Casualty Clearing Stn. 10 cases were transferred to a Convalescent Camp and 20 cases were returned to duty, leaving 133 cases remaining in the Div. Rest Stn.	J.E.P.
"	27/8/16	9 p.m.	Heavy showers of rain again fell during the day. Lieut. E.C. LINDSEY R.A.M.C. reported his arrival for duty with this unit on completion of temporary duty with the 9th East Lancashire Regt. One Officer and 19 other ranks were admitted to the Field Ambulance and one Officer and 11 other ranks were evacuated to a Casualty Clearing Stn. 8 cases were transferred to the Divisional Rest Stn. and 2 cases were returned to duty, leaving 4 Officers and 25 other ranks remaining in the Field Ambulance. – 20 cases were admitted to the Divisional Rest Stn., 5 cases were evacuated to a Casualty Clearing Stn. 10 cases were transferred to a Convalescent Camp and 28 cases were returned to duty, leaving 110 cases remaining.	J.E.P.
"	28/8/16	9 p.m.	The weather still continues showery. – Captain OWENS R.A.M.C. reported his departure this day to take up duty as M.O. i/c 9th Loyal North Lancs Regt. – Lieut. ORAM R.A.M.C. reported his arrival for duty this day as a reinforcement to the Unit. – 16 cases were admitted to the Field Ambulance during the day, one Officer and 8 other ranks were evacuated to a Casualty Clearing Stn., 5 cases were transferred to the Divisional Rest Stn. one man died from wounds, and 3 cases were returned to duty, leaving 3 Officers and 24 other ranks remaining in the Field Ambulance. – 45 cases were admitted to the Divisional Rest Stn. 6 were evacuated to a Casualty Clearing Stn. 17 cases were returned to duty and 10 cases were transferred to a Convalescent Camp, leaving 122 cases remaining in the Divisional Rest Stn.	J.E.P.

1875 Wt. W593/826 1,000,000 4/15 J.B.C. & A. A.D.S.S./Forms/C. 2118.

Instructions regarding War Diaries and Intelligence Summaries are contained in F. S. Regs., Part II. and the Staff Manual respectively. Title Pages will be prepared in manuscript.

WAR DIARY
or
~~INTELLIGENCE SUMMARY~~

(Erase heading not required.)

Army Form C. 2118

Place	Date	Hour	Summary of Events and Information	Remarks and references to Appendices
LOCRE	29/8/16	9 p.m.	Rain has fallen throughout the day, ending in a thunderstorm this evening. Captain R. St.A. HEATHCOTE R.A.M.C. reported his arrival to-day for duty with the Unit as a Reinforcement. — One Officer and 21 other ranks were admitted to the Field Ambulance, one Officer and 11 other ranks were evacuated to a Casualty Clearing Stn. 5 cases were transferred to the Divisional Rest Stn. and 2 cases were returned to duty, leaving 3 Officers and 27 other ranks remaining in the Field Ambulance. — 12 cases were admitted to the Divisional Rest Stn. 9 cases were evacuated to a Casualty Clearing Stn. 17 cases were returned to duty and 10 cases were transferred to a Convalescent Camp, leaving 98 cases remaining in the Divisional Rest Station.	J.E.P.
"	30/8/16	9 p.m.	Heavy rain has fallen throughout the day. The A.D.M.S. visited the Field Ambulance at 11 a.m. One Officer and 17 other ranks were admitted to the Field Ambulance, one Officer and 7 other ranks were evacuated to a Casualty Clearing Stn. 17 cases were transferred to the Divisional Rest Stn. and one case was sent to duty, leaving 3 Officers and 19 men remaining in the Field Ambulance. — 25 cases were admitted to the Divisional Rest Stn. 3 cases were evacuated to a Casualty Clearing Stn. and 21 cases were returned to duty, leaving 99 cases remaining in the Divisional Rest Stn.	J.E.P.
"	31/8/16	9 p.m.	The day has been fine and no rain has fallen. — One Officer and 32 other ranks were admitted to the Field Ambulance, 12 cases were evacuated to a Casualty Clearing Stn. 6 cases were transferred to the Divisional Rest Station, one wounded man died, and two Officers and one man were returned to duty, leaving 2 Officers and 31 other ranks remaining in the Field Ambulance. — 23 cases were admitted to the Divisional Rest Stn. and 15 cases were ~~[illegible]~~ returned to duty, leaving 107 cases remaining in the Divisional Rest Station. — Work is being carried on daily on Horse and Vehicle standings, also on draining and levelling the grounds.	J.E.P.

J.E. Powell Lieut. Colonel R.A.M.C.
O.C. 57th Field Ambulance.

1875 Wt. W593/826 1,000,000 4/15 J.B.C. & A. A.D.S.S./Forms/C. 2118.

Sept. 1916

S

140/1734

19th Div.

57th Field Ambulance.

1305
1-10-16

To A.D.M.S.
19th Division

Herewith copy of "War Diary". Period 1-9-16 to 30-9-16. For transmission to D.H.Q.

J. E. Powell
Lt Col
R.A.M.C.
COMMANDING 57TH FIELD AMBULANCE

Confidential

WAR DIARY
or
~~INTELLIGENCE SUMMARY~~
(Erase heading not required.)

Army Form C. 2118

Instructions regarding War Diaries and Intelligence Summaries are contained in F. S. Regs., Part II. and the Staff Manual respectively. Title Pages will be prepared in manuscript.

Place	Date	Hour	Summary of Events and Information	Remarks and references to Appendices
			of 57th Field Ambulance R.A.M.C. from 1.9.16 to 30.9.16 (Volume No. 15)	

1875 Wt. W593/826 1,000,000 4/15 J.B.C. & A. A.D.S.S./Forms/C. 2118.

Instructions regarding War Diaries and Intelligence Summaries are contained in F. S. Regs., Part II. and the Staff Manual respectively. Title Pages will be prepared in manuscript.

WAR DIARY

or

~~INTELLIGENCE SUMMARY~~

(Erase heading not required.)

Army Form C. 2118

Place	Date	Hour	Summary of Events and Information	Remarks and references to Appendices
LOCRE	1/9/16	9 p.m.	The weather has been dull and cloudy but no rain has fallen. Three Officers and 18 other ranks were admitted to the Field Ambulance, one Officer and eleven men were evacuated to a Casualty Clearing, eleven cases were transferred to the Divisional Rest Stn. leaving 4 Officers and 24 other ranks remaining in the Field Ambulance. — 32 cases were admitted to the Divisional Rest Stn. 5 cases were evacuated to a Casualty Clearing Stn. and 8 cases were returned to duty, leaving 126 cases remaining in the Divisional Rest Stn. — E	J.E.P.
"	2/9/16	9 p.m.	The weather continues dull and cloudy but no rain has fallen. — Rendered billeting certificates for the week this morning. — The A.D.M.S. visited the Field Ambulance at 3.30 p.m. Two Officers and 25 other ranks were admitted and 22 cases were transferred from the 59th Field Ambulance, 3 Officers + 18 other ranks were evacuated to a Casualty Clearing Stn. 16 cases were transferred to the Divisional Rest Stn., one case was returned to duty leaving 3 Officers and 39 other ranks remaining in the Field Ambulance. — 35 cases were admitted to the Divisional Rest Stn. 3 cases were evacuated to a Casualty Clearing Stn. and 22 cases were returned to duty, leaving 137 cases remaining in the D.R.S.	J.E.P.
"	3/9/16	9 p.m.	Weather continues dull and cloudy. One Officer and 33 other ranks were admitted to the Field Ambulance One Officer and 38 other ranks were evacuated to a Casualty Clearing Stn. one wounded man died, leaving 3 Officers and 33 other ranks remaining in the Field Ambulance. 10 cases were evacuated to a Casualty Clearing Stn from the Divisional Rest Stn., and 34 cases were returned to duty, leaving 93 cases remaining in the Divisional Rest Station.	J.E.P.

1875 Wt. W593/826 1,000,000 4/15 J.B.C. & A. A.D.S.S./Forms/C. 2118.

Instructions regarding War Diaries and Intelligence Summaries are contained in F. S. Regs., Part II. and the Staff Manual respectively. Title Pages will be prepared in manuscript.

WAR DIARY
or
~~INTELLIGENCE~~ SUMMARY
(Erase heading not required.)

Army Form C. 2118

Place	Date	Hour	Summary of Events and Information	Remarks and references to Appendices
LOCRE	4/9/16	9 p.m.	Heavy showers of rain fell throughout the day. The A.D.M.S. visited the Field Ambulance at 10 a.m. – Five Officers and 35 other ranks were admitted to the Field Ambulance, two Officers and 8 other ranks were evacuated, 20 cases were transferred to the Divisional Rest Stn at METEREN. leaving 6 Officers and 40 other ranks remaining in the Field Ambulance. – No cases were admitted to the Div. Rest Station here, 6 cases were evacuated to a Casualty Clearing Stn. 18 cases were returned to duty and 30 cases were transferred to the Divisional Rest Stn. METEREN. leaving 39 cases remaining in the Divisional Rest Stn.	J.E.P.
"	5/9/16	9 p.m.	Continuous rain fell throughout the day. Visited the Advanced Dressing Stn at LINDENHOEK at 12.15 p.m. – Received orders from the A.D.M.S. to hand over this site to a Canadian Field Ambulance and to move to ~~Nieppe~~ PONT NIEPPE at 10 a.m. on the 7th inst. One section being detached to NIEPPE. – I have detailed B section for this duty. One Officer and 13 other ranks were admitted to the Field Ambulance during the day. One Officer and 13 other ranks were evacuated to a Casualty Clearing Stn. 2 Officers were sent to a Convalescent Camp and 17 cases were sent to the Divisional Rest Stn at METEREN and one case was returned to duty, leaving 4 Officers and 22 other ranks remaining in the Field Ambulance. – Three cases were evacuated from the Divisional Rest Station to a Casualty Clearing Stn. 15 cases were transferred to the Div. Rest Stn. at METEREN and 10 cases were returned to duty, leaving 11 cases remaining in the Divisional Rest Stn.	J.E.P.

1875 Wt. W593/826 1,000,000 4/15 J.B.C. & A. A.D.S.S./Forms/C. 2118.

Instructions regarding War Diaries and Intelligence Summaries are contained in F. S. Regs., Part II. and the Staff Manual respectively. Title Pages will be prepared in manuscript.

WAR DIARY
or
INTELLIGENCE SUMMARY
(Erase heading not required.)

Army Form C. 2118

Place	Date	Hour	Summary of Events and Information	Remarks and references to Appendices
LOCRE	6/9/16	9 p.m.	The day has been fine with bright sunshine. — 9 cases were admitted to the Field Ambulance during the day, two cases were evacuated to a Casualty Clearing Stn. 4 cases were transferred to the Divisional Rest Stn. at METEREN, two Officers were transferred to a Convalescent Station at MONT des CATS., 2 other ranks were returned to duty, leaving 2 Officers and 23 other ranks remaining in the Field Ambulance. — 5 cases from the Divisional Rest Stn. were returned to duty, and 6 cases were transferred to the D.R.S. at Meteren, leaving no cases remaining in the Divisional Rest Stn at LOCRE and this Divisional Rest Stn. was then closed.	J.E.P.
PONT NIEPPE	7/9/16	9 p.m.	The weather continues fine and cool. The Field Ambulance closed at 10 a.m. this morning at LOCRE and handed over to No. 12 Canadian Field Ambulance, the Unit marched then marched here, arriving at 3.30 p.m. and opened up for the Reception of Sick and wounded — B Section of the Unit being detached to NIEPPE where it has also opened up for the reception of sick and wounded. One Officer and 4 other ranks were admitted to the Field Ambulance 6 cases were evacuated to a Casualty Clearing Stn. and 9 cases were transferred to the Divisional Rest Stn. 4 cases were ~~tran~~ returned to duty, and 3 Officers and 8 other ranks were transferred to No 12 Canadian Fd. Ambulance, leaving no cases remaining.	J.E.P.
"	8/9/16	9 p.m.	The weather continues fine. Two cases only were admitted to the Field Ambulance and there are two cases remaining. Captain Smalley, with Lieut ORAM and a Bearer Subdivision took over the Brewery Advanced Dressing Stn at Sq. C. i. d. 4-4 Map Sheet 36 N.W. at 9 a.m. this morning. Lieut FRY reported his departure for temporary duty as M.O. i/c 7th East Lancs Regt. at 10 a.m. this morning.	J.E.P.

1875 Wt. W593/826 1,000,000 4/15 J.B.C. & A. A.D.S.S./Forms/C. 2118.

Army Form C. 2118

Instructions regarding War Diaries and Intelligence Summaries are contained in F. S. Regs., Part II. and the Staff Manual respectively. Title Pages will be prepared in manuscript.

WAR DIARY
or
INTELLIGENCE SUMMARY
(Erase heading not required.)

Place	Date	Hour	Summary of Events and Information	Remarks and references to Appendices
PONT NIEPPE	9/9/16	9 p.m.	The weather continues fine. The A.D.M.S. visited the Field Ambulance this morning and issued verbal orders that B. Section was to be withdrawn from NIEPPE at 10 a.m. to-morrow the 10th inst. to Headquarters and the site at NIEPPE handed over to No. 59 Field Ambulance. I visited the Advanced Dressing Stn. at the BREWERY this afternoon. 13 cases were admitted to the Field Ambulance during the day. 7 cases were evacuated to a Casualty Clearing Stn. leaving 8 cases remaining in the Field Ambulance.	J.E.P.
"	10/9/16	9 p.m.	The day has been fine and warm. B Section rejoined Headquarters this morning at 10 a.m. having handed over the site and billets at NIEPPE to No. 59 Field Ambulance. – 10 sick and 7 wounded cases were admitted to the Field Ambulance, 4 sick and 4 wounded were evacuated to a Casualty Clearing Stn. two cases were transferred to the 59th Field Ambulance, one man died of his wounds and one man was returned to duty leaving 13 cases remaining in the Field Ambulance.	J.E.P.
"	11/9/16	9 p.m.	The weather continues fine. – Six men were admitted to the Field Ambulance during the day; 5 men were evacuated to a Casualty Clearing Stn., one man was returned to duty, leaving 13 cases remaining in the Field Ambulance. – The Personnel have been employed on constructing Horse Lines + other improvements. – ~~the~~ A daily fatigue party ~~—~~ of ~~[illegible]~~ 10 men has been detailed to assist the 94th Field Coy R.E. in the construction of the Aid Posts. – A bathing parade for the Personnel was held at 3 p.m.	J.E.P.
"	12/9/16	9 p.m.	The weather continues fine but cloudy. – 13 cases were admitted to the Field Ambulance during the day, six cases were evacuated to ~~a~~ Casualty Clearing Station, one man was returned to duty leaving 19 cases remaining in the Field Ambulance. – The Personnel are employed in drainage and in the construction of Horse standings.	J.E.P.

1875 Wt. W593/826 1,000,000 4/15 J.B.C. & A. A.D.S.S./Forms/C. 2118.

Army Form C. 2118.

Instructions regarding War Diaries and Intelligence Summaries are contained in F. S. Regs., Part II. and the Staff Manual respectively. Title Pages will be prepared in manuscript.

WAR DIARY
or
INTELLIGENCE SUMMARY
(Erase heading not required.)

Place	Date	Hour	Summary of Events and Information	Remarks and references to Appendices
PONT NIEPPE	13/9/16	9 p.m.	Heavy showers of rain fell during the day. There was a bathing parade for the Personnel in the afternoon. – Work in connection with drainage and the construction of Horse lines is still in progress. – One Officer and 16 men were admitted to the Field Ambulance, One Officer and 3 men were evacuated to a Casualty Clearing Stn. 9 cases were transferred to the Divisional Rest Stn. ~~and~~ leaving 25 cases remaining in the Field Ambulance. – Influenza was the prevailing disease.	J.E.P.
"	14/9/16	9 p.m.	Heavy showers of rain fell again to-day. – I visited the Advanced Dressing Station in the morning. The A.D.M.S visited the Field Ambulance in the afternoon prior to proceeding on Special leave to-morrow. 9 cases were admitted to the Field Ambulance 2 cases were evacuated to a Casualty Clearing Stn. 5 cases were transferred to the Divisional Rest Stn. and two cases were returned to duty, leaving 25 cases remaining in the Fd Amb.	J.E.P.
"	15/9/16	9 p.m.	Lieut. Col J.E Powell departed to take up temporary duty as A.D.M.S. command being assumed by Capt G.P. Kidd. Good progress is being made with the work of laying horse lines etc. as a large supply of material has been received from the R.E. One officer and 12 O.R. were admitted. 1 Officer and 1 O.R. evacuated to C.C.S. Seven O.R. were transferred to D.R.S. leaving 24 cases remaining in the Fd Amb.	G.P.K.
"	16/9/16	9 p.m.	Capt. Beresford Jones proceeded to the A.D.S. to relieve Capt. Smalley who rejoined headquarters. Raids on the enemy trenches were carried out by the Division last night, producing some 20 casualties including 3 officers slightly wounded. Warning having been given arrangements were made accordingly & evacuation was quick & satisfactory. 4 Officers & 30 O.R. were admitted to the F. Amb. ~~to~~ 4 Officers & 11 O.R. evacuated to C.C.S. 4 O.R. transferred to D.R.S. 1 O.R. died at the A.D.S. leaving 33 O.R. remaining. Weather fine & warm all day.	G.P.K.

1875 Wt. W593/826 1,000,000 4/15 J.B.C. & A. A.D.S.S./Forms/C. 2118.

Instructions regarding War Diaries and Intelligence Summaries are contained in F. S. Regs., Part II. and the Staff Manual respectively. Title Pages will be prepared in manuscript.

WAR DIARY
or
~~INTELLIGENCE~~ SUMMARY
(Erase heading not required.)

Army Form C. 2118

Place	Date	Hour	Summary of Events and Information	Remarks and references to Appendices
PONT NIEPPE	17/9/16	9.0 pm	Wire received warning that the Division would move back into Corps reserve on the 19th inst. & entrain shortly afterwards. Visited the A.D.S. to talk over the intended move with O.C. Bearers. 2. Officers & 9. O.R. admitted to the Fd. Amb. 2 Officers & 3 O.R. evacuated to C.C.S. 14. O.R. transferred to D.R.S. – leaving 25 O.R. remaining. Weather remained fine & good progress has been made with the various fatigue works in progress.	GRK
"	18/9/16	9.0 pm	Preliminary orders received re the forthcoming move. Visited A.D.M.S. during the morning re the handing over of stores etc. Weather has turned cold and wet again & much rain fell today. Lieut. G.B. Oram reported his departure for temporary duty with the 9th Welch Reg. 6. O.R. admitted to Fd. Amb. during the day. 3 Evacuated to C.C.S. 11 transferred to D.R.S. leaving 17. O.R. remaining.	GRK
"	19/9/16	9.0 pm	D.A.D.M.S. visited the Fd. Amb. this afternoon with A.D.M.S. 7th Division. Commenced the packing of some of the stores & [illegible] others for handing over. Lieut. Heathcote reported his arrival back for duty on completion of temporary duty with 87th Bt. R.F.A. 9. O.R. admitted. 2 evacuated to C.C.S. 3. transferred to D.R.S. 1. Died. 2. Returned to duty. Leaving 18. O.R. remaining.	GRK

1875 Wt. W593/826 1,000,000 4/15 J.B.C. & A. A.D.S.S./Forms/C. 2118.

Instructions regarding War Diaries and Intelligence Summaries are contained in F. S. Regs., Part II. and the Staff Manual respectively. Title Pages will be prepared in manuscript.

WAR DIARY
or
~~INTELLIGENCE SUMMARY~~
(Erase heading not required.)

Army Form C. 2118

Place	Date	Hour	Summary of Events and Information	Remarks and references to Appendices
PONT NIEPPE	20/9/16	9.0 pm	Received orders that the unit will move out tomorrow handing over to 23 Fd Amb. Completed most of the packing and clearing up of billets etc. An advance party of 23. Fd Amb. arrived in the course of the afternoon and proceeded to take over the A.D.S. at DELANGLE FARM. On completion of relief Capt. Hereford Jones returned to headquarters with the bearer party. Col Brown [illegible] O.C. 23rd Fd Amb. visited and went round the hospital and billets. ~~admitted 8 OR Transferred to DRS 8 OR~~ Admitted 10. OR To CCS 4. OR To DRS 7 OR. To Duty 1. OR Remaining 16. OR. A good deal of rain fell during the day. ~~Capt~~ Lieut A.P. [illegible] reported his arrival back for duty on completion of [illegible] duty with the 7th E. Lancs Reg.	GRR
STRAZEELE	21/9/16	9.0 pm	Billeting certificates were completed and rendered. The hospital and billets were handed over to 23. Fd Amb. and the Ambulance closed at 9.30 Am. The unit moved out at 10.0 Am marching via NIEPPE – BAILLEUL. A halt was made at midday for dinner and the unit arrived at STRAZEELE about 3.0 pm. going into billets and remaining closed. I visited A.D.M.S at MERRIS to report arrival. Weather was fine all day. admitted 8 OR. To DRS 8 OR To Duty 1. OR. Transferred to 23 Fd Amb 15 OR. Remaining nil.	GRR
"	22/9/16	9.0 pm	Day spent in arranging billets & making latrines & incinerator etc. Cars sent out to collect sick of units in vicinity as per A.D.M.S. orders. We have [illegible] 3. cars here with us as a temporary measure. Arrangements being made for various forms of recreation for the men. Lieut. A.P. [illegible] reported his departure on 10 days leave of absence in England.	GRR
"	23/9/16	9.0 pm	I inspected the unit at 10.0 Am. & a board of survey for clothing was held at 11.0 Am. A.D.M.S visited the Ambulance during the morning & went round the billets etc. Weather continues fine & warm.	GRR

Instructions regarding War Diaries and Intelligence Summaries are contained in F. S. Regs., Part II. and the Staff Manual respectively. Title Pages will be prepared in manuscript.

WAR DIARY
or
~~INTELLIGENCE~~ SUMMARY

(Erase heading not required.)

Army Form C. 2118

Place	Date	Hour	Summary of Events and Information	Remarks and references to Appendices
STRAZEELE	24/9/16	9.0pm	Morning spent in fitting new box respirators, all men being passed through a gas chamber to ensure good fitting of the mask. Inspector of motor transport and ADVS 19th Div. visited the unit during the day. Weather still fine and warm.	GR.
"	25/9/16	9.0pm	Fitting of box respirators completed today. The Unit remains closed and no cases are admitted to the Field Ambulance. The weather continues fine and warm. The A.D.M.S. returned from leave at 5 p.m. I handed over to him and returned to the Headquarters of my Unit at 6 p.m. taking over command from Captain G. P. Kidd R.A.M.C. – The Personnel were paid to-day	J.E. Powell Lt. Col.
"	26/9/16	9 p.m.	The weather continues fine and warm. There was a Parade at 10 a.m. and inspection of smoke helmets, the Personnel were then taken for a route march. In the afternoon a lecture on Nursing duties etc was given to the Tent Division. The remainder of the afternoon & evening was taken up with a cricket match.	J.E.P.
"	27/9/16	9 p.m.	The Personnel were taken for a Route march followed by a bathing parade and the issue of clean clothes. Lectures were given to the Bearer division in the afternoon. The weather has been showery & a strong south easterly wind has been blowing.	J.E.P.
"	28/9/16	9 p.m.	The weather has been fine and warm. The Personnel were exercised in Box Respirator drill in the morning. – A Bathing parade, route march & also lectures were given in the afternoon to the Tent Division. The Personnel were also exercised in tent pitching.	J.E.P.

1875 Wt. W593/826 1,000,000 4/15 J.B.C. & A. A.D.S.S./Forms/C. 2118.

Instructions regarding War Diaries and Intelligence Summaries are contained in F. S. Regs., Part II. and the Staff Manual respectively. Title Pages will be prepared in manuscript.

WAR DIARY
or
~~INTELLIGENCE SUMMARY~~
(Erase heading not required.)

Army Form C. 2118

Place	Date	Hour	Summary of Events and Information	Remarks and references to Appendices
STRAZEELE	29/9/16	9 p.m.	The weather has been dull, cloudy and damp and some rain has fallen. The Personnel were exercised in Box Respirator drill. There was also a Bathing parade and lectures were given in the afternoon. The A.D.M.S. visited the Field Ambulance during the evening.	J.E.P.
"	30/9/16	9 p.m.	The weather has been fine but with a cold wind blowing. During the morning the men were exercised in Physical Drill also in Signalling. – During the afternoon lectures were given to the Tent and Bearer Divisions. The health of the Unit is very good.	J.E.P.

J. E. Powell
Lieut. Colonel R.A.M.C.
O.C. No 57 Field Ambulance

1875 Wt. W593/826 1,000,000 4/15 J.B.C. & A. A.D.S.S./Forms/C. 2118.

Oct. 1916

S

19th Div

140/1817

57th Field Ambulance.

Confidential

Instructions regarding War Diaries and Intelligence Summaries are contained in F. S. Regs., Part II. and the Staff Manual respectively. Title Pages will be prepared in manuscript.

WAR DIARY

or

~~INTELLIGENCE SUMMARY~~

(Erase heading not required.)

Army Form C. 2118

Place	Date	Hour	Summary of Events and Information	Remarks and references to Appendices
			— of —	
			57th Field Ambulance R.A.M.C.	
			— for —	
			Period 1st October 1916 to 31st October 1916	
			(Volume No. 16)	

1875 Wt. W593/826 1,000,000 4/15 J.B.C. & A. A.D.S.S./Forms/C. 2118.

Army Form C. 2118

Instructions regarding War Diaries and Intelligence Summaries are contained in F. S. Regs., Part II. and the Staff Manual respectively. Title Pages will be prepared in manuscript.

WAR DIARY
or
~~INTELLIGENCE SUMMARY~~
(Erase heading not required.)

Place	Date	Hour	Summary of Events and Information	Remarks and references to Appendices
STRAZEELE	1/10/16	9 p.m.	The day has been dry though dull and cloudy and the temperature is considerably lower also. – Captain A.B. JONES and Captain R. St.A. HEATHCOTE reported their departure this day on 14 days leave of absence in England on termination of their contract.	J.E.P.
"	2/10/16	9 p.m.	The Personnel were exercised in Squad and Company drill during the morning. Lieut. & Quartermaster Bennett reported his departure this day on 10 days special leave to England. The weather has been very wet, it has rained almost continuously throughout the day. Received orders to-night for the entrainment of the division on the 5th inst.	J.E.P.
"	3/10/16	9 p.m.	Rain fell throughout the morning, but the weather cleared in the afternoon and the majority of the tents were struck and packed, the men being moved into billets.	J.E.P.
"	4/10/16	9 p.m.	Rain again fell during the morning, but the weather cleared in the afternoon and the remainder of the tents were struck and all the equipment packed. Made arrangements and issued the necessary orders for the move of the Unit to-morrow. Rendered Billeting certificates up to to-morrow inclusive to the Maire.	J.E.P.
DOULLENS	5/10/16	12 midnight	The Unit marched off from STRAZEELE at 11.30 a.m. and entrained at BAILLEUL WEST station at 1.30 p.m. In one hour the entrainment was complete. – The train left Bailleul at 4.20 p.m. and arrived at DOULLENS at 12 Midnight. The weather was fine this morning, but on arriving here a steady rain is falling and the conditions of the station yard and roads are bad.	J.E.P.

1875 Wt. W593/826 1,000,000 4/15 J.B.C. & A. A.D.S.S./Forms/C. 2118.

Instructions regarding War Diaries and Intelligence Summaries are contained in F. S. Regs., Part II. and the Staff Manual respectively. Title Pages will be prepared in manuscript.

WAR DIARY
or
~~INTELLIGENCE SUMMARY~~

(Erase heading not required.)

Army Form C. 2118

Place	Date	Hour	Summary of Events and Information	Remarks and references to Appendices
COUIN	6/10/16	9 p.m.	Detrainment at DOULLENS took 2½ hours – The Unit marched off from the Station at 2.30 a.m. and arrived at AUTHIE at 6.15 a.m. a distance of 10 miles. At AUTHIE the Unit rested in Billets until 1 p.m. when on receipt of instructions from the A.D.M.S. the Field Ambulance marched here, arriving at 2 p.m. and taking over from the 2nd/1st Highland Field Ambulance, opened out for the reception of Sick & wounded. – There is accommodation for 200 patients here in huts & the personnel are also accommodated in huts. The A.D.M.S. visited the Field Ambulance at 4 p.m. and the D.D.M.S. and D.A.Q.M.G. XIII Corps visited the Field Ambulance at 5.30 p.m.	J.E.P.
"	7/10/16	9 p.m.	The weather continues very wet and the conditions of the roads and ground generally ~~are~~ very bad, covered with deep mud. – The D.D.M.S. Corps visited the Field Ambulance at 10 a.m. – Eleven cases of sickness were admitted, of which one case was a case of Diphtheria and was evacuated to a C.C.S. leaving 10 cases remaining in the Field Ambulance.	J.E.P.
"	8/10/16	9 p.m.	Two Officers and 46 other ranks were admitted to the Field Ambulance during the day. One Officer and 12 men were evacuated to a Casualty Clearing Station and one man was returned to duty, leaving One Officer and 43 other ranks remaining in the Field Ambulance. The D.D.M.S. Corps visited the Field Ambulance at 2 p.m. – Seven Hospital marquees arrived to-day. – The weather continues very wet.	J.E.P.

1875 Wt. W593/826 1,000,000 4/15 J.B.C. & A. A.D.S.S./Forms/C. 2118.

Army Form C. 2118

Instructions regarding War Diaries and Intelligence Summaries are contained in F. S. Regs., Part II. and the Staff Manual respectively. Title Pages will be prepared in manuscript.

WAR DIARY
or
~~INTELLIGENCE SUMMARY~~

(Erase heading not required.)

Place	Date	Hour	Summary of Events and Information	Remarks and references to Appendices
COUIN	9/10/16	9 p.m.	The weather though still damp has improved and no rain has fallen to-day. – The A.D.M.S. visited the Field Ambulance at 3.30 p.m. – The Personnel were employed in unloading and packing surplus stores & equipment for the Corps Main Dressing Station during the morning and in the afternoon they were employed in pitching Hospital marquees. – One Officer and 39 other ranks were admitted to the Field Ambulance one Officer and 12 men were evacuated to a Casualty Clearing Station one case was transferred to No 58th Field Ambulance, 2 cases were returned to duty leaving one Officer and 67 men remaining.	J.E.P.
"	10/10/16	9 p.m.	Weather improved much and today was quite fine throughout. Most of the day spent in pitching more marquees and making a new road for cars into the hospital field. Flint and chalk being obtained for this purpose from quarries. 34 more marquees & equipment arrived in the evening and were unloaded & stored in hut. 47. O.R. were admitted. 25. O.R. evacuated to C.C.S. 9 O.R. returned to duty leaving 1 Off. & 80 O.R. remaining. One case of Diphtheria – one of Rubella, [illegible] were admitted during the day & evacuated to 2/1 S. Mid. C.C.S.	GBR
"	11/10/16	9 p.m.	Some showers of rain fell in the morning. – One Officer and 49 other ranks were admitted to the Field Ambulance, 30 cases were evacuated to a Casualty Clearing Stn. and 11 cases were returned to duty leaving 2 Officers and 88 other ranks remaining in the Field Ambulance. The Personnel were employed in pitching Hospital marquees and in making a new road through the Field for motor ambulances! – The 1/3 Highland Field Ambulance arrived to-day to be attached to the Corps Main Dressing Stn. and to assist in making roads & pitching the Camp.	J.E.P.

1875 Wt. W593/826 1,000,000 4/15 J.B.C. & A. A.D.S.S./Forms/C. 2118.

Instructions regarding War Diaries and Intelligence Summaries are contained in F. S. Regs., Part II. and the Staff Manual respectively. Title Pages will be prepared in manuscript.

WAR DIARY

or

~~INTELLIGENCE SUMMARY~~

(Erase heading not required.)

Army Form C. 2118

Place	Date	Hour	Summary of Events and Information	Remarks and references to Appendices
COUIN	12/10/16	9 p.m.	The weather has been fine again to-day. The D.D.M.S. XIII Corps visited the Field Ambulance this morning. The Personnel are continuing work on the new road and pitching hospital marquees. – 55 cases were admitted to the Field Ambulance during the day, 18 cases were evacuated to a Casualty Clearing Stn. and 9 cases were returned to duty, leaving 2 Officers and 116 men remaining in the Field Ambulance.	J.E.P.
"	13/10/16	9 p.m.	The weather continues fine. The D.D.M.S. XIII Corps visited the Main Dressing Stn. this morning also the A.D.M.S. 51st Division. Work is being carried on pitching Hospital Marquees and on the new road for motor ambulances. – One Officer and 44 other ranks were admitted to the Field Ambulance, one officer and 21 other ranks were ~~[illegible]~~ evacuated to a Casualty Clearing Station, 30 cases were transferred to the Corps Rest Stn and 6 cases were returned to duty, leaving 2 Officers and 103 other ranks remaining.	J.E.P.
"	14/10/16	9 p.m.	The Tent Division of the 2/1 Highland Field Ambulance arrived here ~~this~~ at 3 p.m. to be attached to this Unit and to assist in Road making etc. – The work of pitching hospital marquees was completed this evening and work on the new road is being continued. – 33 cases were admitted to the Field Ambulance, 10 cases were evacuated to a Casualty Clearing Stn. 64 cases were transferred to the Corps Rest Stn. and one Officer and six men were returned to duty, leaving one Officer and 56 men remaining.	J.E.P.
"	15/10/16	9 p.m.	The day has been fine but it is much colder to-day. – Work on the new road has been continued. – One Officer and 32 other ranks were admitted to the Field Ambulance during the day, one Officer and 23 other ranks were evacuated to a Casualty Clearing Stn. and 31 cases were transferred to the Corps Rest Stn. one man was returned to duty, leaving one Officer and 33 other ranks remaining in the Field Ambulance.	J.E.P.

1875 Wt. W593/826 1,000,000 4/15 J.B.C. & A. A.D.S.S./Forms/C. 2118.

Army Form C. 2118

Instructions regarding War Diaries and Intelligence Summaries are contained in F. S. Regs., Part II. and the Staff Manual respectively. Title Pages will be prepared in manuscript.

WAR DIARY
or
~~INTELLIGENCE SUMMARY~~
(Erase heading not required.)

Place	Date	Hour	Summary of Events and Information	Remarks and references to Appendices
COUIN	16/10/16	9 p.m.	The day has been fine but much colder. In the morning the D.D.M.S. Corps visited the Field Ambulance. – Work was continued on the new road for ambulances. at 2 p.m. I received orders from the A.D.M.S. to hand over the Corps Main Dressing Stn. to the 1/3 Highland Field Ambulance, to close my Unit & be ready to move off to-morrow the 17th inst. with the 56th Infantry Brigade. The afternoon was spent in packing equipment. – at 5.30 p.m. I closed my Unit and handed over charge to the O.C. 1/3 Highland Field Ambulance. Since Noon on the 15/10/16 Two Officers and 65 men were admitted to the Field Ambulance. 26 men were evacuated to a Casualty Clearing Station. 2 Officers and 40 men were transferred to the Corps Rest Station, 12 men were sent to duty and one Officer and 20 men were transferred to the 1/3 Highland Field Ambulance.	J.E.P.
WARLOY	17/10/16	9.30 p.m.	The Unit marched off from COUIN at 9.45 a.m. The transport proceeding with the 57th Brigade Transport and the Personnel proceeding direct here where the Unit arrived at 3 p.m. and went into Billets. The morning was fine but rain has fallen during the afternoon and evening.	J.E.P.
"	18/10/16	9 p.m.	Heavy rain fell this morning but the afternoon has been fine. – Received orders from the A.D.M.S. at 10 a.m. to take over the Officers Hospital and Divisional Rest Station in the Rue de NEUVÉ from the 56th Field Ambulance. This taking over was completed at 12 Noon & this Unit opened for the reception of casualties at that hour. – Captain JONES and Captain HEATHCOTE reported their arrival this day on return from leave.	J.E.P.

Instructions regarding War Diaries and Intelligence Summaries are contained in F. S. Regs., Part II. and the Staff Manual respectively. Title Pages will be prepared in manuscript.

WAR DIARY
or
~~INTELLIGENCE SUMMARY~~
(Erase heading not required.)

Army Form C. 2118

Place	Date	Hour	Summary of Events and Information	Remarks and references to Appendices
WARLOY	19/10/16	9 p.m.	Heavy rain has fallen throughout the day and the condition of the roads and ground is very bad. — The Personnel have been employed in improving the conditions of the ground and also of the marquees for the Patients. — Indented for 12 Oil Stoves for heating the marquees. 9 Officers and 42 other ranks were admitted to the Field Ambulance, One Officer was evacuated to a Casualty Clearing Stn. 22 men were transferred to the Divisional Rest Stn. 2 men were returned to duty leaving 8 Officers and 18 other ranks remaining in the Field Ambulance. 70 cases were admitted to the Divisional Rest Stn. 9 cases were returned to duty leaving 61 cases remaining in the Divisional Rest Stn. The Personnel were paid this evening.	J.E.P.
"	20/10/16	9 p.m.	The day has been clear and fine but cold with an East wind blowing. — The Personnel have been employed storing and checking equipment and on general fatigues. 3 Officers and 22 other ranks ~~were~~ admitted to the Field Ambulance during the day. 6 Officers and 4 other ranks ~~have been~~ were evacuated to a Casualty Clearing Stn. 14 cases were transferred to the Divisional Rest Stn. leaving 5 Officers and 22 men remaining in the Field Ambulance. — 14 cases were admitted to the Divisional Rest Stn. 4 cases were evacuated to a Casualty Clearing Stn. and 13 cases were returned to duty, leaving 58 cases remaining in the Divisional Rest Stn.	J.E.P.

1875 Wt. W593/826 1,000,000 4/15 J.B.C. & A. A.D.S.S./Forms/C. 2118.

Instructions regarding War Diaries and Intelligence Summaries are contained in F. S. Regs., Part II. and the Staff Manual respectively. Title Pages will be prepared in manuscript.

WAR DIARY
or
~~INTELLIGENCE SUMMARY~~
(Erase heading not required.)

Army Form C. 2118

Place	Date	Hour	Summary of Events and Information	Remarks and references to Appendices
WARLOY	21/10/16	9 p.m.	The weather continues dry and cold and the mud is rapidly drying up – Billeting certificates were rendered to-day for the week. 4 Officers and 48 other ranks were admitted to the Field Ambulance, 3 Officers and 10 men were evacuated to a Casualty Clearing Stn. 9 cases were transferred to the Divisional Rest Stn., leaving 6 Officers and 51 other ranks remaining in the Field Ambulance. – Nine cases were admitted to the Divisional Rest Stn. 5 cases were evacuated to a Casualty Clearing Stn. 12 cases were returned to duty, leaving 50 cases remaining in the Divisional Rest Stn. –	J.E.P.
"	22/10/16	9 p.m.	The weather continues dry and cold. – The Personnel were employed making new drains and improving the condition of the roads and paths. – Seven Officers and 22 other ranks were admitted to the Field Ambulance, 4 Officers and 35 other ranks were evacuated to a Casualty Clearing Stn. 5 cases were transferred to the Divisional Rest Stn. and one case was sent to duty, leaving 9 Officers and 32 men remaining in the Field Ambulance. Eleven cases were admitted to the Divisional Rest Station, 7 cases were evacuated to a Casualty Clearing Stn. and six cases were returned to duty, leaving 48 cases remaining in the Divisional Rest Stn.	J.E.P.
"	23/10/16	9 p.m.	There has been a thick mist throughout the day and a slight drizzling rain this evening. The construction of new drains is being continued – also the checking and storing of blankets and equipment. – A Clothing board was held this morning. Nine Officers and 33 other ranks were admitted to the Field Ambulance during the day. Seven Officers and 24 other ranks were evacuated to a Casualty Clearing Station, 16 cases were transferred to the Divisional Rest Stn. and one Officer and one man were returned to duty, leaving 10 Officers and 35 other ranks remaining in the Field Ambulance. – 16 cases were admitted to the Divisional Rest Stn. 5 cases were evacuated to a Casualty Clearing Stn. and 8 cases were returned to duty leaving 51 cases remaining in the Divisional Rest Stn.	J.E.P.

1875 Wt. W593/826 1,000,000 4/15 J.B.C. & A. A.D.S.S./Forms/C. 2118.

WAR DIARY

or

~~INTELLIGENCE SUMMARY~~

(Erase heading not required.)

Army Form C. 2118

Instructions regarding War Diaries and Intelligence Summaries are contained in F. S. Regs., Part II. and the Staff Manual respectively. Title Pages will be prepared in manuscript.

Place	Date	Hour	Summary of Events and Information	Remarks and references to Appendices
WARLOY	24/10/16	9 p.m.	Rain fell heavily last night & heavy showers have fallen throughout the day making the conditions very bad in the front area. — 5 Officers and 78 other ranks were admitted to the Field Ambulance. 6 Officers and 54 other ranks were evacuated to a Casualty Clearing Stn. 32 cases were transferred to the Divisional Rest. 2 cases were sent to duty, leaving 9 Officers and 25 other ranks remaining in the Field Ambulance. — 32 cases were admitted to the Divisional Rest Stn. 7 cases were evacuated to a Casualty Clearing Stn., leaving 76 cases remaining in the Divisional Rest Stn.	J.E.P.
"	25/10/16	9 p.m.	The weather has continued wet. Four Officers and 130 other ranks were admitted to the Field Ambulance, 3 Officers and 79 other ranks were evacuated to a Casualty Clearing Stn. 46 cases were transferred to the Divisional Rest Stn. 3 Officers and one man were returned to duty, leaving 7 Officers and 29 other ranks remaining in the Field Ambulance. The Prevailing diseases were Influenza and myalgia. 46 cases were admitted to the Divisional Rest Station, 21 cases were evacuated to a Casualty Clearing Stn. 7 cases were transferred to the 91st Field Ambulance and 19 cases were returned to duty, leaving 75 cases remaining in the Divisional Rest Stn.	J.E.P.
"	26/10/16	9 p.m.	A little rain fell in the morning, but the remainder of the day has been quite fine and mild. — I went to the A.D.M.S.'s Office at 9.30 a.m. for a Conference with regard to the medical arrangements for the forward area — I returned at 12.30 p.m. 3 Officers and 103 other ranks were admitted to the Field Ambulance, 5 Officers and 25 other ranks were evacuated to a Casualty Clearing Stn. 42 cases were transferred to the Div. Rest Stn. 4 cases were transferred to the 91st Field Ambulance. One Officer was returned to duty, leaving 4 Officers and 61 other ranks in the Field Ambulance. — 42 cases were admitted to the Divisional Rest Stn. 9 cases were sent to a C.C.S. and 14 cases to duty, leaving 94 cases remaining in D.R.S.	J.E.P.

1875 Wt. W593/826 1,000,000 4/15 J.B.C. & A. A.D.S.S./Forms/C. 2118.

Army Form C. 2118

WAR DIARY
or
~~INTELLIGENCE SUMMARY~~
(Erase heading not required.)

Instructions regarding War Diaries and Intelligence Summaries are contained in F. S. Regs., Part II. and the Staff Manual respectively. Title Pages will be prepared in manuscript.

Place	Date	Hour	Summary of Events and Information	Remarks and references to Appendices
WARLOY	27/10/16	9 p.m.	Rain fell again last night and also this morning. Under the orders of the A.D.M.S. the Bearer Division of this Unit marched off at 10.30 a.m. for BLACKHORSE BRIDGE ~~and~~ to be there held in Reserve. The D.D.M.S. II Corps visited the Officers Hospital, Field Ambulance + Rest Station this morning. Lieut A.P. FRY RAMC reported his departure this day for permanent duty as M.O. i/c 19th Divisional Amm Col. One Officer and 92 other ranks were admitted to the Field Ambulance. 84 cases were evacuated to a Casualty Clearing Stn, 29 cases were transferred to the Divisional Rest Stn, and 2 cases were returned to duty, leaving 5 Officers and 38 other ranks remaining in the Field Ambulance. — 30 cases were admitted to the Divisional Rest Stn. 20 cases were evacuated to a Casualty Clearing Stn. leaving 104 cases remaining in the Divisional Rest Stn.	J.E.P.
"	28/10/16	9 p.m.	The day has been fine and mild and no rain has fallen to-day. The A.D.M.S. visited the Field Ambulance this morning. LIEUT. M. McGILLIVRAY R.A.M.C. S.R. reported his arrival this day as a Reinforcement. — One Officer and 83 other ranks were admitted to the ~~Divisional~~ Field Ambulance, two Officers and 27 other ranks were evacuated to a Casualty Clearing Stn. 21 cases were transferred to the Divisional Rest Stn. and two Officers and 14 other ranks were returned to duty, leaving 2 Officers and 59 other ranks remaining in the Field Ambulance. — 21 cases were admitted to the Divisional Rest Stn. 11 cases were evacuated to a Casualty Clearing Stn. and 5 cases were returned to duty, leaving 109 cases remaining in the ~~Field Ambulance~~ Divisional Rest Stn. — Billeting certificates were rendered for the week, this morning.	J.E.P.

1875 Wt. W593/826 1,000,000 4/15 J.B.C. & A. A.D.S.S./Forms/C. 2118.

Instructions regarding War Diaries and Intelligence Summaries are contained in F. S. Regs., Part II. and the Staff Manual respectively. Title Pages will be prepared in manuscript.

WAR DIARY
or
~~INTELLIGENCE SUMMARY~~
(Erase heading not required.)

Army Form C. 2118

Place	Date	Hour	Summary of Events and Information	Remarks and references to Appendices
WARLOY	29/10/16	9 p.m.	Rain fell again last night and during the morning also and conditions remain very bad & deep mud everywhere. The Field Ambulance was closed today and the whole unit organised as a Divisional Rest Stn. — Two Officers and 74 other ranks were admitted to the Divisional Rest Stn, 61 cases were evacuated to a Casualty Clearing Stn and 23 cases were returned to duty, leaving 4 Officers and 158 other ranks remaining in the Divisional Rest Stn.	J.E.P.
WARLOY	30/10/16	9 p.m.	Very heavy rain has fallen throughout the day. — I visited the Bearer Division of this Unit in the afternoon. — 3 Officers and 75 men were admitted to the Divisional Rest Stn. 36 cases were evacuated to a Casualty Clearing Stn. and 27 cases were returned to duty, leaving 7 Officers and 170 other ranks remaining in the Divisional Rest Stn.	J.E.P.
"	31/10/16	9 p.m.	The day has been quite fine and warm and the main roads are drying rapidly. — Three Officers and 59 other ranks were admitted to the Divisional Rest Stn during the day. Two Officers and 23 other ranks were evacuated to a Casualty Clearing Stn. and 17 cases were returned to duty, leaving 8 Officers and 189 other ranks remaining in the Divisional Rest Stn.	J.E.P.

J. E. Powell
Lieut. Colonel R.A.M.C.
O.C. 57th Field Ambulance

1875 Wt. W593/826 1,000,000 4/15 J.B.C. & A. A.D.S.S./Forms/C. 2118.

Confidential

Army Form C. 2118

14/1862

Instructions regarding War Diaries and Intelligence Summaries are contained in F. S. Regs., Part II. and the Staff Manual respectively. Title Pages will be prepared in manuscript.

WAR DIARY
or
~~INTELLIGENCE SUMMARY~~

(Erase heading not required.)

Vol 17

Place	Date	Hour	Summary of Events and Information	Remarks and references to Appendices
	Nov 1916 S/		19th Div of 57th Field Ambulance from 1. 11. 16 to 30. 11. 16 (Volume No. 17) [illegible] Kidd Cold. R.A.M.C.	

1875 Wt. W593/826 1,000,000 4/15 J.B.C. & A. A.D.S.S./Forms/C. 2118.

SECRET

57th FIELD AMBULANCE
No. 1605
Date 1/12/16
R.A.M.C.

To
A.D.M.S.
19th Division

I forward you herewith War Diary of this unit for the month of November for transmission to D.H.Q.

G. [signature] Capt.
R.A.M.C.
COMMANDING 57th FIELD AMBULANCE

57 FA

Army Form C. 2118

WAR DIARY
or
~~INTELLIGENCE SUMMARY~~
(Erase heading not required.)

[Instructi]ons regarding War Diaries and Intelligence Summaries are contained in F. S. Regs., Part II. and the Staff Manual respectively. Title Pages will be prepared in manuscript.

Place	Date	Hour	Summary of Events and Information	Remarks and references to Appendices
WARLOY	1/11/16	9 p.m.	Rained again last night but has been fine during the day, but the ground does not dry up at all. – Six Officers and 77 other ranks were admitted to the Divisional Rest Stn. 8 Officers and 41 other ranks were evacuated to a Casualty Clearing Stn. 32 cases were sent to duty, leaving six Officers and 193 other ranks remaining in the ~~Field~~ Divisional Rest Stn.	J.E.P.
"	2/11/16	9 p.m.	Some rain fell this morning, but the afternoon and evening has been fine. The A.D.M.S. visited the Field Ambulance this afternoon. Five Officers and 88 other Ranks were admitted to the Divisional Rest Stn. 3 Officers and 41 other ranks were evacuated to a Casualty Clearing Stn. and one Officer and 34 other ranks were returned to duty, leaving 7 Officers and 206 men remaining in the Divisional Rest Stn.	J.E.P.
"	3/11/16	9 p.m.	Rain again fell last night but the day has been fine and clear. Seven Officers and 103 other ranks were admitted to the Divisional Rest Stn. Four Officers and 66 other ranks were evacuated to a Casualty Clearing Stn. and one Officer and 22 men were returned to duty, leaving 9 Officers and 221 other ranks remaining in the Divisional Rest Stn.	J.E.P.
"	4/11/16	9 p.m.	A few showers of rain fell in the morning, otherwise the day has been fine. I visited the Bearer Division in the afternoon. – ~~The~~ Sergeant Major PRIEST was evacuated to a C.C.S. to-day with acute Rheumatism. 4 Officers and 73 other ranks were admitted to the Div. Rest Stn. Six Officers and 54 other ranks were evacuated to a Casualty Clearing Stn. and 38 cases were returned to duty, leaving 7 Officers and 203 other ranks remaining in the Div. Rest Stn.	J.E.P.

1875 Wt. W593/826 1,000,000 4/15 J.B.C. & A. A.D.S.S./Forms/C. 2118.

Instructions regarding War Diaries and Intelligence Summaries are contained in F. S. Regs., Part II. and the Staff Manual respectively. Title Pages will be prepared in manuscript.

WAR DIARY

or

~~INTELLIGENCE SUMMARY~~

(Erase heading not required.)

Army Form C. 2118

Place	Date	Hour	Summary of Events and Information	Remarks and references to Appendices
WARLOY	5/11/16	9 p.m.	The day has been fine with a good drying wind. Under instructions from the A.D.M.S. the Huts and Marquees near the Special Hospital here were taken over this morning from the 91st Field Ambulance, as additional accommodation for the Div. Rest Stn. There is additional accommodation for 200 Patients there. 7 Officers and 110 other ranks were admitted to the Div. Rest Stn. 4 Officers and 98 other ranks were evacuated to a Casualty Clearing Stn. 3 Officers and 32 other ranks were returned to duty, leaving 7 Officers and 183 other ranks remaining in the Divisional Rest Stn.	J.E.P.
"	6/11/16	9 p.m.	Rain again fell during the night but it been fine during the day with the exception of a few showers. The D.M.S. 5th Army visited the Rest Stn. this morning. Three Officers and 76 other ranks were admitted to the Divisional Rest Stn. during the day, two Officers and 52 other ranks were evacuated to a Casualty Clearing Stn. and 24 men were returned to duty, leaving 8 Officers and 183 other ranks remaining in the Divisional Rest Stn.	J.E.P.
"	7/11/16	9 p.m.	Very heavy rain has fallen throughout the day. – Two Officers and 63 other ranks were admitted to the Divisional Rest Stn., and two Officers and 39 other ranks were evacuated to a Casualty Clearing Stn., 20 men were returned to duty, leaving 8 Officers and 187 other ranks remaining in the Divisional Rest Stn.	J.E.P.
"	8/11/16	9 p.m.	The weather has been fine to-day with the exception of a few heavy showers of rain. – Two Officers and 95 other ranks were admitted to the Divisional Rest Stn. one Officer and 40 other ranks were evacuated to a Casualty Clearing Stn., 16 cases were returned to duty, leaving 9 Officers and 206 other ranks remaining in the Divisional Rest Stn. The A.D.M.S. visited the Div. Rest Stn. this afternoon.	J.E.P.

1875 Wt. W593/826 1,000,000 4/15 J.B.C. & A. A.D.S.S./Forms/C. 2118.

Army Form C. 2118

[Ins]tructions regarding War Diaries and Intelligence Summaries are contained in F. S. Regs., Part II. and the Staff Manual respectively. Title Pages will be prepared in manuscript.

WAR DIARY
or
~~INTELLIGENCE SUMMARY~~

(Erase heading not required.)

Place	Date	Hour	Summary of Events and Information	Remarks and references to Appendices
WARLOY	9/11/16	9 p.m.	The day has been fine throughout and the roads have ~~[illegible]~~ dried a little, but it has certainly become colder. – Two Officers and 101 other ranks were admitted to the Divisional Rest Stn., 2 Officers and 71 men were evacuated to a Casualty Clearing Stn. One Officer and 27 men were returned to duty, leaving 8 Officers and 209 men remaining in the Divisional Rest Station.	J.E.P.
"	10/11/16	9 p.m.	The day has again been quite fine throughout. – Three Officers and 116 other ranks were admitted to the Divisional Rest Stn., four Officers and 48 other ranks were evacuated to a Casualty Clearing Stn., 42 cases were returned to duty and one German Prisoner of War died from accidental wounds. – There are 7 Officers and 234 other ranks remaining in the Divisional Rest Stn.	J.E.P.
"	11/11/16	9 p.m.	No rain has fallen during the day, but there has been a thick mist throughout the afternoon and evening. – Three Officers and 136 other ranks were admitted to the Divisional Rest Station, two Officers and 58 other ranks were evacuated to a Casualty Clearing Station, one Officer and 14 men were returned to duty, leaving 7 Officers and 298 other ranks remaining in the Divisional Rest Station. – Billeting certificates were rendered for the week this morning.	J.E.P.
"	12/11/16	9 p.m.	The A.D.M.S. visited the Divisional Rest Station this morning at 11 a.m. – It has been another dull grey day but with no rain. – Seven Officers and 94 other ranks were admitted to the Divisional Rest Station during the day, 6 Officers and 111 other ranks were evacuated to a Casualty Clearing Stn., and 34 cases were returned to duty, leaving 8 Officers and 247 other ranks remaining in the Divisional Rest Stn.	J.E.P.

1875 Wt. W593/826 1,000,000 4/15 J.B.C. & A. A.D.S.S./Forms/C. 2118.

Army Form C. 2118

WAR DIARY
or
~~INTELLIGENCE SUMMARY~~
(Erase heading not required.)

Instructions regarding War Diaries and Intelligence Summaries are contained in F. S. Regs., Part II. and the Staff Manual respectively. Title Pages will be prepared in manuscript.

Place	Date	Hour	Summary of Events and Information	Remarks and references to Appendices
WARLOY	13/11/16	9 p.m.	The day has been dull and grey with a thick mist, but there has been no rain. – Four Officers and 140 other ranks were admitted to the Divisional Rest Stn., and 4 Officers and 130 other ranks were evacuated to a Casualty Clearing Stn., two Officers and 36 other ranks were returned to duty, leaving six Officers and 221 men remaining in the Divisional Rest Stn.	J.E.P.
"	14/11/16	9 p.m.	The weather continues dull and misty but a little colder – No rain has fallen. Five Officers and 98 other ranks were admitted to the Divisional Rest Stn., 3 Officers and 13 other ranks were evacuated to a Casualty Clearing Stn., and two Officers and 21 men were returned to duty, leaving six Officers and 285 men remaining in the Divisional Rest Stn. – I attended a Conference at the A.D.M.S.'s Office at 6·30 p.m. – The Bearer Division of this Unit will take over the A.D.S. at Paisley avenue Sq Q 30 c at 6 a.m. to-morrow 15th inst. from a Field Ambulance of the 39th Division – They will evacuate all cases to LANCASHIRE DUMP.	J.E.P.
"	15/11/16	9 p.m.	The day has been fine and clear but cold. – Five Officers and 92 other ranks were admitted to the Divisional Rest Stn. during the day. – Four Officers and and 29 other ranks were evacuated to a Casualty Clearing Station, and 25 men were returned to duty, 7 Officers and 323 other ranks remaining in the Divisional Rest Stn.	J.E.P.

1875 Wt. W593/826 1,000,000 4/15 J.B.C. & A. A.D.S.S./Forms/C. 2118.

Instructions regarding War Diaries and Intelligence Summaries are contained in F. S. Regs., Part II. and the Staff Manual respectively. Title Pages will be prepared in manuscript.

WAR DIARY
or
~~INTELLIGENCE SUMMARY~~
(Erase heading not required.)

Army Form C. 2118

Place	Date	Hour	Summary of Events and Information	Remarks and references to Appendices
WARLOY	16/11/16	9 p.m.	The day has again been fine, clear & cold, there was a frost last night. — Received orders from the A.D.M.S. at 10 a.m. to send the Quartermaster and a small holding party to East CLAIRFAYE by 12 Noon, to take over the stores and equipment from the 133rd Field Ambulance. — also received a notification that 110 cases were being transferred to this Unit from East CLAIRFAYE. — These cases arrived during the afternoon. Four Officers and 60 other ranks were admitted to the Divisional Rest Stn. up to 12 Noon, three Officers and 64 other ranks were evacuated to a Casualty Clearing Stn. and One Officer and 47 other ranks were returned to duty, leaving 7 Officers and 272 men remaining in the Divisional Rest Stn.	J.E.P.
"	17/11/16	9 p.m.	The weather has again been clear and fine with a cold east wind blowing, there was a hard frost last night. — Four Officers and 208 other ranks were admitted to the Divisional Rest Station during the day, two Officers and 95 other ranks were evacuated to a Casualty Clearing Station, and One Officer and 87 men were returned to duty leaving 8 Officers and 324 men remaining in the Divisional Rest Station.	J.E.P.
"	18/11/16	9 p.m.	There was a slight fall of snow last night which this morning turned to rain. — all roads and the ground generally have become very muddy again. — 124 cases were admitted to the Divisional Rest Stn., 64 cases were evacuated to a Casualty Clearing Stn., and 73 cases were returned to duty, leaving 8 Officers and 283 other ranks remaining in the Divisional Rest Stn. — Billeting Certificates for the week were rendered to-day.	J.E.P.

Instructions regarding War Diaries and Intelligence Summaries are contained in F. S. Regs., Part II. and the Staff Manual respectively. Title Pages will be prepared in manuscript.

WAR DIARY
or
~~INTELLIGENCE SUMMARY~~
(Erase heading not required.)

Army Form C. 2118

Place	Date	Hour	Summary of Events and Information	Remarks and references to Appendices
WARLOY	19/11/16	9 p.m.	Heavy rain fell last night and to-day has been very damp, but no further rain has fallen. – Four Officers and 84 other ranks were admitted to the Divisional Rest Station, 4 Officers and 10 other ranks were evacuated to a Casualty Clearing Station and 22 cases were returned to duty, leaving 8 Officers and 335 other ranks remaining in the Divisional Rest Station.	J.E.P.
"	20/11/16	9 p.m.	The weather has been fine throughout the day. – Six Officers and 104 other ranks were admitted to the Divisional Rest Station, six Officers and 66 other ranks were evacuated to a Casualty Clearing Stn. and 47 men were returned to duty, leaving 8 Officers and 326 other ranks remaining in the Divisional Rest Station.	J.E.P.
"	21/11/16	9 p.m.	The weather has been damp and misty but no rain has fallen to-day. – The A.D.M.S. visited the Divisional Rest Station this afternoon at 3 p.m. and went round the wards. – One Officer and 125 other ranks were admitted to the Divisional Rest Station during the day, one Officer and 139 other ranks were evacuated to a Casualty Clearing Station, and One Officer and 63 other ranks were returned to duty leaving 7 Officers and 249 men remaining in the Divisional Rest Station.	J.E.P.
"	22/11/16	9 p.m.	The day has been fine and clear, but cold, there was a hard frost last night. Two Officers and 114 men were admitted to the Divisional Rest Station to-day, one Officer and 54 men were evacuated to a Casualty Clearing Stn., Two Officers and 35 men were returned to duty leaving 6 Officers and 274 men remaining in the Divisional Rest Station.	J.E.P.

1875 Wt. W593/826 1,000,000 4/15 J.B.C. & A. A.D.S.S./Forms/C. 2118.

Instructions regarding War Diaries and Intelligence Summaries are contained in F. S. Regs., Part II. and the Staff Manual respectively. Title Pages will be prepared in manuscript.

WAR DIARY
or
~~INTELLIGENCE SUMMARY~~
(Erase heading not required.)

Army Form C. 2118

Place	Date	Hour	Summary of Events and Information	Remarks and references to Appendices
WARLOY	23/11/16	9 p.m.	The weather continues fine and clear – There was a hard frost last night. The Bearer Division rejoined the headquarters of the Unit at 11 a.m. this morning from the Advanced Dressing Stn. – Received orders from the A.D.M.S. to transfer by M.A.C. cars to the Rest Stations at VADENCOURT and EAST CLAIRFAYE all patients over one hundred, to-morrow the 24th inst. The remaining hundred patients together with all stores etc. and the whole Officers Hospital and Rest Station are to be handed over to a Field Ambulance of the 4th Army on the afternoon of the 24th inst. This Unit will then march on the morning of the 25th inst. to CANDAS. – 5 Officers and 61 men were admitted to the Divisional Rest Stn., 2 Officers and 24 men were evacuated to a Casualty Clearing Stn. and 52 men were returned to duty, leaving 9 Officers and 259 men remaining in the Divisional Rest Stn.	J.E.P.
"	24/11/16	9 p.m.	The day has been fine but cold, there was frost again last night. – Handed over the Divisional Rest Station this afternoon to the 1/2nd South Midland Field Ambulance. The D.D.M.S. III Corps visited the Divisional Rest Station this morning. – One Officer and 39 men were admitted to the Divisional Rest Station, 3 Officers and 24 men were evacuated to a Casualty Clearing Stn. one Officer and 54 men were returned to duty, 82 men were transferred to EAST CLAIRFAYE D.R.S. and 81 men to VADENCOURT D.R.S. and Six Officers and 57 men were transferred to the 1/2 South Midland Field Ambulance leaving no cases remaining and this Unit closed.	J.E.P.

Instructions regarding War Diaries and Intelligence Summaries are contained in F. S. Regs., Part II. and the Staff Manual respectively. Title Pages will be prepared in manuscript.

WAR DIARY
or
~~INTELLIGENCE SUMMARY~~
(Erase heading not required.)

Army Form C. 2118

Place	Date	Hour	Summary of Events and Information	Remarks and references to Appendices
CANDAS	25/11/16	9 p.m.	The Unit marched off from WARLOY at 9 a.m. and arrived here at 4 p.m. and went into billets. The day has been very wet, heavy rain falling all day. Received orders to proceed to VACQUERIE to-morrow	J.E.P.
VACQUERIE	26/11/16	9 p.m.	The day has been wet again. The Unit marched from CANDAS at 10 a.m. and arrived here at 12 Noon. The afternoon has been spent in preparing empty houses for the reception of sick. The A.D.M.S. visited the Field Ambulance at 3 p.m. and the Brigadier General of the 56th Brigade at 4 p.m.	J.E.P.
"	27/11/16	9 p.m.	The weather has been ~~dry~~ but cold to-day. — The Personnel have been employed in preparing for the reception of sick and in clearing up the surroundings of billets. — Nine cases were admitted to the Field Ambulance this morning and there are 9 cases remaining in the Field Ambulance. — The A.D.M.S. visited the Unit at 3.30 p.m.	J.E.P.
"	28/11/16	9 p.m.	The day has been cold and foggy and there was a frost last night. — Lieut. F. HANNIGAN R.A.M.C. reported his arrival for duty this day and is posted to B Section. — Captain H. DEW R.A.M.C. was evacuated sick with ? influenza to the Officers Hospital GEZAINCOURT. — 11 cases were admitted to the Field Ambulance to-day and 3 cases were evacuated to a Casualty Clearing Station, leaving 17 cases remaining in the Field Ambulance.	J.E.P.

1875 Wt. W593/826 1,000,000 4/15 J.B.C. & A. A.D.S.S./Forms/C. 2118.

Instructions regarding War Diaries and Intelligence Summaries are contained in F. S. Regs., Part II. and the Staff Manual respectively. Title Pages will be prepared in manuscript.

WAR DIARY
or
~~INTELLIGENCE SUMMARY~~
(Erase heading not required.)

Army Form C. 2118

Place	Date	Hour	Summary of Events and Information	Remarks and references to Appendices
VACQUERIE	29/11/16	9 p.m.	Lieut Col. T.E. Powell having reported his departure on 10 days leave in England, command was assumed by Capt. G.P. Kidd R.A.M.C. Weather again dull and misty and still very cold. Extra stretchers and blankets were drawn from C.C.S today for equiping the hospital. 1. Off and 29 O.R. were admitted today. 1 Off & 8 O.R. evacuated to C.C.S leaving 38 O.R. remaining.	G.P.K.
"	30/11/16	9. p.m	A.D.M.S visited the unit at 11.0 A.m and talked over arrangements for forming a Divisional Rest Station, Indent forward to C.R.E for material required for building bath house etc. Weather continues dull and cold. 28. O.R. were admitted today. 16. O.R. evacuated to C.C.S ~~leaving~~ 4. O.R. were returned to duty. leaving 46. O.R. remaining.	G.P.K.

G.P. Kidd.
Capt R.A.M.C
O.C. 57th Field Ambulance

1875 Wt. W593/826 1,000,000 4/15 J.B.C. & A. A.D.S.S./Forms/C. 2118.

Dec. 1916

S/

19th Div.

140/90

57th Field Ambulance

Confidential.

Army Form C. 2118

Instructions regarding War Diaries and Intelligence Summaries are contained in F. S. Regs., Part II. and the Staff Manual respectively. Title Pages will be prepared in manuscript.

WAR DIARY
or
INTELLIGENCE SUMMARY
(Erase heading not required.)

Vol 18

Place	Date	Hour	Summary of Events and Information	Remarks and references to Appendices
			of 57th Field Ambulance R A M C for period 1st December 1916 to 31st December 1916 (volume 18)	

O.C. Lt Col R A M C
57th Field Amb

1875 Wt. W593/826 1,000,000 4/15 J.B.C. & A. A.D.S.S./Forms/C. 2118.

57th FIELD AMBULANCE
No. 831
Date 1/1/17
R. A. M. C.

To/ A.D.M.S.
19th Division

I forward you, herewith, War Diary of this unit, for the period 1/12/16 to 31/12/16, for transmission to G.H.Q.

G A Reid Capt
for Lt Col
R.A.M.C.
COMMANDING 57TH FIELD AMBULANCE

Instructions regarding War Diaries and Intelligence Summaries are contained in F. S. Regs., Part II. and the Staff Manual respectively. Title Pages will be prepared in manuscript.

WAR DIARY
or
~~INTELLIGENCE~~ SUMMARY
(Erase heading not required.)

Army Form C. 2118

Place	Date	Hour	Summary of Events and Information	Remarks and references to Appendices
VACQUERIE	1/12/16	9.0 pm	Weather continues fine and cold. Sharp frost again last night. Capt. A. Heathcote reported his departure for temporary duty as M.O. i/c. 10th Worc. Reg. Lieut. J. Hannigan RAMC (T.C) reported his arrival for duty with the unit 16. O.R. admitted. 5. O.R. evacuated to CCS. 9 OR sent to duty. leaving 58. OR. remaining.	GHX
"	2/12/16	9.0 pm	D.D.M.S. V Corps with A.D.M.S. visited the unit in the morning and inspected all the arrangements for forming a D.R.S. Obtained 400 Kilos of straw for palliasses and 400 extra blankets, so that we now have plenty of accommodation. 4. Off. & 33 O.R. admitted. 1. O.R. (Sick) transferred from 59. FA. 4. Off. & 7. O.R. to CCS 4 O.R. to duty. Leaving 81 O.R. remaining.	GHX
"	3/12/16	9.0 pm	A.D.M.S. visited the unit in the morning. Lieut. J. Hannigan reported his departure for duty with 9th Division. Two Nissen huts were delivered today which will still further relieve the strain on the accommodation. Capt. H.R. Dew reported his return to duty from CCS. GEZAINCOURT. 5. Off. & 37 O.R. admitted. 1. O.R. transferred from 59. FA. 5. Off. & 11. O.R. to CCS. 9. O.R. to duty. Leaving 99. O.R. remaining. Weather continues fine & cold.	GHX

1875 Wt. W593/826 1,000,000 4/15 J.B.C. & A. A.D.S.S./Forms/C. 2118.

Instructions regarding War Diaries and Intelligence Summaries are contained in F. S. Regs., Part II. and the Staff Manual respectively. Title Pages will be prepared in manuscript.

WAR DIARY
or
~~INTELLIGENCE SUMMARY~~
(Erase heading not required.)

Army Form C. 2118

Place	Date	Hour	Summary of Events and Information	Remarks and references to Appendices
YACQUERIE	4/12/16	9.0pm	Capt. A.B. Jones RAMC reported his departure for duty with D.D.M.S. 7 Corps. Weather remains fine and cold. 1. Off. & 28. O.R. Admitted. 1 Off. & 14. O.R. to C.C.S. 20. O.R. to Duty. Leaving 93. O.R. remaining.	G.A.K.
"	5/12/16	9.0pm	Lieut. Dawson RAMC (58th F.Amb) reported his arrival for temporary duty during the present shortage of medical Officers. A.D.M.S. visited the unit during the afternoon and expressed himself as satisfied with the progress being made with the work in hand. Three Nissen huts have now been delivered and a fatigue party of R.E. arrived today and commenced erecting same. 29. O.R. admitted. 11. O.R. to CCS 15. O.R. to Duty. Leaving 96. O.R. remaining.	G.A.K.
"	6/12/16	9.0pm	Good progress is being made with the erecting of huts, bathroom etc. No tubs for use as baths have been obtained yet & this is holding back the treatment of scabies cases. 1 Off. & 30. O.R. Admitted. 1 Off. & 12. O.R. to CCS 7 O.R. to duty. 107 O.R. remaining	G.A.K.
"	7/12/16	9.0pm	I visited the A.D.M.S. during the morning to discuss several minor points about the running of the D.R.S. The personnel have now been moved out of the large room over the receiving room and this is now available for patients, accommodating over 100. 15. O.R. Admitted 1. O.R. trans from 59 F.A. 11 O.R. to CCS 6. O.R. to duty. Leaving 106. O.R. remaining	G.A.K.

1875 Wt. W593/826 1,000,000 4/15 J.B.C. & A. A.D.S.S./Forms/C. 2118.

Instructions regarding War Diaries and Intelligence Summaries are contained in F. S. Regs., Part II. and the Staff Manual respectively. Title Pages will be prepared in manuscript.

WAR DIARY
or
INTELLIGENCE SUMMARY
(Erase heading not required.)

Army Form C. 2118

Place	Date	Hour	Summary of Events and Information	Remarks and references to Appendices
YACQUERIE	8/12/16	9.0 pm	A.D.M.S. visited the unit during the morning and inspected all the work in progress – expressing himself satisfied with the same. Some difficulty is being found in getting the necessary amount of material from the R.E. at present. 31. O.R. Admitted. 14. O.R. to C.C.S. 7. O.R. to Duty. Leaving 116. O.R. remaining	[illegible]
"	9/12/16	9.0 pm	Weather has turned wet again and a good deal of rain fell during day. Capt. A. W. Heathcote reported his departure for permanent duty as M.O. i/c 7th E. Lanc. Regiment. 19. O.R. Admitted. 5 O.R. to C.C.S. 7. O.R. to Duty. Leaving 123. O.R. Remaining.	[illegible]
"	10/12/16	9.0 pm	Medical arrangements were amended today as a V Corps Rest Station has now been opened in BEAUVAL. This will take all Scabies cases and also the usual type of rest camp case. The accommodation here will therefore not all be required and more space can now be used for recreation purposes. A.D.M.S. visited the unit during the afternoon. 23. O.R. admitted. 8 O.R. transferred from 89 F.A. 6. O.R. to C.C.S. 9. O.R. to Duty. Leaving 139 O.R. remaining.	[illegible]
"	11/12/16	9.0 pm	All Scabies cases were transferred to D.R.S. this morning. Tubs have now been obtained for the bath room which will now be available for ordinary patients & the personnel. Lieut. J.D. WRIGHT (RAMC – T.C.) reported his arrival for duty with this unit. Lieut Col. T.E. Powell reported his arrival back for duty from 10 days leave of absence in England and reassumed command of the unit. 38. O.R. Admitted. 13. O.R. to C.C.S. 23. O.R. (Suspected Dysentery Carriers) to Infectious C.C.S. 34. O.R. (Scabies) to D.R.S. 15. O.R. to Duty. Leaving 92. O.R. remaining.	[illegible]

Army Form C. 2118

WAR DIARY
or
~~INTELLIGENCE SUMMARY~~

(Erase heading not required.)

Instructions regarding War Diaries and Intelligence Summaries are contained in F. S. Regs., Part II. and the Staff Manual respectively. Title Pages will be prepared in manuscript.

Place	Date	Hour	Summary of Events and Information	Remarks and references to Appendices
VACQUERIE	12/12/16	9.0 pm	A heavy fall of snow took place this morning. – Captain J.P. H[illegible] reported his departure this evening on 10 days leave of absence to England. 17 cases were admitted to the Field Ambulance during the day, 9 cases were transferred to a Casualty Clearing Stn., and 15 cases were returned to duty, leaving 85 cases remaining in the Field Ambulance.	J.E.P.
"	13/12/16	9 pm	It has been damp and misty all day and snow is again falling this evening. Captain A.W. YOUNG R.A.M.C. reported his arrival for duty this evening. – 28 cases were admitted to the Field Ambulance, 9 cases were transferred to a Casualty Clearing Stn. and 22 cases were sent to the Corps Rest Station and 15 cases were returned to duty, leaving 67 cases remaining in the Field Ambulance.	J.E.P.
"	14/12/16	9 pm	The weather continues damp and cold. The A.D.M.S. visited the Field Ambulance this morning, and held a Medical Board on 7 P.B. men attached to the Town Major GEZAINCOURT. – In the afternoon at 2.30 p.m. the A.D.M.S. again came and delivered a lecture to Regimental and junior Medical Officers on their Sanitary duties. – One Officer and 38 other ranks were admitted, one Officer and 9 other ranks were transferred to a Casualty Clearing Station, 17 cases were sent to the Corps Rest Station and 8 cases were returned to duty, leaving 73 cases remaining in the Field Ambulance.	J.E.P.

1875 Wt. W593/826 1,000,000 4/15 J.B.C. & A. A.D.S.S./Forms/C. 2118.

Instructions regarding War Diaries and Intelligence Summaries are contained in F. S. Regs., Part II. and the Staff Manual respectively. Title Pages will be prepared in manuscript.

WAR DIARY
or
~~INTELLIGENCE~~ SUMMARY

(Erase heading not required.)

Army Form C. 2118

Place	Date	Hour	Summary of Events and Information	Remarks and references to Appendices
VACQUERIE	15/12/16	9 p.m.	Slight rain has fallen throughout the day, and the roads and ground generally are very muddy. – 30 cases were admitted to the Field Ambulance during the day – Two cases were transferred to a Casualty Clearing Station and 12 cases to the Corps Rest Station and one man was sent to duty, leaving 86 cases remaining in the Field Ambulance.	J.E.P.
"	16/12/16	9 p.m.	The weather has been damp and foggy. – Billeting certificates for the week were rendered to-day. – 13 cases were admitted to the Field Ambulance during the day. 21 cases were transferred to Casualty Clearing Station and 11 cases to the V Corps Rest Station and 8 men were returned to duty, leaving 59 cases remaining.	J.E.P.
"	17/12/16	9 p.m.	The day has been cold and damp. 21 cases were admitted to the Field Ambulance, 6 cases were transferred to a Casualty Clearing Str. 11 cases to the Corps Rest Str. and 3 cases were returned to duty, leaving 60 cases remaining in the Field Ambulance.	J.E.P.
"	18/12/16	9 p.m.	There was a slight frost last night & the weather continues cold. – The A.D.M.S. visited the Field Ambulance this morning. – 17 cases were admitted to the Field Ambulance – 17 cases were sent to the Corps Rest Station, 10 cases were sent to a Casualty Clearing Str. and 6 cases were returned to duty, leaving 44 cases remaining.	J.E.P.

1875 Wt. W593/826 1,000,000 4/15 J.B.C. & A. A.D.S.S./Forms/C. 2118.

Instructions regarding War Diaries and Intelligence Summaries are contained in F. S. Regs., Part II. and the Staff Manual respectively. Title Pages will be prepared in manuscript.

WAR DIARY
or
~~INTELLIGENCE SUMMARY~~
(Erase heading not required.)

Army Form C. 2118

Place	Date	Hour	Summary of Events and Information	Remarks and references to Appendices
VACQUERIE	19/12/16	9 p.m.	There was a hard frost last night. The D.D.M.S. V Corps visited the Field Ambulance this morning. Captain A.W. YOUNG R.A.M.C. reported his departure this day for temporary duty as M.O. i/c 15th Worcester Regt. The Personnel had a short route march this morning. They have also had baths and a clean issue of underclothing. – There were 23 admissions to the Field Ambulance during the day, no cases were sent to a Casualty Clearing Stn., 9 cases were sent to the Corps Rest Stn., and two cases were returned to duty, leaving 56 cases remaining in the Field Ambulance.	J.E.P.
"	20/12/16	9 p.m.	There was another hard frost last night and to-day has been bright and clear but very cold. – Sent a permanent fatigue party of one N.C.O. and 24 men to No. 29 C.C.S. GEZAINCOURT this morning, under instructions from the A.D.M.S. – One Officer and 17 other ranks were admitted to the Field Ambulance during the day, one Officer and 6 men were transferred to a Casualty Clearing Stn., and six men were sent to the Corps Rest Stn. and 7 men were returned to duty, leaving 54 men remaining in the Field Ambulance.	J.E.P.
"	21/12/16	9 p.m.	There was a thaw last night and it has been raining nearly all day, but it still continues very cold. – The Personnel are still fully employed making a horse standing in front of the Horse trough, building a new Incinerator and a new Oven etc in the Cookhouse. – 27 cases were admitted to the Field Ambulance during the day, 7 cases were transferred to a Casualty Clearing Stn. 8 cases to the Corps Rest Stn. and two cases ~~were~~ returned to duty, leaving 64 cases remaining in the Field Ambulance.	J.E.P.

Instructions regarding War Diaries and Intelligence Summaries are contained in F. S. Regs., Part II. and the Staff Manual respectively. Title Pages will be prepared in manuscript.

WAR DIARY
or
~~INTELLIGENCE SUMMARY~~
(Erase heading not required.)

Army Form C. 2118

Place	Date	Hour	Summary of Events and Information	Remarks and references to Appendices
VACQUERIE	22/12/16	9 p.m.	Heavy rain fell this morning and it has been damp all day, but it is not nearly so cold. – The Personnel are whitewashing the Kitchens, Dining Halls & Billets, assisting local farmers in agricultural work and ~~[illegible]~~ carrying out numerous billet improvements. – 11 cases were admitted to the Field Ambulance during the day, 6 cases were transferred to a Casualty Clearing Station, 6 cases were sent to the Corps Rest Station and 5 cases were returned to duty, leaving 58 cases remaining in the Field Ambulance.	J.E.P.
"	23/12/16	9 p.m.	Heavy rain fell again last night, but it has been very mild during the day. Billeting certificates for the week were rendered to-day. – Work in Billets is being steadily carried on. – One Officer and 21 other ranks were admitted to the Field Ambulance, one Officer and 7 other ranks were evacuated to a Casualty Clearing Station, 16 men were transferred to the Corps Rest Station, and 9 men were returned to duty, leaving 47 men remaining in the Field Ambulance.	J.E.P.
"	24/12/16	9 p.m.	The weather has been fine and mild. – The A.D.M.S. visited the Field Ambulance at 12 Noon. – 11 cases were admitted during the day, and 11 cases were evacuated to a Casualty Clearing Stn. and 2 men were returned to duty, leaving 45 men remaining in the Field Ambulance.	J.E.P.
"	25/12/16	9 p.m.	Christmas Day. – The day has been kept as a holiday as much as possible. – The weather is again very stormy. – Captain G.P. KIDD R.A.M.C. reported his arrival back for duty from 10 days leave of absence in England. – 14 cases were admitted to the Field Ambulance during the day, 9 cases were sent to the Corps Rest Station and 16 were returned to duty, leaving 34 cases remaining in the Field Ambulance.	J.E.P.

1875 Wt. W593/826 1,000,000 4/15 J.B.C. & A. A.D.S.S./Forms/C. 2118.

Instructions regarding War Diaries and Intelligence Summaries are contained in F. S. Regs., Part II. and the Staff Manual respectively. Title Pages will be prepared in manuscript.

WAR DIARY
or
~~INTELLIGENCE SUMMARY~~
(Erase heading not required.)

Army Form C. 2118

Place	Date	Hour	Summary of Events and Information	Remarks and references to Appendices
VACQUERIE	26/12/16	9 p.m.	The weather was fine and mild to-day, but it is raining again to-night. – Ten cases were admitted to the Field Ambulance during the day, 7 cases were evacuated to a Casualty Clearing Station, leaving 37 cases remaining in the Field Ambulance.	J.E.P.
"	27/12/16	9 p.m.	There was a slight frost last night and to-day has been fine but colder. – Went to see the ~~[illegible]~~ A.D.M.S. at his Office this morning. 22 cases were admitted to the Field Ambulance during the day, one case was evacuated to a Casualty Clearing Stn. and 2 cases were returned to duty, leaving 56 cases remaining in the Field Ambulance.	J.E.P.
"	28/12/16	9 p.m.	There was a hard frost last night and to-day is very cold. – The A.D.M.S. proceeded on leave this morning and I am acting for him during his absence. – 28 cases were admitted to the Field Ambulance. 15 cases were evacuated to a Casualty Clearing Stn., 19 cases were sent to the Corps Rest Stn. and 4 cases were returned to duty, leaving 48 cases remaining in the Field Ambulance.	J.E.P.
"	29/12/16	9 p.m.	A thaw has set in to-day and it is raining heavily to-night. Two Officers and 28 men were admitted to the Field Ambulance during the day, 2 Officers and 7 men were evacuated to a Casualty Clearing Stn., 8 cases were sent to the Corps Rest Stn., and 4 men were returned to duty, leaving 57 cases remaining in the Field Ambulance.	J.E.P.

1875 Wt. W593/826 1,000,000 4/15 J.B.C. & A. A.D.S.S./Forms/C. 2118.

Army Form C. 2118

Instructions regarding War Diaries and Intelligence Summaries are contained in F. S. Regs., Part II. and the Staff Manual respectively. Title Pages will be prepared in manuscript.

WAR DIARY
or
~~INTELLIGENCE SUMMARY~~
(Erase heading not required.)

Place	Date	Hour	Summary of Events and Information	Remarks and references to Appendices
VACQUERIE	30/12/16	9 p.m.	The weather continues very wet and the roads are inundated. Billeting certificates for the week were ~~m~~ rendered this morning. Numerous repairs and improvements to the Billets are still being carried out. – 14 cases were admitted to the Field Ambulance during the day, 15 cases were sent to the Corps Rest Stn., and 3 men were returned to duty, leaving 53 cases remaining in the Field Ambulance.	J.E.P.
"	31/12/16	9 p.m.	Rain has again fallen to-day and the condition of the roads is bad. – 25 cases were admitted to the Field Ambulance, 5 cases were evacuated to the Casualty Clearing Stn., and 20 cases were transferred to the Corps Rest Station, and 2 men were returned to duty, leaving 51 cases remaining in the Field Ambulance.	J.E.P.

J.E. Powell
Lieut. Colonel RAMC
O.C. 57th Field Ambulance

1875 Wt. W593/826 1,000,000 4/15 J.B.C. & A. A.D.S.S./Forms/C. 2118.

1917
S

19th Div.

140/9

57th Field Ambulance

Confidential

WAR DIARY

or

~~INTELLIGENCE SUMMARY~~

(*Erase heading not required.*)

Army Form C. 2118

Instructions regarding War Diaries and Intelligence Summaries are contained in F. S. Regs., Part II. and the Staff Manual respectively. Title Pages will be prepared in manuscript.

Vol 19

Place	Date	Hour	Summary of Events and Information	Remarks and references to Appendices
			of 57th Field Ambulance R.A.M.C. for Period 1st January 1917 to 31st January 1917. (Volume 19) J. E. Powell Lt Col 57TH FIELD AMBULANCE	

1875 Wt. W593/826 1,000,000 4/15 J.B.C. & A. A.D.S.S./Forms/C. 2118.

Instructions regarding War Diaries and Intelligence Summaries are contained in F. S. Regs., Part II. and the Staff Manual respectively. Title Pages will be prepared in manuscript.

WAR DIARY

or

~~INTELLIGENCE SUMMARY~~

(Erase heading not required.)

Army Form C. 2118

Place	Date	Hour	Summary of Events and Information	Remarks and references to Appendices
VACQUERIE	1/1/17	9 p.m.	Another wet and rainy day. – ~~[illegible]~~ The closed Incinerator was completed to-day and numerous repairs to the Billets have been carried out. – Captain A.A. SMALLEY, R.A.M.C. reported his departure on leave to England for 10 days, this evening. – 24 cases were admitted to the Field Ambulance during the day, 9 cases were evacuated to a Casualty Clearing Stn., 10 cases were sent to the Corps Rest Stn., and 2 cases were returned to duty, leaving 54 cases remaining in the Field Ambulance.	J.E.P.
"	2/1/17	9 p.m.	The weather continues very wet and stormy. – 7 cases only were admitted to the Field Ambulance during the day, 11 cases were evacuated to a Casualty Clearing Stn., and 11 cases were sent to the Corps Rest Stn., and 2 men were returned to duty, leaving 37 cases remaining in the Field Ambulance.	J.E.P.
"	3/1/17	9 p.m.	Another wet and windy day. – 12 cases were admitted to the Field Ambulance during the day, 4 cases were evacuated to a Casualty Clearing Stn., and 11 cases were sent to the Corps Rest Stn., and one case was sent to duty leaving 33 cases remaining in the Field Ambulance. – The Personnel of the Unit were paid to-day.	J.E.P.
"	4/1/17	9 p.m.	The weather continues very wet. – One Officer and 18 other ranks were admitted to the Field Ambulance during the day, 3 cases were evacuated to a Casualty Clearing Station, 7 cases were transferred to the Corps Rest Stn., and one case was sent to duty, leaving 46 cases remaining in the Field Ambulance.	J.E.P.

1875 Wt. W593/826 1,000,000 4/15 J.B.C. & A. A.D.S.S./Forms/C. 2118.

Army Form C. 2118

Instructions regarding War Diaries and Intelligence Summaries are contained in F. S. Regs., Part II. and the Staff Manual respectively. Title Pages will be prepared in manuscript.

WAR DIARY
or
~~INTELLIGENCE SUMMARY~~
(Erase heading not required.)

Place	Date	Hour	Summary of Events and Information	Remarks and references to Appendices
VACQUERIE	5/1/17	9 p.m.	To-day has been dry and fine but colder. – 28 other ranks were admitted to the Field Ambulance during the day, 12 cases were evacuated to a Casualty Clearing Station, and 9 cases were transferred to the Corps Rest Station and 2 cases were returned to duty, leaving One Officer and 45 other ranks remaining in the Field Ambulance.	J.E.P.
"	6/1/17	9 p.m.	The weather has again been dry but cold. – The D.D.M.S. V Corps visited the Field Ambulance this morning and expressed his satisfaction with everything. 18 cases were admitted to the Field Ambulance during the day, 2 cases were evacuated to a Casualty Clearing Stn. and 10 cases were sent to the Corps Rest Station leaving One Officer and 51 men remaining in the Field Ambulance	J.E.P.
"	7/1/17	9 p.m.	The weather continues dry and cold there was a slight frost last night. – 21 cases were admitted to the Field Ambulance during the day, 8 cases were evacuated to a Casualty Clearing Stn. and 16 men were sent to the Corps Rest Stn. – One officer was returned to duty leaving 48 cases remaining in the Field Ambulance. Orders were received from the A.D.M.S. for this Unit to close here on the 9th inst and march to BEAUQUESNE and on the 10th inst. to move to COIGNEUX and open a Main Dressing Station.	J.E.P.
"	8/1/17	9 p.m.	Some snow and rain has fallen to-day & the weather is very cold. – The afternoon was spent in packing equipment. – 26 cases were admitted during the day, 16 cases were evacuated to a Casualty Clearing Stn., 19 cases were transferred to the Corps Rest Station and 7 cases were returned to duty, leaving 32 cases remaining in the Field Ambulance	J.E.P.

1875 Wt. W593/826 1,000,000 4/15 J.B.C. & A. A.D.S.S./Forms/C. 2118.

Army Form C. 2118

Instructions regarding War Diaries and Intelligence Summaries are contained in F. S. Regs., Part II. and the Staff Manual respectively. Title Pages will be prepared in manuscript.

WAR DIARY
or
~~INTELLIGENCE SUMMARY~~
(Erase heading not required.)

Place	Date	Hour	Summary of Events and Information	Remarks and references to Appendices
BEAUQUESNE	9/1/17	9 p.m.	It has been dry to-day with a cold North wind blowing. This morning One Officer and 3 other ranks were admitted to the Field Ambulance. One Officer and 18 other ranks were evacuated to a Casualty Clearing Stn., 15 cases were transferred to the Corps Rest Stn., and 2 cases were returned to duty, leaving no cases remaining in the Field Ambulance. – The Unit marched off from VACQUERIE at 9.45 a.m. reaching BEAUQUESNE at 3.30 p.m. and going into Billets there.	J.E.P.
COIGNEAUX	10/1/17	9 p.m.	The Unit marched off from BEAUQUESNE at 10.30 a.m. and arrived here at 3.30 p.m. and took over the Corps Main Dressing Station at once from the 95th Field Ambulance. – The day has been dry but very cold.	J.E.P.
"	11/1/17	9 p.m.	To-day is very cold and some snow has fallen. – The Personnel have been employed in whitewashing huts, unpacking and moving stores, preparing a new receiving room and operating room, quarrying chalk and carting chalk, pitching marquees, draining and constructing foundations for new marquees. – One sick and 10 wounded have been admitted to the Field Ambulance. One sick and 8 wounded were evacuated to a Casualty Clearing Stn. leaving two wounded remaining in the Field Ambulance.	J.E.P.
"	12/1/17	9 p.m.	The weather continues very cold and wet, showers of hail and rain have fallen throughout the day. – The Personnel have been employed in quarrying and carting chalk, pitching and camouflaging marquees, draining and constructing foundations for marquees. – The Operating room and special accommodation for gassed cases have been completed. 22 wounded were admitted to the Field Ambulance, 18 wounded were evacuated to Casualty Clearing Stn. and one man died, leaving 5 cases remaining	J.E.P.

1875 Wt. W593/826 1,000,000 4/15 J.B.C. & A. A.D.S.S./Forms/C. 2118.

Instructions regarding War Diaries and Intelligence Summaries are contained in F. S. Regs., Part II. and the Staff Manual respectively. Title Pages will be prepared in manuscript.

WAR DIARY

or

~~INTELLIGENCE SUMMARY~~

(Erase heading not required.)

Army Form C. 2118

Place	Date	Hour	Summary of Events and Information	Remarks and references to Appendices
COIGNEAUX	13/1/17	9 p.m.	The weather continues cold, showers of snow and sleet have again fallen. – The Personnel have again been employed in quarrying chalk constructing foundations for marquees making drains and clearing roads of mud etc. – Issued a third blanket to each man who is sleeping under canvas during this inclement weather. One wounded man only was admitted to the Field Ambulance during the day, no cases were evacuated, leaving six cases remaining in the Field Ambulance.	J.E.P.
"	14/1/17	9 p.m.	The weather continues cold and damp. – The Personnel have been employed on work in connection with the construction of the Corps Main Dressing Station. – The A.D.M.S. Division visited the Field Ambulance this afternoon. – One wounded man only was admitted to the Field Ambulance during the day, 4 cases were evacuated to a Casualty Clearing Stn. leaving 3 cases remaining in the Field Ambulance.	J.E.P.
"	15/1/17	9 p.m.	There was a hard frost last night & to-day has been dry but cold. – The D.D.M.S. Corps visited the Field Ambulance this morning. – The Personnel continue to be fully employed on work for the construction of the Corps Main Dressing Station. – applied to the A.D.M.S. for extra transport to expedite the work. – Reply received that none was available. – 5 wounded cases were admitted during the day, and 5 cases were evacuated to a Casualty Clearing Stn. and one man died leaving 2 cases remaining.	J.E.P.
"	16/1/17	9 p.m.	There was a hard frost again last night & the weather continues very cold but dry. The Personnel continue fully employed at the Corps Main Dressing Stn. – I visited the Sanitary Section in the afternoon. – 3 wounded cases were admitted during the day, no cases were evacuated, 2 cases were returned to duty, leaving 3 wounded remaining in the Field Ambulance.	J.E.P.

Instructions regarding War Diaries and Intelligence Summaries are contained in F. S. Regs., Part II. and the Staff Manual respectively. Title Pages will be prepared in manuscript.

WAR DIARY
or
~~INTELLIGENCE SUMMARY~~
(Erase heading not required.)

Army Form C. 2118

Place	Date	Hour	Summary of Events and Information	Remarks and references to Appendices
COIGNEAUX	17/1/17	9 p.m.	Six inches of snow fell last night & some snow has fallen throughout the day. All the Personnel are still employed in quarrying, draining and laying the foundation for marquees. Four wounded were admitted to the Field Ambulance during the day and 5 cases were evacuated to a Casualty Clearing Stn., leaving two cases remaining in the Field Ambulance.	J.E.P.
"	18/1/17	9 p.m.	The weather continues very cold but dry. 5 wounded other ranks were admitted during the day to the Field Ambulance, 4 cases were evacuated to a Casualty Clearing Station leaving 3 cases remaining in the Field Ambulance. – During the afternoon I visited No. 23 Field Ambulance at BERTRANCOURT to see an improvised apparatus for Oxygen administration in gas cases.	J.E.P.
"	19/1/17	9 p.m.	There was a hard frost last night and the snow is still lying thickly on the ground. – The D.M.S. Fifth Army visited the Main Dressing Station this morning. – One wounded O.R. only was admitted to the Field Ambulance during the day, leaving 4 cases remaining in the Field Ambulance.	J.E.P.
"	20/1/17	9 p.m.	Severe frost continues and the ground is now very hard. – Two cases were admitted to the Field Ambulance during the day, 3 cases were sent to ~~the~~ a Casualty Clearing Station and one case was returned to duty leaving 2 cases remaining in the Field Ambulance. – Billeting certificates for the week were rendered to-day. Four Officers and 62 men from the 2/2 W.R. Field Ambulance of the 62nd Division arrived here to-day at 4 p.m. to be attached to this Unit for instruction.	J.E.P.

1875 Wt. W593/826 1,000,000 4/15 J.B.C. & A. A.D.S.S./Forms/C. 2118.

Army Form C. 2118

WAR DIARY
or
~~INTELLIGENCE SUMMARY~~
(Erase heading not required.)

Instructions regarding War Diaries and Intelligence Summaries are contained in F. S. Regs., Part II. and the Staff Manual respectively. Title Pages will be prepared in manuscript.

Place	Date	Hour	Summary of Events and Information	Remarks and references to Appendices
COIGNEAUX	21/1/17	9 p.m.	Severe frost continues and the ground is now very hard and dry. — Much snow is still lying on the ground. — 5 wounded other ranks were admitted to the Field Ambulance during the day, 2 cases were evacuated to a Casualty Clearing station, leaving 5 cases remaining in the Field Ambulance.	J.E.P.
"	22/1/17	9 p.m.	The hard frost still continues. — Snow fell again in the afternoon. — Received orders from the A.D.M.S. to take over the Advanced Dressing Stations and Posts at HEBUTERNE and SAILLY DELL from the 58th Field Ambulance to-morrow, the 23rd inst., so in the afternoon went to HEBUTERNE and SAILLY DELL with my Bearer Division officer to arrange for taking them over to-morrow. The A.D.M.S. visited the Field Ambulance during the evening. — 5 severely gassed cases were admitted to the Field Ambulance during the night, so I wired for Captain FRIEDLANDER R.A.M.C. the Specialist Gas Officer, and he arrived in the afternoon. — 13 cases were admitted to the Field Ambulance, 10 cases were evacuated to C.C.S. and 3 died, leaving 5 remaining.	J.E.P.
"	23/1/17	9 p.m.	The cold has become still more intense. — The Bearer Division under Captain SMALLEY left this morning and took over charge of the Advanced Dressing Stn. and Posts at HEBUTERNE and SAILLY DELL from the 58th Field Ambulance. I visited the Advanced Dressing Stn. at SAILLY DELL in the afternoon. 14 cases were admitted to the Field Ambulance, 8 cases were evacuated and 2 cases died, leaving 8 cases remaining in the Field Ambulance.	J.E.P.

1875 Wt. W593/826 1,000,000 4/15 J.B.C. & A. A.D.S.S./Forms/C. 2118.

Instructions regarding War Diaries and Intelligence Summaries are contained in F. S. Regs., Part II. and the Staff Manual respectively. Title Pages will be prepared in manuscript.

WAR DIARY
or
~~INTELLIGENCE SUMMARY~~
(Erase heading not required.)

Army Form C. 2118

Place	Date	Hour	Summary of Events and Information	Remarks and references to Appendices
COIGNEAUX	24/1/17	9 p.m.	The severe frost still continues. The Personnel are still employed all day on the work of constructing the Corps Main Dressing Station. – In the afternoon I visited the Advanced Dressing Station at SAILLY DELL also the Advanced Dressing Station at HEBUTERNE and the Soup Kitchen there. – Eight wounded were admitted during the day, 4 cases were evacuated and one case was returned to duty leaving 11 cases slightly wounded remaining in the Field Ambulance.	J.E.P.
"	25/1/17	9 p.m.	The same intense frost continues. – a detachment of one Officer and 18 N.C.Os + men of the 2/2 West Riding Field Ambulance left headquarters this morning for 3 days duty and instruction at the advanced Dressing Station at HEBUTERNE. The Personnel are continuing work on the construction of the Corps Main Dressing Station. – Eleven wounded other ranks were admitted to the Field Ambulance during the day, 6 cases were evacuated and 2 cases were returned to duty leaving 14 cases remaining in the Field Ambulance.	J.E.P.
"	26/1/17	9 p.m.	The Weather continues very cold, hard frost and East Wind. – Work is still continuing on the construction of the Corps Main Dressing Stn. – 13 cases were admitted to the Field Ambulance during the day, 2 men died from wounds and one man was returned to duty, leaving 24 cases remaining in the Field Ambulance.	J.E.P.
"	27/1/17	9 p.m.	The severe cold weather continues. There were 24 degrees of frost last night. – Billeting certificates for the week were rendered this morning. – 16 cases were admitted to the Field Ambulance ~~this morning~~ during the day, 19 cases were evacuated, one man died and one man was returned to duty leaving 13 cases remaining in the Field Ambulance.	J.E.P.

1875 Wt. W593/826 1,000,000 4/15 J.B.C. & A. A.D.S.S./Forms/C. 2118.

Instructions regarding War Diaries and Intelligence Summaries are contained in F. S. Regs., Part II. and the Staff Manual respectively. Title Pages will be prepared in manuscript.

WAR DIARY
or
~~INTELLIGENCE SUMMARY~~
(Erase heading not required.)

Army Form C. 2118

Place	Date	Hour	Summary of Events and Information	Remarks and references to Appendices
COIGNEAUX	28/1/17	9 p.m.	The same intensely cold weather continues. – Work is still being continued on the Corps Rest Station though the ground being now so very hard, it is difficult to carry on and impossible to pitch marquees. – One Officer and 10 men were admitted to the Field Ambulance during the day, one Officer and 5 men were evacuated and 8 men were sent to the Corps Rest Station, leaving 10 men remaining in the Field Ambulance.	J.E.P.
"	29/1/17	9 p.m.	There is no change in the weather. – One section of the 2/2 W.R. Field Ambulance rejoined the Headquarters of their own Unit this morning and were relieved here by another section of the same Unit. – I visited the Advanced Dressing Stations at SAILLY DELL and HEBUTERNE also the Soup Kitchens at the latter place this afternoon. – One Officer and 3 other ranks wounded were admitted during the day, one Officer and 3 O.R. were evacuated, 4 cases were sent to the Corps Rest Stn. and 3 cases were returned to duty, leaving 3 cases remaining in the Field Ambulance.	J.E.P.
"	30/1/17	9 p.m.	Some snow has again fallen throughout the day and evening, the frost continues. – Seven wounded were admitted to the Field Ambulance during the day and 7 cases were evacuated to a Casualty Clearing Station, leaving 3 cases remaining in the Field Ambulance. – Work is being continued on the construction of the Corps Main Dressing Station.	J.E.P.

Instructions regarding War Diaries and Intelligence Summaries are contained in F. S. Regs., Part II. and the Staff Manual respectively. Title Pages will be prepared in manuscript.

WAR DIARY

or

~~INTELLIGENCE SUMMARY~~

(Erase heading not required.)

Army Form C. 2118

Place	Date	Hour	Summary of Events and Information	Remarks and references to Appendices
COIGNEAUX	31/1/17	9 p.m.	The weather continues the same – very hard frost each day. – 8 cases were admitted to the Field Ambulance during the day, 5 cases were evacuated to Casualty Clearing Stn. and one man died leaving 5 cases remaining in the Field Ambulance. – I visited the Advanced Dressing Stations at SAILLY DELL and HEBUTERNE in the afternoon.	J.E.P.

J. E. Powell
Lieut. Colonel R.A.M.C.
O.C. 57th Field Ambulance

1875 Wt. W593/826 1,000,000 4/15 J.B.C. & A. A.D.S.S./Forms/C. 2118.

Feb. 1917

5

19th Div

140/1997

57th Field Ambulance

Instructions regarding War Diaries and Intelligence Summaries are contained in F. S. Regs., Part II. and the Staff Manual respectively. Title Pages will be prepared in manuscript.

WAR DIARY *of No 57 Field Amb 19th Div*
or
~~INTELLIGENCE SUMMARY~~
(Erase heading not required.)

Vol XX — February 1917. *Vol 20*

Army Form C. 2118

Place	Date	Hour	Summary of Events and Information	Remarks and references to Appendices
COIGNEAUX	1/2/17	9 p.m.	There was a very slight thaw this morning, but there is a severe frost again to-night. The A.D.M.S. visited the Field Ambulance this afternoon. One officer and 29 other ranks wounded were admitted during the day. One officer and 31 other ranks were evacuated to Casualty Clearing Stn. One man died leaving 2 cases remaining in the Field Ambulance.	J.E.P.
"	2/2/17	9 p.m.	The severe frost continues. — Work is being continued on the construction of the Corps Main Dressing Stn. but the ground is frozen so hard that the work is being somewhat delayed. — Only one wounded other rank was admitted during the day, one case was discharged to duty and one man died leaving one wounded man remaining in the Field Ambulance.	J.E.P.
"	3/2/17	9 p.m.	The severe cold weather continues without change. — Billeting certificates were rendered for the week this morning. — The personnel of the Unit were paid to-day. — One officer and 4 other ranks wounded were admitted to the Field Ambulance during the day. 3 cases were evacuated to a Casualty Clearing Station, and one officer and one man died of wounds leaving one case remaining in the Field Ambulance.	J.E.P.
"	4/2/17	9 p.m.	There is no change in the weather. — Three other ranks wounded were admitted to the Field Ambulance during the day, and 3 cases were evacuated to a Casualty Clearing Station, leaving one case remaining in the Field Ambulance. A party of one officer & 19 N.C.O.s & men ~~[illegible]~~ of the 2/2 W.R. Field Ambulance were sent up to the Advanced Dressing Stn. this morning for instruction.	J.E.P.

1875 Wt. W593/826 1,000,000 4/15 J.B.C. & A. A.D.S.S./Forms/C. 2118.

Instructions regarding War Diaries and Intelligence Summaries are contained in F. S. Regs., Part II. and the Staff Manual respectively. Title Pages will be prepared in manuscript.

WAR DIARY
or
~~INTELLIGENCE SUMMARY~~
(Erase heading not required.)

Army Form C. 2118

Place	Date	Hour	Summary of Events and Information	Remarks and references to Appendices
COIGNEAUX	5/2/17	9 p.m.	The severe frost continues. Eight cases were admitted to the Field Ambulance during the day, six cases were evacuated to a Casualty Clearing Stn. and one man died, leaving two cases remaining in the Field Ambulance. – Three Nissen huts have been received to-day and are awaiting erection by the R.E. for the use of the R.A.M.C. personnel.	J.E.P.
"	6/2/17	9 p.m.	There is no change in the weather. Work on the Corps Main Dressing Station is being continued. One Officer and four men were admitted to the Field Ambulance during the day, one case was evacuated to a Casualty Clearing Station, leaving One Officer and 5 men remaining in the Field Ambulance.	J.E.P.
"	7/2/17	9 p.m.	There is still no change in the weather – a North Easterly wind is blowing. – I visited the Advanced Dressing Stations at HEBUTERNE this afternoon. 14 cases were admitted to the Field Ambulance during the day, 9 cases were evacuated, leaving One Officer and 10 other ranks remaining in the Field Ambulance.	J.E.P.
"	8/2/17	9 p.m.	The weather continues the same. – The D.M.S. Fifth Army visited the Field Ambulance this morning. – Two other ranks wounded were admitted to the Field Ambulance during the day, 9 cases were evacuated, one man died and two cases were returned to duty leaving One Officer and 2 other ranks remaining in the Field Ambulance. A party of 4 men from the 81st Field Coy R.E. arrived to-day for the erection of the Nissen huts.	J.E.P.

1875 Wt. W593/826 1,000,000 4/15 J.B.C. & A. A.D.S.S./Forms/C. 2118.

Instructions regarding War Diaries and Intelligence Summaries are contained in F. S. Regs., Part II. and the Staff Manual respectively. Title Pages will be prepared in manuscript.

WAR DIARY

or

~~INTELLIGENCE SUMMARY~~

(Erase heading not required.)

Army Form C. 2118

Place	Date	Hour	Summary of Events and Information	Remarks and references to Appendices
COIGNEAUX	9/2/17	9 p.m.	The severe cold weather continues with an East wind to-day. – LIEUT. J. D. WRIGHT R.A.M.C. reported his departure to-day for temporary medical charge of the 9th Bn. Welsh Regiment. Captain T. O'BRIEN reported his departure from Headquarters for duty at the advanced Dressing Stn. in relief of Lieut. WRIGHT. – Two wounded other ranks were admitted to the Field Ambulance during the day, two wounded were evacuated leaving One Officer and 2 other ranks remaining.	J.E.P.
"	10/2/17	9 p.m.	There is no change in the weather. – The A.D.M.S. visited the Field Ambulance in the afternoon. – Three sick and 18 wounded other ranks were admitted during the day, 15 cases were evacuated and one case was returned to duty, leaving One Officer and 7 other ranks remaining in the Field Ambulance. – Billeting certificates for the week were rendered to-day.	J.E.P.
"	11/2/17	9 p.m.	The weather is a little milder to-day but it is still freezing this evening. – The D.D.M.S. V Corps visited the main Dressing Station this afternoon and expressed his satisfaction with all he saw. – One Officer and 8 wounded men were admitted during the day, One Officer and 11 men were evacuated to a Casualty Clearing Stn. one man died & one man was returned to duty, leaving 3 cases remaining in the Field Ambulance.	J.E.P.

1875 Wt. W593/826 1,000,000 4/15 J.B.C. & A. A.D.S.S./Forms/C. 2118.

Army Form C. 2118

WAR DIARY
or
~~INTELLIGENCE SUMMARY~~
(Erase heading not required.)

Instructions regarding War Diaries and Intelligence Summaries are contained in F. S. Regs., Part II. and the Staff Manual respectively. Title Pages will be prepared in manuscript.

Place	Date	Hour	Summary of Events and Information	Remarks and references to Appendices
COIGNEAUX	12/2/17	9 p.m.	The weather has become much milder and it is thawing this evening. – Three wounded other ranks were admitted during the day, two cases were evacuated, leaving 4 cases remaining in the Field Ambulance. – Work is being continued on the construction of the Corps Main Dressing Stn. and erection of Nissen huts.	J.E.P.
"	13/2/17	9 p.m.	There was a frost again last night, but it is thawing once more to-day & the weather is certainly milder than it has been for some time. – The D.D.M.S. XIII Corps visited the Main Dressing Station this morning and expressed his pleasure at the amount of work carried out there. – One Officer and two other ranks were admitted to the Field Ambulance, 6 other ranks were evacuated, leaving One Officer remaining.	J.E.P.
"	14/2/17	9 p.m.	There is a frost each night now, but it thaws during the day. – I visited the Advanced Dressing Stations at SAILLY DELL and HEBUTERNE this afternoon and saw the work being carried out in the cellars near the HEBUTERNE (N) A.D.S. to increase the accommodation there. – This cellar will take 20 stretcher cases and 15 sitting cases. – Four other ranks wounded were admitted to the Field Ambulance, 3 cases were evacuated to C.C.S. and one man died, leaving One Officer remaining.	J.E.P.
"	15/2/17	9 p.m.	It continues to freeze at night and thaw by day. – Captain YOUNG R.A.M.C. proceeded to the Advanced Dressing Station to-day for duty in place of Captain O'BRIEN. – I called at the Office of the A.D.M.S. in the morning. – Four wounded other ranks were admitted to the Field Ambulance, one case was evacuated to the Special Operating Centre AUTHIE, leaving One Officer and 3 other ranks remaining.	J.E.P.

1875 Wt. W593/826 1,000,000 4/15 J.B.C. & A. A.D.S.S./Forms/C. 2118.

Instructions regarding War Diaries and Intelligence Summaries are contained in F. S. Regs., Part II. and the Staff Manual respectively. Title Pages will be prepared in manuscript.

WAR DIARY
or
~~INTELLIGENCE SUMMARY~~
(Erase heading not required.)

Army Form C. 2118

Place	Date	Hour	Summary of Events and Information	Remarks and references to Appendices
COIGNEAUX	16/2/17	9 p.m.	There was a hard frost last night, but it has thawed all day and some rain has fallen this evening. – Twelve other ranks wounded were admitted during the day, 8 cases were evacuated leaving one Officer and and 7 other ranks remaining in the Field Ambulance.	J.E.P.
"	17/2/17	9 p.m.	The day has been damp and foggy and heavy rain fell this evening – the ground is already very heavy and muddy. – I visited the Advanced Dressing Stations at SAILLY DELL and HEBUTERNE in the afternoon, work is being carried out to increase the accommodation for stretcher cases at HEBUTERNE (North). Billeting certificates for the week were rendered to-day. ~~[illegible]~~ One Officer and 5 other ranks were admitted during the day and One Officer and 9 other ranks were evacuated, and 2 cases were returned to duty, leaving One Officer & One man remaining.	J.E.P.
"	18/2/17	9 p.m.	The weather continues damp and foggy. – Captain T. O'BRIEN was discharged to duty this day. – 3 other ranks wounded were admitted to the Field Ambulance to-day. One Officer was returned to duty, leaving four cases remaining in the Field Ambulance.	J.E.P.
"	19/2/17	9 p.m.	The weather continues damp and foggy. – Orders from the A.D.M.S. were received this afternoon for the Unit to move to LOUVENCOURT at Noon on the 21st inst. – The Bearer Division will be relieved at HEBUTERNE to-morrow the 20th inst. by the 93rd Field Ambulance, the 95th Field Ambulance relieving this unit at the Main Dressing Station. – Two wounded other ranks were admitted during the day, two cases were evacuated, and one case returned to duty, leaving 3 cases remaining.	J.E.P.

1875 Wt. W593/826 1,000,000 4/15 J.B.C. & A. A.D.S.S./Forms/C. 2118.

Instructions regarding War Diaries and Intelligence Summaries are contained in F. S. Regs., Part II. and the Staff Manual respectively. Title Pages will be prepared in manuscript.

WAR DIARY
or
~~INTELLIGENCE SUMMARY~~
(Erase heading not required.)

Army Form C. 2118

Place	Date	Hour	Summary of Events and Information	Remarks and references to Appendices
COIGNEAUX	20/2/17	9 p.m.	The weather continues damp and foggy. – The Bearer Division was relieved by a detachment of the 93rd Field Ambulance and returned from HEBUTERNE to Headquarters. – Six cases were admitted to the Field Ambulance and six cases were evacuated leaving three cases remaining.	J.E.P.
LOUVENCOURT	21/2/17	9 p.m.	There is no change in the weather which continues very damp and misty. – Billeting certificates were rendered up to date at COIGNEAUX. The Unit handed over the Main Dressing Station at COIGNEAUX to No. 95 Field Ambulance at 12 Noon and marched to LOUVENCOURT where we took over the Field Ambulance site and opened up for the reception of sick. – One wounded other rank was admitted prior to 12 Noon, and 3 wounded were evacuated and one case returned to duty, leaving no cases remaining.	J.E.P.
"	22/2/17	9 p.m.	Rain has fallen off & on throughout the day & the condition of the roads is very bad. The Personnel have been employed throughout the day in preparing the huts etc. for the reception of the sick also in cleaning up and draining the surroundings which are very bad. – 15 other ranks sick were admitted to the Field Ambulance, one case of Measles was evacuated leaving 14 cases remaining in the Field Ambulance.	J.E.P.
"	23/2/17	9 p.m.	The weather is damp and misty. – Work is being continued on the improvement of the surroundings. – Under orders from the A.D.M.S. one N.C.O. & 19 men were sent as a permanent fatigue party to the A.D.S. at COLINCAMPS. – 57 other ranks sick were admitted to the Field Ambulance during the day. 14 cases were evacuated to C.C.S., 6 cases were transferred to No. 22 Field Ambulance, 18 cases were sent to the Corps Rest Station, leaving 33 cases remaining in the Field Ambulance.	J.E.P.

Instructions regarding War Diaries and Intelligence Summaries are contained in F. S. Regs., Part II. and the Staff Manual respectively. Title Pages will be prepared in manuscript.

WAR DIARY
or
~~INTELLIGENCE SUMMARY~~
(Erase heading not required.)

Army Form C. 2118

Place	Date	Hour	Summary of Events and Information	Remarks and references to Appendices
LOUVENCOURT	24/2/17	9 p.m.	The weather continues damp and misty. – Billeting certificates for the week were rendered to-day ~~and~~ Two Officers and 35 other ranks sick were admitted during the day. Two Officers and 17 O.R. were evacuated to a Casualty Clearing Stn. six cases were transferred to the Corps Rest Station and 2 cases (scabies) were sent to the 22nd Field Ambulance and six cases were returned to duty, leaving 37 cases remaining in the Field Ambulance. The A.D.M.S. visited the Field Ambulance this afternoon.	J.E.P.
"	25/2/17	9 p.m.	There is no change in the weather. – Orders were received from the A.D.M.S. for the Bearer Division to hold itself in readiness to move at an hours notice. – 36 cases were admitted to the Field Ambulance during the day. 21 cases were evacuated to a Casualty Clearing Stn. of these 21 13 were cases of suspected dysentery carriers being sent in for ~~[illegible]~~ examination, 13 cases were sent to the Corps Rest Station, 2 cases of scabies were sent to the 22nd Field Ambulance and 2 cases were returned to duty, leaving 35 cases remaining in the Field Ambulance	J.E.P.
"	26/2/17	9 p.m.	The day has been fine and clear and mild but the mud and the condition of the roads continues very bad. – Received orders from the A.D.M.S. for the Bearer Division of this unit to move at 9 a.m. to-morrow morning to COLINCAMPS to take over the A.D.S. there from No. 59 Field Ambulance. – Two Officers and 23 other ranks were admitted to the Field Ambulance during the day. Two Officers and 11 other ranks were evacuated to a Casualty Clearing Stn., 14 cases were sent to the Corps Rest Stn., and 5 cases were returned to duty, leaving 28 cases remaining in the Field Ambulance.	J.E.P.

1875 Wt. W593/826 1,000,000 4/15 J.B.C. & A. A.D.S.S./Forms/C. 2118.

Army Form C. 2118

Instructions regarding War Diaries and Intelligence Summaries are contained in F. S. Regs., Part II. and the Staff Manual respectively. Title Pages will be prepared in manuscript.

WAR DIARY
or
~~INTELLIGENCE SUMMARY~~
(Erase heading not required.)

Place	Date	Hour	Summary of Events and Information	Remarks and references to Appendices
LOUVENCOURT	27/2/17	9 pm.	The weather continues fine and mild, but the mud is not diminishing yet. – The Bearer Division of this Unit under Captain A.A. SMALLEY left at 9 a.m. to-day for COLINCAMPS Advanced Dressing Stn. to relieve and assist No. 59 Field Ambulance. I visited the advanced Dressing Station at COLINCAMPS in the afternoon. Fortyseven cases were admitted during the day, 16 cases were evacuated to a Casualty Clearing Stn. 9 cases were sent to the Corps Rest Stn. and 5 cases were returned to duty, leaving 45 cases remaining in the Field Ambulance.	J.E.P.
"	28/2/17	9 pm.	The day has been damp and misty. – Sixtyone cases were admitted to the Field Ambulance during the day, ten cases were evacuated to a Casualty Clearing Stn. twelve cases were sent to the Corps Rest station and two cases were returned to duty, leaving 82 cases remaining in the Field Ambulance.	J.E.P.

J.E. Powell
Lieut Colonel RAMC
O.C. 57th Field Ambulance

1875 Wt. W593/826 1,000,000 4/15 J.B.C. & A. A.D.S.S./Forms/C. 2118.

Mar. 1917.

S

19th Div.

[illegible]

57th Field Ambulance

57 Fd amb
Vol 21

Army Form C. 2118

Instructions regarding War Diaries and Intelligence Summaries are contained in F. S. Regs., Part II. and the Staff Manual respectively. Title Pages will be prepared in manuscript.

WAR DIARY
or
~~INTELLIGENCE SUMMARY~~
(Erase heading not required.)

Place	Date	Hour	Summary of Events and Information	Remarks and references to Appendices
LOUVENCOURT	1/3/17	9 p.m.	The weather has been mild, fine and clear. — Under orders from the A.D.M.S. 19th Division, one Tent Subdivision with two Officers left this morning for duty at the Corps Rest Station at VAUCHELLES. — I recalled Captain O'BRIEN from the Advanced Dressing Stn. for duty at Headquarters. — One Officer and 33 other ranks were admitted to the Field Ambulance during the day, one Officer and 17 other ranks were evacuated to a Casualty Clearing Stn., and 27 cases were sent to the Corps Rest Stn., and six cases returned to duty, leaving 65 cases remaining in the Field Ambulance.	J.E.P.
"	2/3/17	9 p.m.	There was a slight frost last night, but to-day has been fine and clear. — Orders from the A.D.M.S. were received for the Bearer Division to hand over the Advanced Dressing Stn. at COLINCAMPS to the 31st Division to-morrow & to return to Headquarters. — 28 cases were admitted to the Field Ambulance during the day, 16 cases were evacuated to a Casualty Clearing Stn., and 22 cases were sent to the Corps Rest Stn. and 5 cases were returned to duty leaving 50 cases remaining in the Field Ambulance.	J.E.P.
"	3/3/17	9 p.m.	There was another slight frost last night, to-day is fine and clear. — The Bearer Division returned to Headquarters from the COLINCAMPS Advanced Dressing Stn. this afternoon. — One Officer and 7 other ranks were admitted during the day, one Officer and 15 other ranks were evacuated to a Casualty Clearing Stn., 9 cases were sent to the Corps Rest Stn., and 5 cases were returned to duty, leaving ~~..~~ 28 cases remaining in the Field Ambulance.	J.E.P.

1875 Wt. W593/826 1,000,000 4/15 J.B.C. & A. A.D.S.S./Forms/C. 2118.

Instructions regarding War Diaries and Intelligence Summaries are contained in F. S. Regs., Part II. and the Staff Manual respectively. Title Pages will be prepared in manuscript.

WAR DIARY
or
~~INTELLIGENCE SUMMARY~~
(Erase heading not required.)

Army Form C. 2118

Place	Date	Hour	Summary of Events and Information	Remarks and references to Appendices
LOUVENCOURT	4/3/17	9 p.m.	There was a hard frost last night but to-day is fine and clear and the road is drying up a little. — 25 cases were admitted to the Field Ambulance during the day, 16 cases were evacuated to a Casualty Clearing Station and 5 cases were returned to duty, leaving 32 cases remaining in the Field Ambulance.	J.E.P.
"	5/3/17	9 p.m.	There was a heavy fall of snow last night, but it has been thawing to-day. – The personnel of the Unit were paid to-day. – One Officer and 19 men were admitted to the Field Ambulance during the day. One Officer & 4 men were sent to a Casualty Clearing Stn., 4 cases were sent to the Corps Rest Stn. and 7 cases ~~were~~ returned to duty, leaving 33 cases remaining in the Field Ambulance.	J.E.P.
"	6/3/17	9 p.m.	The thaw continues, and the condition of the roads is again bad. – The A.D.M.S. 19th Division visited the Field Ambulance this morning and expressed his pleasure with everything he saw. – Thirty two cases were admitted to the Field Ambulance during the day, 13 cases were evacuated to a Casualty Clearing Station and 11 cases were sent to the Corps Rest Stn. and 4 cases were returned to duty, leaving 37 cases remaining in the Field Ambulance.	J.E.P.
"	7/3/17	9 p.m.	The weather has been damp, misty and cold. 25 cases were admitted to the Field Ambulance during the day, 2 cases were evacuated to a Casualty Clearing Stn., 6 cases were sent to the V Corps Rest Stn., and 6 cases were returned to duty, leaving 48 cases remaining in the Field Ambulance.	J.E.P.

1875 Wt. W593/826 1,000,000 4/15 J.B.C. & A. A.D.S.S./Forms/C. 2118.

Instructions regarding War Diaries and Intelligence Summaries are contained in F. S. Regs., Part II. and the Staff Manual respectively. Title Pages will be prepared in manuscript.

WAR DIARY

or

~~INTELLIGENCE SUMMARY~~

(Erase heading not required.)

Army Form C. 2118

Place	Date	Hour	Summary of Events and Information	Remarks and references to Appendices
LOUVENCOURT	8/3/17	9 p.m.	There was a hard frost last night and snow with a strong N.E. wind to-day. The roads have dried up very well as a result of the wind. – Orders were received from the A.D.M.S. 19th Division for the Unit to close here at 12 Noon to-day and to march to-morrow under the orders of the G.O.C. 56th Brigade. – 44 cases were admitted to the Field Ambulance during the day, 18 cases were evacuated to a Casualty Clearing Stn. and 42 cases were sent to the Corps Rest Stn. and 32 cases were returned to duty, leaving no cases remaining.	J.E.P.
BRETEL	9/3/17	9 p.m.	There was a hard frost again last night and snow fell during the day. – The Unit marched off at 9.45 a.m. and arrived here at 2 p.m. – One case was admitted to the Field Ambulance during the day and evacuated to No. 1 New Zealand Stationary Hospital, leaving no cases remaining.	J.E.P.
LIGNY SUR CANCHE	10/3/17	9 p.m.	There was a thaw last night and the roads were heavy and muddy. – The Unit marched off at 10.30 a.m. and arrived here at 4.30 p.m. – Seven cases were admitted to the Field Ambulance during the day, 5 cases were evacuated to a Casualty Clearing Stn. and two cases were sent to the Corps Rest Stn. leaving no cases remaining.	J.E.P.
"	11/3/17	9 p.m.	The Unit is resting here to-day. The day is mild and fine. 13 cases were admitted to the Field Ambulance during the day and 13 cases were evacuated leaving no cases remaining. – Three cases of measles have occurred in the Unit – all sanitary precautions have been taken.	J.E.P.

1875 Wt. W593/826 1,000,000 4/15 J.B.C. & A. A.D.S.S./Forms/C. 2118.

Instructions regarding War Diaries and Intelligence Summaries are contained in F. S. Regs., Part II. and the Staff Manual respectively. Title Pages will be prepared in manuscript.

WAR DIARY
or
~~INTELLIGENCE SUMMARY~~

(Erase heading not required.)

Army Form C. 2118

Place	Date	Hour	Summary of Events and Information	Remarks and references to Appendices
SIRACOURT	12/3/17	9 p.m.	The weather is damp and mild. The Unit marched off at 8.30 a.m. and arrived here at SIRACOURT at 12.30 p.m. – During the day ten cases were admitted to the Field Ambulance and ten cases were evacuated to No 12. Stationary Hospital leaving no cases remaining in the Field Ambulance.	J.E.P.
SAINS LES PERNES	13/3/17	9 p.m.	The weather continues damp and mild with a thick mist this morning. The Unit marched off at 8.30 a.m. and arrived here at 2.15 p.m. after a twelve mile march. – Sixteen cases were admitted to the Field Ambulance during the day & 16 cases were evacuated to No. 12 Stationary Hospital leaving no cases remaining.	J.E.P.
"	14/3/17	9 p.m.	Lt. Col. J. E. Powell having proceeded today on ten days special leave of absence in England, temporary command was assumed by Capt. G. P. Kidd RAMC. The unit rested today and was visited during the afternoon by G.O.C. 56th Inf. Brigade. One more case of measles occurred in the unit today and was evacuated. Fourteen (14) cases were admitted to the Field Ambulance during the day and evacuated to No. 12. Stationary Hospital	G.P.K.
LIVOSSART	15/3/17	9 p.m.	The unit marched at 10.0 A.M. and arrived here at midday after a short march. We expect to rest here for several days and the billets are good. Ten (10) cases were admitted to the Field Ambulance during the day and evacuated to CCS LILLERS. The men have marched well throughout the past week, only two falling out through sore feet.	G.P.K.

1875 Wt. W593/826 1,000,000 4/15 J.B.C. & A. A.D.S.S./Forms/C. 2118.

Army Form C. 2118

Instructions regarding War Diaries and Intelligence Summaries are contained in F. S. Regs., Part II. and the Staff Manual respectively. Title Pages will be prepared in manuscript.

WAR DIARY
or
~~INTELLIGENCE SUMMARY~~

(Erase heading not required.)

Place	Date	Hour	Summary of Events and Information	Remarks and references to Appendices
KIVOSSART	16/3/17	9. pm	Unit rested here today. Men occupied in washing and repacking waggons. Capt. T.A. O'Brien RAMC reported his departure for duty as M.O. i/c 8 Gloster Reg. Capt. J.L. Cochrane MC RAMC reported his arrival for duty with this unit. No cases were admitted or evacuated today.	[illegible initials]
"	17/3/17	9. pm	Unit rested again here today – the weather being fine and warm. Orders received for continuation of the march tomorrow – billetting party went on this evening to new area. 37. Cases were admitted during the day and evacuated to CCS LILLERS.	[illegible initials]
ISBERGUES	18/3/17	9. pm	Unit marched off at 8.30 AM and arrived here at 2.30 pm. Weather again fine and warm. Men marched well again – no one falling out. Orders received for move again tomorrow morning to HAZEBROUCK area. 18. Cases admitted during the day and evacuated to CCS AIRE.	[illegible initials]
LYNDE	19/3/17	9. pm	Unit marched off at 9.0 AM. and arrived here at 2.0 pm. Weather again fine though cold. Billets again very good. 24. Cases were admitted during the day and evacuated to CCS AIRE	[illegible initials]
RECQUES	20/3/17	9. pm	Unit marched off at 8.0 AM and arrived here at 5.30 pm after a march of nearly 20 miles. The men marched very well indeed under trying conditions as there was a strong head wind and rain & sleet for the greater part of the way. 15. Cases were admitted during the day – 14. being evacuated to No. 10. Stat. Hosp ST. OMER and 1. (German measles) to No. 7. Stat. Hosp MALASSISSE.	[illegible initials]

Instructions regarding War Diaries and Intelligence Summaries are contained in F. S. Regs., Part II. and the Staff Manual respectively. Title Pages will be prepared in manuscript.

WAR DIARY
or
~~INTELLIGENCE SUMMARY~~
(Erase heading not required.)

Army Form C. 2118

Place	Date	Hour	Summary of Events and Information	Remarks and references to Appendices
RECQUES	21/3/17	9. pm	Opened a small Hospital for 20 stretcher cases in a school building. Issued medical arrangements through the Brigade for the collection of sick etc. in the Brigade area. The nine cases admitted during the day – 1 Evacuated to Stat. H. [illegible] and 8. remained.	[illegible]
"	22/3/17	9. pm	G.O.C 56th Inf. Brigade visited the unit during the morning. Weather still very cold with some snow and rain. Arrangements have now been made for dealing with all cases including Eye, Dental & Scabies cases. ADMS visited the unit during the afternoon and expressed himself as satisfied with all arrangements made. 9. Cases admitted during the day – 1 Evacuated to Stat. H.P.	[illegible]
"	23/3/17	9/pm	Arrangements have been now made for baths in this area and all men of the unit were bathed this morning. One barn in the village was opened as a ward for slight cases today in addition to the building already occupied. This gives considerably more accommodation. 20. Cases were admitted during the day and 14. Evacuated to C.C.S. leaving 14. remaining.	(initials)
"	24/3/17	9/pm	Weather still cold, though fine. Some frost last night. The two barns being now fitted up for wards, this gives accommodation for about 50 cases. Capt. A. W. Young (?) has been detailed as Sanitary Officer for the area and is carrying out daily inspection of units sanitary arrangements. 1. Officer & 25 O.R. admitted during the day. 1. Off & 8. O.R. Evacuated to C.C.S. leaving 31. O.R. remaining.	(initials)

1875 Wt. W593/826 1,000,000 4/15 J.B.C. & A. A.D.S.S./Forms/C. 2118.

Army Form C. 2118

Instructions regarding War Diaries and Intelligence Summaries are contained in F. S. Regs., Part II. and the Staff Manual respectively. Title Pages will be prepared in manuscript.

WAR DIARY
or
~~INTELLIGENCE SUMMARY~~
(Erase heading not required.)

Place	Date	Hour	Summary of Events and Information	Remarks and references to Appendices
RECQUES	25/3/17	9. pm	Weather still fine but cold. Routine morning parades have now been started and kit inspections are being held in order to get the unit completely reequipped before moving up to the line again. 36. O.R. admitted during the day. 10. Evacuated to Stat. HP. 1. to Duty. 1. Cases of German measles admitted & evacuated – leaving 51. O.R. remaining.	GFK
"	26/3/17	9. pm	The morning was occupied with kit inspections and physical drill and the Bearer Div. sent for a route march in the afternoon. 34. O.R. admitted during the day. 24. Evacuated to CCS 8. to Duty. leaving 53 remaining.	GFK
"	27/3/17	9. pm	Weather still very cold and uncertain with some snow. Lt. Col. J.E. Powell reported his arrival back for duty from leave in England and re-assumed command of the unit. 1. Off. & 34. O.R. admitted during the day. 1. Off. & 26 O.R. evacuated. 2. Cases of German measles evacuated to No. 7 Stat. HP 5. O.R. to duty leaving 56. O.R. remaining.	GFK
"	28/3/17	9 pm	Weather has been fine but cold, there was some frost last night. – 28 cases were admitted to the Field Ambulance and 24 cases were evacuated to No. 10 Stationary Hospital and 9 cases were returned to duty, leaving 51 cases remaining. Following an Inspection Parade the men were exercised in squad & Company drill. – A Kit inspection was also held. – I made a complete inspection of the Hospital, billets & transport this morning.	J.E.P.

1875 Wt. W593/826 1,000,000 4/15 J.B.C. & A. A.D.S.S./Forms/C. 2118.

Instructions regarding War Diaries and Intelligence Summaries are contained in F. S. Regs., Part II. and the Staff Manual respectively. Title Pages will be prepared in manuscript.

WAR DIARY
or
~~INTELLIGENCE SUMMARY~~
(Erase heading not required.)

Army Form C. 2118

Place	Date	Hour	Summary of Events and Information	Remarks and references to Appendices
RECQUES	29/3/17	9pm	Heavy rain has fallen throughout the morning. – No parades or drill was possible in the morning. One Officer and 28 other ranks were admitted to the Field Ambulance during the day, one Officer and 18 other ranks were evacuated to No. 10 Stationary Hospital and 4 cases were returned to duty, leaving 57 cases remaining in the Field Ambulance.	J.E.P.
"	30/3/17	9pm	Heavy showers of rain and hail fell throughout the morning, but the weather cleared later. – 39 cases were admitted to the Field Ambulance during the day. 29 cases were ~~admitted to~~ evacuated to No. 10 Stationary Hospital and 10 cases were returned to duty leaving 57 cases remaining in the Field Ambulance.	J.E.P.
"	31/3/17	9pm	The weather continues cold and showery with fine intervals but with a strong S.W. Wind blowing. 23 cases were admitted to the Field Ambulance during the day, 19 cases were evacuated to No. 10 Stationary Hospital and 6 cases were returned to duty, leaving 55 cases remaining in the Field Ambulance. – The Personnel following an Inspection Parade were exercised in Physical drill in the morning and taken for a route march in the afternoon. Orders have been received from the 56th Brigade, that this Unit will march with the Brigade from the present area on Monday 2nd April	J.E.P.

J. E. Powell
Lieut. Colonel RAMC
O.C. 57th Field Ambulance

1875 Wt. W593/826 1,000,000 4/15 J.B.C. & A. A.D.S.S./Forms/C. 2118.

April. 1917.

19th Div.

140/2086

No. 57. F. A.

Instructions regarding War Diaries and Intelligence Summaries are contained in F. S. Regs., Part II. and the Staff Manual respectively. Title Pages will be prepared in manuscript.

WAR DIARY
or
~~INTELLIGENCE SUMMARY~~
(Erase heading not required.)

Army Form C. 2118

57 Fd Amb
Vol 22

Place	Date	Hour	Summary of Events and Information	Remarks and references to Appendices
RECQUES	1/4/17	9 p.m.	The weather continues cold with showers of rain and snow. — 33 cases were admitted to the Field Ambulance during the day, and 66 cases were evacuated to No. 10 Stationary Hospital and 6 cases were returned to duty, leaving 16 cases remaining. — The increase in evacuations is due to the necessity of closing the Field Ambulance prior to the move to-morrow. — The Personnel are employed in closing the Unit and packing wagons etc.	J.E.P.
WIZERNES	2/4/17	9 p.m.	There was a hard frost last night and a heavy snowstorm this afternoon. The Unit marched from RECQUES at 9.30 a.m. and arrived in billets here at 2 p.m. Two Officers and 45 other ranks were admitted to the Field Ambulance during the day, & two Officers and 50 other ranks were evacuated and 11 cases were returned to duty, leaving no cases remaining in the Field Ambulance.	J.E.P.
"	3/4/17	9 p.m.	There was a very heavy fall of snow last night and also this morning, but the afternoon was fine & clear. — Twenty three cases were admitted to the Field Ambulance during the day and 23 cases were evacuated, leaving no cases remaining in the Field Ambulance.	J.E.P.
LA WATTINE	4/4/17	9 p.m.	The morning was damp with showers of rain, but the afternoon was fine & clear. — The Unit marched at 10.50 a.m. from WIZERNES and arrived here at 4 p.m. and opened up for the reception of sick. — Two Officers and 19 other ranks were admitted during the day and also evacuated leaving no cases remaining in the Field Ambulance.	J.E.P.

1875 Wt. W593/826 1,000,000 4/15 J.B.C. & A. A.D.S.S./Forms/C. 2118.

Instructions regarding War Diaries and Intelligence Summaries are contained in F. S. Regs., Part II. and the Staff Manual respectively. Title Pages will be prepared in manuscript.

WAR DIARY
or
~~INTELLIGENCE SUMMARY~~
(Erase heading not required.)

Army Form C. 2118

Place	Date	Hour	Summary of Events and Information	Remarks and references to Appendices
LA WATTINE	5/4/17	9 p.m.	There was a hard frost last night and to-day has been cold but fine. – This village is the dirtiest the Unit has ever been billeted in, and the Personnel have been employed all day in cleaning up the surroundings. – The G.O.C. 57th Infantry Brigade visited the Field Ambulance this morning. – Four cases only were admitted during the day and four cases were evacuated leaving no cases remaining in the Field Ambulance.	J.E.P.
"	6/4/17	9 p.m.	The weather continues cold with a N.W. wind and some light showers of rain. Nine cases were admitted to the Field Ambulance during the day, 5 cases were evacuated to No. 10 Stationary Hospital, leaving 4 cases remaining in the Field Ambulance. – The Personnel have been employed on cleaning the roads and yards of the village, also on drainage and general sanitation.	J.E.P.
"	7/4/17	9 p.m.	There was a fall of snow last night and some frost also. – It is cold and showery to-day. The Personnel are still fully employed on cleaning roads and farm yards, removing manure to the fields and drainage etc. – Seventeen cases were admitted to the Field Ambulance during the day, 8 cases were evacuated to No. 10. Stationary Hospital leaving 13 cases remaining in the Field Ambulance. – There was a parade of men for inoculation with T.A.B. vaccine this afternoon.	J.E.P.
"	8/4/17	9 p.m.	There was frost again last night but to-day has been very fine with bright sunshine. Fourteen cases were admitted to the Field Ambulance during the day and 14 cases were evacuated, and one case was returned to duty, leaving 12 cases remaining in the Field Ambulance.	J.E.P.

1875 Wt. W593/826 1,000,000 4/15 J.B.C. & A. A.D.S.S./Forms/C. 2118.

Army Form C. 2118

Instructions regarding War Diaries and Intelligence Summaries are contained in F. S. Regs., Part II. and the Staff Manual respectively. Title Pages will be prepared in manuscript.

WAR DIARY
or
~~INTELLIGENCE SUMMARY~~
(Erase heading not required.)

Place	Date	Hour	Summary of Events and Information	Remarks and references to Appendices
LA WATTINE	9/4/17	9 p.m.	It has rained heavily last night and to-day is cold and cloudy with some showers. — Eleven cases were admitted to the Field Ambulance during the day, eight cases were evacuated and one case was returned to duty, leaving 14 cases remaining in the Field Ambulance. — Following an inspection parade the Personnel were exercised in Squad and Company drill during the morning. — Route march & football in the afternoon.	J.E.P.
"	10/4/17	9 p.m.	The weather continues very cold. there was a heavy fall of snow last night, and showers of snow have fallen during the day. — Captain H.R. DEW R.A.M.C. reported his departure for England this day on termination of his contract. — Captain J.L. COCHRANE R.A.M.C. also reported his departure this day on 14 days leave to England. — Sixteen cases were admitted to the Field Ambulance during the day, 9 cases were evacuated and 2 cases were returned to duty, leaving 19 cases remaining in the Field Ambulance.	J.E.P.
"	11/4/17	9 p.m.	There was frost again last night and to-day is a cold and stormy day with some showers. — Following the usual inspection Parade the Personnel were exercised in Physical Drill and also taken for a Route march. — Eleven cases were admitted to the Field Ambulance, 10 cases were evacuated and 2 cases were returned to duty, leaving 18 cases remaining in the Field Ambulance.	J.E.P.
"	12/4/17	9 p.m.	To-day has been another cold and stormy day with some bright intervals. — Fourteen cases were admitted to the Field Ambulance during the day, 10 cases were evacuated and 3 cases were returned to duty, leaving 19 cases remaining in the Field Ambulance.	J.E.P.

1875 Wt. W593/826 1,000,000 4/15 J.B.C. & A. A.D.S.S./Forms/C. 2118.

Army Form C. 2118

Instructions regarding War Diaries and Intelligence Summaries are contained in F. S. Regs., Part II. and the Staff Manual respectively. Title Pages will be prepared in manuscript.

WAR DIARY
or
~~INTELLIGENCE SUMMARY~~
(Erase heading not required.)

Place	Date	Hour	Summary of Events and Information	Remarks and references to Appendices
LA WATTINE	13/4/17	9 p.m.	The weather is a little warmer to-day, but it is still cloudy. – The Personnel have been employed on road fatigues and drainage, also Squad and Company drill and Physical exercises in the morning. – One Officer and 115 other ranks were admitted to the Field Ambulance. One Officer and 112 other ranks were evacuated and three men were returned to duty, leaving 19 cases remaining in the Field Ambulance.	J.E.P.
"	14/4/17	9 p.m.	The weather continues fine, but there is still a cold wind blowing which dries up the ground rapidly. – The Personnel were exercised in Physical drill and also were sent for a short route march. – Seven cases were admitted to the Field Ambulance during the day, and eight cases were evacuated and five cases were returned to duty, leaving 13 cases remaining in the Field Ambulance. – The A.D.M.S. visited the Field Ambulance in the afternoon.	J.E.P.
"	15/4/17	9 p.m.	The weather is much milder, but a fine rain has been falling most of the day. – Ten cases were admitted to the Field Ambulance, and six cases were evacuated and four cases were returned to duty, leaving 13 cases remaining in the Field Ambulance.	J.E.P.
"	16/4/17	9 p.m.	The weather has been fine to-day. – Orders have been received from the 57th Infantry Bde. for the Unit to march with the Brigade at 8.30 a.m. to-morrow from this area to HALLINES. – The Personnel have been employed in cleaning wagons and packing. One Officer and 14 other ranks were admitted to the Field Ambulance and one Officer and 15 other ranks were evacuated, 4 men were returned to duty, leaving 8 cases remaining in the Field Ambulance.	J.E.P.

1875 Wt. W593/826 1,000,000 4/15 J.B.C. & A. A.D.S.S./Forms/C. 2118.

Instructions regarding War Diaries and Intelligence Summaries are contained in F. S. Regs., Part II. and the Staff Manual respectively. Title Pages will be prepared in manuscript.

WAR DIARY
or
~~INTELLIGENCE SUMMARY~~
(Erase heading not required.)

Army Form C. 2118

Place	Date	Hour	Summary of Events and Information	Remarks and references to Appendices
HALLINES	17/4/17	9 p.m.	The weather has been very wet and cold nearly all day. The Unit marched off at 8.30 a.m. from LAWATTINE and arrived here at 12.30 p.m. – One Officer and 31 other ranks were admitted to the Field Ambulance during the day. One Officer and 33 other ranks were evacuated and six men were returned to duty, leaving no cases remaining in the Field Ambulance.	J.E.P.
LE CINQ RUES	18/4/17	9 p.m.	The weather has again been very wet raining all day but it has been warmer. Nineteen cases were admitted to the Field Ambulance during the day and 19 cases were evacuated to a Casualty Clearing Station in HAZEBRUCK leaving no cases remaining in the Field Ambulance. The Unit marched off at 7.30 a.m. and arrived here at 2.30 p.m.	J.E.P.
BERTHEN	19/4/17	9 p.m.	The day has again been very wet but is much milder. The Unit marched off at 9.45 a.m. and arrived here in the 58th Infantry Brigade training area at 3.30 p.m. and opened up for the reception of sick from the Brigade. – One Officer and 31 other ranks were admitted to the Field Ambulance during the day and one Officer and 31 other ranks were evacuated leaving no cases remaining.	J.E.P.
"	20/4/17	9 p.m.	To-day has been fine and mild all day. – Four cases only were ~~evacuated~~ admitted to the Field Ambulance and no cases were evacuated during the day. The Personnel have been employed in preparing the Hospital, cleaning up the farm yards, making kitchens, latrines etc.	J.E.P.

1875 Wt. W593/826 1,000,000 4/15 J.B.C. & A. A.D.S.S./Forms/C. 2118.

Instructions regarding War Diaries and Intelligence Summaries are contained in F. S. Regs., Part II. and the Staff Manual respectively. Title Pages will be prepared in manuscript.

WAR DIARY
or
~~INTELLIGENCE SUMMARY~~
(Erase heading not required.)

Army Form C. 2118

Place	Date	Hour	Summary of Events and Information	Remarks and references to Appendices
BERTHEN	21/4/17	9 p.m.	The weather has been dry and mild but cloudy. – The Personnel are employed in erecting and improving Kitchens and Latrines etc. and in cleaning up the Farm yards and drains etc. – The A.D.M.S. visited the Unit this afternoon. – Ten cases were admitted to the Field Ambulance during the day, two cases were evacuated and two cases were transferred to No. 59 Field Ambulance, leaving ten cases remaining in the Field Ambulance.	J.E.P.
"	22/4/17	9 p.m.	The weather continues fine, but there is still a cold wind blowing from the North East. Ten cases were admitted to the Field Ambulance and three cases were transferred to No. 59 Field Ambulance, leaving 17 cases remaining in the Field Ambulance. Lieut F. HUMPHREYS R.A.M.C. reported his arrival for duty this day.	J.E.P.
"	23/4/17	9 p.m.	The weather continues fine and is not so cold to-day. – The Personnel have been exercised in Physical drill & Company drill this morning, in the afternoon a Route march & Bathing parade was held. – A Clothing Board was held in the morning at 11:30 a.m. Captain A.W. YOUNG R.A.M.C. reported his departure this morning on taking over medical charge of the 9th Bn. Welsh Regt. – Captain J.D. WRIGHT R.A.M.C. reported his arrival for duty this morning. – 20 cases were admitted to the Field Ambulance during the day, 5 cases were transferred to No. 59 Field Ambulance and one case was returned to duty, leaving 31 cases remaining in the Field Ambulance.	J.E.P.
"	24/4/17	9 p.m.	Weather continues fine but with a cold N.E. wind blowing. – The Personnel were exercised in Squad and Company drill and Physical drill in the morning. – Bathing Parade and football in the afternoon. – Twelve cases were admitted to the Field Ambulance during the day, four cases were evacuated to a Casualty Clearing Station and seven cases were transferred to No. 59 Field Ambulance and seven cases were returned to duty, leaving 25 cases remaining in the Field Ambulance.	J.E.P.

1875 Wt. W593/826 1,000,000 4/15 J.B.C. & A. A.D.S.S./Forms/C. 2118.

Instructions regarding War Diaries and Intelligence Summaries are contained in F. S. Regs., Part II. and the Staff Manual respectively. Title Pages will be prepared in manuscript.

WAR DIARY
or
~~INTELLIGENCE SUMMARY~~
(Erase heading not required.)

Army Form C. 2118

Place	Date	Hour	Summary of Events and Information	Remarks and references to Appendices
BERTHEN	25/4/17	9 p.m.	The day has been cloudy and cold with some light showers of rain. Eleven cases were admitted to the Field Ambulance during the day, three cases were evacuated to a Casualty Clearing Station and seven cases were transferred to No. 59 Field Ambulance and two cases were returned to duty, leaving twenty four cases remaining in the Field Ambulance.	J.E.P.
"	26/4/17	9. p.m	Lt. Col. J.E. Powell having reported his departure for temporary duty as A.D.M.S. 19th Div. temporary command was assumed by Capt. G.P. Kidd R.A.M.C. Weather remains fine & has been much warmer today. One Off. & 5. O.R. admitted during the day. 1. Off & 1. O.R. evacuated to C.C.S. 7 O.R. transferred to 59. Fd. Amb. 2. O.R. to duty. Leaving 19. O.R. remaining	G.P.K.
"	27/4/17	9. p.m	Capt. J.L. Cochrane W.L. R.A.M.C. reported his arrival back for duty from 14 days leave in England Orders received from A.D.M.S. that unit will move to BAILLEUL on the 1st with advance party to go on the 29th inst. 13. O.R. admitted during the day. 3. O.R. to C.C.S. 3. O.R. Transferred to 59. Fd Amb. 2. O.R. to duty Leaving 24. O.R. remaining.	G.P.K.
"	28/4/17	9. p.m	Weather remains fine and has now become much warmer. 5. O.R. admitted during the day. 8. O.R. transferred to 59 Fd. Amb. 1. O.R. to Duty. Leaving 20. O.R. remaining	G.P.K.

1875 Wt. W593/826 1,000,000 4/15 J.B.C. & A. A.D.S.S./Forms/C. 2118.

Instructions regarding War Diaries and Intelligence Summaries are contained in F. S. Regs., Part II. and the Staff Manual respectively. Title Pages will be prepared in manuscript.

WAR DIARY
or
~~INTELLIGENCE SUMMARY~~

(Erase heading not required.)

Army Form C. 2118

Place	Date	Hour	Summary of Events and Information	Remarks and references to Appendices
BERTHEN	29/4/17	~~9 pm~~ 12.0 noon	Orders received at 7.30 a.m. cancelling orders as to pending move to BAILLEUL. I visited ADMS at 10.30 A.M. and learned that unit will probably move to the YPRES area tomorrow. Orders received at 2.0 pm for two advanced parties to proceed to 71. F Amb at VLAMERTINGHE MILL to proceed from there to two ADS near the line. These parties under Capt. Smalley RAMC & Capt Cochrane RAMC left at 3.0 pm. The hospital was cleared of all patients & closed down at 2.0 pm the unit being packed & ready to move at short notice. ADMS visited the unit in the evening to give detailed	[initials]
		9.0 pm	orders as to taking over new area tomorrow. Orders received for advanced parties to proceed tomorrow to take over MDS & ADS from 71. F Amb. 23rd Div. 1. Off & 14. O.R. admitted during the day. 1. Off & 2 O.R. evacuated to CCS 5. O.R. transferred to 59. F Amb. 3. O.R. to duty. Leaving 24. O.R. remaining.	
"	30/4/17	12.0 noon	Capt. Brandon RAMC was evacuated to CCS yesterday evening. Advanced parties for MDS & ADS left at 8.0 A.M. under Capt. Wright RAMC. 1. Off & 1. O.R. were admitted during the 24 hrs. to midday today. 1 Off evacuated to CCS. 13. O.R. transferred to 59. F Amb. 1. O.R. to duty. Leaving 11. O.R. remaining on the books, all these being at the IX Corps Scabies hospital. I visited the MDS at VLAMERTINGHE MILL during the morning to arrange with OC 71. F Amb for the taking over. I called in & saw ADMS on the way back. Working party of 1 NCO & 20 men who have been attached to 58. F Amb for duty, reported their arrival back this morning.	[initials]
		9.0 pm	Lieut. H.S. Johnston RAMC (T.C.) reported his arrival for duty.	

[signature]
Capt RAMC
a/O.C. 57th F Amb

1875 Wt. W593/826 1,000,000 4/15 J.B.C. & A. A.D.S.S./Forms/C. 2118.

Army Form C. 2118.

SECRET

Instructions regarding War Diaries and Intelligence Summaries are contained in F. S. Regs., Part II. and the Staff Manual respectively. Title Pages will be prepared in manuscript.

WAR DIARY
or
INTELLIGENCE SUMMARY
(Erase heading not required.)

Vol 23

Place	Date	Hour	Summary of Events and Information	Remarks and references to Appendices
			WAR DIARY No 57 FIELD AMBULANCE 19th Division Vol XXIII May 1st to 31st 1917	

2449 Wt. W14957/M90 750,000 1/16 J.B.C. & A. Forms/C.2118/12.

Instructions regarding War Diaries and Intelligence Summaries are contained in F. S. Regs., Part II. and the Staff Manual respectively. Title Pages will be prepared in manuscript.

WAR DIARY
or
~~INTELLIGENCE SUMMARY~~
(Erase heading not required.)

Army Form C. 2118

Place	Date	Hour	Summary of Events and Information	Remarks and references to Appendices
VLAMERTINGHE	1/5/17	9.0pm	Unit marched off at 7.30 AM and arrived here at 11.30 AM. Outgoing unit had already moved out and taking over was completed. The unit being opened for the reception of sick and wounded. Capt. Johnson MC RAMC and party from [illegible] Fd Amb. reported their arrival & proceeded at midday to take over ADS at Asylum YPRES. Afternoon was occupied in making various alterations in the MDS. I visited the ADS at the Asylum YPRES during the afternoon. The MDS here is quite satisfactory but the evacuation from the front line to ADS appears to present some difficulty owing to the danger of moving about in the front area in daylight. No cases were admitted or evacuated up to 12.0 noon today.	[initials]
"	2/5/17	12.0 noon	ADMS visited the MDS this morning and expressed himself as quite satisfied with all arrangements made. The men are still being occupied in necessary alterations & general cleaning up of the place.	
		9.0pm	I visited all three ADS's this evening and found everything working quite satisfactorily. 2. Off & 8. OR (S) and 5. Off & 9. OR (W) were admitted during the day – all being evacuated to CCS leaving 11 OR remaining – these being at IX Corps Rest Hospital. The weather remains fine and warm.	[initials]
"	3/5/17	9.0pm	A rush of cases came in at midday today owing to heavy shelling of billets in YPRES – about 45 cases being dealt with between noon & 2.0 pm. Most of these were from the 6th Wilts & 5th S.W.B's. The weather continues fine & very warm. 2. OR (S) and 5. OR (W) were admitted up to noon today. 5. OR evacuated to CCS leaving 2. OR Remaining.	[initials]

1875 Wt. W593/826 1,000,000 4/15 J.B.C. & A. A.D.S.S./Forms/C. 2118.

Instructions regarding War Diaries and Intelligence Summaries are contained in F. S. Regs., Part II. and the Staff Manual respectively. Title Pages will be prepared in manuscript.

WAR DIARY
or
~~INTELLIGENCE SUMMARY~~
(Erase heading not required.)

Army Form C. 2118

Place	Date	Hour	Summary of Events and Information	Remarks and references to Appendices
VLAMERTINGHE	4/5/17	9.0 pm	A marquee was fitted up today for the reception of gassed cases and a small ward for the reception of special or severe cases requiring keeping for some hours. I visited ~~inspected~~ the transport lines of the unit near POPERINGHE during the afternoon. 6. O.R. (S) & 1. Off. & 39. O.R. (W) were admitted up to noon. 4. O.R. (S) & 1. Off. & 30. O.R. (W) evacuated to CCS. 2 O.R. (S) & 11. O.R. (W) sent to DRS. Leaving no cases remaining.	[illegible]
"	5/5/17	9.0 pm	ADMS visited the unit during the morning to inspect improvised stretcher suspension for Thomas' Leg Splints. Alterations & improvements to the M.D.S. are now almost completed. 1 Off & 9. O.R. (S) & 2. O.R. (W) admitted up to noon. 1. Off. & 2 O.R. (S) & 1 O.R. (W) evacuated to CCS. Leaving 7. O.R. (S) and 2. O.R. (W) remaining.	[illegible]
"	6/5/17	9.0 pm	Another small rush of cases from the Barracks YPRES was dealt with about midday. The weather remains very fine but has been cooler the last two days. 14. O.R. (S) & 12. O.R. (W) were admitted up to noon. 7. O.R. (S) & 2. O.R. (W) evacuated to CCS. 11. O.R. (S) and 2. O.R. (W) transferred to DRS. 1. O.R. (W) returned to Duty. Leaving 3. O.R. (S) and 9. O.R. (W) remaining.	[illegible]
"	7/5/17	9.0 pm	I visited the A.D.S.'s during the afternoon and found everything quite satisfactory. Work is proceeding with the small dugout collecting post for walking wounded close to the Asylum. The weather was cooler towards evening with a slight shower of rain. 13. O.R. (S) and 1. Off + 20. O.R. (W) admitted up to noon. 4. O.R. (S) and 1. Off. & 23. O.R. (W) evacuated to CCS. 5. O.R. (S) & 4. O.R. (W) transferred to D.R.S. 2. O.R. (W) Died. Leaving 7. O.R. (S) remaining.	[illegible]

Instructions regarding War Diaries and Intelligence Summaries are contained in F. S. Regs., Part II. and the Staff Manual respectively. Title Pages will be prepared in manuscript.

WAR DIARY
or
~~INTELLIGENCE~~ SUMMARY
(Erase heading not required.)

Army Form C. 2118

Place	Date	Hour	Summary of Events and Information	Remarks and references to Appendices
VLAMERTINGHE	8/5/17	9.0pm	D.D.M.S. IX. Corps visited and inspected the hospital during the morning and expressed himself as quite satisfied with all arrangements. Preliminary Rame 19 Div. order received to the effect that the Div. will move back to the IX Corps (DIEPENDAAL) sector about the 11th – 13th inst. I visited and inspected the units transport lines at POPERINGHE during the afternoon & found everything quite satisfactory. 1. Off. + 7. O.R. (S) and 17. O.R. (W) admitted up to noon. 1. O.R. (S) + 8. O.R. (W) evacuated to C.C.S. 5. O.R. (S) transferred to D.R.S. 1. O.R. (W) to duty. Leaving 1. Off. + 8. O.R. (W) and 8. O.R. (S) remaining.	[initials]
"	9/5/17	12.0 midnight	Order received that the unit will hand over to No. 69. Fd Amb. 23 Div. on the 11th inst. & move to a new area. O.C. 69. Fd Amb. visited us in the morning to discuss arrangements for taking over. I relieved Capt. Johnson [illegible] at the Asylum YPRES [illegible] early tomorrow. I visited and [illegible] in the evening. Advanced parties from 69. Fd Amb. arrived at 5.0 pm & proceeded up to take over the A.D.S. at [illegible] for the [illegible]. This taking over was completed about midnight and our A.D.S. parties returned in the early hours of the morning. 1. Off. + 19. O.R. (S) + 1. Off. + 5. O.R. (W) admitted up to noon. 1 Off. + [illegible] O.R. (S) + 1 Off. + [illegible] O.R. (W) evacuated to C.C.S. 1. Off. + 6. O.R. (S) + 5. O.R. (W) transferred to D.R.S. 1. O.R. (W) ~~[illegible]~~ ~~Leaving~~ 1. O.R. (S) ~~to duty~~. Leaving 16 O.R. (S) + 2. O.R. (W) remaining. The weather remains fine & warm. All equipment was sorted and checked during the day with a view to handing over & all lists prepared for handing over.	[initials]

1875 Wt. W593/826 1,000,000 4/15 J.B.C. & A. A.D.S.S./Forms/C. 2118.

Instructions regarding War Diaries and Intelligence Summaries are contained in F. S. Regs., Part II. and the Staff Manual respectively. Title Pages will be prepared in manuscript.

WAR DIARY

or

~~INTELLIGENCE SUMMARY~~

(Erase heading not required.)

Army Form C. 2118

Place	Date	Hour	Summary of Events and Information	Remarks and references to Appendices
VLAMERTINGHE	10/5/17	9.0 pm	Most of the equipment was packed during the day. Advanced party from 69 F Amb arrived during the afternoon & commenced taking over. One party proceeded to the Asylum & RHES & took over the ADS, our party under Capt J.D. Wright RAMC returning to headquarters. ~~[illegible]~~ 1. Off & 13. OR (S) & 3. Off & 18 OR (W) admitted up to noon. 1. Off (S) & 1. Off & 7 OR (W) evacuated to CCS 20. OR (S) & 3. (OR(W)) transferred to DRS. Leaving 12. OR (S) & 2. Off & 7 OR (W) remaining.	[signature]
BERTHEN	11/5/17	2.0 pm	Handing over being completed the unit marched off at 9.0 Am & arrived here at 12.45 p.m. The same billets were taken over as previously occupied, the unit remaining closed as the Brigade does not move in till the 13th inst. The weather was very hot and the march trying owing to heat and dust on the roads. 1. Off & 16. OR (S) & 1. Off & 5 OR (W) admitted up to noon. 1 Off & 1. OR (S) & 1 Off & 3. OR (S) evacuated to CCS 27. OR (S) & 2. Off & 9. OR (W) transferred to DRS. Leaving 3. OR (S) remaining on the books, these being at Scabies Hospital CAESTRE	[signature]
		9.0 pm	The afternoon was occupied in erecting tents & settling into the new billets.	
"	12/5/17	9.0 pm	Weather still fine & warm. The unit remained closed today. Capt. J.D. Wright RAMC reported his departure for temp duty as MO i/c 250 Coy RE. Lt Col J.E. Powell RAMC having reported his arrival back for duty from temp duty as ADMS, reassumed command of the unit this evening. Capt. T. Brandon RAMC reported his arrival back for duty on discharge from CCS. 2. Cases remained on the books – both being at Scabies Hospital CAESTRE	[signature]

1875 Wt. W593/826 1,000,000 4/15 J.B.C. & A. A.D.S.S./Forms/C. 2118.

Instructions regarding War Diaries and Intelligence Summaries are contained in F. S. Regs., Part II. and the Staff Manual respectively. Title Pages will be prepared in manuscript.

WAR DIARY
or
~~INTELLIGENCE SUMMARY~~
(*Erase heading not required.*)

Army Form C. 2118

Place	Date	Hour	Summary of Events and Information	Remarks and references to Appendices
BERTHEN	13/5/17	9 p.m.	It has been another fine hot day. – The Unit opened up for the reception of sick this morning, but no cases have been admitted up to the present. – Orders were received this evening for one Section of the Field Ambulance with 2 Horse Ambulances and 3 motor ambulances to march with the 58th Brigade back to the REcques Training area. – I detailed B Section for this duty. I visited the A.D.M.S. this evening.	J.E.P.
"	14/5/17	9 p.m.	The weather continues fine and warm with a few light showers of rain. – B Section of this Unit under Captain Kidd R.A.M.C. marched at 2:30 p.m. this afternoon into billets at THIUSHOOK preparatory to marching with the 58th Brigade tomorrow into a new training area. – Two cases were admitted to the Field Ambulance during the day and two cases were returned to duty, leaving 2 cases remaining.	J.E.P.
"	15/5/17	9 p.m.	The weather has been cool and cloudy. – Under orders from the A.D.M.S. 2 N.C.O.s and 30 other ranks left at 5 p.m. to be attached to No. 58 Field Ambulance as a working party on construction of an advanced Dressing station and Regt. Aid Post. 19 other ranks were admitted to the Field Ambulance during the day leaving 21 cases remaining in the Field Ambulance.	J.E.P.
"	16/5/17	9 p.m.	The day has been cool and cloudy and quite heavy rain has fallen throughout this evening. Lieut. F. HUMPHREYS RAMC reported his departure this day for permanent duty as M.O. i/c 1st South Lancs Regt. – Two cases were admitted to the Field Ambulance during the day and 8 cases were evacuated to a Casualty Clearing Station, leaving 15 cases remaining in the Field Ambulance.	J.E.P.

1875 Wt. W593/826 1,000,000 4/15 J.B.C. & A. A.D.S.S./Forms/C. 2118.

Army Form C. 2118

Instructions regarding War Diaries and Intelligence Summaries are contained in F. S. Regs., Part II. and the Staff Manual respectively. Title Pages will be prepared in manuscript.

WAR DIARY
or
~~INTELLIGENCE SUMMARY~~
(Erase heading not required.)

Place	Date	Hour	Summary of Events and Information	Remarks and references to Appendices
BERTHEN	17/5/17	9 p.m.	Rain fell throughout the night and also this morning until noon, since that time the weather has been fine and cool. — Captain A.A. SMALLEY R.A.M.C. left this morning to be attached for 6 days to the Advanced Dressing Station at KLEINE VIERSTRAAT to get to know the line thoroughly. — One case was admitted to the Field Ambulance during the day. 4 cases were evacuated to a Casualty Clearing Stn. and one case was returned to duty, leaving eleven cases remaining in the Field Ambulance.	J.E.P.
"	18/5/17	9 p.m.	The day has been fine and warm throughout. — One Officer and 18 other ranks were admitted to the Field Ambulance during the day, and one Officer and 18 other ranks were evacuated and one case was returned to duty, leaving 10 cases remaining in the Field Ambulance.	J.E.P.
"	19/5/17	9 p.m.	The weather continues fine and warm. — One Officer and seven men were admitted to the Field Ambulance during the day and one Officer and 7 men were evacuated, leaving 10 cases remaining. — Received verbal instructions this evening from the A.D.M.S. to send an advance Party to Westoutre to-morrow to prepare a camp for this Unit to move into shortly	J.E.P.
"	20/5/17	9 p.m.	It has been another fine and warm day. One Officer and 18 other ranks were admitted to the Field Ambulance and one Officer and 7 other ranks were evacuated leaving 21 cases remaining in the Field Ambulance. — I visited the A.D.M.S. in the morning and also went over the ground selected for the formation of a Divisional Rest Station by this Unit. — Submitted Indents on C.R.E. for material & also sent an advance party forward to begin pitching the camp.	J.E.P.

1875 Wt. W593/826 1,000,000 4/15 J.B.C. & A. A.D.S.S./Forms/C. 2118.

Instructions regarding War Diaries and Intelligence Summaries are contained in F. S. Regs., Part II. and the Staff Manual respectively. Title Pages will be prepared in manuscript.

WAR DIARY
or
~~INTELLIGENCE SUMMARY~~
(Erase heading not required.)

Army Form C. 2118

Place	Date	Hour	Summary of Events and Information	Remarks and references to Appendices
BERTHEN	21/5/17	9 p.m.	The weather continues fine and warm. – The Headquarters of the Field Ambulance closed today and all equipment packed for to-morrow's move. – Ten cases were admitted to B Section and 9 cases were evacuated, 6 cases were returned to duty, leaving 15 cases remaining in the Section of the Field Ambulance.	J.E.P.
WESTOUTRE	22/5/17	9 p.m.	Heavy rain fell last night and throughout the morning but the weather cleared in the afternoon. – The Headquarters of the Unit marched at 9 a.m. and arrived here at 10.30 a.m. and proceeded with the preparation of the camp. – Twelve cases were admitted to B Section, two cases were evacuated, leaving 26 cases remaining in the Section of the Field Ambulance.	J.E.P.
"	23/5/17	9 p.m.	The day has been fine clear and warm. – The Personnel have been employed on the construction of Kitchens, Ablution benches, Bath House, Latrines and Incinerators for the Divisional Rest Station. – The A.D.M.S. visited the Camp in the morning. – One Officer and 4 other ranks were admitted to the Field Ambulance Section and one Officer & 3 other ranks were evacuated & one case was returned to duty, leaving 26 cases remaining in the Section.	J.E.P.
"	24/5/17	9 p.m.	The weather continues fine and warm. – Work is being continued all day on the formation of the Divisional Rest Station. – 12 other ranks were admitted to the Field Ambulance during the day, 9 cases were evacuated to a Casualty Clearing Stn. and 3 cases were returned to duty, leaving 26 cases remaining in the Field Ambulance	J.E.P.

1875 Wt. W593/826 1,000,000 4/15 J.B.C. & A. A.D.S.S./Forms/C. 2118.

Instructions regarding War Diaries and Intelligence Summaries are contained in F. S. Regs., Part II. and the Staff Manual respectively. Title Pages will be prepared in manuscript.

WAR DIARY

or

~~INTELLIGENCE SUMMARY~~

(Erase heading not required.)

Army Form C. 2118

Place	Date	Hour	Summary of Events and Information	Remarks and references to Appendices
WESTOUTRE	25/5/17	9 p.m.	The weather continues fine and warm. – Work is being continued on the formation of the Divisional Rest Stn. – B. Section rejoined Headquarters at 5.30 p.m. the Transport having marched by road and the Personnel having come by train to BAILLEUL. Two Officers and 19 other ranks were admitted to B. Section during the day, 2 Officers and 35 other ranks were evacuated and ten cases were returned to duty leaving no cases remaining and the Unit is now closed for the reception of sick.	J.E.P.
"	26/5/17	9 p.m.	The weather continues fine and warm. – Work is being continued on the formation of a Divisional Rest Station, 5 more marquees were pitched to-day. – The A.D.M.S. held a conference of Bearer Division Officers and Regimental Medical Officers this afternoon at No. 59 Field Ambulance, which I attended – the subject for the conference was future operations.	J.E.P.
"	27/5/17	9 p.m.	The day has been fine and warm and clear. – Work is still being continued all day on the Divisional Rest Station which is now nearing completion. – Captain WARD RAMC reported his departure this day for England on completion of his contract.	J.E.P.
"	28/5/17	9 p.m.	The weather continues fine and warm. – Captain J.L. COCHRANE R.A.M.C. was posted to the Advanced Dressing Stn. ~~to attain~~ to-day to obtain a good knowledge of the line. – I visited the Advanced Dressing Stn and three of the Regimental aid Posts this morning. – The Personnel are still fully employed on the completion of the Divisional Rest Stn. – Road repairing and drainage etc.	J.E.P.

1875 Wt. W593/826 1,000,000 4/15 J.B.C. & A. A.D.S.S./Forms/C. 2118.

Army Form C. 2118

Instructions regarding War Diaries and Intelligence Summaries are contained in F. S. Regs., Part II. and the Staff Manual respectively. Title Pages will be prepared in manuscript.

WAR DIARY

or

~~INTELLIGENCE SUMMARY~~

(Erase heading not required.)

Place	Date	Hour	Summary of Events and Information	Remarks and references to Appendices
WESTOUTRE	29/5/17	9 p.m.	The day has been cool and cloudy but no rain has fallen. – The Personnel have been busy all day on the completion of the Divisional Rest Station. – Twelve reinforcements were received from the Base to-day. – Orders were received from the A.D.M.S. for the Bearer Division of this Unit to take over to-morrow the Advanced Dressing Stn. from the No. 58 Field Ambulance.	J.E.P.
"	30/5/17	9 p.m.	The day has been fine and warm. – The Bearer Division took over the advanced Dressing Stn., at KLEINE VIERSTRAAT this morning from No. 58 Field Ambulance. – I visited the advanced Dressing Stn. and all the Regimental aid Posts on the Divisional Front in company with the A.D.M.S. – The A.D.M.S. visited the Divisional Rest Stn. yesterday and expressed himself as pleased with all the work that has been carried out.	J.E.P.
"	31/5/17	9 p.m.	The weather continues fine and warm. – The Divisional Rest Station has now been completed and is ready for the reception of sick. – This afternoon I attended a conference of Bearer Division and Regimental Medical Officers with the A.D.M.S.	J.E.P.

J.E. Powell
Lieut. Colonel R.A.M.C.
O.C. 57th Field Ambulance

1875 Wt. W593/826 1,000,000 4/15 J.B.C. & A. A.D.S.S./Forms/C. 2118.

Army Form C. 2118.

Instructions regarding War Diaries and Intelligence Summaries are contained in F. S. Regs., Part II. and the Staff Manual respectively. Title Pages will be prepared in manuscript.

WAR DIARY
or
INTELLIGENCE SUMMARY
(Erase heading not required.)

Vol 24.

Place	Date	Hour	Summary of Events and Information	Remarks and references to Appendices
			WAR DIARY No 57 Fd Amb Vol XXIV June 1st - 30th (inclusive)	

2449 Wt. W14957/M90 750,000 1/16 J.B.C. & A. Forms/C.2118/12.

Instructions regarding War Diaries and Intelligence Summaries are contained in F. S. Regs., Part II. and the Staff Manual respectively. Title Pages will be prepared in manuscript.

WAR DIARY
or
~~INTELLIGENCE SUMMARY~~
(Erase heading not required.)

Army Form C. 2118

Place	Date	Hour	Summary of Events and Information	Remarks and references to Appendices
WESTOUTRE	1/6/17	9 p.m.	The weather continues fine and warm. – The A.D.M.S. visited the Unit at 10.30 a.m. and in company with him I proceeded to LA CLYTTE and discussed the evacuation of the wounded with the O.C. No. 58 Field Ambulance. – In the afternoon I visited the Advanced Dressing Station. Captain COCHRANE was relieved by Lieut JOHNSTON at the A.D.S.	J.E.P.
"	2/6/17	9 p.m.	The weather still continues fine and hot and the roads are now very dusty. – The ADMS visited the Unit at 11 a.m. – Under verbal instructions from the A.D.M.S. this Unit took over this afternoon at 5 p.m. the School premises from No. 59 Field Ambulance, this building will give accommodation for 50 cases & the more serious "lying" sick cases will be kept there.	J.E.P.
"	3/6/17	9 p.m.	It has been another hot fine day. – The water in the Horse lines has been exhausted and a fresh watering place for the horses has had to be found some distance away. – I visited the ~~ADS~~ Advanced Dressing Station in the afternoon and made arrangements with regard to the equipping of the New Aid Posts at P.1.O. & Poppy Lane. – Lieut. JOHNSTON returned to Headquarters from the A.D.S.	J.E.P.
"	4/6/17	9 p.m.	The weather continues very hot and dusty. – The A.D.M.S. visited the Unit this morning and inspected the arrangements made in the School premises for the reception of sick. – I saw in the afternoon the Commanding Officers of the Bearer Division and arranged the distribution of the Bearers during the forthcoming operations.	J.E.P.

1875 Wt. W593/826 1,000,000 4/15 J.B.C. & A. A.D.S.S./Forms/C. 2118.

Army Form C. 2118

Instructions regarding War Diaries and Intelligence Summaries are contained in F. S. Regs., Part II. and the Staff Manual respectively. Title Pages will be prepared in manuscript.

WAR DIARY

or

~~INTELLIGENCE SUMMARY~~

(Erase heading not required.)

Place	Date	Hour	Summary of Events and Information	Remarks and references to Appendices
WESTOUTRE	5/6/17	9 p.m.	The day has been very hot throughout. – attended a conference at 10 a.m. this morning at the A.D.M.S.'s Office. – Received orders this morning for the Unit to open up for the reception of sick and receive transfers this afternoon from No. 59 Field Ambulance. 47 cases were transferred from No. 59 Field Ambulance during the evening. – I visited the Advanced Dressing Station in the afternoon and made arrangements for the evacuation of casualties from a "Raid" which took place at 3 p.m. – This only resulted in 16 casualties and these were easily evacuated.	J.E.P.
"	6/6/17	9 p.m.	Weather somewhat cooler today & some rain fell towards evening. Bearer Division under Capt. Smalley left for the ADS at 6.0 p.m. and Lt. Col. J.E. Powell DSO also went to the ADS to take over command of all the Div. Bearer Divisions in view of offensive operations commencing tomorrow. Lt. E. Evans RAMC (T.C.) reported his arrival for duty with the unit. 21. O.R. (S) & 2. O.R. (W) were transferred from 59 F. Amb. up to noon. 1 Off. & 40. O.R. admitted 1. Off & 1. O.R. evacuated to C.C.S. leaving 62. O.R. remaining in the D.R.S.	G.H.K.
"	7/6/17	9. p.m.	Weather still very warm but a heavy thunder storm passed over in the evening. I saw the A.D.M.S. in the morning & settled several points about the evacuation of cases from the D.R.S. 44. O.R. were admitted to the D.R.S. up to noon 17. O.R. evacuated to C.C.S. 1. O.R. transferred to 32. F. Amb. leaving 88. O.R. remaining.	G.H.K.

1875 Wt. W593/826 1,000,000 4/15 J.B.C. & A. A.D.S.S./Forms/C. 2118.

WAR DIARY

or

~~INTELLIGENCE SUMMARY~~

(Erase heading not required.)

Army Form C. 2118

Instructions regarding War Diaries and Intelligence Summaries are contained in F. S. Regs., Part II. and the Staff Manual respectively. Title Pages will be prepared in manuscript.

Place	Date	Hour	Summary of Events and Information	Remarks and references to Appendices
WESTOUTRE	8/6/17	9.0 pm	Weather still very hot, occasional showers of rain towards evening. The D.R.S. is becoming gradually filled up as we are unable to send cases to the Corps Rest Station at present. 1. Off & 69. O.R. admitted to the D.R.S. 1. Off. + 19. O.R. evacuated to C.C.S. 1. O.R. to Duty. Leaving 137. O.R. remaining.	G.A.K.
"	9/6/17	9.0 pm	Admissions were much fewer today and we should not be overcrowded now as the Corps Rest Station will be able to take in cases tomorrow. 1. Off. + 39. O.R. admitted. 1. Off. + 9. O.R. evacuated to C.C.S. 2. O.R. to duty. Leaving 156. O.R. remaining in the D.R.S. The weather remains fine and very hot.	G.A.K.
"	10/6/17	9.0 pm	Weather much cooler today. Active operations being now over, cars and horsed transport lent to other units have now returned to the unit. The A.D.S. is now being evacuated by ~~our~~ cars of this unit in the normal manner. Lt. Col. J.E. Powell D.S.O. returned to unit headquarters from the A.D.S. Corps Rest Station was able to take in cases today & 20. O.R. were transferred there, thus increasing our accommodation here. 2. Off. + 44. O.R. admitted. 2. Off. + 9. O.R. evacuated to C.C.S. 17. O.R. to duty. Leaving 176. O.R. remaining in the D.R.S. (including 3. O.R. at IX C.R.S.)	G.A.K.
"	11/6/17	9 pm	Weather continues much cooler & it is cloudy – some rain fell during the day. – I visited the A.D.S. during the ~~morning~~ afternoon. – One Officer & 42 O.R. admitted during the day. One Officer & 8 O.R. evacuated to a C.C.S. and one case returned to duty. Leaving 208 Cases remaining in the D.R.S. including 24 cases remaining in the Corps Rest Stn.	J.E.P.

Army Form C. 2118

WAR DIARY
or
~~INTELLIGENCE SUMMARY~~
(Erase heading not required.)

Instructions regarding War Diaries and Intelligence Summaries are contained in F. S. Regs., Part II. and the Staff Manual respectively. Title Pages will be prepared in manuscript.

Place	Date	Hour	Summary of Events and Information	Remarks and references to Appendices
WESTOUTRE	12/6/17	9 p.m.	The day was very hot until 4 p.m. when a very heavy thunderstorm broke over the camp, with very heavy rain, after this the air was much cooler. – The A.D.M.S. visited the Unit at 6 p.m. & I visited the A.D.S. at 7 p.m. – Two Officers and 37 O.R. were admitted during the day and 2 Officers and 9 O.R. were evacuated and 8 O.R. were returned to duty, leaving 228 O.R. remaining in the D.R.S.	J.E.P.
LOCRE	13/6/17	9 p.m.	At 11 p.m. last night I received orders from the A.D.M.S. to hand over the D.R.S. to No. 4 London Field Ambulance this morning and to march to LOCRE and take over the Hospice from No 113 Field Ambulance and open up for the reception of all sick & wounded from the Division. – Also to hand over the Advanced Dressing Stn. to No 59 Field Ambulance and the Bearer Division of this Unit to return to Headquarters. – All these movements have now been completed. – The day has been fine & hot. – Three Officers and 40 O.R. were admitted, 3 Officers & 16 O.R. were evacuated, one case was returned to duty & 24 cases were transferred to No 58 Field Ambulance, leaving 229 ~~cases~~ remaining in the D.R.S.	J.E.P.
"	14/6/17	9 p.m.	The weather continues fine & warm. – The A.D.M.S. visited the Unit this morning & ~~ordered~~ issued orders for two Bearer Subdivisions to proceed to the A.D.S. this evening to meet the emergency of a raid – On completion of the evacuation of the casualties from the raid, one Bearer Subdivision will return to Headqrs., the other remaining in reserve at the A.D.S. – 5 Officers 115 O.R. were admitted & 5 Officers & 44 O.R. were evacuated to a C.C.S. & 2 men died of wounds, leaving 204 cases remaining.	J.E.P.

1875 Wt. W593/826 1,000,000 4/15 J.B.C. & A. A.D.S.S./Forms/C. 2118.

Instructions regarding War Diaries and Intelligence Summaries are contained in F. S. Regs., Part II. and the Staff Manual respectively. Title Pages will be prepared in manuscript.

WAR DIARY
or
~~INTELLIGENCE SUMMARY~~
(Erase heading not required.)

Army Form C. 2118

Place	Date	Hour	Summary of Events and Information	Remarks and references to Appendices
LOCRE	15/6/17	9 pm	The weather continues very hot. – Two Officers and One Bearer Sub-division returned from the line at 2 a.m. this morning. – The Personnel were paid this morning. Three Officers and 63 O.R. were evacuated ~~admitted~~ during the day, one man died from wounds and 4 cases were returned to duty, four Officers and 111 men were admitted during the day, leaving One Officer and 247 men remaining.	J.E.P.
"	16/6/17	9 pm.	It has been another very hot day. – The D.M.S. Army accompanied by the D.D.M.S. Corps and the A.D.M.S. Division visited this Unit to-day at 12.45 p.m. and addressed the officers and men on parade, thanking them, and expressing appreciation of their good work during the recent Offensive, both on behalf of Himself and the Army Commander. — One Officer and 95 other ranks were admitted during the day, Two Officers and 90 O.R. were evacuated and 13 cases were returned to duty leaving 241 cases remaining.	J.E.P.
"	17/6/17	9 pm.	The weather continues very warm. – I visited the A.D.M.S.'s Office in the morning. Lieut. BODDY R.A.M.C. reported his departure to assume temporary medical charge of the 9th Bn. Cheshire Regt. Lieut. JOHNSTON R.A.M.C. reported his departure to assume permanent medical charge of the 8th Bn. Gloucestershire Regt. – One Officer and 78 other ranks were admitted. One Officer and 33 other ranks were evacuated and 3 cases were returned to duty, leaving 283 cases remaining on the books of the Field Ambulance.	J.E.P.

1875 Wt. W593/826 1,000,000 4/15 J.B.C. & A. A.D.S.S./Forms/C. 2118.

Army Form C. 2118

Instructions regarding War Diaries and Intelligence Summaries are contained in F. S. Regs., Part II. and the Staff Manual respectively. Title Pages will be prepared in manuscript.

WAR DIARY
or
~~INTELLIGENCE SUMMARY~~
(Erase heading not required.)

Place	Date	Hour	Summary of Events and Information	Remarks and references to Appendices
LOCRE	18/6/17	9 p.m.	The day has been very hot until 4 p.m. when a heavy thunderstorm broke over the camp and very heavy rain fell. — Captain T. O'BRIEN R.A.M.C. reported himself for duty this afternoon. — Received orders from the A.D.M.S. this evening, to hand over this site to a Field Ambulance of the 36th Division to-morrow and to march to a Camp at R.17. b 5-2 Map Sheet 27 and open there for the reception of sick. Four Officers and 93 O.R. were admitted during the day, 4 Officers and 34 O.R. were evacuated and 10 cases were returned to duty, leaving 330 cases remaining on our books.	J.E.P.
MT. KOKEREELE	19/6/17	9 p.m.	The weather continues hot and oppressive though numerous thunder showers fell throughout the day. — Having handed over the site, stores, buildings and Patients at the Hospice LOCRE the Unit marched off at 3 p.m. and arrived here at 4.30 p.m. and at once opened up for the reception of sick. — The State at 12 Noon was + 5 Officers and 84 O.R. admitted, 5 Officers 56 O.R. evacuated, 2 men died of wounds, and 17 cases were returned to duty, 345 cases on our books.	J.E.P.
"	20/6/17	9 p.m.	Heavy rain fell during the night and some heavy showers have also fallen during the day but the weather still continues warm. — The Personnel have been employed on the drainage of the camp, the improvement of the roads and the general preparation of the Huts for the reception of sick. — 14 other ranks were admitted to the Field Ambulance, 29 cases were evacuated to Casualty Clearing Stn. and 66 cases were transferred to No. 110 Field Ambulance and 22 cases were returned to duty, leaving 247 cases remaining on our books.	J.E.P.

1875 Wt. W593/826 1,000,000 4/15 J.B.C. & A. A.D.S.S./Forms/C. 2118.

Instructions regarding War Diaries and Intelligence Summaries are contained in F. S. Regs., Part II. and the Staff Manual respectively. Title Pages will be prepared in manuscript.

WAR DIARY

or

~~INTELLIGENCE SUMMARY~~

(Erase heading not required.)

Army Form C. 2118

Place	Date	Hour	Summary of Events and Information	Remarks and references to Appendices
MT. KOKEREELE	21/6/17	9 p.m.	Heavy rain fell during the night and it has been much cooler to-day. – The Personnel are still employed on road repairs and drainage. – Under instructions from the A.D.M.S. One Officer and 11 O.R. were this morning sent to take over and hold the Field Ambulance premises at No. 16 RUE de METEREN BAILLEUL from No 33 Field Ambulance. – One Officer and 21 O.R. were admitted during the day, One Officer and 31 O.R. were evacuated to C.C.S. and 48 O.R. were returned to duty, leaving 189 cases still on our books.	J.E.P.
"	22/6/17	9 p.m.	Rain has fallen throughout the day and it is much cooler. – 17 other ranks were admitted during the day, 14 cases were evacuated to a Casualty Clearing Stn., and 16 cases were returned to duty, leaving 176 cases remaining on our books.	J.E.P.
"	23/6/17	9 p.m.	The day has been fine and cool. The A.D.M.S. visited the Unit this morning & expressed his satisfaction with all he saw. – One Officer and 18 O.R. were admitted during the day, One Officer & 12 O.R. were evacuated to C.C.S. and 20 cases were returned to duty, leaving 162 cases remaining on our books. In addition 4 Portuguese were admitted and evacuated.	J.E.P.
"	24/6/17	9 p.m.	The weather continues fine and cool. – I visited my detachment ~~the~~ holding the Field Ambulance site at 16 RUE de METEREN BAILLEUL this morning, and inspected all the Buildings, grounds, stores etc. — One Officer and 37 O.R. were admitted during the day, & One Officer and 15 O.R. were evacuated to a C.C.S. 18 cases were returned to duty, leaving 166 cases remaining on our books	J.E.P.

1875 Wt. W593/826 1,000,000 4/15 J.B.C. & A. A.D.S.S./Forms/C. 2118.

Army Form C. 2118

WAR DIARY

or

~~INTELLIGENCE SUMMARY~~

(Erase heading not required.)

Instructions regarding War Diaries and Intelligence Summaries are contained in F. S. Regs., Part II. and the Staff Manual respectively. Title Pages will be prepared in manuscript.

Place	Date	Hour	Summary of Events and Information	Remarks and references to Appendices
MT. KOKEREELE	25/6/17	9 p.m.	The day has been cool and cloudy and considerable rain has fallen this evening. The D.D.M.S. IX Corps visited the Unit this morning. — Twentyone other ranks were admitted during the day, 13 O.R. were evacuated to a Casualty Clearing Stn. and 20 O.R. were returned to duty, leaving 154 cases still on our books.	J.E.P.
"	26/6/17	9 p.m.	Heavy rain fell during the night, but the day has been fine and clear. — I inspected the detachment of the Unit at BAILLEUL this morning. — I also wrote to the A.D.M.S. on the training of Officer Reinforcements in the duties of Regimental Medical Officers. — One Officer and 22 O.R. were admitted. One Officer and 12 O.R. were evacuated to a Casualty Clearing Stn., and 14 cases were returned to duty, leaving 150 cases remaining on our books. Captain G.P. KIDD proceeded on 10 days leave to England this morning, and Lieut. E. EVANS proceeded on temporary duty as M.O. i/c 9th Bn. Welsh Regiment.	J.E.P.
"	27/6/17	9 p.m.	The day has been fine and warm throughout. — 19 other ranks were admitted during the day, 6 O.R. were evacuated to a Casualty Clearing Stn., and 12 O.R. were returned to duty, leaving 151 O.R. remaining on our books.	J.E.P.
"	28/6/17	9 p.m.	Heavy thunder showers fell during the afternoon and evening. — 22 other ranks were admitted during the day, 12 O.R. were evacuated to a Casualty Clearing Stn., and 15 cases were returned to duty leaving 146 cases remaining on our books. Lieut. & QMr. A. Bennett proceeded on 10 days leave of absence to England to-day.	J.E.P.

1875 Wt. W593/826 1.000.000 4/15 J.B.C. & A. A.D.S.S./Forms/C. 2118.

Army Form C. 2118

Instructions regarding War Diaries and Intelligence Summaries are contained in F. S. Regs., Part II. and the Staff Manual respectively. Title Pages will be prepared in manuscript.

WAR DIARY
or
~~INTELLIGENCE SUMMARY~~
(Erase heading not required.)

Place	Date	Hour	Summary of Events and Information	Remarks and references to Appendices
MT. KOKEREELE	29/6/17	9 p.m.	Heavy rain fell during the night, but it has been fine throughout the day. — Received a warning order from the A.D.M.S. to be ready to move on the morning of 2nd prox. and take over the Hospice, LOCRE from the 49th Field Ambulance. One Officer and 24 O.R. were admitted during the day, 8 O.R. were evacuated to a Casualty Clearing Stn., one man died from accidental wounds and 8 cases were returned to duty, leaving One Officer and 153 O.R. remaining.	J.E.P.
"	30/6/17	9 p.m.	Rain has fallen continuously throughout the day. — One Officer and 27 O.R. were admitted during the day, Two Officers were sent to the Officers Corps Rest Stn., 17 O.R. were evacuated to a Casualty Clearing Stn., & 15 cases were returned to duty, leaving 158 cases remaining on our books.	J.E.P.

J.E. Powell
Lieut. Colonel R.A.M.C.
O.C. 57th Field Ambulance.

1875 Wt. W593/826 1,000,000 4/15 J.B.C. & A. A.D.S.S./Forms/C. 2118.

July 1917

140/2298

No. 57 F. A.

Instructions regarding War Diaries and Intelligence Summaries are contained in F. S. Regs., Part II. and the Staff Manual respectively. Title pages will be prepared in manuscript.

WAR DIARY
or
INTELLIGENCE SUMMARY.
(Erase heading not required.)

Army Form C. 2118.

Vol 25

Place	Date	Hour	Summary of Events and Information	Remarks and references to Appendices
			WAR DIARY No 57 Fd Amb Vol XXV July 1917	

2353 Wt. W2544/1454 700,000 5/15 D. D. & L. A.D.S.S./Forms/C. 2118.

Instructions regarding War Diaries and Intelligence Summaries are contained in F. S. Regs., Part II. and the Staff Manual respectively. Title Pages will be prepared in manuscript.

WAR DIARY
or
~~INTELLIGENCE SUMMARY~~

(Erase heading not required.)

Army Form C. 2118

Place	Date	Hour	Summary of Events and Information	Remarks and references to Appendices
MT. KOKEREELE	1/7/17	9 p.m.	It has been a cold and cloudy day with some showers. – The A.D.M.S. visited the Unit and issued verbal instructions that this site and the Patients at present in were to be handed over to No. 58 Field Ambulance. – This was done at 6 p.m. this evening. – Two Officers and 37 O.R. were ~~[illegible]~~ admitted during the day, two Officers and 25 O.R. were evacuated to a Casualty Clearing Stn., and 11 cases were returned to duty, leaving 159 cases remaining on our books.	J.E.P.
LOCRE	2/7/17	9 p.m.	The day has been fine and warm throughout. – The Unit marched off at 8.30 a.m. & arrived here at 10 a.m. taking over the buildings, stores and Patients from No 49 Field Ambulance at 12 Noon. – One Officer and 8 O.R. were admitted to the Field Ambulance, One Officer & 14 O.R. were evacuated, 34 O.R. were transferred to No. 58 Field Ambulance and 7 cases were returned to duty, leaving 112 cases remaining on our books.	J.E.P.
"	3/7/17	9 p.m.	The weather continues fine and warm. – The Personnel have been engaged in unpacking and rearranging stores etc., cleaning up and increasing the accommodation for Patients. – Four Officers (2 sick & 2 wounded) were admitted, 120 O.R. ~~[illegible]~~ (79 sick & 41 wounded) were admitted, 3 Officers were evacuated 33 O.R. (8 sick & 25 wounded) were evacuated, 2 wounded O.R. died from wounds & 5 O.R. were returned to duty, leaving One Officer & 192 O.R. remaining on our books.	J.E.P.

1875 Wt. W593/826 1,000,000 4/15 J.B.C. & A. A.D.S.S./Forms/C. 2118.

Instructions regarding War Diaries and Intelligence Summaries are contained in F. S. Regs., Part II. and the Staff Manual respectively. Title Pages will be prepared in manuscript.

WAR DIARY
or
~~INTELLIGENCE SUMMARY~~
(Erase heading not required.)

Army Form C. 2118

Place	Date	Hour	Summary of Events and Information	Remarks and references to Appendices
LOCRE	4/7/17	9 p.m.	The weather has been cloudy and much cooler and a few light showers of rain have fallen. LIEUT. BODDY R.A.M.C. reported his departure to-day for temporary duty as M.O. i/c 250th Tunnelling Company. — Two Officers and 72 O.R. were admitted during the day, 33 other ranks were evacuated to a Casualty Clearing Stn. and 10 cases were returned to duty, leaving 3 Officers and 221 O.R. remaining on our books.	J.E.P.
"	5/7/17	9 p.m.	The weather continues dull, cool and cloudy. — 51 O.R. (34 sick + 17 wounded) were admitted to the Field Ambulance during the day, Two Officers and 42 O.R. were evacuated and 11 other ranks were returned to duty, leaving one Officer and 219 O.R. remaining on our books.	J.E.P.
"	6/7/17	9 p.m.	The day has been fine and warm with good visibility. — a Medical Board was held this morning for the reclassification of P.B. men brought before it. — Forty six other ranks (33 sick + 13 wounded) were admitted during the day, 26 cases were evacuated to a Casualty Clearing Stn. and 16 cases were returned to duty, leaving one Officer and 226 O.R. remaining on our books.	J.E.P.
"	7/7/17	9 p.m.	The weather continues fine and warm. — Captain T. O'BRIEN R.A.M.C. reported his departure this day on 14 days leave of absence to England. — Four Officers (One sick + 3 wounded) + 74 other ranks (32 sick + 42 wounded) were admitted during the day, 3 Officers + 50 other ranks were evacuated to a Casualty Clearing Stn. 2 men died of wounds, + 16 cases were returned to duty, leaving 2 Officers and 237 other ranks remaining on our books	J.E.P.

1875 Wt. W593/826 1.000,000 4/15 J.B.C. & A. A.D.S.S./Forms/C. 2118.

Instructions regarding War Diaries and Intelligence Summaries are contained in F. S. Regs., Part II. and the Staff Manual respectively. Title Pages will be prepared in manuscript.

WAR DIARY
or
~~INTELLIGENCE SUMMARY~~
(Erase heading not required.)

Army Form C. 2118

Place	Date	Hour	Summary of Events and Information	Remarks and references to Appendices
LOCRE	8/7/17	9 p.m.	Heavy rain fell this morning and it has been showery throughout the day. – Captain G.P. KIDD R.A.M.C. reported his arrival this morning on return from 10 days leave in England. LIEUT. E. EVANS R.A.M.C. reported his arrival on completion of temporary duty as M.O. i/c 9th Welsh Regt. – Three Officers and 60 O.R. were admitted during the day, Two Officers & 51 O.R. were evacuated, One Officer & 12 O.R. were returned to duty, two men died of wounds, leaving Two Officers and 232 other ranks remaining on our books.	J.E.P.
"	9/7/17	9 p.m.	The day has been dull and cloudy. – The A.D.M.S. visited the Field Ambulance this morning and visited all the Wards etc. – Four Officers and 60 O.R. were admitted during the day, Two Officers and 29 O.R. were evacuated and 8 cases were returned to duty, leaving 4 Officers and 255 O.R. remaining on our books.	J.E.P.
"	10/7/17	9 p.m.	Lt. Col. J.E. POWELL DSO reported his departure this morning on 10 days leave of absence in England and temporary command was assumed by Capt. G.P. KIDD. A court of Enquiry was held this morning to determine the illegal absence of a man of this unit. The weather remains dull & cloudy & somewhat colder. A.D.M.S. visited and inspected the hospital during the evening. 114. O.R. were admitted during the day. 42. O.R. were evacuated to C.C.S. 1. O.R. Died. 18. O.R. were returned to duty. Leaving 4. Off. & 308. O.R. remaining.	G.P.K.

1875 Wt. W593/826 1.000,000 4/15 J.B.C. & A. A.D.S.S./Forms/C. 2118.

Instructions regarding War Diaries and Intelligence Summaries are contained in F. S. Regs., Part II. and the Staff Manual respectively. Title Pages will be prepared in manuscript.

WAR DIARY
or
~~INTELLIGENCE SUMMARY~~
(Erase heading not required.)

Army Form C. 2118

Place	Date	Hour	Summary of Events and Information	Remarks and references to Appendices
LOCRE.	11/7/17	9.0 pm	The weather remains fine and warm. Lt. & Qm. A. BENNETT reported his arrival back for duty from ten days leave of absence in England. 1. Off. & 46. O.R. were admitted during the day 47. O.R. evacuated to CCS 3. O.R. to D.R.S. 1. O.R. Died. 3. O.R. transferred to 48. F^d Amb. 36. O.R. to Duty. Leaving 2 Off. & 267. O.R. remaining.	[initials]
"	12/7/17	9.0 pm	A.D.M.S visited the hospital during the morning for the purpose of examining prospective P.B. cases. Inspector of Catering 2nd Army visited the unit during the afternoon and inspected the cook house and messing arrangements for the personnel. He expressed himself as quite satisfied with all existing arrangements and also gave various useful advice. 40. O.R. admitted during the day 1. Off. & 25. O.R evacuated to CCS. 3. O.R. trans. to 48. F^d Amb 2. O.R. died. 18. O.R. to Duty. Leaving 1. Off & 259. O.R. remaining.	[initials]
"	13/7/17	9.0 pm	Weather still fine and very hot. 44. O.R. were admitted during the day. 22. O.R. Evacuated to CCS 18. O.R. to duty. Leaving 1. Off. & 263 O.R. remaining. 143 of these being at D.R.S and Corps Scabies Hosp. The hospital is not at all unduly crowded at present and should not become so at the present rate of admissions. A fairly large no. of cases from "other divisions" are still being admitted. Cases from the 19 Div. being quite few.	[initials]
"	14/7/17	9.0 pm	Orders received to take over A.D.S at DOME HOUSE on the 16th inst. The CCS's in BAILLEUL being now closed owing to hostile shelling, cases are now being evacuated to HAZEBROUCK. 3. Off. & 83. O.R. admitted during the day. 2. Off. & 51. O.R evacuated to CCS 1. O.R. died. 20. O.R. to Duty. Leaving 2. Off. & 274. O.R. remaining.	[initials]

1875 Wt. W593/826 1,000,000 4/15 J.B.C. & A. A.D.S.S./Forms/C. 2118.

Instructions regarding War Diaries and Intelligence Summaries are contained in F. S. Regs., Part II. and the Staff Manual respectively. Title Pages will be prepared in manuscript.

WAR DIARY
or
~~INTELLIGENCE SUMMARY~~

(Erase heading not required.)

Army Form C. 2118

Place	Date	Hour	Summary of Events and Information	Remarks and references to Appendices
LOCRE.	15/7/17	9.0 pm	D.D.M.S. IX Corps together with A.D.M.S. visited the unit the morning to give verbal instructions that a "Surgical Team" including nursing sisters will be attached to the hospital from tomorrow, for the purpose of doing major operations & treating serious surgical cases here during the temporary closing of the BAILLEUL CCS. Arrangements have been made for them to have the theatre and one ward of 30 beds. 2. Off & 56. O.R. admitted. 1. Off. & 28. O.R. evacuated to CCS. 2. Off. to Officers Rest. 1. Off & 11. O.R. to duty leaving 291. O.R. remaining.	[initials]
"	16/7/17	12.0 hm	A.D.S. party under Capt. COCHRANE RAMC left at 9.0 A.m to take over the A.D.S. at DOME HOUSE. A.D.M.S. visited the unit during the morning for the purpose of seeing prospective P.B. cases.	
		9.0 pm	Operating team from No 53. CCS under Capt THOMAS RAMC, consisting of 2. M.O.'s, 3. nursing sisters and 4. orderlies, reported their arrival for duty under instructions from D.M.S. 2nd Army. A.D.M.S. visited the unit again during the evening. 1. Off. & 72. O.R. admitted. 1. Off. & 49. O.R. evacuated to CCS. 20. O.R. to duty. Leaving 296. O.R. remaining, 164 of these being at D.R.S. and Corps Scabies hospital.	[initials]
"	17/7/17		The weather remains fine and warm. I visited the A.D.M.S. in the morning to settle various points about the disposal of gassed cases. I visited the A.D.S. in the afternoon & found everything there quite satisfactory. A.D.M.S. visited the unit during the evening. 5 Off. & 86. O.R. admitted. 2 Off & 65. O.R. to CCS. 12. O.R. to duty. Leaving 3. Off & 303. O.R. remaining.	[initials]

Instructions regarding War Diaries and Intelligence Summaries are contained in F. S. Regs., Part II. and the Staff Manual respectively. Title Pages will be prepared in manuscript.

WAR DIARY
or
~~INTELLIGENCE SUMMARY~~
(Erase heading not required.)

Army Form C. 2118

Place	Date	Hour	Summary of Events and Information	Remarks and references to Appendices
LOCRE	18/7/17	9.0 pm	The weather has been considerably cooler today and a good deal of rain has fallen. The "Operating team" are now well settled down and several major operations have been performed since they arrived. They are watching all serious cases from the Corps Area. 4. Off & 94. O.R. (including 1. German P.O.W.) admitted. 3. Off. & 32. O.R. evacuated to CCS 20. O.R. to duty. Leaving 4. Off. & 347 O.R. remaining (199. at DRS & Corps Scabies HP)	GPK.
"	19/7/17	9.0 pm	ADMS visited the hospital during the morning for the purpose of seeing prospective P.B. cases. DDMS IX Corps. visited the unit in the afternoon and inspected all arrangements made for the accomodation of the "Operating team". 4. Off. & 82. O.R. (including 1 German POW) admitted. 2. Off. & 46 O.R. evacuated to CCS 2. O.R. died. 1. Off. & 7. O.R. to duty. Leaving 3. Off & 380 O.R. remaining (237 at DRS & Scabies HP)	GPK.
"	20/7/17	9.0 pm	Consulting Physician to the 2nd Army visited the hospital in the morning and inspected the ward set apart for the "Operating team". The weather remains fine and warm. 1. Off. & 98 O.R. admitted. 65. O.R. evacuated to CCS. 3. O.R. died 37 O.R. to duty. 4. Off & 371 O.R. remained (231. being at DRS and Corps scabies hospital)	GPK.
"	21/7/17	12.0 noon	Lieut J.A.A. BODDY reported his arrival back for duty with the unit, from temporary duty with 250. Tunnelling Coy. RE. Arrangements have now been made whereby cases from the Special ward can be evacuated direct to Ambulance Train at TROIS ARBRES, these cases being put onto the books of No. 53. CCS before evacuation.	
		9.0 pm	I relieved Capt. COCHRANE at the ADS this afternoon. Lieut EVANS taking his place. The Off. hosp in BAILLEUL has now reopened and we are to close down the Off wards here with the exception of two beds, the remainder to be given over to the nursing sisters. 2. Off. & 97 O.R. admitted. 48 O.R. to CCS. 35. O.R. to duty. 6. Off & 385 O.R. remained.	GPK.

1875 Wt. W593/826 1,000,000 4/15 J.B.C. & A. A.D.S.S./Forms/C. 2118.

Army Form C. 2118

Instructions regarding War Diaries and Intelligence Summaries are contained in F. S. Regs., Part II. and the Staff Manual respectively. Title Pages will be prepared in manuscript.

WAR DIARY
or
~~INTELLIGENCE SUMMARY~~
(Erase heading not required.)

Place	Date	Hour	Summary of Events and Information	Remarks and references to Appendices
LOCRE	22/7/17	6 p.m.	Lieut Col. J.E. POWELL DSO reported his arrival back for duty and reassumes command from this date. 4 Off. & 98. O.R. admitted. 2. Off & 33. O.R. to C.C.S. 4. Off to Officers Rest Hosp. 5. O.R. died ~~remaining~~ 23. O.R. to duty. Leaving 427 O.R. remaining (262. being at D.R.S. & Scabies H.P.	GHK.
"	23/7/17	9 p.m.	The A.D.M.S. visited the Field Ambulance this morning. Captain F. O'BRIEN RAMC reported his arrival back for duty from 14 days leave in England, this morning. — I visited the A.D.S. at DOME HOUSE at 5 p.m. and explored the track from there to ONRAET FARM A.D.S. and arranged that in future all cases will be carried direct from DOME HOUSE to ONRAET FARM & there loaded on the Tramway, I therefore withdrew the two motor ambulances from DOME HOUSE & VOORMEZEELE. — 10 Officers & 144 O.R. admitted. 7 Officers & 83 O.R. evacuated. 5 men died & 7 were returned to duty, leaving 7 Officers and 484 O.R. remaining on our books.	J.E.P.
"	24/7/17	9 p.m.	The weather continues fine and warm. – Two Officers and 120 O.R. were admitted during the day and two officers and 105 O.R. were evacuated, one Officer & 5 O.R. died of wounds and one Officer & 34 O.R. were returned to duty, leaving 5 Officers and 460 O.R. remaining on our books, of which 279 are at the Divisional Rest Stn. & Corps Scabies Stn. The A.D.M.S. visited the Field Ambulance this evening.	J.E.P.

Instructions regarding War Diaries and Intelligence Summaries are contained in F. S. Regs., Part II. and the Staff Manual respectively. Title Pages will be prepared in manuscript.

WAR DIARY
or
~~INTELLIGENCE SUMMARY~~

(Erase heading not required.)

Army Form C. 2118

Place	Date	Hour	Summary of Events and Information	Remarks and references to Appendices
LOCRE	25/7/17	9 p.m.	Heavy rain fell throughout the morning, but the weather cleared in the afternoon, though visibility remained poor. – Captain T. O'BRIEN R.A.M.C. reported his departure this day for temporary medical charge of the 7th South Lancashire Regt. and Lieut. J. A. BODDY R.A.M.C. reported his departure for temporary duty at No. 17 C.C.S. Fifth Army. Four Officers and 171 O.R. were admitted during the day, three Officers and 119 O.R. were evacuated, 10 O.R. died of wounds, and 11 men were returned to duty leaving six Officers and 491 O.R. remaining on our books.	J.E.P.
"	26/7/17	9 p.m.	The day has been fine and warm throughout. – I visited the A.D.S. at DOME HOUSE this evening and made arrangements with regard to marking out the tracks for walking wounded. – I also saw the G.O.C. 57th Inf. Brigade with regard to the recent admissions of gassed cases from the 10th Royal Warwicks. Two Officers and 102 O.R. were admitted, 4 Officers and 78 O.R. were evacuated one man died of wounds, and 11 O.R. were returned leaving 4 Officers & 503 O.R. remaining on our books, of which 343 are at the D.R.S. & Scabies Stn.	J.E.P.
"	27/7/17	9 p.m.	The weather continues fine and warm. The A.D.M.S. visited the Field Ambulance this morning. – Under instructions from the D.M.S. 2nd Army the Surgical Team rejoined No. 53 C.C.S. at 6 p.m. this evening, 3 Officers & 13 O.R. patients were transferred with them. – Five Officers and 133 O.R. were admitted during the day 5 Officers and 85 O.R. were evacuated, one man died of wounds, and 36 O.R. were returned to duty leaving 4 Officers and 514 O.R. remaining on our books.	J.E.P.

1875 Wt. W593/826 1,000,000 4/15 J.B.C. & A. A.D.S.S./Forms/C. 2118.

Army Form C. 2118.

WAR DIARY
or
~~INTELLIGENCE SUMMARY~~
(Erase heading not required.)

Instructions regarding War Diaries and Intelligence Summaries are contained in F. S. Regs., Part II. and the Staff Manual respectively. Title Pages will be prepared in manuscript.

Place	Date	Hour	Summary of Events and Information	Remarks and references to Appendices
LOCRE	28/7/17	9 p.m.	The weather continues fine and hot. – Captain H. B. OWENS R.A.M.C. having reported his arrival for duty with this Unit is taken on the strength from this date. – Four Officers and 107 O.R. were admitted during the day, 8 Officers and 90 O.R. were evacuated, 3 men died of wounds and 36 O.R. were returned to duty, leaving 492 O.R. remaining on our books, of which 324 O.R. are in the D.R.S. & Scabies Dressing Stn.	J.E.P.
"	29/7/17	9 p.m.	A thunderstorm with heavy rain occurred in the morning. – Major General T. BRIDGES G.O.C. Division inspected the Field Ambulance this morning and expressed his satisfaction with all he saw. — At 3.30 p.m. I received a message from Lieut. E. EVANS R.A.M.C. Officer i/c A.D.S. stating that they had been badly shelled with Gas & H.E. shells for the past 48 hours and were in need of rest and relief – So I sent Captain A.A. SMALLEY & 4 Bearer Squads up in relief at 5 p.m. & also visited the A.D.S. myself at 5 p.m. – The concrete Dug-out has been partly blown in. Four Officers and 130 O.R. were admitted during the day, 3 Officers and 87 O.R. were evacuated 2 men died of their wounds and 50 cases were returned to duty, leaving one Officer and 483 O.R.	J.E.P.
"	30/7/17	9 p.m.	The day has been cloudy and dull and rain fell throughout the morning but cleared later. – The A.D.M.S. visited the Field Ambulance in the morning and also in the evening – I sent Captain H.B. OWENS R.A.M.C. with 6 Bearer Squads as a reinforcement to the A.D.S. at 5 p.m. making two Officers & 13 Bearer Squads and a Dressing Stn. party. Lieut. E. EVANS & Lieut. J.A. BODDY reported their arrival back for duty. 118 O.R. were admitted during the day and 83 O.R. were evacuated, 3 men died of their wounds, and 29 men were returned to duty, leaving one Officer and 486 O.R. remaining.	J.E.P.

Instructions regarding War Diaries and Intelligence Summaries are contained in F. S. Regs., Part II. and the Staff Manual respectively. Title Pages will be prepared in manuscript.

WAR DIARY
or
~~INTELLIGENCE SUMMARY~~

(Erase heading not required.)

Army Form C. 2118.

Place	Date	Hour	Summary of Events and Information	Remarks and references to Appendices
LOCRE	31/7/17	9 p.m.	The day has been dull and cloudy and rain began falling about 7 p.m. – The 19th Division attacked at 3.50 a.m. and carried all objectives, taking part in the general attack of the army. Casualties were light. 9 Officers and 113 O.R. were admitted, 8 Officers and 91 O.R. were evacuated, 5 cases were returned to duty, leaving (2 Officers) and 523 O.R. remaining on our books. – All arrangements worked smoothly and easily. – Surgeon-General MACPHERSON D.D.G.M.S. the D.D.M.S. & the A.D.M.S. visited the Field Ambulance during the day. – This Unit only dealt with the wounded who were stretcher cases, not with walking wounded.	J.E.P.

J. E. Powell
Lieut. Colonel R.A.M.C.
O.C. 57th Field Ambulance

2449 Wt. W14957/M90 750,000 1/16 J.B.C. & A. Forms/C.2118/12.

Aug. 1917

140/2364

No. 57. F. A.

19

Instructions regarding War Diaries and Intelligence Summaries are contained in F. S. Regs., Part II. and the Staff Manual respectively. Title Pages will be prepared in manuscript.

WAR DIARY
or
INTELLIGENCE SUMMARY
(Erase heading not required.)

Army Form C. 2118.

57 Fd Amb
Vol 26

Place	Date	Hour	Summary of Events and Information	Remarks and references to Appendices
LOCRE	1/8/17	9 p.m.	The day has been wet and stormy throughout. – Six Officers and 133 O.R. were admitted during the day, Five Officers and 127 O.R. were evacuated to a Casualty Clearing Stn. Six men died of wounds, and One Officer and 27 O.R. were returned to duty, leaving Two Officers and 496 O.R. remaining on our books, 413 O.R. being at the D.R.S. & C.S.C.	J.E.P.
"	2/8/17	9 p.m.	The weather has again been wet and stormy. ADMS visited the unit during the morning for the purpose of seeing prospective P.B. cases. Two Officers & 70. O.R. admitted during the day. One Officer & 78 O.R. evacuated to CCS. Two O.R. died. 76. O.R. returned to duty. Leaving three Officers & 410 O.R. on our books 331 O.R. being at DRS & CSS.	G.H.
"	3/8/17	9 p.m.	Weather again wet and stormy. Capt A.R. SMALLEY RAMC reported his departure on ten days leave of absence in England. I recalled Capt OWENS RAMC from the A.D.S. for duty at the M.D.S. and also recalled four bearer squads as the amount of work is not so great now. 3. Off. & 84. O.R. admitted during the day. 1. Off & 38. O.R. evacuated to C.C.S. 2. Off. to Off. Rest Station. 4. O.R. died. 64. O.R. to duty. Leaving 3. Off. & 392 O.R remaining on the books. (272 O.R. being at D.R.S. and C.S.S.)	G.H.
"	4/8/17	9 p.m.	Lieut E. EVANS RAMC reported his departure on termination of contract and is struck off the strength from this date. The ADMS visited the hospital during the morning. 2. Off. & 189 O.R. admitted. 3. Off. & 39. O.R. evacuated to CCS. 1. O.R. died. 85. O.R. to Duty. Leaving 2. Off. & 456 O.R. on our books. (238. at DRS. & C.S.S.)	G.H.

2449 Wt. W14957/M90 750,000 1/16 J.B.C. & A. Forms/C.2118/12.

Instructions regarding War Diaries and Intelligence Summaries are contained in F. S. Regs., Part II. and the Staff Manual respectively. Title Pages will be prepared in manuscript.

WAR DIARY
or
INTELLIGENCE SUMMARY
(Erase heading not required.)

Army Form C. 2118.

Place	Date	Hour	Summary of Events and Information	Remarks and references to Appendices
LOCRE	5/8/17	9.0 pm	The weather has improved today & has been quite dry and warm. A very large number of sick have been admitted during the last three days owing to the bad conditions in the forward area. Most of these are suffering from trench feet or "Exhaustion" & should be fit for duty after a short period at the D.R.S. 2. Off. & 155. O.R. admitted during the day. 1. Off. & 49. O.R. evacuated to C.C.S. 1. O.R. Died 47. O.R. to duty. Leaving 3. Off. & 514. O.R. remaining on the books (307. O.R. being at D.R.S. and C.S.S.)	[illegible]
"	6/8/17	9.0 pm	ADMS visited the hospital in the morning to see prospective A.B. cases. The weather has kept better again today and the number of sick admitted has much decreased as a result. Warning order received that we shall hand over to a F. Amb of the 37th Div. on the 8th inst. and move to BOESCHEPE FARM. Capt. T.A. O'BRIEN reported his arrival back for duty from temp. duty as MO 4/7. 8. Lancs 2. Off. & 174 O.R. admitted. 1. Off. & 100 O.R. evacuated to C.C.S. 38. O.R. to duty Leaving 4. Off. & 550. O.R. remaining on the books. (346. O.R. being at D.R.S. & C.S.S.)	[illegible]
"	7/8/17	12.0 noon	Operation orders received for tomorrows move – handing over to be completed by noon tomorrow. ADMS visited the hospital during the morning.	
		9.0 pm	Orders received to hand over tomorrow to the 49. F. Amb 37th Div. O.C. 49. F. Amb. called to make arrangements re handing over. O.C. 48. F. Amb also called re taking over of the A.D.S. Advanced party 49. F. Amb. arrived at 6.0 pm. to commence taking over. 2. Off. & 105 O.R. admitted during the day. 3. Off. & 44. O.R. evacuated to C.C.S. 2. Off. to C.R.S. 1. O.R. died. 36. O.R. to duty. Leaving 1. Off. & 574 O.R. remaining (379. O.R. at D.R.S. and C.S.S.)	[illegible]

Instructions regarding War Diaries and Intelligence Summaries are contained in F. S. Regs., Part II. and the Staff Manual respectively. Title Pages will be prepared in manuscript.

WAR DIARY
or
~~INTELLIGENCE SUMMARY~~

(Erase heading not required.)

Army Form C. 2118.

Place	Date	Hour	Summary of Events and Information	Remarks and references to Appendices
MONT KOKERELE	8/8/17	12. noon	Orders received that the Division will continue the move on the 12th inst. to a training area. the personnel to move by train and the transport by road. The hospital and equipment at the HOSPICE LOCRE were handed over during the morning to No. 49. Fd Amb. 37th Division	
		9.0 pm	Handing over completed, the unit marched off at 3.0 pm and arrived here at 4.45. The ADMS visited the unit during the evening to give verbal instructions re the forthcoming move. Lieut J.A.A BODDY reported his departure on 10 days special leave of absence to England. Capt. T.A O'BRIEN reported his departure for temp duty as M.O. i/c 19. DRS. 2 Off. & 114. OR admitted during the day. 2. Off & 66. OR to CCS. 1. Off. & 46. OR transferred to No 49. Fd Amb. 113. OR to duty. Remaining 463 OR on the books: all these being at DRS or CCS.	[illegible]
"	9/8/17	9 p.m.	The weather continues showery. — Captain G.P. KIDD in charge of the transport of the Unit marched off at 9 a.m. this morning. Captain A.P. FRY proceeded by car in charge of an advance party for billeting in the new area. — An advance party from No. 96 Field Ambulance arrived at 4 p.m. and took over this site together with stores and patients this evening. — 14 cases were admitted to the Field Ambulance 7 cases were evacuated to a C.C.S. 271 cases were transferred to No. 58 Field Ambulance and 167 cases were returned to duty, leaving 32 cases remaining of which 25 cases are at the Corps Scabies Station.	J.E.P.

2449 Wt. W14957/M90 750,000 1/16 J.B.C. & A. Forms/C.2118/12.

Army Form C. 2118.

Instructions regarding War Diaries and Intelligence Summaries are contained in F. S. Regs., Part II. and the Staff Manual respectively. Title Pages will be prepared in manuscript.

WAR DIARY
or
~~INTELLIGENCE SUMMARY~~

(Erase heading not required.)

Place	Date	Hour	Summary of Events and Information	Remarks and references to Appendices
QUESQUES	10/8/17	10 p.m.	It has again being showery with bright intervals throughout the day. – The Personnel marched off at 7.25 a.m. under Captain H. B. OWENS and entrained at BAILLEUL at 9.30 a.m. and detrained at WIZERNES at 3 p.m. and marched 14 miles here where they arrived at 10 p.m. and went into billets. – 22 O.R. were admitted to the Field Ambulance, 11 O.R. were evacuated to a C.C.S. 12 O.R. were transferred to No. 58 Field Ambulance and 6 O.R. were transferred to No. 96 Field Ambulance, leaving 25 cases remaining on our books.	J.E.P.
ALINCTHUN CHATEAU	11/8/17	9 p.m.	The Weather continues showery. – The Personnel marched at 9.20 a.m. and arrived here at 12.20 p.m. – The Transport of the Unit arrived here at 6.20 p.m. – The Unit has opened up for the reception of sick of the 56th Inf Brigade. – There have been no admissions to the Field Ambulance to-day.	J.E.P.
"	12/8/17	9 p.m.	Heavy rain fell in the night, but the day has been fine and warm throughout. – The A.D.M.S. visited the Field Ambulance in the afternoon. – The Personnel have been employed in preparing wards for the reception of the sick and in cleaning up the surroundings. 7 O.R. sick were admitted to the Field Ambulance during the day, none were evacuated.	J.E.P.
"	13/8/17	9 p.m.	The weather has continued fine and warm. – The Personnel have been employed on general fatigues. – An anti-gas box respirator parade was also held. – Eleven O.R. were admitted to the Field Ambulance during the day, one case was evacuated and 2 cases were returned to duty, leaving 40 cases remaining.	J.E.P.

2449 Wt. W14957/M90 750,000 1/16 J.B.C. & A. Forms/C.2118/12.

Instructions regarding War Diaries and Intelligence Summaries are contained in F. S. Regs., Part II. and the Staff Manual respectively. Title Pages will be prepared in manuscript.

WAR DIARY
or
~~INTELLIGENCE SUMMARY~~
(Erase heading not required.)

Army Form C. 2118.

Place	Date	Hour	Summary of Events and Information	Remarks and references to Appendices
ALINCTHUN CHATEAU	14/8/17	9 p.m.	Heavy rain fell in the night but to-day has been fine and warm. – The Personnel of the Unit were paid this morning. – They were also exercised in Physical drill. Captain H.B. OWENS reported his departure this day for temporary duty as M.O. i/c 9th Loyal North Lancs Regt. – Three O.R. were admitted to the Field Ambulance during the day, 4 O.R. were evacuated and 10 O.R. were returned to duty, leaving 29 O.R. remaining.	J.E.P.
"	15/8/17	9 p.m.	Rain fell last night again and also the whole of the morning, but the remainder of the day has been fine. – Eight O.R. were admitted to the Field Ambulance during the day, five cases were evacuated and two cases were returned to duty, leaving 31 O.R. remaining in the Field Ambulance, of which 13 are at the Corps Scabies Station.	J.E.P.
"	16/8/17	9 p.m.	The day has been fine but cool throughout. – The Personnel were employed on general fatigues and were also taken on a route march. – The acting Brigadier-General 56th Inf. Brigade visited the Field Ambulance in the morning. – Ten O.R. were admitted to the Field Ambulance during the day, 4 cases were evacuated and 3 cases were returned to duty, leaving 34 cases remaining.	J.E.P.
"	17/8/17	9 p.m.	The weather continues fine and a little warmer. – Captain A.A. SMALLEY reported his arrival on return from 12 days leave of absence. – The Personnel were employed in General fatigues and also exercised in Physical Drill. – Only two O.R. were admitted to the Field Ambulance during the day, 4 O.R. were evacuated and one man was returned to duty, leaving 31 O.R. remaining.	J.E.P.

2449 Wt. W14957/M90 750,000 1/16 J.B.C. & A. Forms/C.2118/12.

Instructions regarding War Diaries and Intelligence Summaries are contained in F. S. Regs., Part II. and the Staff Manual respectively. Title Pages will be prepared in manuscript.

WAR DIARY
or
~~INTELLIGENCE SUMMARY~~
(Erase heading not required.)

Army Form C. 2118.

Place	Date	Hour	Summary of Events and Information	Remarks and references to Appendices
ALINCTHUN CHATEAU	18/8/17	9 p.m.	The weather continues fine and cool. – The Personnel were employed on general fatigues and also taken on a Route march. – Seven O.R. were admitted during the day to the Field Ambulance, two O.R. were evacuated and one case was returned to duty, leaving 35 O.R. remaining on our books of which 11 O.R. are at the Corps Scabies Stn.	J.E.P.
"	19/8/17	9 p.m.	The weather continues fine and cool. Seven O.R. were admitted to the Field Ambulance and four O.R. were evacuated, three O.R. were returned to duty, leaving 35 O.R. remaining in the Field Ambulance, of which 10 O.R. are at the Corps Scabies Stn.	J.E.P.
"	20/8/17	9 p.m.	Lt. Col. J.E. POWELL DSO reported his departure for temporary duty as A.D.M.S. 19th Div. temporary command of the unit being assumed by Capt. G.P. KIDD. Pte. J.A.A. BODDY reported his arrival back for duty from ten days leave of absence in England. The personnel were sent for a route march again this morning, the weather being still fine & cool. 10 O.R. admitted during the day. 5. O.R. Evacuated. 11. O.R. to duty. Leaving 29. O.R. remaining	G.P.K.
"	21/8/17	9 p.m.	The weather still remains fine & cool. Orders received that the 56th & 57th Inf. Brigades are changing billetting areas. Medical arrangements will remain the same, this unit now administering the 57th Bde which will move into this area tomorrow. 12. O.R. admitted during the day. 1. O.R. Evacuated. 6. O.R. to Duty. Leaving 34. O.R. remaining. 2. O.R. at Corps Scabies Stn.	G.P.K.
"	22/8/17	9. p.m.	Lt. J.A. BODDY reported his departure for temporary duty with 7th N. Lancs Reg. and Capt OWENS reported his arrival back for duty. 4. O.R. admitted during the day. 3. O.R. Evacuated. Leaving 35 O.R. remaining 1. O.R. at C.S.S.	G.P.K.

2449 Wt. W14957/M90 750,000 1/16 J.B.C. & A. Forms/C.2118/12.

Instructions regarding War Diaries and Intelligence Summaries are contained in F. S. Regs., Part II. and the Staff Manual respectively. Title Pages will be prepared in manuscript.

WAR DIARY
or
~~INTELLIGENCE SUMMARY~~
(Erase heading not required.)

Army Form C. 2118.

Place	Date	Hour	Summary of Events and Information	Remarks and references to Appendices
ALINCTHUN CHATEAU	23/8/17	9.0 pm	The weather has not been so good to-day, a good deal of rain having fallen. Capt H.B. OWENS reported his departure on 14 days leave of absence to England. 1. O.R. admitted during the day. 3. O.R. evacuated. 5. O.R. to Duty. Leaving 28. O.R. remaining.	[illegible]
"	24/8/17	9.0 pm	The weather is still uncertain and a good deal cooler. Warning orders received that the unit will probably move from this area about the 27th inst. 3. O.R. admitted during the day. 1. O.R. evacuated. 1. O.R. to duty. Leaving 29 O.R. remaining.	[illegible]
"	25/8/17	9.0 pm	Orders received that all Transport of the unit will move tomorrow 26th inst. The morning was spent in striking and packing tents and stores. 1. Off. + 7. O.R. admitted during the day. 1. Off + 7. O.R. evacuated. 7. O.R. to duty. Leaving 20. O.R. remaining.	[illegible]
"	26/8/17	1.0 pm	Billeting parties under Lt. + Qr.Mr. A. Bennett left by car at 10.30 AM for the new area. All packing was completed by noon and the Transport under Capt [illegible] marched off at 12.15 pm they will proceed to LUMBRES tonight + thence to the WALLON CAPPEL area by two stages.	[illegible]
		9.0 pm	1. Off. + 8. O.R. admitted during the day. 1. Off. + 10. O.R. evacuated. Leaving 18. O.R. remaining.	
"	27/8/17	9.0 pm	All remaining patients were evacuated during the day + the hospital closed in the evening. A.D.M.S. visited the unit during the morning to see prospective R.B. areas. Orders received that the unit will move by bus tomorrow to the [illegible] area. 4. O.R. admitted during the day. 4. O.R. evacuated. 1. O.R. to duty. Leaving nil remaining. After a heavy storm last night there was continuous rain almost all day to-day. Capt A.P. FRY reported his arrival back for duty from ten days leave of absence in England.	[illegible]
EY HOUCK	28/8/17	9.0 pm	The unit moved at 7.30 AM by bus and arrived here by noon. The transport joined up after arrival here, having marched from ARQUES this morning. Orders received that the unit will move to the MERRIS area tomorrow by march. Billeting party under Lt. + Qr.Mr. A. BENNETT left at 2.0 pm by car for MERRIS. No cases were admitted to-day.	[illegible]

2449 Wt. W14957/M90 750,000 1/16 J.B.C. & A. Forms/C.2118/12.

Army Form C. 2118.

Instructions regarding War Diaries and Intelligence Summaries are contained in F. S. Regs., Part II. and the Staff Manual respectively. Title Pages will be prepared in manuscript.

WAR DIARY
or
~~INTELLIGENCE SUMMARY~~

(Erase heading not required.)

Place	Date	Hour	Summary of Events and Information	Remarks and references to Appendices
STRAZEELE	29/8/17	6.0 pm	The unit marched off at 9.15 AM and arrived here at 2.0 pm. The billets are quite satisfactory and there is sufficient accommodation for all personel. ADMS visited the unit in the afternoon to give verbal instructions re medical arrangements. The unit will remain "open" here but no cases will be retained at present owing to lack of accommodation. All cases will be evacuated to CCS or transferred to DRS. 11 O.R. were admitted during the day & evacuated to No 15 CCS HAZEBROUCK.	GHK
"	30/8/17	9.0 pm	The unit was occupied throughout the day in cleaning up billets & settling down. Capt. T.A. O'BRIEN reported his arrival back for duty from MO i/c 19 DAC. 7. O.R. were admitted up to noon. Leaving 8. O.R. remaining. The weather remains very uncertain and a good deal of rain has fallen the last few days.	GHK
"	31/8/17	9.0 pm	Lt. Col. J.E. Powell DSO reported his arrival back for duty and reassumes command of the unit from this date. The weather improved today & looks decidedly more settled. 7. O.R. were admitted up to noon. 5. O.R. evacuated to CCS. 2. O.R. transferred to 58 F[d] Amb leaving 8. O.R. remaining. 3 being at DRS.	GHK

J.E. Powell
Lieut. Colonel RAMC
O.C. 57th Field Ambulance

2449 Wt. W14957/M90 750,000 1/16 J.B.C. & A. Forms/C.2118/12.

Sept. 1917
S

140/2438

No. 57 7.0

24

Instructions regarding War Diaries and Intelligence Summaries are contained in F. S. Regs., Part II. and the Staff Manual respectively. Title Pages will be prepared in manuscript.

WAR DIARY
or
~~INTELLIGENCE SUMMARY~~
(Erase heading not required.)

57 Fd Amb

Vol 27

Army Form C. 2118.

Place	Date	Hour	Summary of Events and Information	Remarks and references to Appendices
STRAZEELE	1/9/17	9 p.m.	The weather is dull cloudy and cool with some light showers. – One Officer and five other ranks were admitted to the Field Ambulance during the day 1 Officer & 1 O.R. were evacuated to a Casualty Clearing Stn., 4 O.R. were transferred to the 19th Div. Rest Stn. and 4 O.R. were transferred to No. 58 Field Ambulance leaving 4 cases remaining in the Field Ambulance.	J.E.P.
"	2/9/17	9 p.m.	The weather continues cool dull and cloudy. – Five other ranks (sick) were admitted during the day, three other ranks were evacuated to a Casualty Clearing Station, two cases were transferred to the 19th Divisional Rest Stn., and 3 cases were transferred to No. 58 Field Ambulance, leaving one case remaining.	J.E.P.
"	3/9/17	9 p.m.	The day has been fine, warm and clear. The Personnel were exercised in Physical Drill in the morning & paid later in the day. – One Officer and five other ranks were admitted to the Field Ambulance, four cases O.R. were evacuated to a Casualty Clearing Station, one O.R. was transferred to the 19th Divisional Rest Stn., and One Officer was transferred to the Corps Officers Rest Stn., leaving one case remaining.	J.E.P.
"	4/9/17	9 p.m.	The weather continues fine, warm and clear. – The Personnel went for a route march and attended Bathing parades in the morning. – Three other ranks were admitted to the Field Ambulance, one case was evacuated to a Casualty Clearing Stn., and two cases were transferred to the 19th Divisional Rest Stn., leaving one case remaining in the Field Ambulance. – Ten A.S.C. (H.T.) Batmen were sent to their Base Depot Havre to-day having been replaced by ten P.B. Infantry men.	J.E.P.

2449 Wt. W14957/M90 750,000 1/16 J.B.C. & A. Forms/C.2118/12.

Army Form C. 2118.

Instructions regarding War Diaries and Intelligence Summaries are contained in F. S. Regs., Part II. and the Staff Manual respectively. Title Pages will be prepared in manuscript.

WAR DIARY
or
INTELLIGENCE SUMMARY
(Erase heading not required.)

Place	Date	Hour	Summary of Events and Information	Remarks and references to Appendices
STRAZEELE	5/9/17	9 p.m.	The weather continues fine and warm and clear. – The Personnel were exercised in Physical Drill during the morning. Eleven other ranks (sick) were admitted during the day, 2 cases were evacuated to a Casualty Clearing Stn., 2 cases were transferred to the Divisional Rest Stn., and 3 cases were transferred to No. 58 Field Ambulance leaving 5 cases remaining in the Field Ambulance.	J.E.P.
TYRONE FARM Sq. M36a.9-4 Sheet 28	6/9/17	9 p.m.	The day has been fine with the exception of two Thunder Storms with heavy rain one at 4 a.m. and one at 7 p.m. – In accordance with instructions received from the A.D.M.S. The Unit marched out from STRAZEELE at 10 a.m. and arrived here at 1.30 p.m. where the Unit remains closed only collecting sick from the 58th Infantry Bde. and conveying them to the 58th Field Ambulance. – During the morning Two Officers and one O.R. (sick) were admitted to the Field Ambulance. Two Officers and one O.R. were evacuated to a Casualty Clearing Stn., one O.R. was transferred to the 19th Divisional Rest Stn. and 4 cases were transferred to No. 58 Field Ambulance leaving no cases remaining.	J.E.P.
"	7/9/17	9 p.m.	The weather has been dull, cloudy and hazy to-day. – The Personnel have been employed in general fatigues cleaning up the camp site. – The sick of the 58th Inf. Brigade were collected by the Unit's Ambulance cars and conveyed to No. 58 Field Ambulance. I attended a conference at 6 p.m. at the A.D.M.S.'s Office of Field Ambulance Commanders with the A.D.M.S.	J.E.P.

2449 Wt. W14957/M90 750,000 1/16 J.B.C. & A. Forms/C.2118/12.

Instructions regarding War Diaries and Intelligence Summaries are contained in F. S. Regs., Part II. and the Staff Manual respectively. Title Pages will be prepared in manuscript.

WAR DIARY
or
~~INTELLIGENCE SUMMARY~~
(Erase heading not required.)

Army Form C. 2118.

Place	Date	Hour	Summary of Events and Information	Remarks and references to Appendices
TYRONE FARM DRANOUTRE	8/9/17	9 p.m.	To-day has again been dull, cloudy and hazy. – The Personnel were employed in general fatigues and were also taken for a route march. – 1st Lieut. C.H. PHILLIPS M.O.R.C. U.S.A. reported his arrival for duty this day with the Unit. – Captain H.B. OWENS RAMC also reported his arrival for duty on return from 14 days leave of absence in England.	J.E.P.
"	9/9/17	9 p.m.	The weather has been fine, clear and warm throughout the day. – During the afternoon together with my Bearer Division Officer, Captain SMALLEY R.A.M.C., I visited Norfolk Lodge Advanced Dressing Stn. and all the Regimental Aid Posts served from there. – We also visited the site of the proposed new A.D.S. at crater VESUVIUS.	J.E.P.
"	10/9/17	9 p.m.	The weather has continued fine. – The Personnel were exercised in Physical Drill during the morning. – Operation Orders were received in the afternoon from the A.D.M.S. detailing this Unit to take over the A.D.S. at Norfolk Lodge on the 11th inst. and be responsible for the evacuation of the front line, and to take over the main Dressing Stn. at the Hospice LOCRE on the 12th inst. – Made arrangements to carry these orders out.	J.E.P.
"	11/9/17	9 p.m.	The weather still continues fine warm and clear. – Under instructions received from the A.D.M.S. Captain T. O'BRIEN R.A.M.C. reported his departure this day for England to report to the R.A.M.C. Training Centre BLACKPOOL for duty in MESOPOTAMIA. Captain OWENS & an advance party of 20 men reported their departure at 9.30 a.m. to take over NORFOLK LODGE A.D.S. – Captain SMALLEY and the remainder of the Bearer Division left at 1.30 p.m. – I visited the A.D.M.S. 19th Division in the morning.	J.E.P.

2449 Wt. W14957/M90 750,000 1/16 J.B.C. & A. Forms/C.2118/12.

Army Form C. 2118.

WAR DIARY
or
~~INTELLIGENCE SUMMARY~~

(Erase heading not required.)

Instructions regarding War Diaries and Intelligence Summaries are contained in F. S. Regs., Part II. and the Staff Manual respectively. Title Pages will be prepared in manuscript.

Place	Date	Hour	Summary of Events and Information	Remarks and references to Appendices
LOCRE	12/9/17	9 p.m.	The weather has been fine to-day, though cloudy. – The Unit marched off at 9:20 a.m. and arrived at the HOSPICE, LOCRE at 10 a.m. taking over from No. 49 Field Ambulance was completed by 12 Noon. – I visited the A.D.M.S. in the morning and the Advanced Dressing Stn. in the evening. The D.D.M.S. IX Corps visited the Unit in the afternoon.	J.E.P.
"	13/9/17	9 p.m.	The weather has continued fine though cloudy and cooler and a little rain has fallen this evening. – Two Officers and 68 O.R. were transferred from 37th Division Field Ambulances, two Officers and 74 O.R. were admitted, one Officer and 16 O.R. were evacuated to a Casualty Clearing Stn. leaving 3 Officers and 126 O.R. remaining in the Field Ambulance. – Of the above numbers 21 are wounded and 9 gassed (shell).	J.E.P.
"	14/9/17	9 p.m.	Some rain fell during the night but it has been fine throughout the day. The A.D.M.S. visited the Field Ambulance during the evening. – One Officer and 96 O.R. were admitted during the day, 40 O.R. were evacuated to a Casualty Clearing Station, Two Officers and 45 O.R. were transferred to the Rest Station. One man died of wounds, 6 O.R. were transferred to No. 50 Field Ambulance and 4 cases were returned to duty leaving Two Officers and 126 O.R. remaining.	J.E.P.

2449 Wt. W14957/M90 750,000 1/16 J.B.C. & A. Forms/C.2118/12.

Army Form C. 2118.

Instructions regarding War Diaries and Intelligence Summaries are contained in F. S. Regs., Part II. and the Staff Manual respectively. Title Pages will be prepared in manuscript.

WAR DIARY
or
~~INTELLIGENCE SUMMARY~~

(Erase heading not required.)

Place	Date	Hour	Summary of Events and Information	Remarks and references to Appendices
LOCRE	15/9/17	9 p.m.	The weather still continues fine though some rain fell during the night. — Captain B. SAMUEL reported his arrival this afternoon with a Dental Wagon for duty with the IX Corps. — Captain A.P. FRY R.A.M.C. also reported his arrival for duty on completion of temporary duty with the 9th Loyal North Lancs. Four Officers and 91 O.R. were admitted during the day. 4 Officers and 43 O.R. were evacuated to a Casualty Clearing Stn. One Officer and 38 O.R. were sent to the Rest Stn. One man died of wounds, 3 cases were transferred to the 50th Field Ambulance and 10 O.R. were returned to duty leaving One Officer and 122 O.R. remaining.	J.E.P.
"	16/9/17	9 p.m.	To-day has been fine and clear. — 86 O.R. were admitted to the Field Ambulance during the day. One Officer and 68 O.R. were evacuated to a Casualty Clearing Stn. 27 O.R. were transferred to the Divisional Rest Stn., 7 cases were transferred to the 50th F.A. and two cases were returned to duty leaving 104 O.R. remaining in the Field Ambulance. — A conference was held here this afternoon by the A.D.M.S. with the Field Ambulance Commanders, Bearer Division Officers and Regimental Medical Officers.	J.E.P.

2449 Wt. W14957/M90 750,000 1/16 J.B.C. & A. Forms/C.2118/12.

Instructions regarding War Diaries and Intelligence Summaries are contained in F. S. Regs., Part II. and the Staff Manual respectively. Title Pages will be prepared in manuscript.

WAR DIARY
or
~~INTELLIGENCE SUMMARY~~
(Erase heading not required.)

Army Form C. 2118.

Place	Date	Hour	Summary of Events and Information	Remarks and references to Appendices
LOCRE	17/9/17	9 p.m.	The weather has continued dry, but cloudy with a good deal of wind. – The D.D.M.S. Corps visited the Unit in the afternoon and inspected all the arrangements made and expressed his satisfaction. – Two Officers and 103 O.R. were admitted to the Field Ambulance during the day, 57 O.R. were evacuated to a Casualty Clearing Stn., 33 O.R. were transferred to the Div. Rest Stn. and 10 O.R. to the 50th Field Ambulance and 11 O.R. were returned to duty, leaving 2 Officers and 91 O.R. remaining.	J.E.P.
"	18/9/17	9 p.m.	The day has been cloudy and dull & some fine rain has fallen. – Captain Smalley & the Bearer Division returned to Headquarters at 4 p.m. this afternoon having handed over the A.D.S. at Norfolk Bridge to No. 59th Field Ambulance. One Officer and 82 O.R. were admitted during the day, one Officer and 39 O.R. were evacuated to a Casualty Clearing Stn., 14 cases were transferred the Div. Rest Stn. 4 cases were transferred to the 50th Field Ambulance, one man died of wounds and 5 cases were returned to duty, leaving two Officers and 110 O.R. remaining.	J.E.P.
"	19/9/17	9 p.m.	The weather has been fine and clear. – The Bearer Division under Captain Smalley left at 2 p.m. to report for duty to O.C. No 58 Field Ambulance. All motor ambulances left this Unit at 5.30 p.m. for duty with the 58th Field Ambulance for the evacuation of casualties from the front line. – Five Officers and 117 O.R. were admitted during the day, 3 Officers and 74 O.R. were evacuated to a Casualty Clearing Stn., 32 O.R. were sent to the Div. Rest Stn., 3 men died of wounds, 28 men were transferred to the 50th Fd. Ambulance leaving 4 Officers and 90 O.R. remaining.	J.E.P.

2449 Wt. W14957/M90 750,000 1/16 J.B.C. & A. Forms/C.2118/12.

Instructions regarding War Diaries and Intelligence Summaries are contained in F. S. Regs., Part II. and the Staff Manual respectively. Title Pages will be prepared in manuscript.

WAR DIARY
or
~~INTELLIGENCE SUMMARY~~
(Erase heading not required.)

Army Form C. 2118.

Place	Date	Hour	Summary of Events and Information	Remarks and references to Appendices
LOCRE	20/9/17	9 p.m.	Heavy rain fell in the night but to-day has been fine. – Zero hour was 5.40 a.m. and the first casualty from the attack arrived here at 9 a.m. – The D.D.M.S. Corps visited the Field Ambulance at 10.15 a.m. and again at 3 p.m. – The A.D.M.S. visited the Main Dressing Stn. at 4 p.m. During the day 22 Officers wounded and 236 O.R. wounded were admitted, dressed and evacuated with the exception of some severe cases who were unfit to continue the journey. During the afternoon it was necessary to have seven dressing tables working to keep pace with the casualties arriving, but there was never at any time an undue accumulation of cases.	J.E.P.
"	21/9/17	9 p.m.	The day has been fine and clear. – The A.D.M.S. visited the Main Dressing Stn. at 11.30 a.m. Captain A.A. SMALLEY R.A.M.C. reported his arrival for duty this evening, on completion of duty with the Bearer Division. – Six Officers and 107 other ranks wounded were admitted during the day and evacuated to C.C.S. with the exception of the more serious cases who were temporarily unfit to travel further.	J.E.P.
"	22/9/17	9 p.m.	The weather continues fine but the mornings and evenings are now cold. – One Officer and 102 O.R. were admitted during the day, one Officer and 94 O.R. were evacuated to a Casualty Clearing Stn., 3 other ranks were sent to the Divisional Rest Stn. 2 O.R. were transferred to 37th Division Field Ambulances, 3 men died of wounds, and one man was returned to duty, leaving two Officers and 21 other ranks remaining in the Field Ambulance.	J.E.P.

2449 Wt. W14957/M90 750,000 1/16 J.B.C. & A. Forms/C.2118/12.

Army Form C. 2118.

Instructions regarding War Diaries and Intelligence Summaries are contained in F. S. Regs., Part II. and the Staff Manual respectively. Title Pages will be prepared in manuscript.

WAR DIARY
or
~~INTELLIGENCE SUMMARY~~

(Erase heading not required.)

Place	Date	Hour	Summary of Events and Information	Remarks and references to Appendices
LOCRE	23/9/17	9 p.m.	The weather continues fine. Two N.C.O.s and 9 Bearer Squads of the Bearer Division returned to the Headquarters of the Unit this evening on completion of duty. – Rendered a report to the A.D.M.S. on the recent operations. Six Officers and 94 O.R. were admitted during the day. Six Officers and 57 O.R. were evacuated to a Casualty Clearing Stn., one man was transferred to No. 50 Field Ambulance, one man was returned to duty and two officers and two other ranks died of wounds, leaving 34 O.R. remaining in the Fd. Ambulance.	J.E.P.
"	24/9/17	9 p.m.	The weather continues fine and warm. – The A.D.M.S. visited the Field Ambulance this morning. – Eleven cases of Shell gas poisoning were admitted during the day. Twelve Officers and 179 O.R. were admitted during the day, Ten Officers and 100 O.R. were evacuated, 10 O.R. were sent to the Div. Rest Stn., 2 men died of their wounds, 7 O.R. were transferred to No. 50 Fd. Ambulance and 3 O.R. were returned to duty, leaving two Officers and 91 O.R. remaining.	J.E.P.
"	25/9/17	9 p.m.	The weather still continues fine and warm with cloudless skys. – Sent up Captain A.P. FRY to Norfolk Bridge A.D.S. in relief of Captain OWENS who returned to Headquarters for duty. – I also sent up 3 Bearer Squads as reinforcements to the A.D.S., making eleven squads in all. – Twenty cases of shell gas poisoning were admitted during the day, none of them were severe. – Nine Officers and 289 O.R. were admitted during the day, 5 Officers and 172 O.R. were evacuated to C.C.S. – One Officer and 34 O.R. were sent to the Rest Stns., 2 men died of wounds, 7 O.R. were transferred to No. 50 Fd. Ambulance and 4 men were returned to duty, leaving 5 Officers and 161 O.R. remaining.	J.E.P.

2449 Wt. W14957/M90 750,000 1/16 J.B.C. & A. Forms/C.2118/12.

Army Form C. 2118.

Instructions regarding War Diaries and Intelligence Summaries are contained in F. S. Regs., Part II. and the Staff Manual respectively. Title Pages will be prepared in manuscript.

WAR DIARY
or
INTELLIGENCE SUMMARY

(Erase heading not required.)

Place	Date	Hour	Summary of Events and Information	Remarks and references to Appendices
LOCRE	26/9/17	9 p.m.	The day has been much colder and cloudy but no rain has fallen during the day. Twelve gassed (Shell) cases were admitted during the day, none of them severe. Four Officers and 298 other ranks were admitted during the day, six Officers and 223 other ranks were evacuated to a Casualty Clearing Stn., two Officers and 71 O.R. were sent to the Corps + Divisional Rest Stns. 7 men died, 33 O.R. were transferred to No. 50 Field Ambulance and 4 men were returned to duty, leaving one Officer and 121 other ranks remaining.	J.E.P.
"	27/9/17	9 p.m.	Some rain fell in the night but to-day has been fine. – Three gassed cases were admitted during the day, all slight + due to Shell gas. – Ten Officers and 204 O.R. were admitted during the day, 4 Officers and 124 O.R. were evacuated to a Casualty Clearing Stn., One Officer and 51 O.R. were sent to the Corps and Divisional Rest Stns. 4 men died of wounds. 17 O.R. were transferred to No. 50 Field Ambulance and 10 O.R. were returned to duty, leaving six Officers and 119 O.R. remaining in the Field Ambulance.	J.E.P.
"	28/9/17	9 p.m.	The weather continues fine and warm. – Eleven Bearer squads arrived from the A.D.S. for 48 hours rest. Eight Officers and 187 O.R. were admitted during the day, 8 Officers and 117 O.R. were evacuated to a Casualty Clearing Stn., Two Officers and 53 O.R. were sent to the Corps + Divisional Rest Stns., 4 men died of wounds, 21 O.R. were transferred to No. 50 Field Ambulance, 4 men were returned to duty, leaving 4 Officers and 107 O.R. remaining.	J.E.P.

2449 Wt. W14957/M90 750,000 1/16 J.B.C. & A. Forms/C.2118/12.

Instructions regarding War Diaries and Intelligence Summaries are contained in F. S. Regs., Part II. and the Staff Manual respectively. Title Pages will be prepared in manuscript.

WAR DIARY
or
~~INTELLIGENCE SUMMARY~~
(Erase heading not required.)

Army Form C. 2118.

Place	Date	Hour	Summary of Events and Information	Remarks and references to Appendices
LOCRE	29/9/17	9 p.m.	The weather continues fine and warm, — [illegible] admitted during the day, none of them were serious. — [illegible] were admitted during the day, five Officers and 10[illegible] O.R. were evacuated to a Casualty Clearing Stn., two Officers and 3[illegible] O.R. were sent to the [illegible] Divisional Rest Stn., 3 men died of wounds, 9 men were transferred to No. 50 Field Ambulance and 9 men were returned to duty, leaving two Officers and 133 O.R. remaining in the Field Ambulance.	[illegible]
"	30/9/17	9 p.m.	The weather still continues fine and clear, — Two Officers and [illegible]5 O.R. were admitted with Shell gas poisoning during the day, none of them were serious. — Six Officers and 245 O.R. were admitted during the day, five Officers and 203 O.R. were evacuated to a Casualty Clearing Stn., [illegible] O.R. were sent to the Divisional Rest Stn., no Officers and 5 [illegible] died of wounds, 9 men were transferred to No. 50 Field Ambulance and 12 men were returned to duty, leaving two Officers and 100 O.R. remaining in the Field Ambulance.	[illegible]

[illegible] Powell
Lieut. Colonel R.A.M.C.
O.C. 57th Field Ambulance

2449 Wt. W14957/M90 750,000 1/16 J.B.C. & A. Forms/C.2118/12.

Oct. 1917

S

No. 57. 7. A.

15

Instructions regarding War Diaries and Intelligence Summaries are contained in F. S. Regs., Part II. and the Staff Manual respectively. Title pages will be prepared in manuscript.

WAR DIARY

~~or~~

~~INTELLIGENCE SUMMARY.~~

(*Erase heading not required.*)

Army Form C. 2118.

Vol 28

Place	Date	Hour	Summary of Events and Information	Remarks and references to Appendices
			OF	
			No 57 FIELD AMBULANCE.	
			FROM. 1. 10. 17 TO. 31. 10. 17	
			VOLUME. No 28.	

A5834 Wt. W4973/M687 750,000 8/16 D. D. & L. Ltd. Forms/C.2118/13.

Instructions regarding War Diaries and Intelligence Summaries are contained in F. S. Regs., Part II. and the Staff Manual respectively. Title Pages will be prepared in manuscript.

WAR DIARY
or
~~INTELLIGENCE SUMMARY~~
(Erase heading not required.)

Army Form C. 2118.

Place	Date	Hour	Summary of Events and Information	Remarks and references to Appendices
LOCRE	1/10/17	9 p.m.	To-day again has continued fine, warm and clear. – The A.D.M.S. visited the Main Dressing Station this morning and inspected all proposed F.B. cases. 14 O.R. were admitted with Shell gas poisoning, none of them bad severe cases. Fourteen Officers and 271 O.R. were admitted during the day, seven Officers and 183 O.R. were evacuated to a Casualty Clearing Stn., One Officer and 58 O.R. were sent to the Corps & Divisional Rest Stns. respectively, 10 O.R. died of wounds, 14 O.R. were transferred to No. 50 Field Ambulance, and 5 cases were returned to duty, leaving 8 Officers and 101 O.R. remaining.	J.F.P.
"	2/10/17	9 p.m.	The weather continues fine and clear. – Lieut. C.H. PHILLIPS M.O.R.C. U.S.A. reported his departure for temporary duty as M.O. i/c 8th Bn. Gloucester Regt. – Captain A.P. FRY R.A.M.C. reported his arrival for duty at Headquarters, having been recalled from the A.D.S. Norfolk Bridge. – Six Officers and 225 O.R. were admitted during the day, 9 Officers and 142 O.R. were evacuated to a Casualty Clearing Stn., One Officer and 51 O.R. were sent to the Corps & Divisional Rest Stns. respectively, One Officer and 9 O.R. died of wounds, six cases were transferred to No. 50 Field Ambulance, and 5 men were returned to duty, leaving 3 Officers and 113 O.R. remaining.	J.F.P.

2449 Wt. W14957/M90 750,000 1/16 J.B.C. & A. Forms/C.2118/12.

Instructions regarding War Diaries and Intelligence Summaries are contained in F. S. Regs., Part II. and the Staff Manual respectively. Title Pages will be prepared in manuscript.

WAR DIARY

or

~~INTELLIGENCE SUMMARY~~

(Erase heading not required.)

Army Form C. 2118.

Place	Date	Hour	Summary of Events and Information	Remarks and references to Appendices
LOCRE	3/10/17	9 pm	Rain fell during the night & this morning was [illegible] and dull [illegible] the same throughout the day. — The A.D.M.S. visited [illegible] morning. — 51 cases of Shell gas poisoning were admitted [illegible] These cases were severe. — 13 Officers and [illegible] day. 11 Officers and 175 O.R. were evacuated to [illegible] was sent to the Divisional Rest Stn. [illegible] 24 cases were transferred to No. 50 Field Ambulance [illegible] to duty leaving 2 Officers and 110 O.R. remaining in the [illegible]	
"	4/10/17	9 pm	Rain fell again last night & to-day has been [illegible] The A.D.M.S. visited the Main Dressing Stn. during the morning [illegible] Shell gas poisoning were admitted during the day, [illegible] Three Officers and 241 O.R. were admitted during the day. [illegible] Officers and 170 O.R. were evacuated to a Casualty Clearing Stn., 62 O.R. were sent to the Divisional Rest Stn. — One officer and 3 men died of wounds, 13 O.R. were transferred to No 50 Field Ambulance and 15 O.R. were returned to duty, leaving 4 Officers and 87 O.R. remaining in the Field Ambulance. Two wounded German Prisoners of War were admitted during the day.	J.E.P.

2449 Wt. W14957/M90 750,000 1/16 J.B.C. & A. Forms/C.2118/12.

Army Form C. 2118.

WAR DIARY
or
~~INTELLIGENCE SUMMARY~~
(Erase heading not required.)

Instructions regarding War Diaries and Intelligence Summaries are contained in F. S. Regs., Part II. and the Staff Manual respectively. Title Pages will be prepared in manuscript.

Place	Date	Hour	Summary of Events and Information	Remarks and references to Appendices
LOCRE	5/10/17	9 p.m.	The weather has become much colder but remained dry until this evening when more rain fell. Ten Officers and 194 O.R. were admitted during the day. 9 Officers and 140 O.R. were evacuated to a Casualty Clearing Stn., three Officers and 82 O.R. were sent to the Corps & Divisional Rest Stations respectively. 8 men died of wounds. 10 men were transferred to No. 50 Field Ambulance and 23 O.R. were returned to duty, leaving 2 Officers and 6[illegible] O.R. remaining in the Field Ambulance.	J.E.P.
"	6/10/17	9 p.m.	The weather has been cold and wet throughout the day. — Only 5 cases of Shell gas poisoning were admitted during the day, none of them were severe. — Eight Officers and 172 O.R. were admitted during the day. Seven Officers and 101 O.R. were evacuated to a Casualty Clearing Stn., 31 O.R. were sent to the Divisional Rest Stn., six men died of wounds, 14 O.R. were transferred to No. 50 Field Ambulance, and 3 men were returned to duty, leaving three Officers and 85 other ranks remaining in the Field Ambulance.	J.E.P.
"	7/10/17	9 p.m.	The weather continues cold and wet. — 4 cases of Shell gas poisoning were admitted during the day, they were all slight cases. Four Officers and 138 O.R. were admitted during the day, 4 Officers and 95 O.R. were evacuated to a Casualty Clearing Stn., One Officer and 32 O.R. were ~~[illegible]~~ sent to the Corps & Divisional Rest Stns. respectively, 3 men died of wounds, 10 cases were transferred to No. 50 Field Ambulance, 7 men were returned to duty leaving two Officers and 76 O.R. remaining.	J.E.P.

2449 Wt. W14957/M90 750,000 1/16 J.B.C. & A. Forms/C.2118/12.

Instructions regarding War Diaries and Intelligence Summaries are contained in F. S. Regs., Part II. and the Staff Manual respectively. Title Pages will be prepared in manuscript.

WAR DIARY
or
~~INTELLIGENCE SUMMARY~~

(Erase heading not required.)

Army Form C. 2118.

Place	Date	Hour	Summary of Events and Information	Remarks and references to Appendices
LOCRE	8/10/17	9 p.m.	To-day has been fine and warmer. – The A.D.M.S. visited the [illegible] this morning. – [illegible] paid the Personnel of the [illegible] this afternoon. Six Officers and 127 O.R. were admitted during the day, two Officers and 55 O.R. were evacuated to a Casualty Clearing Stn., 23 cases were sent to the Divisional Rest Stn., Two Officers and 3 O.R. died of their wounds. 3[illegible] O.R. were transferred to No. 50 Field Ambulance, and eleven men were returned to duty, leaving 4 Officers and 80 O.R. remaining.	
"	9/10/17	9 p.m.	Heavy rain fell again last night, but this morning was fine and [illegible] with a strong west wind. – Four Officers and 120 other ranks were admitted to the Field Ambulance during the day. – Four Officers and 73 O.R. were evacuated to a Casualty Clearing Stn., 25 cases were sent to the Divisional Rest Stn. One Officer and 11 other ranks were returned to duty, one man died of wounds and 18 cases were transferred to No. 50 Field Ambulance leaving 3 Officers and 72 other ranks remaining.	J.E.P.
"	10/10/17	9 p.m.	This morning was showery, but the remainder of the day has been fine with a drying wind. – The A.D.M.S. visited the Field Ambulance in the afternoon. – 16 cases of trench feet were admitted during the day. – Four Officers and 187 O.R. were admitted during the day, 3 Officers and 77 O.R. were evacuated to a C.C.S., 25 other ranks were sent to the Divisional Rest Stn., two men died of wounds, 15 cases were transferred to No. 50 Field Ambulance and 9 cases were returned to duty, leaving 4 Officers and 131 O.R. remaining.	J.E.P.

2149. Wt. W14957/M90 750,000 1/16 J.B.C. & A. Forms/C.2118/12.

Army Form C. 2118.

WAR DIARY
or
~~INTELLIGENCE SUMMARY~~
(Erase heading not required.)

Instructions regarding War Diaries and Intelligence Summaries are contained in F. S. Regs., Part II. and the Staff Manual respectively. Title Pages will be prepared in manuscript.

Place	Date	Hour	Summary of Events and Information	Remarks and references to Appendices
LOCRE	11/10/17	9 p.m.	The day has been fine and clear though cold. – Eleven cases of Diarrhoea were admitted & 9 cases of Trench feet during the day. – a Total of 7 Officers and 201 O.R. were admitted during the day, 6 Officers and 132 O.R. were evacuated to a C.C.S., One Officer and 53 O.R. were sent to the Corps and Divisional Rest Stns., respectively, One Officer 17 O.R. were transferred to No. 50 Field Ambulance, 2 men died of wounds, 9 men were returned to duty, leaving 3 Officers and 119 O.R. remaining.	J.E.P.
"	12/10/17	9 p.m.	The day has been dull, cloudy & cold & some rain has fallen. – The A.D.M.S. visited the Unit this morning. – 12 cases of Diarrhoea and 30 cases of Trench feet were admitted during the day. – a total of 4 Officers & 223 O.R. were admitted during the day, 4 Officers & 128 O.R. were evacuated to a C.C.S. 1 Officer & 41 O.R. were sent to the Corps & Divisional Rest Stns., 5 men died of wounds, 5 men were returned to duty and 34 cases were transferred to No. 50 Field Ambulance, leaving 2 Officers & 129 O.R. remaining in the Field Ambulance.	J.E.P.

2449 Wt. W14957/M90 750,000 1/16 J.B.C. & A. Forms/C.2118/12.

Instructions regarding War Diaries and Intelligence Summaries are contained in F. S. Regs., Part II. and the Staff Manual respectively. Title Pages will be prepared in manuscript.

WAR DIARY

or

~~INTELLIGENCE SUMMARY~~

(Erase heading not required.)

Army Form C. 2118.

Place	Date	Hour	Summary of Events and Information	Remarks and references to Appendices
LOCRE	13/10/17	9 p.m.	The day has been very cold, wet and stormy. – 21 cases of trench feet were admitted during the day. – Four Officers and 160 O.R. were admitted during the day, two Officers and 92 O.R. were evacuated to a Casualty Clearing Stn., One Officer and 35 O.R. were transferred to the Corps & Divisional Rest Stns. One Officer and 5 O.R. died of wounds. 10 O.R. were transferred to No. 50 Field Ambulance 3 men were returned to duty, leaving 2 Officers and 144 O.R. remaining.	J.E.P.
LOCRE	14/10/17	9 p.m.	The day has been fine and clear. – Captain OWENS R.A.M.C. reported his departure this morning for permanent duty as M.O. i/c Royal Engineers. – The A.D.M.S. & A.A. & Q.M.G. visited the Main Dressing Stn. this afternoon. – 33 cases of trench feet were admitted during the day. – a total of 4 Officers and 217 O.R. were admitted during the day, one Officer and 128 O.R. were evacuated to C.C.S., one Officer & 36 O.R. were sent to the Divisional Rest Stn. & Corps Rest Stn., 3 men died of wounds & 15 cases were transferred to No. 50 F.A. & 4 men were returned to duty leaving 4 Officers & 175 O.R. remaining.	J.E.P.
"	15/10/17	9 p.m.	The day has been fine & clear, though a few light showers of rain fell this evening. Only 5 cases of trench feet have been admitted to-day. – a total of 3 Officers and 131 O.R. were admitted during the day, 2 Officers and 109 O.R. were evacuated to a C.C.S. One Officer & 3 O.R. were sent to the Corps & Divisional Rest Stns., one man died of wounds, 16 cases were transferred to No. 50 F.A. & 10 men were returned to duty, leaving 4 Officers & 167 O.R. remaining.	J.E.P.

Instructions regarding War Diaries and Intelligence Summaries are contained in F. S. Regs., Part II. and the Staff Manual respectively. Title Pages will be prepared in manuscript.

WAR DIARY
or
~~INTELLIGENCE SUMMARY~~
(Erase heading not required.)

Army Form C. 2118.

Place	Date	Hour	Summary of Events and Information	Remarks and references to Appendices
LOCRE	16/10/17	9 p.m.	The day has been dull, cold and cloudy but no rain has fallen. – Lieut Phillips M.O.R.C. U.S.A. reported his arrival for duty on completion of temporary duty as M.O. i/c 8th Bn. Gloucester Regt. – The A.D.M.S. visited the Main Dressing Stn. this morning. – 21 cases of Trench feet were admitted during the day. Five Officers and 248 O.R. were admitted during the day, 5 Officers and 198 O.R. were evacuated to a C.C.S. 2 Officers and 36 O.R. were sent to the Corps and Divisional Rest Stns., six men died of wounds, 18 cases were transferred to No. 50 Field Ambulance and 5 cases were returned to duty, leaving 2 Officers and 152 O.R. remaining.	
"	17/10/17	9 p.m.	Rain fell during the night but to-day has been fine though cold. – 4 Officers and 139 O.R. were admitted with shell gas poisoning during the day, none of these cases were serious. – 12 cases of Trench foot were admitted during the day. – A total of 4 Officers and 303 O.R. were admitted during the day, 4 Officers and 221 O.R. were evacuated to a Casualty Clearing Stn., two Officers and 36 O.R. were sent to the Corps + Divisional Rest Stns. respectively, 2 men died of their wounds, 8 men were transferred to No. 50 Field Ambulance and 11 men were returned to duty, leaving 177 O.R. remaining.	J.E.P.

2449 Wt. W14957/M90 750,000 1/16 J.B.C. & A. Forms/C.2118/12.

Army Form C. 2118.

Instructions regarding War Diaries and Intelligence Summaries are contained in F. S. Regs., Part II. and the Staff Manual respectively. Title Pages will be prepared in manuscript.

WAR DIARY
or
~~INTELLIGENCE SUMMARY~~

(Erase heading not required.)

Place	Date	Hour	Summary of Events and Information	Remarks and references to Appendices
LOCRE	18/10/17	9 p.m.	Rain fell again last night but to-day has been fine and clear. – Four Officers and 94 O.R. were admitted suffering from Shell gas poisoning, none of them were severe cases. – No Trench feet cases were admitted. – a total of 10 Officers and 202 O.R. were admitted during the day, 5 Officers and 155 O.R. were evacuated to a C.C.S. One Officer and 37 O.R. were sent to the Corps & Divisional Rest Stns, two Officers and one man died of wounds, 22 O.R. were transferred to No. 133 Field Ambulance, 12 O.R. were returned to duty, leaving 2 Officers and 152 O.R. remaining in the Field Ambulance.	J.E.P.
"	19/10/17	9 p.m.	The day has been dull and cloudy and some rain has fallen. – 8 cases of Trench feet were admitted and 30 cases of Shell gas poisoning. – a Total of 5 Officers and 136 O.R. were admitted during the day, 3 Officers and 93 O.R. were evacuated to a C.C.S., One Officer and 37 O.R. were sent to the Corps & Divisional Rest Stns., 6 cases were transferred to No. 133 Field Ambulance and 13 O.R. were returned to duty, leaving 3 Officers and 139 O.R. remaining.	J.E.P.
"	20/10/17	9 p.m.	The day has been fine and clear. – 19 cases of Shell gas poisoning were admitted – all were slight. – Only 2 cases of Trench feet were admitted. – a total of 112 O.R. were admitted during the day, One Officer and 57 O.R. were evacuated to a C.C.S., One Officer and 28 O.R. were sent to the Divisional Rest Stn., & Corps Rest Stn., 3 men died of wounds, 17 O.R. were transferred to No. 133 Field Ambulance, 11 O.R. were returned to duty, leaving One Officer and 135 O.R. remaining in the Field Ambulance.	J.E.P.

2449 Wt. W14957/M90 750,000 1/16 J.B.C. & A. Forms/C.2118/12.

Army Form C. 2118.

Instructions regarding War Diaries and Intelligence Summaries are contained in F. S. Regs., Part II. and the Staff Manual respectively. Title Pages will be prepared in manuscript.

WAR DIARY
or
~~INTELLIGENCE SUMMARY~~
(Erase heading not required.)

Place	Date	Hour	Summary of Events and Information	Remarks and references to Appendices
LOCRE	21/10/17	9 p.m.	The weather continues fine and bright but with a ground haze. – 30 cases of Shell gas poisoning were admitted during the day, only 2 cases of Trench feet were admitted. – A Total of 2 Officers and 87 O.R. were admitted during the day, 2 Officers and 82 O.R. were evacuated to a Casualty Clearing Stn., 26 O.R. were sent to the Divisional Rest Stn., 2 men died of wounds, 9 men were transferred to 133 Field Ambulance and One Officer and 17 men were returned to duty, leaving 86 O.R. remaining in the Field Ambulance.	J.E.P.
"	22/10/17	9 p.m.	Some rain fell early this morning, but it soon cleared to a bright fine day. – The A.D.M.S. visited the Unit & held a "P.B." Board this morning. 19 cases of Shell gas poisoning were admitted during the day but only two cases of Trench feet were admitted. – A total of One Officer and 110 O.R. were admitted during the day, One Officer and 62 O.R. were evacuated to a Casualty Clearing Stn., 21 cases were sent to the Divisional Rest Stn., 2 men were transferred to No. 133 Field Ambulance, 3 men were returned to duty leaving 108 O.R. remaining in the Field Ambulance of which 27 O.R. are at the Corps Scabies Hospital.	J.E.P.

Army Form C. 2118.

Instructions regarding War Diaries and Intelligence Summaries are contained in F. S. Regs., Part II. and the Staff Manual respectively. Title Pages will be prepared in manuscript.

WAR DIARY
or
~~INTELLIGENCE SUMMARY~~
(Erase heading not required.)

Place	Date	Hour	Summary of Events and Information	Remarks and references to Appendices
LOCRE	23/10/17	9 p.m.	It has been a pouring wet day. – 18 cases of Shell gas poisoning were admitted but only one case of Trench foot was admitted. – A total of one Officer and 122 O.R. were admitted during the day, one Officer and 63 O.R. were evacuated to a Casualty Clearing Stn., 28 cases were sent to the Divisional Rest Stn., 12 cases were transferred to No. 133 Field Ambulance and 11 cases were returned to duty, leaving 116 O.R. remaining in the Field Ambulance.	J.E.P.
"	24/10/17	9 p.m.	The day has been fine and clear though cold. – 10 cases of Shell gas poisoning were admitted during the day and two cases of Trench foot were admitted. – A total of 5 Officers and 120 O.R. were admitted 5 Officers and 71 O.R. were evacuated to C.C.S., 29 O.R. were sent to the Divisional Rest Stn., 4 men died of wounds & 9 men were transferred to No. 133 Field Ambulance & 5 men were returned to duty, leaving 120 O.R. remaining in the Field Ambulance.	J.E.P.
"	25/10/17	9 p.m.	Heavy rain fell last night, but to-day is fine though with a very strong West wind blowing. – Lieut. J.A. BODDY R.A.M.C. reported his departure this day for temporary duty at No. 44 C.C.S. – 17 cases of Shell gas poisoning were admitted during the day and 2 cases of Trench feet. – A total of 3 Officers and 108 O.R. were admitted during the day, 68 O.R. were evacuated to a C.C.S., one Officer and 30 O.R. were sent to the Corps & Divisional Rest Stns. one man died of wounds, 10 men were transferred to No 133 Field Ambulance & 4 men were returned to duty, leaving 2 Officers & 115 O.R. remaining.	J.E.P.

2449 Wt. W14957/M90 750,000 1/16 J.B.C. & A. Forms/C.2118/12.

Army Form C. 2118.

WAR DIARY
or
~~INTELLIGENCE SUMMARY~~
(Erase heading not required.)

Instructions regarding War Diaries and Intelligence Summaries are contained in F. S. Regs., Part II. and the Staff Manual respectively. Title Pages will be prepared in manuscript.

Place	Date	Hour	Summary of Events and Information	Remarks and references to Appendices
LOCRE	26/10/17	9.0 pm	Lieut. Col. J.E. Powell DSO RAMC reported his departure on 14 days leave of absence to England. Temporary command was assumed by Capt. G.P. Kidd RAMC. Capt. H.B. Jones reported his departure for temporary duty at 44. C.C.S. in relief of Lieut. J.A.A. Doddy who returned to this unit. Rain fell almost throughout the day until evening. 1. Off. & 117 O.R. were admitted during the day. 1. Off. & 92 O.R. evacuated to C.C.S. 20. O.R. transferred to D.R.S. 4. O.R. transferred to 133. F.A. 7. O.R. to duty. Leaving 2. Off. & 109. O.R. remaining, including 20. O.R. at Corps Scabies HP.	GPK.
"	27/10/17	9.0 pm	The weather has been quite fine again all day, but a good deal colder. The ADMS visited the hospital during the morning & went round the wards. 5. Off. & 78. O.R. were admitted during the day. 3. Off. & 30 O.R. evacuated to C.C.S. 28. O.R. transferred to D.R.S. 7. O.R. transferred to 133. F.A. 10. O.R. returned to duty. Leaving 4. Off. & 112. O.R. remaining, including 18. O.R. at Corps Scabies HP.	GPK.
"	28/10/17	9.0 pm	The weather remained fine & cold throughout the day. The number of sick admissions has fallen considerably during the last week - especially in the case of trench feet - very few of these are now coming down from the line. 3. Off. & 75. O.R. were admitted during the day. 3. Off. & 61. O.R. evacuated to C.C.S. 2. Off. & 25. O.R. transferred to Corps & Div. Rest Stations. 10. O.R. transferred to 133. F.A. 10. O.R. to duty. Leaving 2. Off. & 91. O.R. remaining, including 19. O.R. at Corps Scabies HP.	GPK.
"	29/10/17	9.0 pm	ADMS visited the hospital during the morning to see prospective P.B. cases. 3. Off. & 69. O.R. were admitted during the day. 2. Off. & 31 O.R. evacuated to C.C.S. 1. Off. & 74 O.R. transferred to Corps & Div. Rest Stations. 5. O.R. transferred to 133. F.A. 4. O.R. to duty. Leaving 2. Off. & 96. O.R. remaining, including 20. O.R. at Corps Scabies HP.	GPK.

2449 Wt. W14957/M90 750,000 1/16 J.B.C. & A. Forms/C.2118/12.

Army Form C. 2118.

Instructions regarding War Diaries and Intelligence Summaries are contained in F. S. Regs., Part II. and the Staff Manual respectively. Title Pages will be prepared in manuscript.

WAR DIARY
or
~~INTELLIGENCE SUMMARY~~

(Erase heading not required.)

Place	Date	Hour	Summary of Events and Information	Remarks and references to Appendices
LOCRE	30/10/17.	9.0 pm	Material having now been obtained for the erection of an ablution hut and an extension to the horse standings – this work is being put in hand. Lieut E.R. CHAMNESS M.O.R.C. U.S.A. reported his arrival for duty with the unit and is taken on the strength from this date. He is posted to C Section of the Fd Amb. 7 Off & 86 O.R. were admitted during the day. 7 Off & 37 O.R. evacuated to C.C.S. 27 O.R. Transferred to D.R.S. 1 O.R. died. 1 O.R. transferred to 133 F.A. 5 O.R. to duty. Leaving 2 Off & 111 O.R. remaining, including 19 O.R. at Corps Scabies HP.	[initials]
"	31/10/17	9.0 pm	D.D.M.S. IX Corps visited and inspected the hospital during the morning. He impressed upon me the necessity for cutting down the number of evacuations. I have therefore increased the number of medical beds by thirty and taken one group of marquees into use as a surgical ward for slight cases. This marquee has been fitted with a stove and should be quite warm enough for the purpose as it has a wood floor. 1 Off & 59 O.R. were admitted during the day. 31 O.R. evacuated to C.C.S. 1 Off & 32 O.R. to Corps & D.R.S. 1 O.R. died. 8 O.R. transferred to 133 F.A. 6 O.R. to duty. Leaving 2 Off & 91 O.R. remaining, including 17 O.R. at Corps Scabies HP.	[initials]

[signature]
Capt RAMC
for O.C.
Commanding 57th Fd Amb.

2449 Wt. W14957/M90 750,000 1/16 J.B.C. & A. Forms/C.2118/12.

26

Nov. 1917

(S)

140/2078

Vol 29

War Diary

of 57th Field Ambulance R.A.M.C.

From 1-11-17 to 30-11-17. Volume 29.

Confidential

Instructions regarding War Diaries and Intelligence Summaries are contained in F. S. Regs., Part II. and the Staff Manual respectively. Title Pages will be prepared in manuscript.

WAR DIARY
or
~~INTELLIGENCE SUMMARY~~
(Erase heading not required.)

Army Form C. 2118.

Place	Date	Hour	Summary of Events and Information	Remarks and references to Appendices
LOCRE	1/11/17	9.0 pm	The A.D.M.S. visited the hospital during the morning. [illegible] to arrange for the bearers coming down from the line on the 3rd inst. 2. Off + 69. O.R. were admitted during the day. 1. Off. + 28. O.R. evacuated to C.C.S. 1. Off + 26. O.R. to Corps + D.R.S. 3. O.R. transferred to 133. F.A. 3. O.R. to duty. Leaving 2. Off. + 90. O.R. remaining.	GHK.
"	2/11/17	9.0 pm	The A.D.M.S. visited the unit again this morning. The weather remains damp and rather cold, but not much rain has fallen during the last few days. 2. Off + 62. O.R. were admitted during the day. 1. Off + 28 O.R. evacuated to C.C.S. 14. O.R. to D.R.S. 4. O.R. transferred to 133. F.A. 10. O.R. to duty. Leaving 3. Off + 96. O.R. remaining, including 20. O.R. at Corps Scabies H.P.	GHK.
"	3/11/17	9.0 pm	Orders received that a party of 1. Off. + 12. O.R. will proceed for duty at the Corps Scabies Hospital tomorrow. CAPT. J. L. COCHRANE returned to headquarters this afternoon after ten days duty at the A.D.S. 4. Off + 85. O.R. were admitted during the day. 1. Off + 32. O.R. evacuated to C.C.S. 2. Off + 28. O.R. to Corps + D.R.S. 8. O.R. transferred to 133. F.A. 5. O.R. to duty. Leaving 4. Off + 108. O.R. remaining, including 22. O.R. at Corps Scabies H.P.	GHK.
"	4/11/17	9.0 pm	D.D.M.S. Anzac Corps visited and inspected the hospital and grounds during the morning. Lieut. E.R. CHAMNESS M.O.R.C. U.S.A. reported his departure with 12. O.R. at 1.0 pm to report for duty at Corps Scabies H.P. at CAESTRE, as ordered by A.D.M.S. 1. Off. + 97. O.R. were admitted during the day. 1. Off. + 35. O.R. evacuated to C.C.S. 22. O.R. to D.R.S. 1. O.R. died 7. O.R. transferred to 50. F.A. 6. O.R. to duty. Leaving 4. Off + 136. O.R. remaining, including 34. O.R. at Corps Scabies H.P. The weather remains fine but still damp and rather cold. A good deal of work has been done in the camp during the last few days in the way of improving drains etc.	GHK.

2449 Wt. W14957/M90 750,000 1/16 J.B.C. & A. Forms/C.2118/12.

Instructions regarding War Diaries and Intelligence Summaries are contained in F. S. Regs., Part II. and the Staff Manual respectively. Title Pages will be prepared in manuscript.

WAR DIARY
or
~~INTELLIGENCE SUMMARY~~
(Erase heading not required.)

Army Form C. 2118.

Place	Date	Hour	Summary of Events and Information	Remarks and references to Appendices
LOCRE	5/11/17	9.0 pm	A.D.M.S. visited the hospital during the morning to see prospective P.B. cases. 2 Off. & 40 O.R. Gassed. were admitted from the 7th K.O.R.L. this afternoon. About half of these are being kept as they are mostly Batt. H.Q. Staff. 90. O.R. were admitted during the day. 46 O.R. evacuated to C.C.S. 21 O.R. to D.R.S. 5. O.R. transferred to 50 F.A. 2. Off & 4. O.R. to duty. Leaving 2. Off & 148. O.R. remaining, including 45. O.R. at Corps Scabies Hosp.	[illegible]
"	6/11/17	9.0 pm	Orders received this evening that the unit will move from here on the 10th inst to a training area. Verbal orders received from D.D.M.S. to send all surplus Equipment to 19 Fd Amb for storage. 2. Off & 110. O.R. were admitted during the day. 1. Off & 36. O.R. evacuated to C.C.S. 1. Off & 24. O.R. to Corps D.R.S. 5. O.R. transferred to 50 F.A. 8. O.R. to duty. Leaving 2. Off & 185 O.R. remaining, including 43 O.R. at Corps Scabies Hosp.	[illegible]
"	7/11/17	9.0 pm	I visited the A.D.M.S. in the morning to settle points with regard to forthcoming move. I also visited O.C. 59 F.A. with regard to stores being sent to them today. Orders received that we shall be under 58. Brigade for the move and operation orders received from them. 3. Off & 62 O.R. were admitted during the day. 3. Off & 42. O.R. evacuated to C.C.S. 35. O.R. to D.R.S. 6. O.R. transferred to 50. F.A. 12. O.R. to duty. Leaving 2. Off & 182. O.R. remaining, including 43. O.R. at Corps Scabies Hospital.	[illegible]
"	8/11/17	9.0 pm	A certain amount of packing was done today and various work about the camp completed. Billeting party for the new area left at 8.0 a.m. as per 58 Bde O.O. 2. Off & 81. O.R. were admitted during the day. 1. Off & 29. O.R. to C.C.S. 29. O.R. to D.R.S. 5. O.R. transferred to 50. F.A. 8. O.R. to duty. Leaving 3. Off & 162. O.R. remaining, including 43. O.R. at Corps Scabies Hosp.	[illegible]

2449 Wt. W14957/M90 750,000 1/16 J.B.C. & A. Forms/C.2118/12.

Instructions regarding War Diaries and Intelligence Summaries are contained in F. S. Regs., Part II. and the Staff Manual respectively. Title Pages will be prepared in manuscript.

WAR DIARY
or
~~INTELLIGENCE SUMMARY~~

(Erase heading not required.)

Army Form C. 2118.

Place	Date	Hour	Summary of Events and Information	Remarks and references to Appendices
LOCRE	9/11/17	9.0 pm	D.A.D.M.S. 5th Aust. Div. visited & went round the premises in the morning. Advanced party of 49. F. Amb. arrived at 4.0 pm to commence taking over. A.D.M.S. visited the unit at midday to arrange various small points. Almost all the packing was completed by the evening. 2. Off & 64. O.R. were admitted during the day. 2. Off & 24 O.R. evacuated to C.C.S. 32. O.R. to D.R.S. 9 (O.R.) transferred to 50. F.A. 1. Off & 12. O.R. to duty. Leaving 2. Off & 149. O.R. remaining, including 47. O.R. at Corps Scabies Hosp.	G.W.K.
STRAZEELE	10/11/17	10.0 pm	Handing over was completed early. The unit marched off at 10.30 AM and arrived here at 1.30 going into billets in the village. Orders received from 58. Bde that the Bde Group will proceed by march to the EBBLINGHAM area tomorrow. 4. Off & 46. O.R. were admitted up to 10.0 AM. when the books were closed. 4. Off & 31. O.R. evacuated to C.C.S. 2. Off & 57 O.R. to Corps & Div. Rest Camps. 3. O.R. transferred to 50. F.A. 18. O.R. to duty. 43. O.R. transferred to 49. F.A. Leaving no cases actually remaining but 43. on the books at Corps Scabies HP.	G.W.K.
EBBLINGHAM	11/11/17	6.0 pm	Lieut E.R. Channer reported his departure for temp. Med. duty with 5. S.W.B. Lieut & Qr.M. T. Armitage RAMC reported his arrival for duty with this unit in relief of Lieut & Qm. A. Bennett M.C. RAMC. ordered to England on duty. The unit marched off at 10.30 AM. & arrived here at 3.30. The billets here are very bad and on first sight there appears to be no accommodation for keeping patients at all.	G.W.K.
		9.0 pm	Lieut Col. J.E. Powell D.S.O. RAMC reported his arrival back for duty from leave of absence in England and reassumes command from this date. No cases were admitted or evacuated today.	

2449 Wt. W14957/M90 750,000 1/16 J.B.C. & A. Forms/C.2118/12.

Army Form C. 2118.

Instructions regarding War Diaries and Intelligence Summaries are contained in F. S. Regs., Part II. and the Staff Manual respectively. Title Pages will be prepared in manuscript.

WAR DIARY
or
INTELLIGENCE SUMMARY

(Erase heading not required.)

Place	Date	Hour	Summary of Events and Information	Remarks and references to Appendices
EBLINGHAM	12/11/17	9 p.m.	The day has been fine and clear throughout. – Lieut. & Q.M. BENNETT M.C. reported his departure this day for England to report to the A.D.M.S. WOOLWICH. – Lieut. C.H. PHILLIPS MORC U.S.A. reported his departure this day for permanent duty as M.O. i/c 8th North Staffordshire Regt. – The A.D.M.S. visited the Unit this afternoon – There is no accommodation here for the retention of sick. – 5 O.R. were admitted & 5 O.R. were evacuated to No 15 C.C.S., 9 cases were returned to duty, leaving 33 O.R. remaining in the Corps Scabies station.	J.E.P.
"	13/11/17	9 p.m.	The weather continues fine. – The A.D.M.S. visited the Unit this morning. – Captain J.L. Cochrane M.C. reported his departure this day for temporary duty as M.O. i/c 10th Bn. Royal Warwickshire Regt. – The men were exercised in squad drill during the morning. – One Officer and 22 O.R. sick were ~~[illegible]~~ admitted during the day, One Officer and 21 O.R. were evacuated to No 15 C.C.S. & 4 men were returned to duty, leaving 30 O.R. remaining at the Corps Scabies Stn.	J.E.P.
"	14/11/17	9 p.m.	The day has been cold dull and misty. – The Personnel have been exercised in Physical Drill, Squad Drill etc., also in general fatigues for the improvement of the camp. – One Officer and 18 O.R. were admitted during the day, One Officer and 15 O.R. were evacuated to No. 15 C.C.S., leaving 33 O.R. remaining, who are at the Corps Scabies Stn.	J.E.P.

Army Form C. 2118.

Instructions regarding War Diaries and Intelligence Summaries are contained in F. S. Regs., Part II. and the Staff Manual respectively. Title Pages will be prepared in manuscript.

WAR DIARY
or
~~INTELLIGENCE SUMMARY~~

(Erase heading not required.)

Place	Date	Hour	Summary of Events and Information	Remarks and references to Appendices
EBLINGHAM	15/11/17	9 p.m.	The weather continues fine, but the ground is still very damp. – The Personnel are employed on a continuous programme of training in the mornings & football matches in the afternoon. – 18 O.R. were admitted to the Field Ambulance during the day & 18 O.R. were evacuated to No 15 C.C.S., one man was returned to duty, leaving 32 O.R. remaining in the Field Ambulance.	J.E.P.
"	16/11/17	9 p.m.	The weather continues dry but foggy. – Captain KIDD reported his departure on 14 days leave to England. – Lieut. BODDY reported his departure for England to report to the War Office. — The Personnel were employed on the training Programme. – 10 O.R. were admitted during the day and 10 O.R. were evacuated to No. 15 C.C.S., 11 O.R. were returned to duty, leaving 21 cases remaining.	J.E.P.
"	17/11/17	9 p.m.	It has been another typical November day, dry but foggy. – The A.D.M.S. visited the Unit this morning and made new arrangements with regard to the reception of sick by No. 15 C.C.S. — Billetting certificates for the week were rendered to-day. – One Officer and 14 O.R. were admitted to the Field Ambulance during the day, 3 O.R. were transferred to the Divisional Rest Stn. & 4 O.R. were returned to duty, leaving 3 Officers and 75 O.R. remaining in the Field Ambulance.	J.E.P.

2449 Wt. W14957/M90 750,000 1/16 J.B.C. & A. Forms/C.2118/12.

Army Form C. 2118.

Instructions regarding War Diaries and Intelligence Summaries are contained in F. S. Regs., Part II. and the Staff Manual respectively. Title Pages will be prepared in manuscript.

WAR DIARY
or
~~INTELLIGENCE SUMMARY~~

(Erase heading not required.)

Place	Date	Hour	Summary of Events and Information	Remarks and references to Appendices
EBLINGHAM	18/11/17	9 p.m.	There is no change in the weather. – The morning was occupied in the inspection of the mens billets and kits. – Thirteen O.R. were admitted to the Field Ambulance during the day, three O.R. were returned to duty, leaving 3 Officers and 85 O.R. remaining on the books of the Field Ambulance.	J.E.P.
"	19/11/17	9 p.m	The weather still continues dry but foggy. – The Personnel went for a Route march in the morning and Bathing parades in the afternoon. – One Officer and 13 O.R. were admitted to the Field Ambulance during the day, 2 O.R. were evacuated & 2 O.R. were returned to duty, leaving four Officers and 94 O.R. remaining.	J.E.P.
"	20/11/17	9 p.m.	There is no change in the weather. The Personnel of the Unit were all paid this morning. – The programme of training is being carried out. – One Officer and 22 other ranks were admitted during the day, 4 other ranks were sent to the Divisional Rest Stn., and one man was returned to duty, leaving 5 Officers and 111 O.R. remaining.	J.E.P.
"	21/11/17	9 p.m.	Heavy rain fell last night and a thick driving mist has continued throughout the day & it is also colder. – The Personnel went for a Route march this morning. Thirteen other ranks were admitted during the day, two Officers and 15 O.R. were evacuated to the Base, two O.R. were evacuated to No. 50 C.C.S. and one man was returned to duty, leaving 3 Officers & 106 O.R. remaining. — Captains Cochrane & Jones reported their arrival for duty, also Lieut Chamners MORC USA reported his arrival for duty	J.E.P.

2449 Wt. W14957/M90 750,000 1/16 J.B.C. & A. Forms/C.2118/12.

Army Form C. 2118.

Instructions regarding War Diaries and Intelligence Summaries are contained in F. S. Regs., Part II. and the Staff Manual respectively. Title Pages will be prepared in manuscript.

WAR DIARY

or

~~INTELLIGENCE SUMMARY~~

(Erase heading not required.)

Place	Date	Hour	Summary of Events and Information	Remarks and references to Appendices
EBLINGHAM	22/11/17	9 p.m.	The weather continues wet & the ground is very muddy. – Programme of training continues. – Captain H.B. Jones reported his departure for temporary duty with No.59 Field Ambulance & Lieut Chamney M.O.R.C. reported his departure for temporary duty as M.O. i/c 8th N. Staffords. The A.D.M.S. visited the Unit this morning for a Medical Board. – One Officer & and 17 O.R. were admitted during the day, 3 men were evacuated to a C.C.S. 4 men were transferred to No.59 Field Ambulance (D.R.S.) and 6 men were returned to duty leaving 4 Officers and 110 O.R. remaining.	J.E.P.
"	23/11/17	9 p.m.	The day has been fine & mild throughout. – The Personnel went for a route march this morning. – Sixteen other ranks ~~sick~~ were admitted during the day three other ranks were transferred to No.59 Field Ambulance and five men were returned to duty, leaving 4 Officers and 118 other ranks remaining.	J.E.P.
"	24/11/17	9 p.m.	The weather continues fine but with a strong S.W. wind blowing which dries the ground well. – The A.D.M.S. visited the Unit this morning. – The programme of training for the Personnel is still being carried out. – 13 other ranks were admitted sick during the day, 14 other ranks were evacuated to the Base, one man was returned to duty, leaving 4 Officers and 116 O.R. remaining.	J.E.P.

2449 Wt. W14957/M90 750,000 1/16 J.B.C. & A. Forms/C.2118/12.

Army Form C. 2118.

Instructions regarding War Diaries and Intelligence Summaries are contained in F. S. Regs., Part II. and the Staff Manual respectively. Title Pages will be prepared in manuscript.

WAR DIARY
or
~~INTELLIGENCE SUMMARY~~

(Erase heading not required.)

Place	Date	Hour	Summary of Events and Information	Remarks and references to Appendices
EBLINGHAM	25/11/17	9 p.m.	The weather continues dry but it has become much colder and there is a S.W. gale blowing. Six other ranks were admitted to the Field Ambulance during the day, five cases were transferred to No. 59 Field Ambulance (D.R.S.) – One Officer and two O.R. were returned to duty, leaving three Officers and 115 O.R. remaining.	J.E.P.
"	26/11/17	9 p.m.	A strong S.W. wind continues to blow & the ground has dried up very much. – 1st Lieut Croop M.O.R.C. U.S.A. & 1st Lieut Deck M.O.R.C. U.S.A. reported their arrival for duty this morning. – The programme of training for the Personnel is being carried out steadily. – Seven other ranks were admitted to the Field Ambulance during the day, two other ranks were returned to duty, leaving 3 Officers and 120 O.R. remaining.	J.E.P.
"	27/11/17	9 p.m.	Heavy rain fell last night & throughout the morning, interfering with the outdoor training programme – lectures in billets were given in place of drills. – Fourteen other ranks were admitted to the Field Ambulance during the day, 4 other ranks were transferred to No. 59 Field Ambulance (D.R.S.) and 8 O.R. were returned to duty leaving 3 Officers and 122 other ranks remaining.	J.E.P.
"	28/11/17	9 p.m.	The day has been fine and much milder. – Five other ranks were admitted to the Field Ambulance during the day, two Officers and 26 other ranks were evacuated to the Base, One Officer and four other ranks were returned to duty, leaving 97 other ranks remaining.	J.E.P.

2449 Wt. W14957/M90 750,000 1/16 J.B.C. & A. Forms/C.2118/12.

Instructions regarding War Diaries and Intelligence Summaries are contained in F. S. Regs., Part II. and the Staff Manual respectively. Title Pages will be prepared in manuscript.

WAR DIARY
or
~~INTELLIGENCE SUMMARY~~
(Erase heading not required.)

Army Form C. 2118.

Place	Date	Hour	Summary of Events and Information	Remarks and references to Appendices
EBLINGHAM	29/11/17	9 p.m.	The weather continues fine and mild. – The A.D.M.S. the Division inspected the Unit including the Transport on parade this morning. – He also held a medical Board on proposed P.B. men. – 14 other ranks were admitted to the Field Ambulance during the day, three cases were evacuated to a Casualty Clearing Station, and four men were returned to duty, leaving 107 other ranks remaining.	J.E.P.
"	30/11/17	9 p.m.	The morning was fine and mild, but it came on to rain in the afternoon. – The programme of training for the Personnel is still being carried on. – Sixteen other ranks were admitted during the day to the Field Ambulance, one other rank was evacuated to a C.C.S. and one man was returned to duty, leaving 121 other ranks remaining, 7 other ranks being at the IX Corps Scabies Station.	J.E.P.

J.E. Powell
Lieut. Colonel R.A.M.C.
O.C. 57th Field Ambulance

2449 Wt. W14957/M90 750,000 1/16 J.B.C. & A. Forms/C.2118/12.

Dec 1917 (S) II Army only 2

140/2696

CONFIDENTIAL. Vol 30

War Diary

of 57th Field Ambulance. R.A.M.C.

From 1-12-17 to 31-12-17.

Volume 30.

Instructions regarding War Diaries and Intelligence Summaries are contained in F. S. Regs., Part II. and the Staff Manual respectively. Title Pages will be prepared in manuscript.

WAR DIARY
or
~~INTELLIGENCE SUMMARY~~
(Erase heading not required.)

Army Form C. 2118.

Place	Date	Hour	Summary of Events and Information	Remarks and references to Appendices
EBLINGHEM	1/12/17	9 p.m.	The weather has become much colder to-day. – Billeting certificates for the week were rendered. – The A.D.M.S. visited the Unit in the morning. – Four other ranks were admitted during the day, 28 other ranks were evacuated to the Base, and 4 cases were transferred to No. 59 Field Ambulance (D.R.S.) and 2 cases returned to duty, leaving 88 cases remaining.	J.E.P.
"	2/12/17	9 p.m.	The weather continues very cold with a Northerly wind blowing. – The G.O.C. Division inspected the Personnel and Transport of the Unit this afternoon. – Captain KIDD R.A.M.C. reported his arrival back from leave this afternoon. – Ten other ranks were admitted to the Field Ambulance during the day, 4 men were returned to duty, leaving 94 other ranks remaining.	J.E.P.
"	3/12/17	9 p.m.	There was a frost last night and the ground is hard and dry to-day – a cold North wind still continues blowing. Seven other ranks were admitted to the Field Ambulance during the day, one man was evacuated to a Casualty Clearing Stn, and one man was returned to duty, leaving 99 other ranks remaining.	J.E.P.
"	4/12/17	9 p.m.	It froze hard again last night and some snow fell in the morning, but the remainder of the day has been fine. – Two Officers and 16 other ranks were admitted to the Field Ambulance during the day, 3 men were returned to duty, leaving two Officers and 112 other ranks remaining.	J.E.P.

2449 Wt. W14957/M90 750,000 1/16 J.B.C. & A. Forms/C.2118/12.

Army Form C. 2118.

Instructions regarding War Diaries and Intelligence Summaries are contained in F. S. Regs., Part II. and the Staff Manual respectively. Title Pages will be prepared in manuscript.

WAR DIARY
or
~~INTELLIGENCE SUMMARY~~

(Erase heading not required.)

Place	Date	Hour	Summary of Events and Information	Remarks and references to Appendices
EBLINGHEM	5/12/17	9 p.m.	It froze hard again last night & to-day is fine and cold. Received during the night a warning order that the Division would entrain on the 8th inst. – All training and competitions are indefinitely postponed. – Captain Cochrane left at 7.30 a.m. this morning in charge of a billeting party. – Seven other ranks were admitted to the Field Ambulance during the day, fifteen other ranks were evacuated to the Base and two men were returned to duty, leaving two Officers and 102 other ranks remaining in the Field Ambulance.	J.E.P.
"	6/12/17	9 p.m.	The hard frost continues with fine clear weather during the day. – Definite orders were received for the Unit to entrain at 20.26 on the 7th inst. – The Personnel were occupied in packing wagons etc. – Two Officers and 18 other ranks were admitted to the Field Ambulance during the day, four Officers and 107 O.R. were evacuated to C.C.S. preparatory to the move of the Unit and six other ranks were returned to duty, leaving 7 other ranks remaining in the Fd. Amb.	J.E.P.
Arques	7/12/17	8 p.m.	A thaw set in last night and to-day is damp. – No cases were admitted or evacuated to-day, the Unit being closed for the move. – The motor ambulances proceeded as a convoy by road and the Personnel and transport of the Unit marched from Billets at EBLINGHEM at 3.30 p.m. entraining there at 8 p.m.	J.E.P.

2449 Wt. W14957/M90 750,000 1/16 J.B.C. & A. Forms/C.2118/12.

Instructions regarding War Diaries and Intelligence Summaries are contained in F. S. Regs., Part II. and the Staff Manual respectively. Title Pages will be prepared in manuscript.

WAR DIARY
or
~~INTELLIGENCE SUMMARY~~
(Erase heading not required.)

Army Form C. 2118.

Place	Date	Hour	Summary of Events and Information	Remarks and references to Appendices
GOMIECOURT	8/12/17	9 p.m.	The day has been mild and damp with a mist and slight rain. – The Unit arrived at BEAUMETZ-les-Loges at 7 a.m. and detrained and marched to a Camp at HENDECOURT by 9·30 a.m. Received Brigade orders at 10 a.m. to march again at 2 p.m. to GOMIECOURT where we arrived in billets at 5 p.m. – Six other ranks sick were admitted and evacuated to C.C.S. during the day.	J.E.P.
ETRICOURT	9/12/17	9 p.m.	Heavy rain fell last night and it has rained steadily all day to-day. – At 1 a.m. I received orders from Brigade Headquarters to march to ETRICOURT at 8·15 a.m. a distance of 16 miles, we arrived here at 4 p.m. and went in to camp. Thirty six other ranks sick were admitted and evacuated to C.C.S. during the day.	J.E.P.
METZ-en-COUTURE	10/12/17	9 p.m.	The weather continues damp and the roads and ground are very muddy. – Received orders from the A.D.M.S. at 11·30 p.m. to march here to-day and take over from No. 16 Field Ambulance, billets and stores for Headquarters here, a Walking Wounded Collecting Post at TRESCAULT and an A.D.S. at Sq L 31 c 2-4 Map sheet 57c. The Unit marched at 10 a.m. and all reliefs were completed by 3 p.m. One other rank sick was admitted and evacuated during the day, and the seven other ranks at the IX Corps Scabies Stn. were transferred to No. 96 Field Ambulance leaving no cases remaining and the Unit has closed for all admissions.	J.E.P.

2449 Wt. W14957/M90 750,000 1/16 J.B.C. & A. Forms/C.2118/12.

Instructions regarding War Diaries and Intelligence Summaries are contained in F. S. Regs., Part II. and the Staff Manual respectively. Title Pages will be prepared in manuscript.

WAR DIARY
or
~~INTELLIGENCE SUMMARY~~
(Erase heading not required.)

Army Form C. 2118.

Place	Date	Hour	Summary of Events and Information	Remarks and references to Appendices
METZ en COUTURE	11/12/17	9 p.m.	The weather continues damp and very cold and the roads are in bad condition in the front area. – I visited the A.D.M.S. at D.H.Q. in the morning and in the afternoon I visited the Walking Wounded Post and also the A.D.S. – Under instructions from the A.D.M.S. Two clerks proceeded to No. 21 C.C.S. for 19th Division clerical work there, also Captain J.L. Cochrane M.C. and one Tent Sub Division reported to O.C. No. 2y Field Ambulance for duty at the Walking Wounded Dressing Station at FINS.	J.E.P.
METZ en COUTURE	12/12/17	9 p.m.	There was a slight frost last night and to-day is fine but cold, but the roads continue very ~~[illegible]~~ muddy. – The Personnel are employed in cleaning out stores and cellars. – Local sick are seen here in the morning, and any local wounded are also attended to prior to evacuation.	J.E.P.
"	13/12/17	9 p.m.	The weather continues very cold and damp. – The remainder of the Personnel are employed in attending to local sick and wounded and also cleaning out and improving billets. – Serious sick & wounded are sent direct to C.C.S. at YTRES, sitting & walking sick & wounded are sent to the M.D.S. at FINS. – One Officer and one other rank were admitted and evacuated to C.C.S.	J.E.P.
"	14/12/17	9 p.m.	The weather is milder again and some rain has fallen throughout the day. – Three Officers and 16 other ranks were admitted and evacuated to C.C.S. during the day. – Received a warning order from the A.D.M.S. 19th Division at 8 p.m. to be ready to move and take over the V Corps Rest Station on the 16th inst.	J.E.P.

2449 Wt. W14957/M90 750,000 1/16 J.B.C. & A. Forms/C.2118/12.

Instructions regarding War Diaries and Intelligence Summaries are contained in F. S. Regs., Part II. and the Staff Manual respectively. Title Pages will be prepared in manuscript.

WAR DIARY
or
~~INTELLIGENCE SUMMARY~~
(Erase heading not required.)

Army Form C. 2118.

Place	Date	Hour	Summary of Events and Information	Remarks and references to Appendices
METZ EN COUTURE	15/12/17	9 p.m.	The weather has become colder again, but the day has been bright and clear. Equipment has been packed etc. preparatory to moving to-morrow – In the afternoon I sent a small advance Party to the V Corps Rest Stn. to take over & I also went there myself to make arrangements for taking over. Three other ranks sick were admitted and evacuated to C.C.S. during the day.	J.E.P.
BUS	16/12/17	9 p.m.	The Unit marched off at 9 a.m. & arrived here at 11 a.m. & took over the Rest Station from No 1/6 London Field Ambulance. – The weather is cold & some snow has fallen. – We took over 409 Patients from No. 6 London Field Ambulance, 5 Officers and 121 other ranks were admitted. 5 Officers and 231 O.R. were evacuated to C.C.S. and 30 other ranks were sent to the Corps Rest Stn., 101 cases were sent to duty leaving 225 other ranks remaining.	J.E.P.
"	17/12/17	9 p.m.	A Blizzard has blown all last night & all to-day also. – The D.D.M.S. V Corps visited the Rest Station this morning. – The Personnel are employed cleaning up and arranging the wards & attending to the Patients. – ~~[illegible]~~ 131 other ranks were admitted during the day, 3 Officers and 115 were evacuated to C.C.S., 30 other ranks were transferred to the Corps Rest Stn. and 79 cases were returned to duty, leaving 227 cases remaining.	J.E.P.

2449 Wt. W14957/M90 750,000 1/16 J.B.C. & A. Forms/C.2118/12.

Army Form C. 2118.

Instructions regarding War Diaries and Intelligence Summaries are contained in F. S. Regs., Part II. and the Staff Manual respectively. Title Pages will be prepared in manuscript.

WAR DIARY
or
~~INTELLIGENCE SUMMARY~~
(Erase heading not required.)

Place	Date	Hour	Summary of Events and Information	Remarks and references to Appendices
BUS	18/12/17	9 p.m.	There was a hard frost last night and a strong East wind blowing to-day. The erection of 5 new Nissen huts has been commenced to-day. Six Officers and 207 other ranks were admitted and transferred to this Unit during the day, seven Officers and 169 other ranks were evacuated to a Casualty Clearing Stn., 30 cases were sent to the Corps Rest Stn., and 5 cases were returned to duty, leaving One Officer and 230 other ranks remaining.	J.E.P.
BUS	19/12/17	9 p.m.	The hard frost continues & the weather is still bitterly cold. — The D.D.M.S. V Corps visited the Unit in the morning & the A.D.M.S. visited the Unit in the afternoon. I visited the Corps Main Dressing Stn. in the morning to arrange about the admission & transference of "Sick". — Two Officers and 282 other ranks were admitted and transferred to this Rest Stn., during the day, 3 Officers & 191 other ranks were evacuated to a Casualty Clearing Stn., 30 cases were sent to the Corps Rest Stn., and 54 cases were returned to duty, leaving One Officer and 238 other ranks remaining.	J.E.P.
"	20/12/17	9 p.m.	The same bitter weather continues — The erection of the Nissen Huts is being carried on. Seven Officers and 243 other ranks were admitted and transferred to this Unit during the day, eight Officers and 105 other ranks were evacuated to a C.C.S., 30 cases were sent to the Corps Rest Stn., and 57 cases were returned to duty, leaving 289 other ranks remaining.	J.E.P.

2449 Wt. W14957/M90 750,000 1/16 J.B.C. & A. Forms/C.2118/12.

Instructions regarding War Diaries and Intelligence Summaries are contained in F. S. Regs., Part II. and the Staff Manual respectively. Title Pages will be prepared in manuscript.

WAR DIARY
or
~~INTELLIGENCE SUMMARY~~

(Erase heading not required.)

Army Form C. 2118.

Place	Date	Hour	Summary of Events and Information	Remarks and references to Appendices
BUS	21/12/17	9 p.m.	The hard frost continues and the ground is now very hard and still covered with snow. – Seven Officers and 274 other ranks were admitted and transferred to this Unit during the day, seven Officers and 137 other ranks were evacuated to C.C.S. and 87 cases were sent to the Corps Rest Stn, and 34 men were returned to duty, leaving 305 other ranks remaining.	J.E.P.
"	22/12/17	9 p.m.	The same severe weather continues. – The Personnel of the Unit were paid to-day. One Officer and 278 other ranks were admitted and transferred to this Unit during the day, one Officer and 198 other ranks were evacuated to a C.C.S., 99 other ranks were transferred to the Corps Rest Stn. and 11 other ranks were returned to duty, leaving 275 other ranks remaining.	J.E.P.
"	23/12/17	9 p.m.	There was a severe frost again last night & it continues very cold. – The D.A.D.M.S. V Corps called this morning. – Four Officers and 236 other ranks were admitted and transferred to this Unit during the day, 4 Officers and 153 other ranks were evacuated to a C.C.S., 101 other ranks were transferred to the Corps Rest Stn. and 38 men were returned to duty, leaving 219 men remaining. – Bt. Major A. WALKER T.F. and Captain A.G. BUCHANAN T.F. R.A.M.C. reported themselves for duty with this Unit this morning.	J.E.P.
"	24/12/17	9 p.m.	The same severe cold weather continues. – The A.D.M.S. 19th Divn visited the Unit for a Medical Board in the afternoon and then inspected the whole Rest Station and expressed his complete satisfaction with what he saw. — Three Officers and 214 O.R. were admitted and transferred to this Unit during the day, 4 Officers and 122 O.R. were evacuated to C.C.S., 65 O.R. were sent to the Corps Rest Stn., & 18 men returned to duty, leaving 228 O.R. remaining.	J.E.P.

2449/ Wt. W14957/M90 750,000 1/16 J.B.C. & A. Forms/C.2118/12.

Army Form C. 2118.

Instructions regarding War Diaries and Intelligence Summaries are contained in F. S. Regs., Part II. and the Staff Manual respectively. Title Pages will be prepared in manuscript.

WAR DIARY
or
~~INTELLIGENCE SUMMARY~~

(Erase heading not required.)

Place	Date	Hour	Summary of Events and Information	Remarks and references to Appendices
BUS	25/12/17	9 p.m.	Some rain fell last night and a definite thaw appears to have set in. – A Parade Service C of E was held here by the Senior Chaplain at 11:30 a.m. for the Personnel & Patients. Four Officers and 213 other ranks were admitted and transferred during the day to this Unit. Four Officers and 87 other ranks were evacuated to Casualty Clearing Stn., and 58 other ranks were sent to the Corps Rest Stn., and 16 other ranks were returned to duty, leaving 280 other ranks remaining.	J.E.P.
"	26/12/17	9 p.m.	Heavy snow fell all last night and frost has again set in. – The D.D.M.S. V Corps made a thorough inspection of this Rest Station this morning and ~~made~~ expressed his satisfaction with all he saw. – Two Officers and 138 other ranks were admitted and transferred to this Unit during the day, two Officers and 76 O.R. were evacuated to a C.C.S. and 65 O.R. were sent to the Corps Rest Stn., leaving 277 other ~~ranks~~ remaining	J.E.P.
"	27/12/17	9 p.m.	The severe frost is still continuing, the atmosphere is foggy. – The erection of Nissen Huts is still being carried on – 3 huts have now been erected and 3 more remain to be erected. Two Officers and 323 other ranks were admitted and transferred to this Unit during the day, two Officers and 130 other ranks were evacuated to C.C.S., and 58 O.R. sent to the Corps Rest Station, and 36 men returned to duty, leaving 376 O.R. remaining.	J.E.P.
"	28/12/17	9 p.m.	The hard frost continues and in addition there is a strong N.E. wind blowing & the atmosphere is much clearer. – One Officer and 258 other ranks were admitted and transferred to this Unit during the day, One Officer and 120 O.R. were sent to a Casualty Clearing Stn. 116 other ranks were transferred to the Corps Rest Stn. 12 O.R. were transferred to the 63rd Div. Rest Stn., and 32 cases were returned to duty, leaving 354 cases remaining.	J.E.P.

2449 Wt. W14957/M90 750,000 1/16 J.B.C. & A. Forms/C.2118/12.

Instructions regarding War Diaries and Intelligence Summaries are contained in F. S. Regs., Part II. and the Staff Manual respectively. Title pages will be prepared in manuscript.

WAR DIARY

or

~~INTELLIGENCE SUMMARY.~~

(Erase heading not required.)

Army Form C. 2118.

Place	Date	Hour	Summary of Events and Information	Remarks and references to Appendices
BUS	29/12/17	9 p.m.	The weather continues very cold and dry and the atmosphere ~~[illegible]~~ clear. — The D.D.M.S. V Corps visited the Rest Stn. this morning, also the A.D.M.S. 17th Division. Seven Officers and 232 other ranks were admitted and transferred to this Unit during the day, five Officers and 131 O.R. were evacuated to a Casualty Clearing Stn., 59 O.R. were transferred to the Corps Rest Stn., and 30 cases were returned to duty, leaving two Officers and 366 other ranks remaining.	J.E.P.
"	30/12/17	9 p.m.	A slight thaw has set in to-day. — Seven Officers and 203 other ranks were admitted and transferred to this Unit during the day, six Officers and 90 other ranks were evacuated to a Casualty Clearing Stn., two Officers and 125 O.R. were sent to the Corps Rest Stn. and 29 cases were returned to duty, leaving one Officer and 325 other ranks remaining.	J.E.P.
"	31/12/17	9 p.m.	There was a severe frost again last night and an East wind blowing. — The A.D.M.S. visited the Rest Station this afternoon and held a Board on Suspected "B" cases. — One Officer and 270 other ranks were admitted and transferred to this Unit during the day. One Officer and 153 O.R. were evacuated to a C.C.S. 72 other ranks were transferred to the Corps Rest Stn., and 27 cases were returned to duty, leaving one Officer and 338 O.R. remaining.	J.E.P.

J.E. Powell
Lieut. Colonel R.A.M.C.
O.C. 54th Field Ambulance

D. D. & L., London, E.C.
(A8004) Wt. W1771/M2'31 750,000 5/17 Sch. 52 Forms/C2118/14

Jany. 1918 7 Vol 31

War Diary

of 57th Field Ambulance, R.A.M.C.

From 1-1-18 to 31-1-18

Volume 31

Instructions regarding War Diaries and Intelligence Summaries are contained in F. S. Regs., Part II. and the Staff Manual respectively. Title pages will be prepared in manuscript.

WAR DIARY
or
~~INTELLIGENCE SUMMARY~~.
(*Erase heading not required.*)

Army Form C. 2118.

Place	Date	Hour	Summary of Events and Information	Remarks and references to Appendices
BUS	1/1/18	9 p.m.	There was a further fall of snow last night followed by frost and an East wind. – The erection of the Nissen huts is not yet quite completed. – Six Officers and Three hundred and three other ranks were admitted and transferred to this Unit during the day, seven Officers and 104 O.R. were evacuated to C.C.S., 108 O.R. were transferred to the Corps Rest Stn. and 30 cases were returned to duty, leaving 399 other ranks remaining.	J.E.P.
"	2/1/18	9 p.m.	A slight thaw has set in to-day and some rain has fallen this morning. – The D.D.M.S. V Corps visited the Rest Stn. this morning. – Six Officers and 213 other ranks were admitted and transferred to this Unit during the day, six Officers and 104 O.R. were evacuated to a C.C.S. and 107 other ranks were transferred to the Corps Rest Stn. and 30 men were returned to duty, leaving 371 cases remaining.	J.E.P.
"	3/1/18	9 p.m.	More snow fell again last night and the frost has once more set in. – The D.D.M.S. Corps again visited the Rest Stn. this morning and gave me verbal warning orders about the reception of sick from the 47th Division in place of the 19th Division. The New A.D.M.S. 19th Division Colonel HARTIGAN visited and inspected the Rest Station in the afternoon. – Six Officers and 244 other ranks were admitted and transferred to this Unit during the day, five Officers and 123 other ranks were evacuated to C.C.S., one Officer and 96 O.R. were transferred to the Corps Rest Stn. and 36 cases were returned to duty, leaving 360 other ranks remaining.	J.E.P.

D. D. & L., London, E.C. (A8004) Wt. W1771/M231 750,000 5/17 Sch. 52 Forms/C2118/14

Instructions regarding War Diaries and Intelligence Summaries are contained in F. S. Regs., Part II. and the Staff Manual respectively. Title pages will be prepared in manuscript.

WAR DIARY
or
~~INTELLIGENCE SUMMARY.~~
(Erase heading not required.)

Army Form C. 2118.

Place	Date	Hour	Summary of Events and Information	Remarks and references to Appendices
BUS	4/1/18	9 p.m.	The weather continues very cold with a hard frost at night and foggy ~~during~~ day. — The A.D.M.S. 17th Division visited the Rest Station this afternoon. — Four Officers and two hundred & nineteen other ranks were admitted and transferred to this Unit during the day, 2 Officers & 71 O.R. were evacuated to a C.C.S. and 2 Officers & 96 O.R. were transferred to the Corps Rest Stn., and 15 O.R. were returned to duty, leaving 397 other ranks remaining.	J.E.P.
"	5/1/18	9 p.m.	The weather remains unchanged. — I attended a Conference at 11 a.m. at the A.D.M.S.'s Office. — Three Officers and 214 other ranks were admitted and transferred to this Unit during the day, 3 Officers and 75 O.R. were evacuated to a Casualty Clearing Stn., and 114 other ranks were transferred to the Corps Rest Station and 22 men were returned to duty, leaving 397 men remaining in the Field Ambulance.	J.E.P.
"	6/1/18	9 p.m.	The frost continues with a S.E. wind and thick fog to-day. — Four Officers and 231 other ranks were admitted and transferred to this Unit during the day, four officers and 82 O.R. were evacuated to a C.C.S., and 126 other ranks were transferred to the Corps Rest Stn., and 21 cases were returned to duty, leaving 399 other ranks remaining in the Rest Station.	J.E.P.
"	7/1/18	9 p.m.	A thaw set in last night & heavy rain has fallen throughout last night & to-day also. — But frost has again set in to-night. — The A.D.M.S. visited the Rest Station this afternoon. 3 Officers and 188 O.R. were admitted & transferred to this Rest Stn. Two Officers and 53 O.R. were evacuated to C.C.S. and one Officer & 131 O.R. were sent to the Corps Rest Stn. & 11 O.R. were returned to duty, leaving 392 O.R. remaining.	J.E.P.

D. D. & L., London, E.C. (A8002) Wt W1771/M2 31 750,000 5/17 Sch. 52 Forms/C2118/14

Army Form C. 2118.

Instructions regarding War Diaries and Intelligence Summaries are contained in F. S. Regs., Part II. and the Staff Manual respectively. Title pages will be prepared in manuscript.

WAR DIARY
or
~~INTELLIGENCE SUMMARY.~~

(Erase heading not required.)

Place	Date	Hour	Summary of Events and Information	Remarks and references to Appendices
BUS	8/1/18	9 p.m.	There was a severe frost last night and this morning a heavy fall of snow. – Two officers and 203 other ranks were admitted and transferred to this Unit during the day. One Officer and 84 other ranks were evacuated to a Casualty Clearing Stn., one officer + 119 O.R. were transferred to the Corps Rest Stn. and 11 cases were returned to duty, leaving 381 cases remaining.	J.E.P.
"	9/1/18	9 p.m.	The frost and snow continues. – I attended a conference at the A.D.M.S.'s office in the morning. – The D.D.M.S. Corps visited the Rest Station in the afternoon + expressed his satisfaction with all he saw. – Two officers and 259 other ranks were admitted and transferred to this Unit during the day, two officers and 115 O.R. were evacuated to C.C.S. and 99 O.R. were transferred to the Corps Rest Stn. and 9 men were returned to duty, leaving 415 other ranks remaining.	J.E.P.
"	10/1/18	9 p.m.	The wind changed to the west + heavy rain fell last night + it has been thawing all day to-day. – Five officers and 199 other ranks were admitted and transferred to this Unit during the day, 4 officers and 85 O.R. were evacuated to a C.C.S., one officer and 133 other ranks were transferred to the Corps Rest Stn., and 17 O.R. were returned to duty, leaving 379 O.R. remaining in the Rest Stn.	J.E.P.
"	11/1/18	9 p.m.	The thaw continues with occasional showers of rain. – The D.D.M.S. V Corps visited the Rest Station this morning. – Captain A.A. Smalley + 1 N.C.O. of the Bearer Division visited the front this morning, to visit the medical sites + learn the routes of evacuation. – Four officers + 166 other ranks were admitted and transferred to this Unit during the day, + 4 officers + 116 O.R. were evacuated to C.C.S. + 90 O.R. were transferred to the Corps Rest Stn. + 18 men were returned to duty, leaving 321 other ranks remaining in the Rest Station.	J.E.P.

D. D. & L., London, E.C. (A8004) Wt. W1771/M2 31 750,000 1/17 Sch. 52 Forms/C2118/14.

Instructions regarding War Diaries and Intelligence Summaries are contained in F. S. Regs., Part II. and the Staff Manual respectively. Title pages will be prepared in manuscript.

WAR DIARY
or
~~INTELLIGENCE SUMMARY~~.
(*Erase heading not required.*)

Army Form C. 2118.

Place	Date	Hour	Summary of Events and Information	Remarks and references to Appendices
BUS	12/1/18	9 p.m.	There was a very slight frost last night, but it is thawing again to-day & thaw precautions were adopted from midnight last night. – 129 other ranks were admitted to this Unit during the day 67 other ranks were evacuated to C.C.S. 32 O.R. were transferred to the Corps Rest Station and ten O.R. were returned to duty. – The 47th Division and 63rd Division now keep separate A & D Books in this Rest Stn., and 76 O.R. were transferred to their books – 339 O.R. are now remaining in this Rest Station	J.E.P.
BUS	13/1/18	9 p.m.	There was a slight fall of snow and a slight frost last night, but to-day has been fine and clear & it has been thawing all day. – 113 O.R. were admitted during the day, 70 O.R. were evacuated to a C.C.S. 51 O.R. were transferred to the Corps Rest Stn., & 5 cases were returned to duty, leaving 336 other ranks remaining in the Rest Station.	J.E.P.
BUS	14/1/18	9 p.m.	There ~~was~~ again a slight frost and fall of snow last night, but it is thawing slightly to-day. – The A.D.M.S. 19th Division came in the afternoon to examine proposed "B" men, he also visited all the wards & went round the Camp. – Two Officers and 100 O.R. were admitted during the day 1 Officer and 60 O.R. were evacuated to a C.C.S. 1 Officer & 49 O.R. were transferred to the Corps Rest Stn. & 27 O.R. were returned to duty, leaving 371 O.R. remaining.	J.E.P.
BUS	15/1/18	9 p.m.	Rain fell all last night & to-day also & a complete thaw has now set in. – All thaw precautions have been taken. – Two Officers and 226 other ranks were admitted, one Officer and 111 O.R. were evacuated to a Casualty Clearing Stn., one Officer and 84 O.R. ~~transf~~ were transferred to the Corps Rest Stn. and 27 O.R. were returned to duty, leaving 337 O.R. remaining.	J.E.P.

D. D. & L. London, E.C. (A8094) Wt. W2771/M1 31 750,000 5/17 Sch. 52 Forms/C2118/14

Instructions regarding War Diaries and Intelligence Summaries are contained in F. S. Regs., Part II. and the Staff Manual respectively. Title pages will be prepared in manuscript.

WAR DIARY

or

~~INTELLIGENCE SUMMARY.~~

(Erase heading not required.)

Army Form C. 2118.

Place	Date	Hour	Summary of Events and Information	Remarks and references to Appendices
BUS	16/1/18	9 p.m.	The weather has continued very wet and stormy and has damaged the roofs of several of the Rest Station Huts – Efforts to repair these are being made. I attended a conference at the A.D.M.S.'s Office at 11 a.m. – Two Officers and 211 O.R. were admitted to the Unit during the day. One Officer and 117 O.R. were evacuated to C.C.S. – One Officer and 127 O.R. were transferred to the Corps Rest Stn. 27 men were returned to duty, leaving 293 other ranks remaining in the Rest Station.	J.E.P.
"	17/1/18	9 p.m.	The weather continues very wet and stormy – The G.O.C. 19th Division visited the Rest Station this morning and expressed his satisfaction with the work done here. – Four Officers and 215 O.R. were admitted to the Unit during the day, two Officers and 109 O.R. were evacuated to a Casualty Clearing Stn., 78 O.R. were transferred to the Corps Rest Stn. and 27 men were returned to duty, leaving two Officers and 293 other ranks remaining in the Rest Station.	J.E.P.
"	18/1/18	9 p.m.	The weather has become much warmer, but is damp and showery. – The Personnel are engaged in repairing the roofs of the huts after the damage done by the recent storm. – Large numbers of Trench feet of a severe type are being admitted and nearly all are being evacuated – the conditions in the Trenches are now very bad. – The A.D.M.S. 19th Division visited the Rest Stn. in the afternoon. – Four Officers and 282 other ranks were admitted during the day, 5 Officers and 156 O.R. were evacuated to a C.C.S. 88 other ranks were transferred to the Corps Rest Stn. and 21 men were returned to duty, leaving One Officer and 310 other ranks remaining in the Rest Stn.	J.E.P.

(A8004) Wt. W1771/M2 31 750,000 5/17 D. D. & L., London, E.C. Sch. 52 Forms/C2118/14

Instructions regarding War Diaries and Intelligence Summaries are contained in F. S. Regs., Part II. and the Staff Manual respectively. Title pages will be prepared in manuscript.

WAR DIARY

or

~~INTELLIGENCE SUMMARY.~~

(Erase heading not required.)

Army Form C. 2118.

Place	Date	Hour	Summary of Events and Information	Remarks and references to Appendices
BUS	19/1/18	9 p.m.	The day has been fine and mild throughout. – Repairs to the huts are being continued, a certain amount of tarred felting has been obtained from the C.R.E. – Three Officers and 239 other ranks were admitted to the Rest Station, four Officers and 109 O.R. were evacuated to a C.C.S. 91 O.R. were transferred to the Corps Rest Stn., and 23 men were returned to duty, leaving 326 other ranks remaining in the Rest Station.	J.E.P.
"	20/1/18	9 p.m.	Some rain fell in the night, but to-day has been fine and mild. – Repairs to huts are being continued – a further indent for tarred felt has been made on C.E. Corps. The D.M.S. Army and the A.D.M.S. Division visited the Rest Station this afternoon. One Officer and 197 other ranks were admitted, One Officer and 110 O.R. were evacuated to a C.C.S., 71 other ranks were transferred to the Corps Rest Stn., and 30 men were returned to duty, leaving 312 other ranks remaining in the Rest Stn. –	J.E.P.
"	21/1/18	9 p.m.	The weather continues mild but showery. – Orders were received from the A.D.M.S. to detail two Medical Officers for charge of Regts. – I detailed Captain BOYLE R.A.M.C. for permanent medical charge of the 10th Bn. Worcester Regt. and Captain WALL RAMC for temporary medical charge of the 9th Bn. Welsh Regt. – 178 other ranks were admitted to the Rest Station during the day, 96 O.R. were evacuated to a C.C.S., 62 O.R. were transferred to the Corps Rest Stn., and 20 men were returned to duty, leaving 312 other ranks remaining in the Rest Stn.	J.E.P.

D. D. & L., London, E.C.
(A8004) Wt. W1771/M2 31 750,000 5/17 Sch. 52 Forms/C2118/14

Instructions regarding War Diaries and Intelligence Summaries are contained in F. S. Regs., Part II. and the Staff Manual respectively. Title pages will be prepared in manuscript.

WAR DIARY
or
~~INTELLIGENCE SUMMARY.~~
(Erase heading not required.)

Army Form C. 2118.

Place	Date	Hour	Summary of Events and Information	Remarks and references to Appendices
BUS	22/1/18	9 pm.	The weather continues mild with light showers of rain. – Captain BOYLE and Captain WALL RAMC reported their departure this morning for their respective Battalions. – Captain HARPER M.C. RAMC reported his arrival this evening. – One officer and 209 other ranks were admitted to the Rest Stn. during the day. One officer and 108 other ranks were evacuated to a C.C.S. and 93 O.R. were sent to the Corps Rest Stn., and 14 men were returned to duty, leaving 304 O.R. remaining.	J.E.P.
"	23/1/18	9 pm.	Heavy showers of rain continue to fall and the atmosphere is damp foggy & mild. Captain HARPER M.C. R.A.M.C. reported his departure this morning for the 19th Divisional Wing of the Corps Reinforcement Camp for duty. – Captain A.G. BUCHANAN R.A.M.C. (T.F.) reported his arrival for duty on handing over charge of the 19th Divisional Wing of Corps Reinforcement Camp to Captain HARPER. – Three Officers and 150 O.R. were admitted during the day, two Officers & 81 O.R. were evacuated to C.C.S. & One Officer & 71 O.R. were transferred to the Corps Rest Stn. and 25 men were returned to duty, leaving 277 other ranks remaining.	J.E.P.
"	24/1/18	9 pm.	The weather has been fine and mild. – The G.O.C. Division visited the Rest Station in the afternoon. – 157 other ranks were admitted to the Rest Station during the day, 60 other ranks were evacuated to a C.C.S., 65 O.R. were transferred to the Corps Rest Stn., and 35 O.R. were returned to duty, leaving 273 O.R. remaining in the Rest Station.	J.E.P.

D. D. & L., London, E.C.
(A8004) Wt. W1771/Ma 31 750,000 5/17 Sch. 52 Forms/C2118/14

Army Form C. 2118.

Instructions regarding War Diaries and Intelligence Summaries are contained in F. S. Regs., Part II. and the Staff Manual respectively. Title pages will be prepared in manuscript.

WAR DIARY

or

~~INTELLIGENCE SUMMARY.~~

(Erase heading not required.)

Place	Date	Hour	Summary of Events and Information	Remarks and references to Appendices
BUS	25/1/18	9 p.m.	The weather continues fine, clear and mild. – 105 other ranks were admitted to the Rest Station during the day, 46 O.R. were evacuated to a C.C.S. & 47 O.R. were transferred to the Corps Rest Station and 34 men were returned to duty, leaving 251 other ranks remaining in the Rest Station – ~~[illegible]~~ Personnel are employed in constructing a drying room in connection with the Incinerator & other sanitary appliances.	J.E.P.
BUS	26/1/18	9 p.m.	To-day has been damp and foggy. – Under instructions from the A.D.M.S. 19th Division ~~[illegible]~~ 1st Lieut. R. DECK M.O.R.C. U.S.A. and 32 other ranks R.A.M.C. marched off at 1.30 p.m. for temporary duty at No. 49 C.C.S. – 113 other ranks were admitted to the Rest Station during the day, 38 O.R. were evacuated to a C.C.S. & 45 O.R. were transferred to the Corps Rest Stn., & 37 O.R. were returned to duty, leaving 244 O.R. remaining in the Rest Station.	J.E.P.
BUS	27/1/18	9 p.m.	The weather continues damp and foggy & has become colder. – The D.A.D.M.S. V Corps called and I have arranged that the first course of the Corps School of Instruction for R.A.M.C. will begin on the 4th February. 87 other ranks were admitted during the day, 31 O.R. were evacuated to a C.C.S. & 65 O.R. were transferred to the Corps Rest Stn. & 19 O.R. were returned to duty, leaving 216 O.R. remaining in the Rest Stn.	J.E.P.

D. D. & L., London, E.C.
(A8004) Wt. W1771/M2 31 750,000 5/17 Sch. 52 Forms/C2118/14

Instructions regarding War Diaries and Intelligence Summaries are contained in F. S. Regs., Part II. and the Staff Manual respectively. Title pages will be prepared in manuscript.

WAR DIARY

or

~~INTELLIGENCE SUMMARY.~~

(Erase heading not required.)

Army Form C. 2118.

Place	Date	Hour	Summary of Events and Information	Remarks and references to Appendices
BUS	28/1/18	9 pm	The weather has been fine and clear to-day and there was a slight frost last night. – One Third Army Hut has been received to-day from the R.E. to be erected for the use of the Personnel. – 63 O.R. were admitted to the Rest Station during the day, 18 O.R. were evacuated to a C.C.S. & 30 O.R. were transferred to the Corps Rest Stn. & 22 men were returned to duty, leaving 198 O.R. remaining in the Rest Station.	[illegible]
"	29/1/18	12.0 noon	Lt. Col. J. E. POWELL D.S.O. reported his departure this morning for temporary duty as A.D.M.S. 19th Division during the absence of the A.D.M.S. on leave. Temporary command of the unit was assumed by Capt. G. P. KIDD R.A.M.C.	
		9.0 pm	All unemployed personnel is being occupied in providing lateral splinter proof protection for huts and billets in the camp. Good progress is being made with this work. 76. O.R. admitted during the day. 86. O.R. evacuated to C.C.S. 17. O.R. to C.R.S. 13. O.R. to duty. leaving 218. O.R. remaining in the Rest Station.	[illegible]
"	30/1/18	9.0 pm	The weather remains fine and warm in the day time with slight frosts at night. A good deal of Hostile bombing from aircraft has occurred during the past week & every effort is being made to get all huts & billets protected as soon as possible. The third Army Hut for personnel is now being erected. A good number of models of sanitary appliances have been constructed for demonstration purposes in connection with the School of Instruction commencing next week. 3. Off. & 109. O.R. were admitted during the day. 2. Off. & 44. O.R. evacuated to C.C.S. 1. Off. & 32. O.R. transferred to C.R.S. 21. O.R. to duty. leaving 230. O.R. remaining.	[illegible]

D. D. & L., London, E.C.
(A8004) Wt. W1771/M2 31 750,000 5/17 Sch. 52 Forms/C2118/14

Instructions regarding War Diaries and Intelligence Summaries are contained in F. S. Regs., Part II. and the Staff Manual respectively. Title pages will be prepared in manuscript.

WAR DIARY
or
~~INTELLIGENCE~~ SUMMARY.

(Erase heading not required.)

Army Form C. 2118.

Place	Date	Hour	Summary of Events and Information	Remarks and references to Appendices
BUS	31/1/18	9.5pm	The weather remains fine but has been very foggy all day. O.C. Sanitary Section called in the afternoon to make arrangements about lectures for the School of Training next week. 2 Offs & 83. OR were admitted during the day. 1 Off & 30. OR evacuated to CCS 1 Off & 37. OR transferred to CRS. [illegible] OR to duty. Leaving 232 OR remaining. The past month has been a busy one as far as this unit is concerned, a very large number of cases having been dealt with at the Rest Station. During the month 72 Officers and 5340 OR were admitted and dealt with by the unit; of these [illegible] were returned to duty with their own units.	[illegible]

C. H. Kidd
Capt RAMC
O.C. 57th Field Ambulance

D. D. & L., London, E.C.
(A8004) Wt. W1771/M231 750,000 5/17 Sch. 52 Forms/C2118/14

Feb 1918

26

CONFIDENTIAL

Vol 32

WAR DIARY

OF 57 FIELD AMBULANCE. R.A.M.C.

FROM - 1-2-18 TO 28-2-18

VOLUME 32.

Army Form C. 2118.

WAR DIARY
or
~~INTELLIGENCE SUMMARY.~~
(Erase heading not required.)

Instructions regarding War Diaries and Intelligence Summaries are contained in F. S. Regs., Part II. and the Staff Manual respectively. Title pages will be prepared in manuscript.

Place	Date	Hour	Summary of Events and Information	Remarks and references to Appendices
BUS	1/2/18	9.0pm	There was a thick mist again all day today & the weather has become much colder with sharp frosts at night. Good progress has been made during the past few days in constructing sanitary models for the School of Instruction next week and a good selection of these is now ready. 89. O.R. were admitted during the day. 45. O.R. evacuated to C.C.S. 32. O.R. transferred to C.R.S. 16. O.R. to duty, leaving 228. O.R. remaining in the rest station.	[illegible initials]
"	2/2/18	9.0pm	An extra number of tables and forms were received today and placed in the dining hall. 1. Off. & 101. O.R. were admitted during the day. 1 Off. & 73. O.R. evacuated to C.C.S. 37 O.R. transferred to C.R.S. 10. O.R. to duty, leaving 249. O.R. remaining in the Rest Station	[illegible initials]
"	3/2/18	9.0pm	D.A.D.M.S. and Sanitary Officer [illegible] Corps. called in the morning to make final arrangements with regard to the School of Instruction tomorrow. Five Officers & five N.C.O's reported this evening for the Course commencing tomorrow. a/A.D.M.S. 19th Div. visited the unit and expressed his satisfaction with the amount of work done about the camp in the last few days. 3. Off & 95. O.R. were admitted during the day. 2 Off & 66 O.R. evacuated to C.C.S. 1. Off & 47. O.R. transferred to C.R.S. 12. O.R. to duty. Leaving 240. O.R. remaining	[illegible initials]
"	4/2/18	9.0pm	The R.A.M.C. course of instruction for Officers and N.C.O's commenced today at 9.0 A.M. A.D's.M.S. 17th & 63rd Divs. and a/A.D.M.S. 19th Div. visited the Rest Station during the day. The weather remains fine and has become much warmer. 2. Off & 56. O.R. were admitted during the day. 1. Off. & 37. O.R. evacuated to C.C.S. 1. Off & 46. O.R. transferred to C.R.S. 11. O.R. to duty. Leaving 202. O.R. remaining.	[illegible initials]

D. D. & L., London, E.C.
(A8004) Wt. W1771/M2/31 750,000 5/17 Sch. 52 Forms/C2118/14

Instructions regarding War Diaries and Intelligence Summaries are contained in F. S. Regs., Part II. and the Staff Manual respectively. Title pages will be prepared in manuscript.

WAR DIARY

or

~~INTELLIGENCE SUMMARY.~~

(Erase heading not required.)

Army Form C. 2118.

Place	Date	Hour	Summary of Events and Information	Remarks and references to Appendices
BUS	5/2/18	9.0pm	D.A.D.M.S. 7. Corps called again in the afternoon to enquire if anything further was required for the School of Instruction. 4. Off. & 141. O.R. were admitted during the day. 3. Off & 50. O.R. evacuated to C.C.S. 1. Off & 42. O.R. transferred to C.R.S. 7. O.R. to duty. leaving 244. O.R. remaining.	G.H.R.
"	6/2/18	9.0pm	O.C. Sanitary Section & Corps Gas Officer came & lectured to the Class of Instruction today. A large amount of work was done today in improving the permanent sanitary arrangements of the camp. Both large soak pits being opened up and cleaned out. 118. O.R. were admitted during the day. 42. O.R. evacuated to C.C.S. 56. O.R. transferred to C.R.S. 12. O.R. to duty. leaving 261 O.R. remaining.	G.H.R.
"	7/2/18.	9.0pm	A/A.D.M.S. 19. Div. visited the Rest Station during the morning. The weather has become much warmer again and some rain fell today. 88. O.R. were admitted during the day. 31. O.R. evacuated to C.C.S. 66. O.R. transferred to C.R.S. 8. O.R. to duty. leaving 234. O.R. remaining.	G.H.R.
"	8/2/18	12.0noon	Lieut. R. DECK. M.O.R.C. USA. reported his arrival back yesterday with party ~~ph~~ 32 O.R. from temporary duty at 49. C.C.S. He proceeded this morning under instructions from A.D.M.S. to temporary duty at 56 C.C.S. By same authority a party of 10. O.R. was sent today to temp: duty at 48. C.C.S. and a further party of 12. O.R. to report to O.C. 59. Fd Amb. for duty as a working party. A good deal of rain fell again today but the weather cleared in the evening. 90. O.R. were admitted during the day. 42. O.R. evacuated to C.C.S. 41 O.R. transferred to C.R.S. 9. O.R. to duty. leaving 227 O.R. remaining.	G.H.R.

D. D. & L., London, E.C.
(A8004) Wt. W1771/M2 31 750,000 5/17 Sch. 52 Forms/C2118/14

Army Form C. 2118.

WAR DIARY
or
~~INTELLIGENCE SUMMARY.~~

(Erase heading not required.)

Instructions regarding War Diaries and Intelligence Summaries are contained in F. S. Regs., Part II. and the Staff Manual respectively. Title pages will be prepared in manuscript.

Place	Date	Hour	Summary of Events and Information	Remarks and references to Appendices
BUS	9/2/18	9.0pm	The first course of the RAMC School of Instruction was completed at 4.0 pm today and the officers & NCO's attending reported their departure to rejoin their respective units. 128. O.R. were admitted during the day. 63. O.R. evacuated to C.C.S 36. O.R. transferred to CRS 26. O.R. to duty, leaving 230. O.R. remaining.	[illegible]
"	10/2/18	9.0pm	Officers & NCO's for next weeks course of instruction reported this evening. 93. O.R. were admitted during the day. 40. O.R. evacuated to C.C.S. 40. O.R. transferred to CRS 5. O.R. to duty, leaving 246. O.R. remaining. The weather remains warm & some rain fell again today.	[illegible]
"	11/2/18	9.0pm	The DADMS visited the Rest Station during the afternoon. Capt. H. WALL RAMC reported his arrival back for duty from temporary duty as M.O. 4th 9. Welch Reg. Orders received this evening that the 19 Division will be relieved in the line on the 13th – 15th inst. This unit will not move from here but will continue to administer the Rest Station and RAMC School of Instruction. 69. O.R. were admitted during the day 29. O.R. evacuated to C.C.S 49. O.R. transferred to CRS 6. O.R. to duty, leaving 231 O.R. remaining.	[illegible]
"	12/2/18	9.0pm	80 O.R. were admitted during the day. 45. O.R. evacuated to C.C.S 41. O.R. transferred to CRS 13. O.R. to duty, leaving 211 O.R. remaining. Orders received today that the CRS at MARICOURT is closed for the present, this will mean keeping a larger number of cases here during this period	[illegible]
"	13/2/18	12 noon	Capt. J. L. Cochrane MC RAMC reported his departure this morning on 14 days leave to U.K. D.D.M.S. V. Corps visited the Rest Station this morning and expressed his intention of again visiting & thoroughly inspecting the camp at a later date. 112. O.R. were admitted during the day. 54. O.R. evacuated to C.C.S 26 O.R. transferred to CRS 15. O.R. to duty, leaving 228. O.R. remaining	[illegible]

D. D. & L., London, E.C.
(A8004) Wt. W1771/M2'31 750,000 5/17 Sch. 52 Forms/C2118/14

Instructions regarding War Diaries and Intelligence Summaries are contained in F. S. Regs., Part II. and the Staff Manual respectively. Title pages will be prepared in manuscript.

WAR DIARY
or
~~INTELLIGENCE SUMMARY~~.
(Erase heading not required.)

Army Form C. 2118.

Place	Date	Hour	Summary of Events and Information	Remarks and references to Appendices
BUS.	14/2/18	9.0 pm	The weather has become cold & wet again, some rain fell today. 82 O.R. were admitted during the day. 49. O.R. Evacuated to C.C.S. 38. O.R. to duty. 5. O.R. transferred to 53. F.A. leaving 218. O.R. remaining. A further ward has been opened to accommodate convalescent cases which would otherwise be sent to C.R.S. Officers & Scabies cases are still sent to C.R.S. as before.	G.H.R.
"	15/2/18	11.0 am 9.0 pm	Lieut. Col. J. E. Powell DSO RAMC on completion of temporary duty as A.D.M.S. 19 Div. reported his departure on thirty days leave of absence to England. The A.D.M.S. visited the Rest Station this afternoon and inspected in detail all the wards and the camp arrangements in general. The 19. Div. has now been relieved in the line by the 63. (RN) Div. and is now in the Corps Reserve Area – the three Brigades being billetted in the BARASTRE, ROCQUIGNY and BEAULENCOURT areas respectively. 84. O.R. were admitted during the day. 26. O.R. Evacuated to C.C.S. 19. O.R. transferred to C.R.S. 37. O.R. to duty. leaving 220 O.R. remaining.	G.H.R.
"	16/2/18	9.0 pm	The D.D.M.S. V. Corps visited and thoroughly inspected the Rest Station this morning. He expressed himself as very satisfied with all arrangements and with the amount of work that has been done since his last visit. The second course of the RAMC. School of instruction was completed today and the Officers & N.C.O.s attending returned to their respective units in the afternoon. 64. O.R. were admitted during the day. 71. O.R. evacuated to C.C.S. 6. O.R. transferred to C.R.S. 8. O.R. to duty. leaving 199. O.R. remaining. The weather has become very clear and cold again and there have been hard frosts at night for the last three days.	G.H.R.

D. D. & L., London, E.C.
(A8004) Wt. W1771/M2 31 750,000 5/17 Sch. 52 Forms/C2118/14

Instructions regarding War Diaries and Intelligence Summaries are contained in F. S. Regs., Part II. and the Staff Manual respectively. Title pages will be prepared in manuscript.

WAR DIARY
or
~~INTELLIGENCE SUMMARY.~~

(Erase heading not required.)

Army Form C. 2118.

Place	Date	Hour	Summary of Events and Information	Remarks and references to Appendices
BUS	17/2/18	9.0pm	There was considerable enemy aerial activity last night in this area during which an E.A. dropped an aerial torpedo into this camp which luckily failed to explode. The ADMS visited the Hospital during the afternoon and a lecture was given by the Corps Chemical advisor to Medical Officers of the Division. Five officers & five NCOs for the next course of instruction reported here this evening. 66. OR were admitted during the day. 39. OR evacuated to CCS. 5. OR transferred to CRS. 14 OR to duty, leaving 207 OR remaining.	[illegible initials]
"	18/2/18	9.0pm	The third course of the RAMC School of Instruction commenced this morning. DDMS visited the hospital in the afternoon to inspect prospective "B" men. 61. OR were admitted during the day. 32. OR evacuated to CCS. 11 OR transferred to CRS. 9. OR to duty, leaving 215 OR remaining.	[illegible initials]
"	19/2/18	9.0pm	This afternoon three Medical Officers of the unit including myself attended a Third Army Medical meeting at GREVILLERS on "Surgical Shock" and the treatment thereof. 2 Off & 73. OR were admitted during the day. 43. OR evacuated to CCS. 8. OR transferred to CRS. 13. OR to duty, leaving 2. Off. & 224 OR remaining.	[illegible initials]
"	20/2/18	9.0pm	I visited the Fifth Army School of Sanitation at PERONNE this morning to see various models of new Sanitary appliances. The DDMS V. Corps visited the Rest Camp for a short time this afternoon. 1 Off & 94. OR were admitted during the day. 1 Off & 25. OR evacuated to CCS. 2 Off & 15. OR transferred to CRS. 20. OR to duty, leaving 257 OR remaining. The weather became much warmer today and a warning order was received that thaw precautions will probably come into force shortly.	[illegible initials]

D. D. & L., London, E.C. (A8004) Wt. W1771/M2 31 750,000 5/17 Sch. 52 Forms/C2118/14

Army Form C. 2118.

Instructions regarding War Diaries and Intelligence Summaries are contained in F. S. Regs., Part II. and the Staff Manual respectively. Title pages will be prepared in manuscript.

WAR DIARY
or
~~INTELLIGENCE SUMMARY.~~

(Erase heading not required.)

Place	Date	Hour	Summary of Events and Information	Remarks and references to Appendices
BUS.	21/2/18	9.0pm	I attended a conference at the ADMS Office in the morning when various points were discussed. 1. Off. & 76. O.R. were admitted during the day. [illegible] O.R. evacuated to C.C.S. 15. O.R. transferred to C.R.S. 25. O.R. to duty leaving 1 Off. & 262. O.R. remaining.	E.H.
"	22/2/18	5.0pm	A conference of Medical Officers was held at the Rest Camp today when a lecture on "Gas" was given by Capt Douglas RAMC from GHQ Central Laboratories. ADMS 19th & ADMS 17th Divs. visited the Rest Camp & attended the conference. Notification was received today that Capt. Hooper RAMC is struck off the strength of the unit on being appointed M.O. i/c Third Army School of Instruction. Capt. F. Humphreys RAMC and Lieut. J Acomb RAMC reported their arrival for duty with the unit on their respective Battalions being disbanded.	E.H.
		9.0pm	2. Off. & 70. O.R. were admitted during the day. 2. Off. & 36. O.R. evacuated to C.C.S. 1. Off. & 12. O.R. to C.R.S. 36. O.R. to duty leaving 228. O.R. remaining.	
"	23/2/18	9.0pm	The third course of the RAMC School of Instruction was finished today, and the officers & NCOs attending returned to their respective units. A good deal of work has been done about the camp this week. A new equipment store and canteen have been erected and work commenced on improving the Q.M. stores. 2. Off & 88. O.R. were admitted during the day. 2. Off & 48. O.R. evacuated to C.C.S. 16 O.R. transferred to C.R.S. 19. O.R. to duty leaving 237. O.R. remaining.	E.H.
"	24/2/18	12 noon	D.D.M.S. V. Corps visited the rest station this morning. Ten reinforcements (O.R.) were received today. These are B I and B II men and appear of a very low class of physique. 1. Off. & 78. O.R. were admitted during the day. 1 Off. & 47. O.R. evacuated to C.C.S. 19. O.R. to C.R.S. 10. O.R. to duty Leaving 235. O.R. remaining	E.H.

D. D. & L., London, E.C.
(A8004) Wt. W1771/M231 750,000 5/17 Sch. 52 Forms/C2118/14

Instructions regarding War Diaries and Intelligence Summaries are contained in F. S. Regs., Part II. and the Staff Manual respectively. Title pages will be prepared in manuscript.

WAR DIARY

or

~~INTELLIGENCE SUMMARY~~.

(Erase heading not required.)

Army Form C. 2118.

Place	Date	Hour	Summary of Events and Information	Remarks and references to Appendices
BUS.	25/2/18.	9.0pm	The fourth course of the RAMC School of Instruction was commenced this morning, two officers & six NCOs attending. The ADMS visited and inspected the Rest Station in the afternoon. Orders received that the Division is now held in Army reserve and ready to move at six hours notice. 70. OR. were admitted during the day. 31. OR. evacuated to CCS. 11. OR. transferred to CRS. 19 OR. to duty. Leaving 244. OR. remaining.	ELK
"	26/2/18	9.0pm	The weather has been quite warm for the past few days. 2. Off & 83. OR. were admitted during the day. 26. OR. evacuated to CCS. 5. OR. transferred to CRS. ~~1 Off~~ & 23. OR. to duty. Leaving 2 Off & 272 OR. remaining.	ELK
"	27/2/18	9.0pm	I attended a conference at the ADMS Office this morning. This afternoon I visited Third Army School of Sanitation at ARRAS to see various models there. Orders received this evening that no more Officers or Scabies cases are to be sent to Corps Rest Station at MARICOURT. This will mean that temporary arrangements must be made here for the treatment of Scabies cases. 2. Off & 71. OR. were admitted during the day. 2. Off & 71. OR. Evacuated to CCS. 1. Off & 9. OR. transferred to CRS. 26. OR. to duty. Leaving 1. Off & 237. OR. remaining.	ELK
"	28/2/18	9.0pm	Lieut J.E. CROUP MORC USA reported his departure yesterday for a three day course of instruction at the Third Army School of Sanitation at ARRAS. 1. Off & 79. OR were admitted during the day. 1. Off & 46. OR. Evacuated to CCS. Leaving 244 OR. remaining. The admission rate was very much lower this month than last month. 24. Off. & 2389. OR. were admitted & dealt with during the month. 475 being returned to duty.	ELK

ELK [signature]
Capt RAMC
O.C. 57th Field Ambulance.

D. D. & L., London, E.C. (A8004) Wt. W1771/M231 750,000 5/17 Sch. 52 Forms/C2118/14

17

Vol 33

WAR DIARY

Mar. 1918.

of 57 FIELD AMBULANCE. R.A.M.C

FROM 1-3-18 to 31-3-18

VOLUME 32

Instructions regarding War Diaries and Intelligence Summaries are contained in F. S. Regs., Part II. and the Staff Manual respectively. Title pages will be prepared in manuscript.

WAR DIARY

or

~~INTELLIGENCE SUMMARY~~.

(Erase heading not required.)

Army Form C. 2118.

Place	Date	Hour	Summary of Events and Information	Remarks and references to Appendices
BUS	1/3/18	9 pm	The weather has become much colder again with a lot of wind. Temporary arrangements have now been made for the treatment of Scabies cases here pending the opening of the new CRS at BEAULENCOURT. 1. Off & 114 OR. were admitted during the day. 73 OR. Evacuated to CCS 22 OR. to duty. Leaving 1. Off & 263. OR remaining.	EBL
"	2/3/18	9 pm	I attended with Capt. Smalley a V Corps Medical meeting at 48 CCS this afternoon. ADMS. 19. Div was there and warned me that the unit may be moving from here when the Division moves back into the line in a few days time. Capt. H.M. WALL reported his departure for duty as M.O. i/c 9. Welch Reg. Capt. J.L. Cochrane reported his arrival back for duty from leave in the U.K. 1. Off & 70. OR. were admitted during the day. 1 Off. & 37. OR. Evacuated to CCS. 31. OR. to duty. Leaving 1. Off & 265. OR remaining.	EBL
"	3/3/18	9 pm	I attended a conference at the DDMS. office this morning to discuss the forthcoming move. This unit will be taking over the line from 51. F. Amb. 17th Div. This afternoon I visited O.C. 51. F. Amb. with Capt Smalley to arrange details as to the method of working the line in the new sector. Capt. F.J. Humphrey RAMC reported his departure this evening for duty as M.O. i/c 6th Entrenching Battalion & is struck off the strength. 2. Off & 64. OR were admitted during the day. 2. Off & 36. OR. Evacuated to CCS. 21. OR. to duty. Leaving 1. Off & 274. OR remaining. Further reinforcements of 'B' Category men were received today, these men being of a very low physical standard & apparently of not much use for a F. Ambulance.	EBL

D. D. & L., London, E.C. (A8004) Wt. W1771/M2 31 750,000 5/17 Sch. 52 Forms/C2118/14

Army Form C. 2118.

Instructions regarding War Diaries and Intelligence Summaries are contained in F. S. Regs., Part II. and the Staff Manual respectively. Title pages will be prepared in manuscript.

WAR DIARY
or
~~INTELLIGENCE SUMMARY.~~

(Erase heading not required.)

Place	Date	Hour	Summary of Events and Information	Remarks and references to Appendices
BUS	4/3/18	9.0pm	Orders received today that the Rest Camp will be handed over to 58. Fd Amb on the 6th inst. ADMS visited and inspected the hospital in the afternoon. In the evening I visited O.C. 58 Fd Amb to make preliminary arrangements for the move. All ranks were exercised today in the use of the box respirator, all working parties worked for periods with respirators adjusted and all other men were exercised in marching with masks on. The A.S.C personnel also carried out similar exercises. 72. O.R. were admitted during the day. 43. O.R. evacuated to C.C.S. 1. Off & 23. O.R. to duty. leaving 280. O.R. remaining.	E.K.
"	5/3/18	12.0 Noon	O.C. 58. Fd Amb. came over this morning to see the Rest Station & make detailed arrangements for taking over same tomorrow.	
		9.0pm	Advanced party from 58 Fd Amb. under Capt. McCombie RAMC arrived at 6.0 pm. 1 Off & 96. O.R. were admitted during the day. 1. Off & 75. O.R. evacuated to C.C.S 33. O.R. to duty. leaving 261. O.R. remaining.	E.K.
SANDERS CAMP (Haplincourt)	6/3/18	9.0pm	The Rest Station at BUS and all patients were handed over to 58 Fd Amb this morning, our books being closed at 12.0 noon. The unit moved off at 2.0pm and arrived here at 3.0pm. The unit will be closed in the camp here for the present. Lieut. J.E. Crouse reported his departure for temp duty as M.O. i/c 10th R War Reg. 1. Off & 67 O.R. were admitted up to noon. 1 Off & 82 O.R. evacuated to C.C.S. 36. O.R. to duty. 11. O.R. transferred to 53. Fd Amb. 229. O.R. transferred to 58. Fd Amb. leaving nil remaining.	E.K.
"	7/3/18	9.0pm	The morning was spent in cleaning up the new camp & in gas drill for the unit. In the afternoon I visited the forward area in company with the ADMS to decide sites for A.D.S. and routes for walking wounded etc. in the event of active operations.	E.K.

D. D. & L., London, E.C.
(A8004) Wt. W1771/M2 31 750,000 5/17 Sch. 52 Forms/C2118/14

Instructions regarding War Diaries and Intelligence Summaries are contained in F. S. Regs., Part II. and the Staff Manual respectively. Title pages will be prepared in manuscript.

WAR DIARY

or

~~INTELLIGENCE SUMMARY~~.

(*Erase heading not required.*)

Army Form C. 2118.

Place	Date	Hour	Summary of Events and Information	Remarks and references to Appendices
SANDERS CAMP	8/3/18	9.0pm	I visited the forward area again today with DADMS and OC. 59. FA and bearer officers also visited the forward area to get to know the ground. The personnel were occupied with camp duties, and in Gas drill. Capt. F. J. Humphreys RAMC reported his arrival for duty with the unit & is taken on strength	[illegible]
"	9/3/18	9.0pm	Lieut R. Deck & Lieut J E Cramp M.O's R.C. U.S.A. reported their arrival back for duty today. I attended a conference at ADMS. Office this morning. This afternoon I reconnoitred the HAVRINCOURT WOOD area in company with my bearer officers to arrange routes of evacuation from that area in accordance with Defence Scheme. The weather remains fine & clear with frosts at night.	[illegible]
"	10/3/18	9.0pm	This afternoon I visited the Havrincourt Wood area again in company with my bearer officers & thoroughly reconnoitred all the ground. In the evening I visited the ADMS. & discussed further points with regard to defence scheme.	[illegible]
"	11/3/18	9.0pm	Together with ADMS. I reconnoitred the LOUVERVAL Sector this morning to find battle sites for ADS and routes of evacuation for wounded. The personnel are being occupied in various kinds of training and in improving the camp	[illegible]
"	12/3/18	9.0pm	The weather remains fine and clear with some frost at nights. A good deal of work has been done in improving the camp during the past few days. If possible and if material can be obtained, cover for the horse lines will be erected this week.	[illegible]
"	13/3/18	noon 9.0pm	Together with the ADMS I visited the L.R. Control Officer at BEAUMETZ JUNCTION this morning to arrange for the use of light Railways in the event of active hostilities. ADMS visited the camp this afternoon for a conference of medical Officers of the Division which was held here to discuss arrangements for forthcoming operations.	[illegible]

D. D. & L., London, E.C.
(A8004) Wt. W1771/M2·31 750,000 5/17 Sch. 53 Forms/C2118/14

Instructions regarding War Diaries and Intelligence Summaries are contained in F. S. Regs., Part II. and the Staff Manual respectively. Title pages will be prepared in manuscript.

WAR DIARY
or
~~INTELLIGENCE SUMMARY~~.
(Erase heading not required.)

Army Form C. 2118.

Place	Date	Hour	Summary of Events and Information	Remarks and references to Appendices
SANDERS CAMP.	14/3/18	9.0 pm.	Bearer officers again reconnoitred the forward areas today and all are now well acquainted with the various prospective areas of operations. The personnel were sent for a march this morning and a training system of training is being carried out each day.	[initials]
"	15/3/18	9.0 pm.	Authority has been obtained for drawing material for stabling and this will now be erected as soon as possible. The weather remains fine and is still very cold at nights.	[initials]
"	16/3/18	9.0 pm.	D.D.M.S. [illegible] Corps visited and inspected the camp during the morning. Work is being proceeded with [illegible] [illegible]. The condition of [illegible] [illegible] improvement [illegible] [illegible] is being erected over the ablution [illegible].	[initials]
"	17/3/18	9.0 pm.	The unit attended church parade this morning. Material for stabling has now been drawn and erection of same will commence. A course of lectures on Map Reading for Bearer Officers & N.C.O.s is being held. The first lecture took place tonight by A.D.C. 19 Div.	[initials]
"	18/3/18	9.0 pm.	The unit marched to ROQUIGNY this morning to be tested in Gas training and to have respirators tested in Gas chamber. The ablution bench shed is now completed, also the [illegible] butchers shop in store.	[initials]
"	19/3/18	9.0 pm.	I attended a conference at the A.D.M.S. Office this afternoon. Warning orders received that the Div. will relieve the 17th Div. in the line on the 22nd & 23rd inst. Lt. Col. J.E. POWELL D.S.O. reported his arrival back for duty from one month's leave in the U.K. and reassumes command of the unit from this date.	[initials]

D. D. & L., London, E.C.
(A8004) Wt. W1771/M2 31 750,000 5/17 Sch. 52 Forms/C2118/14

Army Form C. 2118.

Instructions regarding War Diaries and Intelligence Summaries are contained in F. S. Regs., Part II. and the Staff Manual respectively. Title pages will be prepared in manuscript.

WAR DIARY
or
~~INTELLIGENCE SUMMARY.~~
(Erase heading not required.)

Place	Date	Hour	Summary of Events and Information	Remarks and references to Appendices
SANDERS CAMP HAPLINCOURT	20/3/18	9 p.m.	It rained all last night & this morning. I reassumed command & took over charge of the Unit from Major KIDD. – Saw O.C. 51st Field Ambulance with reference to arrangements for taking over the A.D.S. etc. on the 22nd & 23rd insts. The A.D.M.S. & D.D.M.S. each visited the Unit during the morning. In the afternoon I visited O.C. 52nd Field Ambulance to make arrangements for handing over this camp on the 23rd inst.	J.E.P.
Map Sheet 57 C Sq I 35 b 8-3	21/3/18	5.30 a.m.	Weather fine & clear. – Received wires from A.D.M.S. & 58th Bde to "Stand By" ready to move at ½ hours notice to assembly Position. – Warned all ranks & breakfasts ordered.	
		7.30 a.m.	Visited 58th Bde Hdqrs. – No information there, except all quiet on 17th Division front – Enemy seen massing near GEANT.	
		11.55 a.m.	Received Wire from A.D.M.S. "Proceed to assembly Position" Bearer Division & 2 Tent subdivisions proceeded at 12.10 p.m.	J.E.P.
		12.40 p.m.	Met the A.D.M.S. at assembly Position at 12.40 p.m. Sq I 35 b 8-3. – Got in touch with 57th & 58th Inf. Bde Hdqrs., & distributed two runners to each Battalion of the 2 Brigades. – Also sent two clerks to the M.D.S. BEUGNY.	
		5.30 p.m.	Sent two Medical Officers and 10 Bearer squads to form A.D.S. at BEAUMETZ les-CAMBRAI also sent two motor ambulances there & arranged for marking out walking wounded track.	

D. D. & L., London, E.C. (A3004) Wt. W1771/M2 31 750,000 3/17 Sch. 52 Forms/C2118/14

Instructions regarding War Diaries and Intelligence Summaries are contained in F. S. Regs., Part II. and the Staff Manual respectively. Title pages will be prepared in manuscript.

WAR DIARY
or
INTELLIGENCE SUMMARY.
(Erase heading not required.)

Army Form C. 2118.

Place	Date	Hour	Summary of Events and Information	Remarks and references to Appendices
Map Sheet 57c Sq I 35b 8-3	21/3/18	6·30 p.m.	A.D.M.S. visited my Hdqrs. & arranged for stretcher cases to go to FREMICOURT & walking wounded to BEUGNY. Received notification that the 8th Gloster R.A.P was at Sq J 26 c Railway Cutting & the 10th Warwick R.A.P was at J 26 d 5-0	
		9 p.m.	Visited the A.D.S. & found a large number of lying & some walking cases awaiting evacuation — arranged for their evacuation by increased number of cars — Found the position of the A.D.S. far too near the front line and considered dangerous & I decided to evacuate the position as early as possible to-morrow morning — The Officer i/c A.D.S. Captain COCHRANE is in touch with all Regt Aid Posts & is keeping them clear	J.E.P.
"	22/3/18	2 a.m.	Reported personally to the A.D.M.S. on the position.	
		7·30 a.m.	Received report that A.D.S. is not yet clear — Sent Major SMALLEY with 4 more cars to clear it. — arranged for two Horse Ambulances & 3 motor ambulances to wait at Sq I 29 b for clearance of both lying & walking cases. —	
		11 a.m.	The two M.Os. & A D S Party returned from BEAUMETZ leaving all clear. Established a new A.D.S. at I 29 b with a Bearer relay post at VELU Chateau. From I 29 b cases are cleared by car to LOCH Camp FREMICOURT	
		1 p.m.	A.D.M.S arrived & after conference it was decided to move my Hdqrs at once to LOCH Camp FREMICOURT.	

D. D& L. London, E.C. (A8041) Wt. W771/M.31 750,000 8/17 Sch. 52 Forms/C2118/14

Instructions regarding War Diaries and Intelligence Summaries are contained in F. S. Regs., Part II. and the Staff Manual respectively. Title pages will be prepared in manuscript.

WAR DIARY
or
~~INTELLIGENCE SUMMARY.~~
(Erase heading not required.)

Army Form C. 2118.

Place	Date	Hour	Summary of Events and Information	Remarks and references to Appendices
LOCH CAMP FREMICOURT	22/3/18	2 p.m.	This move was completed and all Bde Hdqrs notified. During the afternoon all my Transport was also moved from SANDERS CAMP to a Camp near BAPAUME Water works.	
		4.30 p.m.	Visited 56th Bde Hdqrs & notified situation, also ~~visited~~ reported to the A.D.M.S. at D.H.Q. at 2 p.m. Bearer Division of 59th Field Ambulance was ordered to establish a loading post in BEUGNY & arrange for the evacuation of casualties in 58th Bde to LOCH camp where I established an A.D.S. by 6 p.m. – The Bearer Division of the 58th Field Ambulance was then ordered to relieve the bearer division of the 59th F.A. by 8 a.m. to-morrow morning, the latter then to return to their own Hdqrs.	J.E.P.
"	23/3/18	9 a.m.	Weather fine & clear. – Visited Post at BEUGNY and notified O.C. 58th F.A. Bearer Division that I was evacuating LOCH CAMP & proceeding to H35d near BANCOURT & to change his route of evacuation via HAPLINCOURT accordingly. – Then I proceeded to my A.D.S. at I29b but found that they had already been compelled to evacuate it & retire behind the 57th Bde towards HAPLINCOURT.	J.E.P.
H35d BANCOURT		11 a.m.	Moved my Hdqrs to H35d near BANCOURT & reported the changes to A.D.M.S.	
		1.30 p.m.	My Bearer Division with two medical officers arrived at my new Hdqrs on retirement with the 57th Bde, with the exception of 8 squads still attached to Battalions of the 57th Bde. – The Bearer Division of 58th Fd. Ambulance has also been compelled to retire on H35d from BEUGNY.	
		4 p.m.	The A.D.M.S. visited my Hdqrs. – The transport of all 3 Field Ambulances moved this afternoon to M6c	

D. D. & L., London, E.C. (A8004) Wt. W1771/M231 750,000 5/17 Sch. 52 Forms/C2118/14

Instructions regarding War Diaries and Intelligence Summaries are contained in F. S. Regs., Part II. and the Staff Manual respectively. Title pages will be prepared in manuscript.

WAR DIARY
or
~~INTELLIGENCE SUMMARY.~~
(Erase heading not required.)

Army Form C. 2118.

Place	Date	Hour	Summary of Events and Information	Remarks and references to Appendices
Brickfields Sq N 2 a	23/3/18	7 p.m.	Moved my Headquarters and A.D.S. to the Brickfields at Sq. N 2 a. – The Bearer Division of the 59th Fd. Amb. moved up to H 35 d to evacuate all casualties from the 58th Inf. Bde & also relieve some Bearers of the 57th Fd. Amb. – All 3 Bearer Divisions are now based on H 35 d & it is also the car loading post.	J.E.P.
		8 p.m.	Reported to the A.D.M.S.	
"	24/3/18	4 a.m.	Weather continues fine and clear. Received a report from Major BURTON giving positions of Regt Aid Posts of 56th Bde. as follows & that they were then all intact. 1/4 K. Shropshire L.I. Sq H 36 b 3-6. 8th North Staffords I 26 c 8-6 9th Cheshire I 26 d 8-8	
		6 a.m.	Received a report from Captain COCHRANE that 57th Bde R.A.Ps were as follows 10th Warwicks H 29 b 6-1, 10th Worcesters H 28 d 5-4 8th Glosters H 34 d 6-7	
		8 a.m.	Recd. a report from Major McCOMBIE that the 58th Bde had one combined A.P. for all 3 Battalions at I 20 d 1-9 also that the Regt. M.Os. of the 9th R.W. Fusiliers & 6th Wilts were missing believed prisoners. – Brought up Lieuts DECK & CRISP M.O.R.C. to replace the above casualties. –	J.E.P.
		10 a.m.	The A.D.M.S. visited me at my Headqrs. and informed me he was trying to establish a Dressing Stn. at Sq M 6 c on the BAPAUME – ALBERT Rd.	
		10.30 a.m.	Received a report that two H.D. horses of my unit were lost at H 35 d through shellfire.	
		11 a.m.	Saw all 3 Bearer Division Officers at H 35 d & made arrangements in case of further retirement.	
		1.30 p.m.	Reported the situation to the A.D.M.S.	

D. D. & L., London, E.C. (A6094) Wt. W5771/M2 31 750,000 5/17 Sch. 52 Forms/C2118/14

Instructions regarding War Diaries and Intelligence Summaries are contained in F. S. Regs., Part II. and the Staff Manual respectively. Title pages will be prepared in manuscript.

WAR DIARY
or
~~INTELLIGENCE SUMMARY.~~
(Erase heading not required.)

Army Form C. 2118.

Place	Date	Hour	Summary of Events and Information	Remarks and references to Appendices
Brickfields Sq N2a	24/3/18	4 p.m.	Enemy broke through FREMICOURT and Infantry retired on Red Line in front of BAPAUME & all 3 Bearer Divisions retired on the Brickfield at Sq N 2 d where they are fused and have a car relay there, pushing cars as far as possible up the road to BAPAUME and evacuating all cases to GREVILLERS as an A.D.S. where I made my Headquarters.	J.E.P.
GREVILLERS	24/3/18	5.30 p.m.	Sent Major KIDD back to the A.D.M.S. at ACHIET-LE-PETIT to report our movements & ask for instructions re evacuation of cases. – All Field Ambulance transport moved to site on ACHIET-MIRAMOUNT Rd.	
		8.30 p.m.	Visited O.Cs of Bearer Divisions at KNOTTY Corner north of THILLOY.	
MIRAMOUNT Goods Stn.		9.30 p.m.	Left GREVILLERS & marched to the M.D.S. which had been established on the ACHIET-MIRAMOUNT Rd. at the Goods Station & saw the A.D.M.S. there at midnight.	
"	25/3/18	4 a.m.	Weather has become dull & cloudy. – Remainder of Bearer Divisions arrived in from THILLOY carrying 11 stretcher cases all the way.	
		9 a.m.	Sent out Major McCOMBIE & Captain COCHRANE in two motor ambulances & with 3 Bearer squads to establish car loading posts at G 15 c & G 23 b Map Sheet 57 D.	J.E.P.
		10 a.m.	Having cleared the M.D.S. of all casualties I left for BUCQUOY with the remainder of the 3 Bearer Divisions arriving there at 12 Noon where I saw the A.D.M.S. &	
BUCQUOY		12 Noon	under instructions from him sent out another Horse Ambulance with Captain ROBERTSON & 3 more bearer squads to establish posts at G 29 a. – The position of the 1/4 Shropshire R.A.P. at 9 a.m. was H 31 c 8-0.	

D. D. & L., London, E.C. (A8004) Wt. W1774/M2 31 750,000 5/17 Sch. 52 Forms/C2118/14.

Instructions regarding War Diaries and Intelligence Summaries are contained in F. S. Regs., Part II. and the Staff Manual respectively. Title pages will be prepared in manuscript.

WAR DIARY
or
~~INTELLIGENCE SUMMARY.~~
(Erase heading not required.)

Army Form C. 2118.

Place	Date	Hour	Summary of Events and Information	Remarks and references to Appendices
BUCQUOY	25/3/18	2 p.m.	Majors KIDD & SMALLEY left with 15 squads of bearers to clear the Division now established on the PYS – BIHUCOURT line.	J.E.P.
		5 p.m.	Closed Dressing Stn. at BUCQUOY & retired with remainder of bearers to HEBUTERNE via PUSIEUX collecting cases en route arrived HEBUTERNE	
HEBUTERNE		10 p.m.	Majors KIDD & SMALLEY returned with the 15 Bearer Squads the Infantry having retired to a line in front of HEBUTERNE	
"	26/3/18	6 a.m.	The Dressing Stn. at HEBUTERNE closed & moved under Lt. Col PRESTON to BIENVILLERS, another Dressing Stn. has also opened at SOUASTRE.	J.E.P.
		7 a.m.	A.D.M.S. arrived. – I remain here at present with the Bearer Division forming an A.D.S. & evacuating all cases to SOUASTRE.	
		10 a.m.	Warned that the enemy were just outside HEBUTERNE & we were to retire at once on SOUASTRE. – I retired at once with the Bearer Division [illegible] to SOUASTRE – BIENVILLERS Rd. – Then saw the A.D.M.S. who ordered me to withdraw my BEARER Division to COUTERELLE together with the Transport & surplus Personnel of all 3 Field Ambulances. – Nos. 58 & 59 Field Ambulances remaining to carry out the evacuation of wounded	
COUTERELLE		4.30 p.m.	arrived here with transport.	

D. D. & L., London, E.C.
(A8004) Wt. W1771/M2 31 750,000 5/17 Sch. 52 Forms/C2118/14

Army Form C. 2118.

WAR DIARY
or
~~INTELLIGENCE SUMMARY.~~
(Erase heading not required.)

Instructions regarding War Diaries and Intelligence Summaries are contained in F. S. Regs., Part II. and the Staff Manual respectively. Title pages will be prepared in manuscript.

Place	Date	Hour	Summary of Events and Information	Remarks and references to Appendices
COUTERELLE	27/3/18	9 p.m.	The weather has become cold, cloudy and showery. – The Bearer Division arrived here at 1.30 a.m. and have been resting here all day. The A.D.M.S. visited the camp this evening.	J.E.P.
"	28/3/18	9 p.m.	The weather continues cold & showery. – Received orders from the A.D.M.S. to send a Billeting Party at 10 a.m. this morning for the 2nd Army Area & for the Unit to move by train to-morrow. – Remained resting at COUTERELLE all day.	J.E.P.
CANDAS	29/3/18	9 p.m.	Heavy rain fell throughout the night & it continues showery to-day. – The Unit marched off at 12 Noon to entrain at CANDAS Stn. at 9 p.m. for CAESTRE. The Motor Ambulances proceeded by road at 2 p.m. less 1 car remaining at CANDAS Stn. to collect sick.	J.E.P.
DRANOUTRE	30/3/18	9 p.m.	The weather continues very wet & cold. The Unit detrained at CAESTRE Stn. at 9.30 a.m. & arrived in camp at DRANOUTRE at 2 p.m. where the Unit opened up for the reception of sick. – A.D.M.S. visited the camp at 4 p.m.	J.E.P.
"	31/3/18	9 p.m.	To-day is fine with a high wind. – A.D.M.S. visited the Camp at 12 Noon. Received orders to take over the A.D.S. at KANDAHAR Farm & the evacuation of the Messines sector of the line – wounded to proceed direct to A.D.S. relief to be complete by 10 a.m. to-morrow. – Major SMALLEY proceeded this morning to reconnoitre the line & R.A.Ps. – Major SMALLEY and a Bearer Subdivision proceeded at 8.30 p.m. to take over the A.D.S. & all Bearer posts	J.E.P. J.E. Powell Lt. Col. RAMC O.C. 57th Field Amb.

D. D. & L., London, E.C. (A8004) Wt. W1771/M2 31 750,000 3/17 Sch. 52 Forms/C2118/14

apr. 1918!

Vol 34

140/2985

WAR DIARY

of 57 FIELD AMBULANCE. R.A.M.C.

FROM 1-4-18 to 30-4-18.

VOLUME 34

Confidential

Army Form C. 2118.

Instructions regarding War Diaries and Intelligence Summaries are contained in F. S. Regs., Part II. and the Staff Manual respectively. Title pages will be prepared in manuscript.

WAR DIARY
or
~~INTELLIGENCE SUMMARY.~~

(Erase heading not required.)

Place	Date	Hour	Summary of Events and Information	Remarks and references to Appendices
DRANOUTRE	1/4/18	9.0pm	Orders received that the unit will move from here tomorrow and take over a camp at RAVELSBURG from the 6' Aust. Fd Amb. I visited the new camp in the afternoon & made arrangements for the handing over. The remainder of the A.D.S party under Capt. HUMPHREYS proceeded to the ADS KANDAHAR FARM this morning. An advance party proceeded to RAVELSBERG this evening to commence taking over	GPK
RAVELSBERG CAMP	2/4/18	noon	Lt. Col. J.E. POWELL DSO RAMC on receipt of orders to ~~proceed~~ report to DDMS ETAPLES for duty, reported his departure this morning and is struck off the strength from this date. Temporary command of the unit was assumed by Major G.P. KIDD RAMC. The unit marched off at 10.0 AM. and arrived here at 11.0 AM.	GPK
		9.0pm	The afternoon was spent in arranging wards etc. I visited the ADS & met the ADMS there who had been round the line with Major Smalley this morning. A part of 77. Fd Amb 25th Div. is at present accommodated in this camp. Capt. R.H. JONES RAMC (T.C.) reported his arrival for duty & is taken on the strength.	
"	3/4/18	noon	ADMS 25. Div. called this morning with reference to the part of 77. Fd. Amb. accommodated here. 3. Off & 7. OR were admitted yesterday. 69. OR. transferred from 6. Aust. Fd. Amb. 3. Off & 4. OR to CCS leaving 74. OR. remaining. Orders received that we shall be open here for the reception of sick and their retention up to seven days. A D.R.S. will be run by 59. Fd Amb at HAGEDOORNE.	GPK
		9.0pm	ADMS visited and inspected the camp this morning and approves of all arrangements. A ward with 4 beds for Officers will be opened as soon as the personnel of 77. Fd Amb has gone. 1 Off & 41. OR. were admitted during the day. 14. OR. transferred from 5. Aust. Fd Amb. 1. Off & 47. OR. Evacuated to CCS. 3. OR. to Corps Scabies HP. Leaving 78. OR. remaining	

D. D. & L., London, E.C. (A8004) Wt. W4771/M2031 750,000 5/17 Sch. 52 Forms/C2118/14

Army Form C. 2118.

WAR DIARY
or
~~INTELLIGENCE SUMMARY~~.
(Erase heading not required.)

Instructions regarding War Diaries and Intelligence Summaries are contained in F. S. Regs., Part II. and the Staff Manual respectively. Title pages will be prepared in manuscript.

Place	Date	Hour	Summary of Events and Information	Remarks and references to Appendices
RAVELSBERG CAMP	4/4/18.	9.0pm	The unit has now settled down into the new camp and good progress is being made in replacing lost stores & re-equipping personnel. 46 OR. were admitted during the day. 25 OR. evacuated to CCS 2 OR. to Corps Scabies HP. 12. O.R. to duty. leaving 86. OR. remaining.	[signature]
"	5/4/18	noon. 9.0pm	The personnel of 77. Fd. Amb. left this morning & the huts occupied by them will now be equipped as an officers hospital with four beds. I attended a conference at the ADMS office this morning when various matters in connection with the recent fighting were discussed. I visited the ADS this afternoon to arrange various matters. a foot preparation room will be started there.	[signature]
"	~~[date struck out]~~		43. OR. were admitted during the day. 20. OR. evacuated to C.C.S 4. OR. to Corps Scabies HP. 7 OR. to duty. leaving 98. OR. remaining	
"	6/4/18	9.0pm	I visited the ADS in the afternoon to arrange reliefs of bearers up the line, orders received that the Div. is taking over the WYTSCHAETE sector in addition to the sector at present held, 58. Fd. Amb. will administer this sector and the M.D.S. at YORK STREET. this unit will not be affected. Brig. Gen. WILLAN G.O.C, 56. Inf. Bde, was admitted this afternoon suffering with Trench fever 30. OR. were admitted during the day. 6. OR. to CCS 20. OR. to DRS 1. OR. to Corps Scabies HP. 8. OR. to duty. leaving 83. OR. remaining.	[signature]
"	7/4/18	9.0pm	ADMS visited and thoroughly inspected the hospital this morning and expressed himself as very pleased with all he saw. Major Gen. G.D. JEFFREYS CMG (G.O.C. 19. Div.) visited the hosp. in the evening to see Brig. Gen. WILLAN (G.O.C. 56. Inf. Bde) who is a patient in the hospital. 38. OR. were admitted during the day. 12. OR. to CCS 19. OR. to D.R.S. 4. OR. to Corps Scabies HP. 5. OR. to duty. leaving 81 OR. remaining.	[signature]

D. D. & L., London, E.C.
(A8004) Wt. W1771/M2 31 750,000 3/17 Sch. 52 Forms/C2118/14

Army Form C. 2118.

Instructions regarding War Diaries and Intelligence Summaries are contained in F. S. Regs., Part II. and the Staff Manual respectively. Title pages will be prepared in manuscript.

WAR DIARY
or
~~INTELLIGENCE SUMMARY~~.

(Erase heading not required.)

Place	Date	Hour	Summary of Events and Information	Remarks and references to Appendices
RAVELSBERG	8/4/18	9.0 pm	ADMS visited the Hosp. early this morning to see Brig. Gen. WILLAN. Further stores were drawn from the DRCS today and the Officers wards can now be completely filled up for use. 32. OR. were admitted during the day. 11 OR. evacuated to CCS 4 OR. to DRS. 5. OR. to Corps Scabies HP. 2 OR to duty leaving 91. OR. remaining.	EPK.
"	9/4/18	9.0 pm	Orders received at 6.0 pm to pack all transport as per ADMS instructions for active ~~offensive~~ operations. All cases were evacuated from here during the night. I sent Capt. COCHRANE to get in touch with HQ. 56 Inf. Brigade as liaison officer. Capt. HUMPHREYS reported his departure from the ADS for temp. duty with 1/4 RSLI. 1. Off + 26. OR. were admitted up to noon. 1. Off + 15. OR evacuated to CCS. 13. OR. to DRS 1 OR. to Scabies HP. 3 OR. to duty. leaving 1. Off + 85. OR. remaining.	EPK
"	10/4/18	11.0 am	The enemy commenced an offensive against the Div. front this morning and orders for the withdrawal of the Div. were cancelled. ADMS visited me at 11.0 am and gave instructions for all bearers to be sent up to the ADS which will continue to clear R. Bde front as before. 59 Fd. Amb. have now opened a MDS at HAGEDOORNE and all cases will be evacuated there from the ADS this unit closing at noon today. I sent Capt. Cochrane to get in touch with 56 Bde. HQ again.	EPK
		noon	46. OR. were admitted up to noon. (also 2. Off.) 3. Off + 91. OR. evacuated to CCS. 13. OR. to DRS 3 OR to Corps Scabies HP. 20. OR. to duty 3 OR. trans. to 59 Fd. Amb. 1. OR. died leaving nil remaining.	
		5.0 pm	I visited OC. 59. Fd. Amb. this afternoon to arrange for relief of cars & Horsed Amb. waggons. All cars are now based on 59. Fd. Amb. & relief arranged from there. I sent 3. Horsed Amb. waggons up to ADS. to clear walking wounded & to remain under the orders of OC. ADS.	

(A8004) Wt. W1771/M2 31 750,000 5/17 Sch. 52 Forms/C2118/14 D. D. & L., London, E.C.

Instructions regarding War Diaries and Intelligence Summaries are contained in F. S. Regs., Part II. and the Staff Manual respectively. Title pages will be prepared in manuscript.

WAR DIARY
or
~~INTELLIGENCE SUMMARY.~~

(Erase heading not required.)

Army Form C. 2118.

Place	Date	Hour	Summary of Events and Information	Remarks and references to Appendices
RAVELSBERG.	10/4/18	5.0 pm (cont)	Capt. Cochrane returned from 56. Bde HQ and reported that 1/4 KSLI were established on Hill 63 with an R.A.P. at WHITE GATES (T.18.a.4.8 – Sheet 28) I sent Capt Jones with a car from here to get in touch with the RAP & then to proceed to A.D.S. for duty, as more assistance is required there.	
HAGEDORNE.	11	11.30 pm	Capt. Cochrane visited the A.D.S. again this evening and reported that all was quiet and no cases awaiting evacuation. ADMS visited us at 8.30 pm. and gave orders to move at once to the M.D.S. at HAGEDORNE. The unit moved off within an hour and arrived here at 10.30 pm. Billets being provided by O.C 59. Fd. Amb.	G.K.
11	11/4/18	9.0 Am	Capt. Cochrane visited 56. B.HQ. early this morning & reported situation quite satisfactory. Maj. Smalley came down at 3.0 Am & reported the A.D.S. clear. I proceeded to BERTHEN at 5.30 Am to find new site for M.D.S. Called at HQ Div on way back to report. I sent Capt. Cochrane & a small party to relieve Maj Smalley at the A.D.S. at 9.0 Am.	
		noon.	ADMS visited the M.D.S here.	
BERTHEN		5.0 pm	orders received at 4.0 pm to proceed forthwith to BERTHEN and prepare to open new M.D.S. as enemy reported attacking NEUVE EGLISE and WULVERGHEM from the South. marched off at 3.0 pm & arrived here at 6.0 pm. Requisitioned the school and fitted it up as a M.D.S. Notified ADMS.	G.K.
		10. pm	On completion of fitting up of M.D.S. I returned to HAGEDORNE and learned that the A.D.S. at KANDAHAR FARM had been evacuated this morning, the bearer Div. retiring on DRANOUTRE, with car posts along the NEUVE EGLISE road. I returned to BERTHEN at 9.30 pm with a load of dressings. 19. OR. of the bearer div. reported missing after the retirement yesterday. Believed prisoners.	

D. D. & L., London, E.C. (A8004) Wt. W1771/M2 31 750,000 5/17 Sch. 52 Forms/C2118/14

Instructions regarding War Diaries and Intelligence Summaries are contained in F. S. Regs., Part II. and the Staff Manual respectively. Title pages will be prepared in manuscript.

WAR DIARY
or
~~INTELLIGENCE SUMMARY.~~
(Erase heading not required.)

Army Form C. 2118.

Place	Date	Hour	Summary of Events and Information	Remarks and references to Appendices
BERTHEN	12/4/18	9.0 Am	ADMS visited us here at 9.0 Am & gave orders to open at 10.0. Surplus transport of 58. Fd Amb. reported here during the night.	
		10 Am	OC. MAC called to make arrangements about evacuating our cases.	
		noon	59. Fd. Amb. arrived here at 11.0 Am. having closed the MDS at HAEGEDOORNE. First cases began to arrive about noon.	
		5.0 pm	Maj. Smalley and the Bearer Div. arrived at 3.0 pm having been relieved in the line by 59. Fd Amb. Bearer Div. 58. Fd Amb Bearers still work left sector.	[illegible]
		11.0 pm	About 120 cases have been dealt with up to now, very few of these being from the 19 Div. area, most from Divisions in front of BAILLEUL. The 19 Div. is now in support to the 21st Div. and is holding a line along the VIERSTRAAT - N. EGLISE road	
"	13/4/18	9.0 Am	144. cases dealt with since 6.0 pm last night. Very few since midnight. ADMS visited us at 7.0 Am.	
		11.0 Am	A large number of cases were received this morning from 29 Div. Dressing Station in ST. JANS CAPELL which has had to close owing to hostile shell fire. Orders received that OC 58. Fd Amb. has taken charge of all evacuation from the line.	
		noon	138. cases dealt with since 6.0 Am. Only one of these was from 19 Div.	[illegible]
		4.0 pm	I visited OC. MAC at BOESCHEPE to try & get more cars as we have now nearly 50 lying cases awaiting evacuation. Got 5. cars to work till we are clear.	
		6.0 pm	71 cases dealt with since noon. Now only 13. lying cases remaining.	
		9.0 pm	All cases were cleared by 8.0 pm & the place well cleaned up. Orders received that 59. Fd Amb will open a new MDS at WESTOUTRE tomorrow, when we shall close & be in reserve.	

D. D. & L., London, E.C.
(A8004) Wt. W1771/M2 31 750,000 5/17 Sch. 52 Forms/C2118/14

Instructions regarding War Diaries and Intelligence Summaries are contained in F. S. Regs., Part II. and the Staff Manual respectively. Title pages will be prepared in manuscript.

WAR DIARY
or
~~INTELLIGENCE SUMMARY.~~
(Erase heading not required.)

Army Form C. 2118.

Place	Date	Hour	Summary of Events and Information	Remarks and references to Appendices
BERTHEN	14/4/18	6.0 am	263. cases dealt with since 6.0 pm last night. all cleared.	
		9.0 am	59. Fd Amb marched off at 7.30 to open in WESTOUTRE	
		noon	orders received to close at noon and proceed to the old site of 17. C.C.S at REMY SIDING. D.D.M.S. IX Corps called in for a few minutes. closed at noon, all cases being then clear 76. cases dealt with since 6.0 am. sent off all cars to 59. Fd Amb at WESTOUTRE also 3 officers + 25. OR. to assist them	G.K.
REMY SIDING		9.0 pm	marched off at 12.30 pm and arrived here at 2.0 pm. Plenty of accommodation in a deserted camp. I visited A.D.M.S. and O.C. 59 Fd Amb at A.D.S. WESTOUTRE in the afternoon. the unit was very busy during its short stay at BERTHEN, during the fifty hours we were open, dealing with 776. cases of wounded and at least 100 cases of sick.	
"	15/4/18.	noon	about 120 walking wounded were sent here during the night from the M.D.S. to be accommodated. these were marched off this morning to PROVEN under an NCO all the C.C.S's here having now closed. the morning was spent in collecting salvage + stores in this camp.	G.K.
		9.0 pm	20. Reinforcements (O.R.) arrived this evening - the men being of a good type. 4. Horsed Amb. Waggons reported here for duty. + are to be used for evacuating walking cases which may be sent down here by light Railway.	
"	16/4/18	noon.	A.D.M.S. visited us this morning and issued instructions that we were to receive all walking cases sent here by light Ry. from M.D.S. WESTOUTRE and evacuate them. I have now six horsed Amb. waggons for evacuating purposes, but they are hardly sufficient as the C.C.S's are some distance away.	G.K.
		9.0 pm	I visited the A.D.M.S. + O.C. M.A.C. in the evening to arrange methods of evacuation for walking cases from here.	

D. D. & L., London, E.C.
(A8004) Wt. W1771/M2 31 750,000 5/17 Sch. 52 Forms/C2118/14

Instructions regarding War Diaries and Intelligence Summaries are contained in F. S. Regs., Part II. and the Staff Manual respectively. Title pages will be prepared in manuscript.

WAR DIARY
or
~~INTELLIGENCE SUMMARY.~~
(Erase heading not required.)

Army Form C. 2118.

Place	Date	Hour	Summary of Events and Information	Remarks and references to Appendices
REMY SIDING	17/4/18	noon	All our remaining cases were cleared by MAC during the night. Under instructions from ADMS four squads of bearers were sent up last night to report to O.C. 58. Fd Amb.	
		5.0pm	ADMS visited us at 2.0pm and issued instructions for us to open up as M.D.S here as WESTOUTRE had been evacuated owing to hostile shell fire. Part of the 17 CCS site, occupied by us as billets was fitted up and we opened at once. Car post & ADS is now established on the RENINGHELST - HEKSEN road, ½ mile from R.	
		11.0pm	59. Fd Amb. reported here during the afternoon & are accommodated in the camp. ADMS visited us again at 7.30 pm & gave instructions for Horsed Amb. Waggons to be sent up to the relay post to convey sitting cases to here. This was done. Orders received that our Bearer Div. will relieve 58. Fd Amb. Bearer Div. in the line tomorrow. Capt Cochrane proceeded up the line this evening to relieve Maj Greig of 59. Fd Amb.	GKT.
"	18/4/18	6.0am	46. OR. were admitted from 6.pm last night. of which 9. were 19th Div. & 20. French troops. We have now two MAC cars & two busses attached for evacuation, which should suffice.	
		noon.	Instructions received from ADMS that relief of bearers will not take place today in view of the fact that the Div. is being relieved by the French tonight. 1 off & 45 OR. dealt with since 6-0 am. 1 off & 14. OR. from 19th Div. 3. French OR. We shall now administer a Corps Walking Wounded Station here and all RAMC personnel of the three Fd Ambces will return here to reorganise.	GKT.
		6.0pm.	43. OR. dealt with since noon. 19 of these being 19. Div. & 3. French Troops. Orders received that the Div. is being relieved in the line tonight and all medical personnel will return here as soon as the relief is complete.	
"	19/4/18	6.0am	3. off. & 79. OR. dealt with since 6.0pm last night. 2 off & 26. OR. from 19. Div. 21. OR. French troops. Order received from O.C. Bearers for Maj. Smalley & 8. Squads of bearers to proceed up the line. Left at 7.0 am.	
		noon	Instructions received that our bearers will remain up the line to clear French wounded for the present. 19. OR. dealt with since 6.0 am. 4. from 19. Div. 6. French troops.	GKT.
		6.0pm.	13. OR. dealt with since noon. 1. from 19. Div. 6. French troops.	

Army Form C. 2118.

Instructions regarding War Diaries and Intelligence Summaries are contained in F. S. Regs., Part II. and the Staff Manual respectively. Title pages will be prepared in manuscript.

WAR DIARY
or
~~INTELLIGENCE SUMMARY.~~

(Erase heading not required.)

Place	Date	Hour	Summary of Events and Information	Remarks and references to Appendices
REMY SIDING	20/4/18	9.0pm	1. Off + 24 OR. (W) and 17. OR sick admitted up to noon. 22 of these being trench foot. 1. Off + 27. OR. (W) and 9 OR sick evacuated to CCS. Leaving 8. OR remaining. orders received this evening that the Div. will move to the PROVEN area tomorrow, this unit will stand fast here & continue to take in for the present.	GHK.
"	21/4/18	9.0pm	58. & 59. Fd. Ambces moved to the new area this morning. All the personnel and cars of this unit returned from the line by midday on relief by the French. The remainder of the units transport joined up during the day & the whole unit is now here. Capt. R. M. JONES reported his departure for permanent medical charge of the 10 Worc. Reg. Capt. J. T. HUMPHREYS is also struck off the strength, being appointed M.O. 1/c K.D.L.I. Lieut. R DECK has rejoined the unit and is taken on the strength again. 4. Off + 35. OR (S) and 19. OR. (W) were admitted up to noon. 7. OR. (W) died. 4. Off + 43. OR. (S) and 12. OR. (W) Evacuated to CCS leaving nil remaining.	GHK.
"	22/4/18	9.0pm	ADMS visited us this morning and gave instructions for [illegible] to close. Later orders received that we shall remain [illegible] [illegible] the British artillery units left in [illegible] area. The [illegible] were occupied today in cleaning up the [illegible]	GHK.
"	23/4/18	9.0pm	Equipment and kit inspection were held this morning [illegible] Arrangements were made for evacuating cases from [illegible] and [illegible] in the line. One squad of bearers and [illegible] cars will be kept up the line for this purpose. ADMS notified of arrangements made. 1. OR (W) admitted and evacuated to CCS up to noon today.	GHK.
"	24/4/18	9.0pm	ADMS visited the unit during the morning. The men of the unit were bathed in POPERINGHE today and all blankets disinfected. The evacuation of the gunners is working well now. 4 OR. (W) admitted up to noon. 1 OR. died 1. OR to CCS 2. OR transferred to [illegible] Fd. Amb.	GHK.

D. D. & L., London, E.C. (A8004) Wt. W1771/M731 750,000 5/17 Sch. 52 Forms/C2118/14

Army Form C. 2118.

Instructions regarding War Diaries and Intelligence Summaries are contained in F. S. Regs., Part II. and the Staff Manual respectively. Title pages will be prepared in manuscript.

WAR DIARY
or
~~INTELLIGENCE SUMMARY~~.

(Erase heading not required.)

Place	Date	Hour	Summary of Events and Information	Remarks and references to Appendices
REMY SIDING	25/4/18	noon	There was considerable hostile bombing activity in the POPERINGHE area early this morning, one bomb fell very near this camp. The unit is being occupied in protecting all huts by revetments of earth or sandbags.	
		2.0pm	Orders received that all units of the Div be prepared to move at short notice, the enemy having attacked this morning and believed to have taken MONT KEMMEL.	
		8.0pm	I attended with my bearer officers a conference this afternoon. ADMS gave instructions for all surplus transport to be packed ready to move to join Div. train at short notice. This was done this evening, everything being packed except the M.D.S. equipment.	GJK
		11.0pm	Order received that 56. Bde was moving to OUDERDOM. Capt. COCHRANE went as liaison officer to 56. Bde. HQ.	
"	26/4/18	9.0am	Orders received from ADMS for us to continue running the M.D.S. here. OC 59. Fd Amb. being made responsible for administration of bearers in the forward area. Sent one large car to be at Capt COCHRANE'S disposal until A.D.S. is established. 57. Bde has now moved also to OUDERDOM and 58. Bde is in Div reserve near BUSSEBOOM.	
		5.0pm	I attended a conference at the ADMS office this afternoon. Orders received for us to close at once and take over the administration of the forward area, all cases to be sent now to Lock M.D.S. etc. Sick still to 58. Fd Amb at PROVEN. Major A.A. Smalley proceeded at 3.0pm with the A.D.S. party and nine squads of bearers to get in touch with the Brigades in the forward area.	GJK
		11.30pm	Major Smalley came down and reported that the situation was unchanged, the Div. being still in reserve. I notified ADMS of positions of all RAPs etc. All RMOs now have one squad & 2 runners attached. A.D.S. party is parked near BUSSEBOOM ready to open if necessary, two large cars are there and two Fords working forward to collect odd casualties & sick. 7. OR. Ad & evac. up to noon.	
"	27/4/18	noon.	I visited the A.D.S. in the morning and found the situation unchanged.	
		9.0pm	~~Maj Smalley came down this eve~~ Orders received that 57. Bde was coming back tonight to TUNNELLERS CAMP (PROVEN). 56 Bde remains in its present position, attached to the 49th Div. 58. Bde is to dig & if necessary hold a line from HALLEBAST to VLAMERTINGHE. Lt. Col. C.T. EDMUNDS RAMC having reported his arrival for duty, is taken on the strength & assumes command of the unit from this date.	GJK

D. D. & L., London, E.C.
(A8004) Wt. W1771/M2 31 750,000 5/17 Sch. 52 Forms/C2118/14

Army Form C. 2118.

Instructions regarding War Diaries and Intelligence Summaries are contained in F. S. Regs., Part II. and the Staff Manual respectively. Title pages will be prepared in manuscript.

WAR DIARY
or
~~INTELLIGENCE SUMMARY.~~

(Erase heading not required.)

Place	Date	Hour	Summary of Events and Information	Remarks and references to Appendices
Remy Siding	28/4/18	10 am	I visited the 58th [illegible] Bde with Maj. [illegible] [illegible] [illegible] [illegible] [illegible] cases from them. A.D.M.S. visited the A.D.S. at [illegible] [illegible] casualties at A.D.S. a large dug out [illegible] [illegible] [illegible] [illegible] of Remy Siding.	[illegible]
	29.4.18	8 am	On request of O.C. A.D.S. all available cars were sent up to A.D.S. [illegible] 2 H.A.M's were sent for walking wounded. [illegible] [illegible] to its [illegible] from [illegible] [illegible] [illegible] [illegible] [illegible]	[illegible]
	30.4.18	10. am	Received warning order for 58th Bde [illegible] [illegible] [illegible] [illegible]	
		2 pm	Visited [illegible] Camp & [illegible] Post with a view of [illegible] [illegible]	C. [illegible] [illegible] [illegible]

D. D. & L., London, E.C.
(A8004) Wt. W1771/M2 31 750,000 5/17 Sch. 52 Forms/C2118/14

May 1918.

140/2983.

No. 57 F. A.

174 30 Confidential

WAR DIARY

of 57 FIELD AMBULANCE · R·A·M·C·

From 1-5-18 to 31-5-18

VOLUME 35.

Army Form C. 2118.

35

Instructions regarding War Diaries and Intelligence Summaries are contained in F. S. Regs., Part II. and the Staff Manual respectively. Title pages will be prepared in manuscript.

WAR DIARY
or
~~INTELLIGENCE SUMMARY~~.
(Erase heading not required.)

Place	Date	Hour	Summary of Events and Information	Remarks and references to Appendices
Remy Siding	1-5-18	11 p.m.	Moved with personnel from Remy Siding to Waratah Camp & took over from 64th Fd Amb. All bearer posts taken over by Maj Bradley & posts relieved by 2 p.m.	[illegible]
Waratah Camp	2-5-18	10 a.m.	Visited Trinity Post, Belgian B. Arm. All stretcher cases evacuated by car to Waratah. All w. wounded by hand to Corps Walking Wounded Post at .	[illegible]
Waratah.	3-5-18	2 p.m.	Received orders that 39th Comp. Bde will be relieved by 57th Bde the former withdrawing to Brusse Farm area. Squads & runners allotted to 57 Bde & M.O.s explained the route of evacuation etc	
		3 p.m.	The 98th Bde is under orders of 19th Div. as Divisional reserve. Arranged medical matters with OC 99th F.A.	[illegible]
		5 p.m.	Received orders that 30th Comp Bde will relieve S. A. Bde on night of 5/6th & will be under G.O.C. 19th Div.	
		9 p.m.	Medical relief of 58th Bde by 77th Field Ambulance [illegible]	
Waratah	4-5-18	10 a.m.	Conference of F. A. commanders at A.D.M.S. Office.	
		12 p.m.	Maj. Wright [illegible] of 57th Field Ambulance [illegible] for 30th Composite Bde., [illegible]	
Waratah	5-5-18	3 p.m.	Received news that 30th Bde (comp) will not [illegible] but the 33rd & that the A.D.M.S. 33rd [illegible] necessary arrangements, consequently Maj. Wright's squads returned to 57 F.A. [illegible]	[illegible]
		4 p.m.	Visited 6th Divisional Field Ambulance at [illegible] [illegible] as regards evacuation of sick & walking wounded [illegible]	

D. D. & L., London, E.C.
(A8004) Wt. W1771/M2 31 750,000 5/17 Sch. 52 Forms/C2118/14

Army Form C. 2118.

Instructions regarding War Diaries and Intelligence Summaries are contained in F. S. Regs., Part II. and the Staff Manual respectively. Title pages will be prepared in manuscript.

WAR DIARY
or
~~INTELLIGENCE SUMMARY.~~
*(Erase heading not required.)

Place	Date	Hour	Summary of Events and Information	Remarks and references to Appendices
Waratah Camp	6/5/18.	11 am	Visited Trinity Post. Everything very quiet.	[illegible]
"	7/5/18	10 am	Visited Trinity Post with a view to [illegible] with Belgian [illegible] as an Car Post, & moving cars to H22 & P4. [illegible] who appeared; this was accordingly done at 4 p.m. [illegible] were made against Trinity Post being [illegible]. Matter reported to ADMS.	
"	8/5/18	3 am 6 am 9 am 11 am 12 am	Very heavy & intense bombardment started apparently [illegible] Six squads & 2 cars sent to reinforce Trinity Post 3 extra cars obtained from M.A.C. H.A.W.s [illegible] from [illegible] 124 cases evacuated up to 2 noon. In the afternoon everything very quiet again. 18 reinforcements for this unit arrived. No wounded [illegible]	[illegible]
"	9.5.18.		Very quiet & uneventful day. ADMS visited the camp.	[illegible]
"	10.5.18.	11 am 9 pm	Five squads proceeded to Trinity Post to relieve others. [illegible] Visited Trinity Post. 58th Brigade relieved 57th Brigade. [illegible] of [illegible] taken over by [illegible]. Capt [illegible] returned to 56th Bde.	[illegible]

D. D. & L., London, E.C.
(A8004) Wt. W1771/M2 31 750,000 5/17 Sch. 52 Forms/C2118/14

Army Form C. 2118.

WAR DIARY
or
~~INTELLIGENCE SUMMARY.~~
(Erase heading not required.)

Instructions regarding War Diaries and Intelligence Summaries are contained in F. S. Regs., Part II. and the Staff Manual respectively. Title pages will be prepared in manuscript.

Place	Date	Hour	Summary of Events and Information	Remarks and references to Appendices
Waratah Camp	11.5.18	10.30 am.	Conference of Field Ambulance C.O.s at A.D.M.S. office to discuss the coming move. 2 M.O.s of 59th Field Ambulance returned to them also all their bearers.	CA
"	12.5.18	10 a.m.	Visited Trinity Post & arranged with Maj Smalley details of relief. Saw Capt. Cochrane at 56th Bde HdQrs. also General [illegible] with reference to Capt Cochrane accompanying the [illegible] [illegible] [illegible]. Negative decision arrived at subject to A.D.M.S. approval.	CA
		6.30 p.m.	Vacated Waratah Camp at [illegible] for [illegible] of [illegible] taking [illegible] the following [illegible].	
		8 p.m.	All M.O.s returned to their [illegible].	
MENDINGHEM		[illegible] p.m.	Arrived at Mendinghem [illegible] Camp with 56 F.A.	
"	13.5.18	10 a.m.	[illegible] of 56th Bde collecting [illegible] [illegible] 58 F.A. No definite news of train journey received.	CA
"	14.5.18	10 a.m.	Orders for train journey received. Departure on 15.5.18	CA
"	15.5.18	10 a.m.	Train journey postponed for 16.5.18	CA
"	16.5.18	8 p.m.	Unit left Mendinghem Camp with all its transport to entrain at Proven [illegible] Stn. Successful entraining. [illegible] [illegible] but [illegible]	CA

P.T.O.

D. D. & L., London, E.C.
(A8004) Wt. W1771/M2 31 750,000 5/17 Sch. 52 Forms/C2118/14

Army Form C. 2118.

WAR DIARY

or

~~INTELLIGENCE SUMMARY.~~

(Erase heading not required.)

Instructions regarding War Diaries and Intelligence Summaries are contained in F. S. Regs., Part II. and the Staff Manual respectively. Title pages will be prepared in manuscript.

Place	Date	Hour	Summary of Events and Information	Remarks and references to Appendices
			in the immediate vicinity of Station. All M.O.'s left behind [illegible] of Maj. [illegible] at each entraining station [illegible]. Maj. [illegible] & all cars then to proceed to destination by road. Capt. Cochrane & [illegible] went ahead [illegible]	CP
	17.5.18	10 am	Train journey. [illegible] at all [illegible]	CP
	18.5.18	2 pm	Arrived at detraining station [illegible] detraining ¾ hour. [illegible] proceeded [illegible] march 8–9 kilometres. Very hot [illegible]. Arrived at Aulnay l'Aitre 5 pm [illegible] by Capt. [illegible]	CP
AULNAY L'AITRE	"	5pm	Billets [illegible] good.	
	19.5.18	11 am	Day spent in arranging accommodation [illegible] for [illegible]. All tents pitched in [illegible] field. [illegible] taken over also.	CP
	20.5.18	11 am	Visited by D.D.M.S. VIII Corps.	CP
	21.5.18	3 pm	Visited by A.D.M.S. All scabies of Div. to be [illegible]	CP

D. D. & L., London, E.C.
(A8004) Wt. W1771/M2 31 750,000 5/17 Sch. 82 Forms/C2118/14

Instructions regarding War Diaries and Intelligence Summaries are contained in F. S. Regs., Part II. and the Staff Manual respectively. Title pages will be prepared in manuscript.

WAR DIARY

or

~~INTELLIGENCE SUMMARY.~~

(Erase heading not required.)

Army Form C. 2118.

Place	Date	Hour	Summary of Events and Information	Remarks and references to Appendices
AULNAY L'AITRE	22.5.18	10 am	Scabies cases of Div now treated in Tents. Billet taken over by me as Hospital, accommodation for 50 cases. 5 cases of Scabies.	CW
"	23.5.18	11 a.m.	Nothing to report. Capt. Robertson RAMC att to H.Q. RF sick in quarters.	CW
"	24.5.18	10 am	Fourteen cases of Scabies. Ten cases of mild cases in Infirmary.	CW
	25.5.18	11 am	Capt Robertson evacuated to Chalons with P.U.O. Lieut. Deck M.O.R.C. U.S.A. is attached to H.Q. Thresh disinfector arrived	CW
	26.5.18	11 am	Capt. Cochrane appointed Fly officer to Division.	CW
	27.5.18	10.15 am	The Field Ambulance was inspected by A.D.M.S. 19th Div	CW
	"	11 p.m.	Received warning order that Transport may be required to make an early start, next morning	CW
	28.5.18	10 am	Transport complete left at 10 am to join Divisional Transport near Chalons. All cases evacuated to 62 CCS. All Scabies to duty. Maj. Smalley, Capt Humphreys + Lt Simpson + 110 O.R left at 10 p.m. Myself + Maj Heald +	CW

D. D. & L., London, E.C. (A8004) Wt. W1771/M2 31 750,000 5/17 Sch. 52 Forms/C2118/14

P.T.O.

Instructions regarding War Diaries and Intelligence Summaries are contained in F. S. Regs., Part II. and the Staff Manual respectively. Title pages will be prepared in manuscript.

WAR DIARY
or
~~INTELLIGENCE SUMMARY.~~

(Erase heading not required.)

Army Form C. 2118.

Place	Date	Hour	Summary of Events and Information	Remarks and references to Appendices
AULNAY L'AITRE	28.5.18		remainder of F.A. left one hour later, all in French [illegible]	[illegible]
CHAUMUZY	29.5.18	11 a.m.	arrived at Chaumuzy. Started an M.D.S. at Mill in conjunction with F.A. of 21st Div. Officers W. 10, S. Nil. O.R. W. 177, S. 27. French 2 officers W. &	[illegible]
	"		37 O.R. passed through in the day.	
"	30.5.18	10 a.m.	F.A. of 21st Div left on Division being relieved. Following cases passed through the M.D.S. British Officers S 1, W 31; O.R. S 19, W 336. French 2 officers wounded & 120 O.R. wounded & one P. of War wounded. The immediate vicinity of M.D.S. was somewhat heavily shelled in the afternoon. Prospected Nanteuil in the morning for another M.D.S. site & selected 2 Adrian Huts.	[illegible]
	31.5.18		Prospected for another M.D.S further back selected the school at Boursault. Maj. Kidd myself & party moved there in the evening. Lt Simpson & 20 O.R. left at Nanteuil to assist 5[illegible] F.A. & Maj. [illegible] attached to 59 F.A.	[illegible] Lt Col [illegible] F.A.

D. D. & L., London, E.C.
(A8004) Wt. W1771/M2 31 750,000 5/17 Sch. 52 Forms/C2118/14

27
June 1918.

140/3076.

War Diary

of 57th Field Ambulance R.A.M.C.

From 1-6-18 to 30-6-18

Volume 36.

Army Form C. 2118.

VIII 36

WAR DIARY
or
~~INTELLIGENCE SUMMARY.~~
(*Erase heading not required.*)

Instructions regarding War Diaries and Intelligence Summaries are contained in F. S. Regs., Part II. and the Staff Manual respectively. Title pages will be prepared in manuscript.

Place	Date	Hour	Summary of Events and Information	Remarks and references to Appendices
Boursault	1.6.18	10. am	School at Boursault prepared as an M.D.S. [illegible] 40 cases during the day. Transport [illegible]	[illegible]
"	2.6.18	10. am	Two officers + 22 O.R. sick + [illegible] [illegible] The officers were accommodated in [illegible] + the O.R. in [illegible]	[illegible]
"	3.6.18	10 am	Visited by A.D.M.S. At 4 pm received [illegible] M.D.S. [illegible] a spot selected near Dizy-Magenta. All [illegible] 7 p.m. Moved at 8.30 pm + arrived at [illegible]	[illegible]
Dizy-Magenta	4.6.18.	10 am	Accommodated in champagne factory. Good for [illegible] stretcher cases. Received orders to be ready [illegible] [illegible]	[illegible]
"	5.6.18	10 am	The place is now ready to receive [illegible] 50 cases in by night.	[illegible]
	6.6.18	10 am	Received orders to open as an M.D.S. [illegible] Transport lines [illegible] light duty [illegible] on 7.6.18 ~~[illegible]~~	[illegible]

D. D. & L., London, E.C.
(A8004) Wt. W1771/M2 31 750,000 5/17 Sch. 52 Forms/C2118/14

Instructions regarding War Diaries and Intelligence Summaries are contained in F. S. Regs., Part II. and the Staff Manual respectively. Title pages will be prepared in manuscript.

WAR DIARY
or
~~INTELLIGENCE SUMMARY~~.
(Erase heading not required.)

Army Form C. 2118.

Place	Date	Hour	Summary of Events and Information	Remarks and references to Appendices
Dise – Magenta	7.6.18	10 am	Now working as an M. D. S. Very few cases Evacuated by cars from Hautvillers under charge of French M.T. officer, working very well & no difficulty in evacuations. Officers doing duty Maj Kidd, Maj. Smalley, Lts Deck & Simpson. Capt Humphries with Brown & Lt Walker with Divisional details. Maj. Smalley received a bar to his M.C. All sick evacuated or otherwise disposed of by 2 p.m.	[illegible]
"	8.6.18	10 am	A very quiet day. Nothing to report.	[illegible]
"	9.6.18	10 am	Maj. Wright & his party of N.C.O.s & men left to form D.R.S. at other side of Epernay. Took Simm as Officers Mess.	[illegible]
"	10.6.18	10 am	Very quiet day. 38 sick were sent to 58 F.A.	[illegible]
"	11.6.18	10 am	Very quiet day. Recommendations for immediate awards sent to A.D.M.S. News of possible gas attack in early morning. All precautions taken. Did not materialise.	[illegible]
"	12.6.18	10 am	Very quiet day. Visited Marfaux in the morning. Very few wounded. Still keeping a few sick.	[illegible]
"	14.6.18 to 17.6.18		Very little doing.	[illegible]
"				[illegible]

D. D. & L., London, E.C.
(A8004) Wt. W1771/M2 31 750,000 5/17 Sch. 52 Forms/C2118/14

WAR DIARY

or

INTELLIGENCE SUMMARY.

(Erase heading not required.)

Army Form C. 2118.

Instructions regarding War Diaries and Intelligence Summaries are contained in F. S. Regs., Part II. and the Staff Manual respectively. Title pages will be prepared in manuscript.

Place	Date	Hour	Summary of Events and Information	Remarks and references to Appendices
Disi - Magenta	18.6.18	10 am	Moved entirely from [illegible] & Claudon [illegible] owing to the [illegible] wandering the site. Sick sent to D.R.S. & C.C.S. Buildings in the Farm near Disi turned into a M.D.S. [illegible] three. Transport moved to [illegible] 2b of F.A.	W
"	19.6.18	10 am	Transport over hauled & repainted preparatory for a move. Visited by A.D.M.S. in the afternoon. Visited the Station D.S.	W
"	20.6.18	6 am	Moved from Disi to Le Mesnil by brigade with transport. 10 miles. Pleasant march & good billets at Mesnil	W
Le Mesnil	21.6.18	6 am	Left Le Mesnil for Reuves by bus. Rather poor accommodation for men supplemented by 10 Bell Tents from Corps.	C.T.
Reuves.		7 pm	Transport of Maj. Reid arrived. Hospital for 50 patients established in barn. Visited by A.D.M.S.	C.T.R.
Reuves.	22.6.18	10 am	Few sick in Hospital. All bearers & M.T. given clean shirts. Repainting etc of transport started.	C.T.R.

(A8004) D. D. & L., London, E.C. Wt. W1771/M2031 750,000 3/17 Sch. 52 Forms/C2118/14

Instructions regarding War Diaries and Intelligence Summaries are contained in F. S. Regs., Part II. and the Staff Manual respectively. Title pages will be prepared in manuscript.

WAR DIARY
or
INTELLIGENCE SUMMARY.
(Erase heading not required.)

Army Form C. 2118.

Place	Date	Hour	Summary of Events and Information	Remarks and references to Appendices
Reuves	23. 6. 18.	10am	Visited & inspected by Gen Jeffreys in the morning.	CT
"	24.6 18	10am	An average of 21 sick in Hospital mostly P.U.O. all slight.	CT
"	25.6. 18	10am	Draft of 20 men to unit.	CT
"	26.6. 18	10am	F.G.C.M. on Cpl. Hudson. Verdict guilty & reduced to ranks. Capt. Deck evacuated to C.C.S.	CT
"	27.6. 18	10am	Pte Hudson transferred to 59 F.A.	CT
"	28.6. 18	10am	Transport inspected by Gen. Monkhouse, also by Corps Horse master in the afternoon. All tents returned to Corps. Capt Humphreys proceeded on leave. (14 days on host.)	C.T.
"	29.6 18	10am	All patients evacuated to C.C.S. or duty in view of move at a near date. Capt. Cockraine in one ambulance moved to new area as advanced & billeting party.	C.T.

D. D. & L., London, E.C.
(A8004) Wt. W1771/M2031 750,000 5/17 Sch. 52 Forms/C2118/14

Army Form C. 2118.

WAR DIARY
or
INTELLIGENCE SUMMARY.

(*Erase heading not required.*)

*Instructions regarding War Diaries and Intelligence Summaries are contained in F. S. Regs., Part II. and the Staff Manual respectively. Title pages will be prepared in manuscript.

Place	Date	Hour	Summary of Events and Information	Remarks and references to Appendices
Renves	30.6.18	8.20 am	Unit as a whole moved to Bouzy [illegible] by route march distance 5 kilos. Maj. Sunley & his cars proceeded midday to new area. Lt-Col [illegible] proceeded on leave to U.K.	[illegible]

D. D. & L., London, E.C. (A8004) Wt. W1771/M2 31 750,000 5/17 Sch. 52 Forms/C2118/14

9 July 1918.

Confidential

Vol 37

140/3131.

War Diary

of 57th Field Ambulance - R.A.M.C.

From 1-7-18 to 31-7-18

Volume 37

Instructions regarding War Diaries and Intelligence Summaries are contained in F. S. Regs., Part II. and the Staff Manual respectively. Title pages will be prepared in manuscript.

WAR DIARY
or
~~INTELLIGENCE~~ SUMMARY.

(Erase heading not required.)

Army Form C. 2118.

Place	Date	Hour	Summary of Events and Information	Remarks and references to Appendices
Brussy le Grand	1.7.16	10 a.m.	Unit at Brussy le Grand preparing to [illegible] area. Lt [illegible] acting as [illegible] officer.	
"	2.7.16	6.30 a.m.	Left Brussy le Grand by route march to [illegible] [illegible] by 10.30 a.m.	
"	3.7.16	3 pm	Arrived at Marquel [illegible]. [illegible], personnel arriving at 11 pm.	
Rumilly	4.7.16	10 a.m.	Transport arrived at 9 a.m. Accommodation for the personnel ready by 12 noon. Billets very good indeed	[illegible]
"	5/7/16	9.0 pm	A.D.M.S. visited the unit this afternoon and inspected the hospital etc. He expressed himself as satisfied with all he saw. Medical arrangements for present area (V. Army) received.	[illegible]
"	6/7/16	9.0 pm	Lt. Col. C.T. Edmunds reported his departure for temp. duty as A.D.M.S. Command being assumed temporarily by Major G. P. Kidd. Arrangements made for treating Scabies cases from the Div. here. Good progress is being made with painting of waggons, checking stores etc.	[illegible]

D. D. & L., London, E.C.
(A8004) Wt. W1771/M2 31 750,000 5/17 Sch. 52 Forms/C2118/14

Instructions regarding War Diaries and Intelligence Summaries are contained in F. S. Regs., Part II. and the Staff Manual respectively. Title pages will be prepared in manuscript.

WAR DIARY
or
~~INTELLIGENCE SUMMARY.~~
(Erase heading not required.)

Army Form C. 2118.

Place	Date	Hour	Summary of Events and Information	Remarks and references to Appendices
RUMILLY	7/6/18	9.0pm	A/ADMS visited the unit during the morning. Warning orders and administrative arrangements received from Div. & Bde with reference to possible moves in case of emergency to support the XI or XIII Corps.	[illegible]
"	8/6/18	9.0pm	Lt. A.G. DUNBAR MORC USA reported his arrival for duty and is taken on the strength today. Warning order received that the Bde Group will probably move to a new area on the 13th inst.	[illegible]
"	9/6/18	9.0pm	A/ADMS visited the unit in the morning to inspect "protective" M.D. men. Lt. H.S. DU CRET. MORC USA reported his arrival for duty and was taken on the strength.	[illegible]
"	10/6/18	9.0pm	Major A.A. SMALLEY reported his departure on ten days leave of absence in France. Under Bde arrangements a small party of men were conveyed by bus to Pecault for the purpose of bathing today. Orders received from Div. & Bde for the move on the 13th inst.	[illegible]
"	11/6/18	9.0pm	Lt. M.B. SIMPSON M.O.R.C. USA having been appointed MO to 19. DAC reported his departure today and is struck off the strength.	[illegible]
"	12/6/18	9.0pm	A/ADMS visited the unit today. I visited the new area to arrange billets etc. All patients were cleared during the day and the Hospital closed down. All stores etc. were packed before the evening. A good deal of rain fell.	[illegible]
AMETTES	13/6/18	9.0pm	Transport marched off at 4.30 A.M. & the remainder of the unit by bus at 10.0 AM. arriving here at 2.0 pm. A good barn in the village has been fitted up as a hospital and should provide sufficient accommodation as we can now send cases likely to be well within 10 days to XIII Corps Rest Station (No. 30. CCS) at ALLOUAGNE. Billets are fairly good here though there is some lack of straw in the barns – there is plenty of accommodation for all ranks.	[illegible]

D. D. & L., London, E.C.
(A8004) Wt. W1771/M2131 750,000 5/17 Sch. 52 Forms/C2118/14

Instructions regarding War Diaries and Intelligence Summaries are contained in F. S. Regs., Part II. and the Staff Manual respectively. Title pages will be prepared in manuscript.

WAR DIARY
or
~~INTELLIGENCE SUMMARY.~~
(Erase heading not required.)

Army Form C. 2118.

Place	Date	Hour	Summary of Events and Information	Remarks and references to Appendices
AMETTES	14/7/18	9.0 pm	The men were occupied all day in cleaning up billets and improving existing sanitary arrangements which were in a very bad condition. A report on the sanitary condition of the village was rendered to the A.D.M.S.	E.J.K.
"	15/7/18	9.0 pm	A/ADMS visited the unit today and inspected the hospital and all arrangements. Work – still being continued in cleaning up the billets etc. and a marked improvement has been effected.	E.J.K.
"	16/7/18	9.0 pm	A good deal of rain has fallen again during the past few days. Sick rate in the Brigade is still keeping very low, only 18 cases being in hospital today. ~~Capt. F.J. Humphrey RAMC reported his arrival back from 14 days leave in U.K.~~	E.J.K.
"	17/7/18	9.0 pm	A/ADMS visited the unit this morning. Lt. H.S. Du Cros [illegible] Lt. [illegible] MO i/c 19 DAC during the sickness of the [illegible] [illegible]	E.J.K.
"	18/7/18	9.0 pm	Lt. & QM T. Armitage reported his arrival back from 14 days leave in England. Provisional orders received for possible counter attack. The Div. might be required to [illegible] the area. Reconnaissance will be carried out in due course.	E.J.K.
"	19/7/18	9.0 pm	Weather remains fine and warm. The sick rate in the Brigade is still keeping very low, [illegible] and [illegible]	E.J.K.
"	20/7/18	9.0 pm	Together with [illegible] 19 [illegible] officers I visited and reconnoitred the [illegible] [illegible] the 4th Div. front today with a view to [illegible] sites for RAP [illegible] Maj. A.A. [illegible] reported his arrival back from 13 days leave [illegible] in France.	E.J.K.
"	21/7/18	9.0 pm	57 Bde. moved yesterday from the AUCHEL area to the ST. HILAIRE area yesterday. We now collect sick from 19. Div. units still in the AUCHEL – FERFAY areas. Lt. Col. C.T. Edmunds RAMC reported his arrival back from temporary duty as ADMS 19. Div. & reassumed command of the unit.	E.J.K.

A7092). Wt. W12839/M1297 750,000. 1/17. D. D & L., Ltd. Forms/C2118/14.

Army Form C. 2118.

Instructions regarding War Diaries and Intelligence Summaries are contained in F. S. Regs., Part II. and the Staff Manual respectively. Title pages will be prepared in manuscript.

WAR DIARY
or
~~INTELLIGENCE SUMMARY.~~

(Erase heading not required.)

Place	Date	Hour	Summary of Events and Information	Remarks and references to Appendices
AMETTES	22/7/18.	9.0pm	Dental Surgeon attended at the Hospital this morning. ADMS. visited the unit & inspected the hospital in the evening.	C.P.K.
"	23/7/18	[illegible] 9.0pm	Lt Col. C.T. Edmunds reported his departure on 14 days leave to England this morning. Temporary command was again assumed by Major C.P. Kidd RAMC. Lt. [illegible] MORC USA reported his arrival back for duty from temp duty with DAC	C.P.K.
"	24/7/18	9.0pm	Weather remains warm with some rain. Sick rate still very low.	C.P.K.
"	25/7/18	9.0pm	Inspection held by Div. Gas Officer of Gas Drill & appliances.	C.P.K.
"	26/7/18.	9.0pm	I attended a conference at the ADMS' office this morning to discuss points in connection with schemes of possible operations. Heavy rain fell again this evening.	C.P.K.
"	27/7/18	9.0pm	An inter Field Amb. Transport Competition was held today. This was won by 59 F.A. [illegible] this unit being second, one mark behind. Amended medical arrangements received today.	C.P.K.
"	28/7/18	9.0pm	Sick rate still keeping very low, only 10 cases in hospital today.	C.P.K.
"	29/7/18	9.0pm	ADMS visited the unit and inspected the hospital and all arrangements this afternoon. The DMS. Fifth Army will visit the unit on the 1st inst.	C.P.K.
	30/7/18	9.0pm	57. Bde. moved back to the AUCHEL area today. Med. arrangements amended accordingly.	C.P.K.
"	31/7/18	9.0pm	Lieut. STOLL MORC USA reported his arrival for duty and is taken on the strength from today.	C.P.K.

C.P. Kidd
Major RAMC
Commanding 57. Fd. Amb.

A7092). Wt. W12839/M1297 750,000. 1/17. D. D & L., Ltd. Forms/C2118/14.

16

Aug 1918.

VR 38

14/3200.

War Diary

of 57th Field Ambulance. R.A.M.C.

From 1-8-18 to 31-8-18

Volume. 38

Instructions regarding War Diaries and Intelligence Summaries are contained in F. S. Regs., Part II. and the Staff Manual respectively. Title pages will be prepared in manuscript.

WAR DIARY
or
~~INTELLIGENCE SUMMARY.~~
(Erase heading not required.)

Army Form C. 2118.

Place	Date	Hour	Summary of Events and Information	Remarks and references to Appendices
AMETTES	1/8/18	9.0pm	D.D.V.S. Fifth Army visited & inspected the Transport of the unit this morning. Owing to the C.R.S. being closed for the last two days, accommodation has been rather strained.	E.H.
"	2/8/18	9.0pm	I visited the A.D.M.S. in the morning to settle points regarding disposal of cases from the R.G.A. who have an epidemic of Influenza in the battalions at present.	E.H.
"	3/8/18	9.0pm	Divisional Horse Show & Sports were held today. I saw A.D.M.S. in the afternoon in reference to various points about the D.D.V.S. inspection on the 1st inst. Sick rate is still keeping low, although the R.G.A. still have a good many Influenza cases.	E.H.
"	4/8/18	9.0pm	Warning Order received that the Div is moving into the line on the nights 5/6 & 6/7 to relieve the 3rd Div. I visited the A.D.M.S. in the evening to obtain details as to the forthcoming move.	E.H.
"	5/8/18	9.0pm	I visited the forward area with Major Smalley today. Saw the proposed M.D.S. at LABEUVRIERE – the A.D.S. at ANNEZIN – the forward relay posts and R.A.P.s. I saw O.C. No. 8 & No. 142 Fd Amb. and made arrangements for taking over	
"	6/8/18	12 noon 9.0pm	A.D.S. party, bearers and adv. party for M.D.S. marched off at 10.0 A.M. I proceeded to LABEUVRIERE again at midday. I found that the place was being shelled and one hut was destroyed. I returned to [illegible] & reported this to A.D.M.S. Orders were then changed and we shall now take over the camp from 142 Fd Amb in the BOIS des DAMES. 9 [illegible] will run the M.D.S. in the [illegible]	E.H.
BOIS des DAMES	7/8/18	9.0pm midnight	The unit marched off at 10.0 A.M. & arrived here about 3.0 pm. The men are accommodated in tents & bivouacs & should be fairly comfortable. A.D.M.S. visited us about noon. I went up to the A.D.S. in the morning and found that everything had been taken over satisfactorily there. Information received from [illegible] that the line was being advanced owing to Enemy retirement. I proceeded to the A.D.S. & found that the R.A.P. had already been moved forward [illegible] [illegible] and [illegible] established a new post on the N. bank of the canal. Lt. Col. C.T. Edmunds reported his arrival back from leave and resumed command.	E.H.

A7092). Wt. W12839/M1297 750,000. 1/17. D. D. & L., Ltd. Forms/C2118/14.

Army Form C. 2118.

WAR DIARY
or
INTELLIGENCE SUMMARY.
(Erase heading not required.)

Instructions regarding War Diaries and Intelligence Summaries are contained in F. S. Regs., Part II. and the Staff Manual respectively. Title pages will be prepared in manuscript.

Place	Date	Hour	Summary of Events and Information	Remarks and references to Appendices
BOIS [illegible] JAMES	[illegible]	10 am	Visited the A.D.S. at [illegible] [illegible] post [illegible]. [illegible] [illegible] up. [illegible] [illegible] [illegible] R.E.'s with a view to its being used [illegible]. At 7 p.m. took over the M.D.S. at [illegible] [illegible] Fd. Ambulance, sick to be [illegible] [illegible]. No hostile shelling or bombing in the vicinity.	
Bois [illegible] Dames	9/8/18	10 am	A quiet night. No hostile shelling or bombing. At present Maj. [illegible] is at [illegible] [illegible] & Lt. Stott at [illegible]. [illegible] at the front have changed very little	[illegible]
"	10.8.18	10 am	Nothing to report	[illegible]
"	12.8.18	10 am	Lt. [illegible] left to take charge of D.A.C. vice Lt. [illegible] [illegible] who returned to this unit for duty	[illegible]
"	13.8.18	10 am	No appreciable change in the line. All bearers in the line relieved	[illegible]
"	14.8.18	10 am	Maj. [illegible] relieved Maj. [illegible] at A.D.S.	[illegible]

A7092). Wt. W12839/M1297 750,000. 1/17. D. D & L., Ltd. Forms/C2118/14.

Instructions regarding War Diaries and Intelligence Summaries are contained in F. S. Regs., Part II. and the Staff Manual respectively. Title pages will be prepared in manuscript.

WAR DIARY
or
INTELLIGENCE SUMMARY.
(*Erase heading not required.*)

Army Form C. 2118.

Place	Date	Hour	Summary of Events and Information	Remarks and references to Appendices
Bois des Dames	16.8.18	10am	Nothing to report. Lt Simpson left unit to take temp charge of K.S.L.I.	CP
"	17.8.18	10am	The Consulting Surgeon & Physician visited the M.D.S with the A.D.M.S. New Bridge completed over canal at Long Croix Lt Dunbar returned to F.A.	CP
"	18.8.18	10am	The D.D. of M.S. visited the M.D.S.	CP
"	19.8.18	10am	Visited the A.D.S.	CP
"	20.8.18	10am	Nothing to report	CP
"	21.8.18	10am	All the cases of diarrhoea were transferred to 5? F.A. Col. Frankau gave lecture at M.D.S on the subject of shock with particular reference to recent investigation. D.D.M.S present.	CP
"	22.8.18	10am	Visited Gunnersmill, Burbure Farm & Long Croix & investigated roads leading from the former to the latter places. Car post (adv) moved to Loon.	CP
"	27.8.18	10am	Quiet day nothing to report	CP

A7092). Wt. W12839/M1294 750,000. 1/17. D. D & L., Ltd. Forms/C2118/14.

Instructions regarding War Diaries and Intelligence Summaries are contained in F. S. Regs., Part II. and the Staff Manual respectively. Title pages will be prepared in manuscript.

WAR DIARY
or
INTELLIGENCE SUMMARY.
(Erase heading not required.)

Army Form C. 2118.

Place	Date	Hour	Summary of Events and Information	Remarks and references to Appendices
Bois de Dames	26.8.18	10am	Lecture on "Gas" from a medical point of view by Col. [illegible] of 5th Army	CW
Pont de Revelon	27.8.18	10am	Unit moved to Pont de Revelon, our [illegible] [illegible] in [illegible] Div. [illegible] centre & gas centre. Capt. Harvey joined the F.A. as a [illegible].	CW
"	29.8.18	10am	Went to Loos with Maj Pendred, D.A.D.M.S. & found a site for an A.D.S.	CW
"	30.8.18	10am	Very quiet day. New A.D.S. at Loos being prepared.	CW
"	31.8.18	10am	A.D.S. moved to Loos, [illegible] used as a reserve. [illegible] at A.D.M.S. office	CW

C Ramsay [illegible]
Lt Col RAMC

A7092). Wt. W12839/M1291 750,000. 1/17. D. D & L., Ltd. Forms/C2118/14.

Sept. 1918

VR 39

14d/32.5-9

War Diary

of 57 Field Ambulance. R.A.M.C.

From 1-9-18 to 30-9-18

Volume 39.

Instructions regarding War Diaries and Intelligence Summaries are contained in F. S. Regs., Part II. and the Staff Manual respectively. Title pages will be prepared in manuscript.

WAR DIARY
or
INTELLIGENCE SUMMARY.
(Erase heading not required.)

Army Form C. 2118.

Place	Date	Hour	Summary of Events and Information	Remarks and references to Appendices
Pont de Riviere	1.9.18	10am	Visited Locre. Went round the line with Maj. Bright of 1st FA preparatory to taking over the line	CP
"	2.9.18	10am	58th F.A took over the evacuation of line. Capt Cochrane & 4 squads lent to 58th F.A	CP
"	4.9.18	10am	Capt. Harvey went up to relieve Capt Cochrane.	CP
Annezin.	5.9.18	10am	M.D.S. moved to Annezin. 59th F.A. took over Pont de Riviere also diarrhoea centre. Gas centre moved to Annezin.	CP
"	6.9.18	10am	A.D.M.S. visited the M.D.S.	CP
"	7.9.18	10am	General Jeffreys visited the M.D.S. Col. Miller consulting physician to 5th Army visited the M.D.S.	CP
			Capt Harvey & bearers of 59th F.A returned from A.D.S. Capt Dunbar returned to unit from 59 F.A	
"	9.9.18	10am	Very quiet.	CP

A7092). Wt. W12839/M1291 750,000. 1/17. D. D & L., Ltd. Forms/C2118/14.

Army Form C. 2118.

Instructions regarding War Diaries and Intelligence Summaries are contained in F. S. Regs., Part II. and the Staff Manual respectively. Title pages will be prepared in manuscript.

WAR DIARY
or
INTELLIGENCE SUMMARY.
(Erase heading not required.)

Place	Date	Hour	Summary of Events and Information	Remarks and references to Appendices
Annezin	10.9.18		Visited 113 Siege Battery to investigate some gassed cases	CW
"	11.9.18		Very quiet. Nothing to report.	CW
"	13.9.18		Visited Brewery at Bethune with the idea of it being transformed into an M.D.S.	CW
"	14.9.18		Holding party sent to Brewery at Bethune	CW
"	15.9.18		Capt. Harvey went to 5-8 F.A. for temporary duty	CW
"	16.9.18		N.C.O + 15 men sent to Bethune brewery to clean & make ready for an M.D.S	CW

A7092). Wt. W12839/M1297 750,000. 1/17. D. D & L., Ltd. Forms/C2118/14.

Instructions regarding War Diaries and Intelligence Summaries are contained in F. S. Regs., Part II. and the Staff Manual respectively. Title pages will be prepared in manuscript.

WAR DIARY
or
INTELLIGENCE SUMMARY.
(Erase heading not required.)

Army Form C. 2118.

Place	Date	Hour	Summary of Events and Information	Remarks and references to Appendices
Annezin [illegible]	17.9.18.	10am	Very quiet. Nothing to report.	[illegible]
Annezin [illegible]	18.9.18.	10am	D.D.M.S. visited the M.D.S. also Col. [illegible] the consulting Surgeon of the 5th Army.	[illegible]
Annezin [illegible]	19.9.18.	10am	Very quiet day. Visited Brewery at Bethune, & [illegible] & Military Hosp. where there are still holding parties.	[illegible]
Annezin	20.9.18	10am	Nothing to report.	[illegible]
Annezin	21.9.18	10am	Two squads sent to 58 F.A. Holding party returned from [illegible]. All equipment there handed over to 57th Div.	[illegible]
Annezin	23.9.18	10am	Started preparing Annezin for an advanced operating centre, coming from 54 C.C.S. consisting of 1 Surgeon, 1 anaesthetist & one X ray officer 3 theatre orderlies & 2 ward orderlies. 4 Sisters	[illegible]
Annezin	24.9.18.	10am	D.M.S. visited the M.D.S. work for operating centre proceeding.	[illegible]

A7092). Wt. W12839/M1293 750,000. 1/17. D. D. & L., Ltd. Forms/C2118/14.

Instructions regarding War Diaries and Intelligence Summaries are contained in F. S. Regs., Part II. and the Staff Manual respectively. Title pages will be prepared in manuscript.

WAR DIARY
or
INTELLIGENCE SUMMARY.
(Erase heading not required.)

Army Form C. 2118.

Place	Date	Hour	Summary of Events and Information	Remarks and references to Appendices
Annezin	25.9.18	10am	Advanced operating centre arrived, & took over old main dressing room as a theatre & the two lower wards for the patients. The main dressing room was used with the "Marie" & a new house taken over for walking wounded.	CM
Annezin	26.9.18	10am	Maj General Sir D. Bruce visited the Field Ambulance with Col Cummins.	CM
Annezin	27.9.18	10am	The D.M.S. 1st Army visited the Field Ambulance & also D.D.M.S. XI Corps. The advisability of relieving Field Ambulance going to Brewery at Bethune discussed.	CM
Annezin	28.9.18	10am	Advanced operating centre performed six major operations.	CM
Annezin	29.9.18	10am	Quiet.	CM

A7092). Wt. W12839/M1297 750,000. 1/17. D. D & L., Ltd. Forms/C2118/14.

Army Form C. 2118.

Instructions regarding War Diaries and Intelligence Summaries are contained in F. S. Regs., Part II. and the Staff Manual respectively. Title pages will be prepared in manuscript.

WAR DIARY
or
INTELLIGENCE SUMMARY.
(Erase heading not required.)

Place	Date	Hour	Summary of Events and Information	Remarks and references to Appendices
Annezin	30.9.18	10am	O.C. relieving Field Ambulance came to Annezin, in view of his taking over the Annezin site & also the Brewery at Bethune	
			[illegible] Lt Col RAMC O.C. 57 F.A.	

A7092). Wt. W12839/M1297 750,000. 1/17. D. D & L., Ltd. Forms/C2118/14.

Oct 1918

19 War Diary. 48 40

of 57 Field Ambulance. 140/3327

From 1-10-18 to 31-10-18

Volume 40

Instructions regarding War Diaries and Intelligence Summaries are contained in F. S. Regs., Part II. and the Staff Manual respectively. Title pages will be prepared in manuscript.

WAR DIARY
or
INTELLIGENCE SUMMARY.

(Erase heading not required.)

Army Form C. 2118.

Place	Date	Hour	Summary of Events and Information	Remarks and references to Appendices
Annezin	1.10.18	10am	More busy than usual. About 70 wounded through chiefly K.S.L.I.	[illegible]
Annezin	2.10.18	10am	The Main dressing station at Annezin & the Bureau at Bethune were handed over to Field Ambulance of 74th Div & the 57th Field Amb. with transport moved to new billeting area at Auchel by march route. Capt Cochrane & party joined H.Q. 9th in the evening from Allouagne.	[illegible]
Annezin	3.10.18	10am	At Auchel. Field Ambulance resting. Conference of Field Ambulance Commanders at A.D.M.S. office.	[illegible]
Auchel	4.10.18	10am	Left Auchel. Join Column [illegible] to Sailly [illegible] 5.0 [illegible] Billets at Sailly.	[illegible]
Sailly	5.10.18		At Sailly.	[illegible]

A7092). Wt. W12839/M1293 750,000. 1/17. D. D & L., Ltd. Forms/C2118/14.

Army Form C. 2118.

WAR DIARY
or
INTELLIGENCE SUMMARY.
(Erase heading not required.)

Instructions regarding War Diaries and Intelligence Summaries are contained in F. S. Regs., Part II. and the Staff Manual respectively. Title pages will be prepared in manuscript.

Place	Date	Hour	Summary of Events and Information	Remarks and references to Appendices
Saulty	6.10.18		Dismissed at Saulty closed & awaiting orders to move.	CM
"	7.10.18		Unit moved in busses from Saulty to a spot near the Cambrai - Bapaume Rd between Bourlon wood, arriving about 2 pm.	CM
Bapaume-Cambrai Rd	8.10.18		Visited the A D S at Rumilly of 24th Div.	CM
do	9.10.18		Unit moved to Rumilly at 1.30 pm & formed billets in the village.	CM
Rumilly	10.10.18		Unit closed at Rumilly, collecting sick of affiliated Bde	CM
Rumilly	12.10.18		Unit moved to Rieux on Cambrai - Solesmes road late in afternoon & billeted in factory.	CM

A7092). Wt. W12839/M1297 750,000. 1/17. D. D & L., Ltd. Forms/C2118/14.

Instructions regarding War Diaries and Intelligence Summaries are contained in F. S. Regs., Part II. and the Staff Manual respectively. Title pages will be prepared in manuscript.

WAR DIARY
or
INTELLIGENCE SUMMARY.

(Erase heading not required.)

Army Form C. 2118.

Place	Date	Hour	Summary of Events and Information	Remarks and references to Appendices
Cauroir	13.10.18		Moved to Cauroir in the morning & billeted in the village. Sent party back to [illegible] (24 [illegible]). Visited A.D.S. of 24th Div. at Avesnes. [illegible] collecting [illegible] of Brigade.	
"	14, 15 & 16.10.18		At Cagnoncles. Collecting [illegible] and [illegible] Cambrai.	
Avesnes	7.10.18		Took over [illegible] at Avesnes as an A.D.S. for 24th Div. [illegible] Corps at St Aubert.	
"	18.10.18		Visited the R.A.P. [illegible] of 59th F.A. [illegible]	
"	19.10.18		All quiet.	
"	20.10.18		Attack at 02.00 hrs. 2 sectors [illegible] & left. Cars were [illegible] upon the left sector to begin with the [illegible] carry of R.A.P.s, also on right. Evacuation proceeded very [illegible] [illegible] fully. [illegible]	

A7092). Wt. W12839/M1297 750,000. 1/17. D. D & L., Ltd. Forms/C2118/14.

Instructions regarding War Diaries and Intelligence Summaries are contained in F. S. Regs., Part II. and the Staff Manual respectively. Title pages will be prepared in manuscript.

WAR DIARY
or
INTELLIGENCE SUMMARY.
(Erase heading not required.)

Army Form C. 2118.

Place	Date	Hour	Summary of Events and Information	Remarks and references to Appendices
Avesnes	20.10.18		being dealt with by A.D.S. at St Aubert the evacuating at Avesnes, all cases being evacuated straight to M.D.S. at Cambrai. Explored & found a new site for A.D.S. at Haussy.	CM
"	21.10.18		Went to Haussy in the morning, 5/8 F.A. starting an A.D.S. there at 00.01 hrs. Avesnes evacuated & handed over to F.A. of 61 Div. The new A.D.S. at Haussy clears the right sector & the A.D.S. at St Aubert the left sector. Evacuation rendered very difficult by bad state of roads & traffic.	CM
"	22.10.18		Hd. Qrs of Field Ambulance moved to St Aubert. A.D.S. still at Haussy.	CM
"	23.10.18		Handed over evacuation of line to F.A. of 61st Div at 16.00. Three motor ambulances & a small party left to assist as Division is not relieved until 04.00.	CM

A7092). Wt. W12839/M1293 750,000. 1/17. D. D & L., Ltd. Forms/C2118/14.

Instructions regarding War Diaries and Intelligence Summaries are contained in F. S. Regs., Part II. and the Staff Manual respectively. Title pages will be prepared in manuscript.

WAR DIARY
or
INTELLIGENCE SUMMARY.
(Erase heading not required.)

Army Form C. 2118.

Place	Date	Hour	Summary of Events and Information	Remarks and references to Appendices
Avesnes.	24.10.18		Hd. qrs now at Avesnes. 19th Div. out of the line. Collecting sick of 56th Bde. Kit inspection of whole Field Ambulance.	CR
"	25.10.18		At Avesnes.	CR
"	26.10.18		Field Ambulance & transport moved to Cagnoncles by march route & were billeted in that village.	CR
"	27.10.18		Small detention hospital prepared for 25–30 light cases. All parties engaged in cleaning billets, streets & yards.	CR
	28.10.18		Influenza very prevalent amongst the Horse transport personnel of Field Ambulance. Few cases also in 56th Bde in village.	CR

A7092). Wt. W12839/M1293 750,000. 1/17. D. D & L., Ltd. Forms/C2118/14.

Army Form C. 2118.

Instructions regarding War Diaries and Intelligence Summaries are contained in F. S. Regs., Part II. and the Staff Manual respectively. Title pages will be prepared in manuscript.

WAR DIARY
or
INTELLIGENCE SUMMARY.

(Erase heading not required.)

Place	Date	Hour	Summary of Events and Information	Remarks and references to Appendices
Cagnoncles 29.10.18			Influenza still prevalent amongst all ranks. No serious cases.	[illegible]
Cagnoncles	30.10.18		At Cagnoncles.	[illegible]
"	31.10.18		Influenza still prevalent, but not increasing. About 30 cases daily in the Brigade.	[illegible] Lt Col RAMC OC 57 FA

A7092). Wt. W12839/M1292 750,000. 1/17. D. D & L., Ltd. Forms/C2118/14.

19

Nov 1918

Confidential

WO 95/41

140/34 01

War Diary

of 57th Field Ambulance. R.A.M.C.

From 1-11-18 to 30-11-18

Volume 41.

Army Form C. 2118.

Instructions regarding War Diaries and Intelligence Summaries are contained in F. S. Regs., Part II. and the Staff Manual respectively. Title pages will be prepared in manuscript.

WAR DIARY
or
INTELLIGENCE SUMMARY.
(Erase heading not required.)

Place	Date	Hour	Summary of Events and Information	Remarks and references to Appendices
Cagnoncles.	1.11.18		At Cagnoncles. Twelve cases of influenza evacuated.	CM
Vendegies	2.11.18		F. Amb. moved to Vendegies & bivouacked in the fields.	CM
"	3.11.18		Division went into the line. A.D.S. was established at Artres Chateau, & cases evacuated to Avesnes.	CM
Preseau.	4.11.18		During the day the A.D.S. moved to Preseau & later to Pont [illegible] cases being brought from R.A.P.s in Jenlain by bearers & Ford cars. Great difficulty was experienced in evacuation owing to the inability of getting Fords into Jenlain village due to craters & various other obstructions. Cases now being sent to La Chaussée Farm. All the roads between Jenlain & Vendegies were very bad, congested with traffic & frequently blocked for an hour or more with "ditched" lorries.	CM
Jenlain	5.11.18		A.D.S. moved to house in Jenlain. Evacuation from forward areas now easier as roads improved, but evacuation to back M.D.S. still very long, cars frequently taking six hours to do the whole journey.	CM
Bry.	6.11.18		A.D.S. moved to Bry. Car post at [illegible] & St Waast.	CM

A7092). Wt. W12839/M1297 750,000. 1/17. D. D & L., Ltd. Forms/C2118/14.

Army Form C. 2118.

Instructions regarding War Diaries and Intelligence Summaries are contained in F. S. Regs., Part II. and the Staff Manual respectively. Title pages will be prepared in manuscript.

WAR DIARY
or
INTELLIGENCE SUMMARY.
(Erase heading not required.)

Place	Date	Hour	Summary of Events and Information	Remarks and references to Appendices
Bry	7.11.18		A. D. S. still at Bry with car post at St Vaast & La [Petite Rompe?] owing to roads & weather. [illegible] were [extensively?] used & proved very useful.	[CW?]
St Vaast	8.11.18		A. D. S. moved to centre of St Vaast village. Car post [illegible]. This move took place at 00.01 on 8.11.18.	[CW?]
Taisnières	9.11.18		A. D. S. moved to Taisnières opening at ~~[illegible]~~ 16.00 hrs. R.A.P.s in the village. Not possible to get cars in village owing to bridges blown up.	[CW?]
"	10.11.18		At Taisnières. Very quiet day. Very few casualties. H.Q. [illegible] of Field Ambulance arrived.	[CW?]
"	11.11.18		At Taisnières. No casualties after 06.00 hrs. Armistice signed during day.	[CW?]
"	12.11.18		Fd. Amb. moved to [Feignies?] & [rested?] from old billets.	[CW?]

A7092). Wt. W12839/M1293 750,000. 1/17. D. D & L., Ltd. Forms/C2118/14.

Army Form C. 2118.

Instructions regarding War Diaries and Intelligence Summaries are contained in F. S. Regs., Part II. and the Staff Manual respectively. Title pages will be prepared in manuscript.

WAR DIARY
or
INTELLIGENCE SUMMARY.
(Erase heading not required.)

Place	Date	Hour	Summary of Events and Information	Remarks and references to Appendices
Wargnies le Petit	13.11.18		Fd. Amb. to Wargnies le Petit & billeted in the village.	CW
"	14.11.18		Small detention hosp. opened for [illegible] cases.	CW
"	15.11.18		Collecting local sick & evacuating to Wargnies le Grand.	CW
"	16.11.18		Nothing to report.	CW
Rieux	17.11.18		Field Ambulance to Rieux by road route & billeted in village with 58th Bde.	CW
"	18.11.18		Nothing to report. Collecting & evacuating local sick of 58th Bde.	CW
"	19.11.18		Nothing to report.	CW

A7092. Wt. W12839/M1297 750,000. 1/17. D. D & L., Ltd. Forms/C2118/14.

Instructions regarding War Diaries and Intelligence Summaries are contained in F. S. Regs., Part II. and the Staff Manual respectively. Title pages will be prepared in manuscript.

WAR DIARY
or
INTELLIGENCE SUMMARY.
(Erase heading not required.)

Army Form C. 2118.

Place	Date	Hour	Summary of Events and Information	Remarks and references to Appendices
Rieux	21.11.18		Maj. Smalley + Lt Dunbar + 12 O.R. proceeded to Maubeuge to report to French Commandant to help with returning prisoners.	[illegible]
"	22.11.18.		Received orders that this F.A. would remain in this area after the division had moved.	[illegible]
"	23.11.18		Received orders from XVII Corps to send one section to Rendegies, one section to Cambrai + one to Avesnes. Capt Owens with C sect to Rendegies, + Maj Brown to Cambrai. A. section at Rieux with OC + Capt Ferguson pending departure of 60th Field Ambulance from Avesnes.	[illegible]
"	24.11.18		Visited Avesnes + ascertained that 60th F.A. do not anticipate moving for three days. Quartermaster visited Maubeuge, to settle the rationing of party there	[illegible]

A7092. Wt. W12839/M1297 750,000. 1/17. D. D & L., Ltd. Forms/C2118/14.

Army Form C. 2118.

WAR DIARY
or
INTELLIGENCE SUMMARY.
(*Erase heading not required.*)

Instructions regarding War Diaries and Intelligence Summaries are contained in F. S. Regs., Part II. and the Staff Manual respectively. Title pages will be prepared in manuscript.

Place	Date	Hour	Summary of Events and Information	Remarks and references to Appendices
Rieux	26.XI 18		Nothing to report.	CM
"	27.XI 18		Proceeded to Avesnes took over site of old Corps Main dressing Station.	CM
"	28.XI 18		Capt [illegible] & party reported from [illegible]	CM
"	29.XI 18		At Avesnes.	CM
	30.XI 18		Proceeded by march route to Cambrai & joined Hay Reeds in billets on the way to rejoin the division	C[illegible] [illegible]

[illegible] F.A.

11

Instructions regarding War Diaries and Intelligence Summaries are contained in F. S. Regs., Part II. and the Staff Manual respectively. Title pages will be prepared in manuscript.

WAR DIARY
or
INTELLIGENCE SUMMARY.

(*Erase heading not required.*)

Army Form C. 2118.

WO 95/2042

Place	Date	Hour	Summary of Events and Information	Remarks and references to Appendices
Dec 1918			War Diary of 57 Field Ambulance	140/34 81
			For December 1918. Volume 41	

A7092). Wt. W12839/M1297 750,000. 1/17. D. D & L., Ltd. Forms/C2118/14.

Instructions regarding War Diaries and Intelligence Summaries are contained in F. S. Regs., Part II. and the Staff Manual respectively. Title pages will be prepared in manuscript.

WAR DIARY
or
INTELLIGENCE SUMMARY.
(Erase heading not required.)

Army Form C. 2118.

Place	Date	Hour	Summary of Events and Information	Remarks and references to Appendices
Cambrai	1.12.18		Left Cambrai by route march + reached Favreuil.	
Favreuil	2.12.18		Left Favreuil by march route + reached St Leger, billeting there for night.	
Havernas	3.12.18		Reached Havernas at 16.00 + billeted in Chateau + village	
"	4.12.18		Collecting sick of 56th Bde from neighbouring villages + evacuating to 18 C.C.S.	
	5.12.18		No accommodation in village for Hospital can be found + all cases sent straight to C.C.S.	
"	8.12.18		56th Bde will move from present area date unknown.	
	9.12 to 16th		Nothing to report. Remaining at Havernas collecting 56th Bde sick.	[initials]

A7092). Wt. W12839/M1293 750,000. 1/17. D. D & L., Ltd. Forms/C2118/14.

Instructions regarding War Diaries and Intelligence Summaries are contained in F. S. Regs., Part II. and the Staff Manual respectively. Title pages will be prepared in manuscript.

WAR DIARY

or

INTELLIGENCE SUMMARY.

(Erase heading not required.)

Army Form C. 2118.

Place	Date	Hour	Summary of Events and Information	Remarks and references to Appendices
NOEUX.	17.12.18		Arrived at NOEUX at 1500 hrs. Billeted in camp at Chateau + in village. Collecting sick from 55th Div + evacuating to 6 Stat. Hosp.	
"	18.12.18		Arranged billets for all personnel in village & preparing camp for Hospital.	
"	19.12.18		2 Hosp. Nissen huts promised by C.R.E. one to be used as recreation room for men.	
"	20.12.18		1 Hosp. Hut arrived + erection commenced in village.	
"	21.12.18		2nd Hut arrived for erection in Chateau grounds.	
"	22.12.18		Capt. A.G. Dunbar reported his arrival back from leave in Paris.	

A7092). Wt. W12839/M1297 750,000. 1/17. D. D & L., Ltd. Forms/C2118/14.

Instructions regarding War Diaries and Intelligence Summaries are contained in F. S. Regs., Part II. and the Staff Manual respectively. Title pages will be prepared in manuscript.

WAR DIARY
or
~~INTELLIGENCE SUMMARY.~~
(Erase heading not required.)

Army Form C. 2118.

Place	Date	Hour	Summary of Events and Information	Remarks and references to Appendices
NOEUX	23/12/18	9.0pm.	Good progress has been made with erection of the H.P. Nissen hut in the village.	
	24/12/18	9.0pm	Lt. Col. C.T. Edmunds reported his departure on 14 days special leave to England, temporary command being assumed by Major G.P. Kidd.	
	25/12/18	9.0pm	The day was spent in entertainments & special meals for the personnel.	
	26/12/18	9.0pm	The large Nissen Hut in the Chateau grounds is now being cleared & fitted up as a hospital for detaining and treating slight cases from the Brigade.	
	27/12/18	9.0pm	The hospital is now ready for the reception of slight cases. Cases are now to be kept (excluding Influenza) which are likely to be well in 10 days.	
	28/12/18	9.0pm.	I visited B.R.C.S. stores with reference to indent put in by me for hospital furniture etc, but found that there does not seem to be much prospect of obtaining same for some time. The weather continues very bad with much rain almost every day.	
	29/12/18	9.0pm	I visited M.T. workshops with reference to repairs to our cars as we have now only one car running and this is not sufficient.	
	30/12/18	9.0pm	The recreation hut in the village is now practically finished and the second one is now ready for erection when R.E. material is available.	
	31/12/18	9.0pm.	I sent Capt. Dunbar to relieve Maj. Smalley on temp. duty with [illegible] this army	

G.P. Kidd
Major RAMC
Commanding 1/[illegible] Fd Amb.

A7092). Wt. W12839/M1293 750,000. 1/17. D. D & L., Ltd. Forms/C2118/14.

AD/8/MR.

B.D.M.S., XVII Corps.

SANITARY REPORT OF A.D.M.S. 19th DIVISION
FOR MONTH OF DECEMBER. 1918.

1. During December, the 19th Division has occupied an area West of DOULLENS - re-arrangement of troops continued to take place up to 20th December ; this continual movement of units has greatly retarded the organization of the area.

2. BILLETS.

Mens billets consist of (a) Army huts - (b) Barns. The former have been put up by the troops and are mostly Nissen huts. The latter are for the most part small barns with earth floors and mud walls, damp, draughty and uncomfortable. Wire beds are being made but at present many men are sleeping on the floor. Palliasses have been received for each man in the Division. Tables and forms are required.

Heating is deficient in many of the barns; stoves not being allowed owing to the presence of straw.

Lighting is notably deficient. During the day-time many billets are so dark it is not possible to read in them. During the darkness candles only are available and that in insufficient quantities. On the whole, although progress has been made, living conditions for the majority of men are still very hard.

3. FEEDING.

Rations have been good. Cooking at present in most units is done on Field Cookers and improvised fireplaces.

Unit dining rooms are being made everywhere and along with these unit kitchens are being erected. very few of them are yet in use ; meanwhile kitchen equipment leaves much to be desired.

4. CLOTHING.

There has been a difficulty in obtaining new boots or leather for repairing old ones - this shortage has now been overcome.

Each man has received a third blanket.

5. BATHS & LAUNDRY.

There is plenty of bathing accommodation although the baths themselves are small and scattered all over the Divisional Area. Sufficient clean clothing is also received to enable men's underclothing to be changed every ten days.

/ 6. DISINFECTION.

6. DISINFECTION.

Men are on the whole free from lice. They now receive clean underclothing and baths regularly every ten days. Skin inspections by Regimental Medical Officers are regularly held. Irons and brushes are available in each Company or similar unit.

As soon as can be arranged delousers will be put up at each bath to delouse men's service dress while they bathe.

At present the Foden is making a tour of the Units of the Division completely delousing them platoon by platoon.

7. WATER.

Water is drawn from wells - in some cases organised piped supply is in use. It is chlorinated in water carts under unit arrangements. Certain units being isolated some good distance from a good water point have been allotted water lorries.

8. CONSERVATION.

Latrines are of the deep pit type - practically all now have fly-proof seats, but more superstructures and duckboard tracks are required.

Refuse is burned and buried ; incinerators exist in most villages. Manure is carted into fields.

9. INFECTIOUS DISEASE.

The following cases have been reported during the month :-

Measles ..... 7 cases.
Scarlet Fever ..... 1 case.

The Measles cases came from units as follows :-

(a) 88th Brigade R.F.A. ..... 3 cases.
(b) 1/4th K.S.L.Inf. ..... 3 cases.
(c) 9th Welsh R. ..... 1 case.

Contacts are isolated and medically inspected daily. Billets have been disinfected and the blankets of all contacts passed through the Foden.

10. Influenza & P.U.O. 330 cases of P.U.O. and Influenza have been recorded during the month and of these one hundred and seventy two were diagnosed "Influenza".

As every cases of Pyrexia has been evacuated to Casualty Clearing Station many mild cases have been passed through which in ordinary times would be kept in Field Ambulance.

Diarrhoea - The incidence of this disease has been low.

Scabies. - Nineteen cases of this disease have been recorded.

D F McKenzie

Lieut.Colonel,
A/ A.D.M.S., 19th. Division.

1/1/19.

War Diary

Os.C. Field Ambulances.
M.Os.i/c Units.

A.M.A/59.

The following addition should be made to 19th Division Medical Arrangements No.59 :-

V. DENTAL CASES.

(a) Units whose sick are collected by No.57 Field Ambulance.

Cases will be seen (whether Officers or O.Ranks) by arrangements direct with O.C. No.57 Field Ambulance.

(b) Units whose sick are collected by Nos.58 & 59 Field Ambulances.

Cases will be sent to Field Ambulance on Sundays to see the Dental Surgeon on Mondays. Vacancies however are limited, and the following arrangements necessary for ensuring that the vacancies are all used, and that men are not sent in when they cannot be seen.

M.Os.i/c Units will notify Os.C. Field Ambulance collecting their sick, by 16.00 hours on Saturdays the number of vacancies they desire. Os.C. Field Ambulances will then wire the same evening the number of vacancies allotted, and will arrange for their collection next day.

Officers will be seen any day at No. 18 C.C.S. DOULLENS by direct arrangement between M.O.i/c Unit and O.C. No. 18 C.C.S.

A.D.M.S.,
19th DIVISION.
No.
27/12/18.
Date

[signature]
Major.
D.A.D.M.S. 19th Division.

To all recipients of Medical Arrangements 19th Divn. No. 59.

11

Jan. 1919

19 DIV

Box 1795

57th
FIELD
AMBULANCE.

No.............

Date.............

Vol 43

War Diary

of 57 Field Ambulance. R.A.M.C.

From 1-1-19 to 31-1-19

Volume 43.

Instructions regarding War Diaries and Intelligence Summaries are contained in F. S. Regs., Part II. and the Staff Manual respectively. Title pages will be prepared in manuscript.

WAR DIARY
or
~~INTELLIGENCE SUMMARY.~~
(Erase heading not required.)

Army Form C. 2118.

Place	Date	Hour	Summary of Events and Information	Remarks and references to Appendices
NOEUX	1/1/19	9.0 pm	I visited the A.D.M.S. today re question of shortage of cars. One large car will be sent down by 59. [illegible]. I sent Capt. Dunbar today to relieve Major Smalley for temp. duty with A.A.D.C. Third Army.	[initials]
"	2/1/19	9.0 pm	Lieut & QM. T. Armitage reported his arrival back from leave to England. A [illegible] quantity of material was drawn from the R.E. today for construction purposes.	[initials]
"	3/1/19	9.0 pm	Nothing to report.	[initials]
"	4/1/19	9.0 pm	Confidential report on all Officers as called for in G.R.O. 5822, [illegible] in to A.D.M.S.	[initials]
"	5/1/19	9.0 pm	Nothing to report.	[initials]
"	6/1/19	9.0 pm	a/A.D.M.S. visited the unit this afternoon and inspected the Hospital and all arrangements. D.D.M.S. will probably visit & inspect the unit on the 17th inst.	[initials]
"	7/1/19	9.0 pm	Capt. H.D. Owens reported his departure this morning for England for demobilization, auth. [illegible]	[initials]
"	8/1/19	9.0 pm	A new M.O. having been now posted to 58. Bde R.H.A., the sick of this unit have no longer to be seen by us.	[initials]
"	9/1/19 10/1/19	9.0 pm	Nothing to report.	[initials]
"	11/1/19 12/1/19	9.0 pm -	Nothing to report.	[initials]
	13/1/19 14/1/19 15/1/19	-	The second [illegible] Nissen hut is now almost completed and will be ready for use in a few days. [illegible] work has also been done in improving [illegible] during the past week. Sick admission rate still keeping very low. One case of measles from [illegible]. 15/1/19	[initials]

A7092) Wt. W12839/M1294 750,000. 1/17. D. D & L., Ltd. Forms/C2118/14.

Army Form C. 2118.

Instructions regarding War Diaries and Intelligence Summaries are contained in F. S. Regs., Part II. and the Staff Manual respectively. Title pages will be prepared in manuscript.

WAR DIARY
or
~~INTELLIGENCE SUMMARY~~.

(Erase heading not required.)

Place	Date	Hour	Summary of Events and Information	Remarks and references to Appendices
NOEUX	16/1/19	9.0pm	D.D.M.S. XIII Corps ~~visited~~ visited and inspected the unit & hospital today. He expressed himself as satisfied with everything he saw.	[illegible]
"	17/1/19 18/1/19	9.0pm	Nothing to report.	[illegible]
"	19/1/19 20/1/19	9.0pm	Nothing to report.	[illegible]
"	21/1/19	9.0pm	Order received for early release of Major A.A. Smalley.	[illegible]
"	22/1/19	9.0pm	Lieut Col. C.G. Edmunds reported his arrival back from leave & resumed command of the unit.	[illegible]
"	23.1.19	21.00 hrs	Nothing to report.	[illegible]
"	25.1.19	21 hrs	Brig. Gen. Heath inspected the unit. Also the A.D.M.S. 19th Div.	[illegible]
"	27.1.19	21 hrs	Maj. Smalley left for England to be demobilised under A.D.M.S. [illegible]	[illegible]
"	28.1.19	21 hrs.	Sgt. Maj. Doran ASC left the unit for demobilisation.	[illegible]
"	29.1.19	21 hrs	Conference of O.C. F.A.s & [illegible] at A.D.M.S. office to discuss the new [illegible] of F.A. as 2 sections.	[illegible]
"	30.1.19	21 hrs.	Sgt. Maj. Wyse, 1 Sergeant & 6 men left at 09.00 hrs en route for S.D.M.S. Rouen via 59 Field Ambulance, for duty in connection with medical [illegible]	[illegible]
				[illegible]

A7092). Wt. W12839/M1291 750,000. 1/17. D. D & L., Ltd. Forms/C2118/14.

Feb. 1919 11

140/3524

War Diary VIII 44

of 57 Field Ambulance FRANCE

From 1-2-19 to 28-2-19

Volume 44.

Instructions regarding War Diaries and Intelligence Summaries are contained in F. S. Regs., Part II. and the Staff Manual respectively. Title pages will be prepared in manuscript.

WAR DIARY
or
INTELLIGENCE SUMMARY.

(Erase heading not required.)

Army Form C. 2118.

Place	Date	Hour	Summary of Events and Information	Remarks and references to Appendices
NOEUX	1.2.19	21.00	Nothing to report.	
"	3.2.19	21.00	At present 6 cases in Hosp.	
"	5.2.19	21.00	The Divisional Commander inspected the Hospital & billets.	
"	6.2.19	21.00	Nothing to report.	
"	7.2.19	21.00	ditto.	
"	9.2.19	21.00.	ditto.	
"	11.2.19	21.00.	Owing to intense cold & fuel difficulty, the large Hospital Nissen was closed & the patients put into a smaller hut.	
"	13.2.19	21.00	Nothing to report	
"	15.2.19	21.00	Two men demobilised. Cases from 1st Div. Art. now sent to us by M.A.C. car	
"	16.2.19	21.00	Two men demobilised. Maj. Read [illegible]	
"	18.2.19	21.00	Nothing to report	

A7092). Wt. W12839/M1293 750,000. 1/17. D. D & L., Ltd. Forms/C2118/14.

Instructions regarding War Diaries and Intelligence Summaries are contained in F. S. Regs., Part II. and the Staff Manual respectively. Title pages will be prepared in manuscript.

WAR DIARY
or
INTELLIGENCE SUMMARY.

(Erase heading not required.)

Army Form C. 2118.

Place	Date	Hour	Summary of Events and Information	Remarks and references to Appendices
NSEUX?	21.2.19	21.00	Seven? men demobilised.	[illegible]
"	22.2.19	21.00	Nothing to report.	[illegible]
"	23.2.19	21.00	Conference at A.D.M.S. Office [illegible] arrangements [illegible] of H.D. [illegible] to [illegible] Field Ambulance.	[illegible]
"	24.2.19	21.00	Capt. [illegible] evacuated to [illegible] of [illegible] Bde [illegible] to [illegible] Hospital.	[illegible]
"	25.2.19	21.00	Nothing to report.	[illegible]
"	26.2.19	21.00	Capt. [illegible] left [illegible] to take over [illegible] [illegible] Bde.	[illegible]

A7092. Wt. W12839/M1293 750,000. 1/17. D. D. & L., Ltd. Forms/C2118/14.

140/3551

Mar. 1919

War Diary Vol 45

of 57 Field Ambulance

from 1-3-19 to 31-3-19

Volume 45.

Instructions regarding War Diaries and Intelligence Summaries are contained in F. S. Regs., Part II. and the Staff Manual respectively. Title pages will be prepared in manuscript.

WAR DIARY

or

INTELLIGENCE SUMMARY.

(Erase heading not required.)

Army Form C. 2118.

Place	Date	Hour	Summary of Events and Information	Remarks and references to Appendices
MOEUX	1.3.19	21.00	Nothing to report	
"	2.3.19	21.00	Maj [illegible] arrived back from leave	
"	3.3.19	21.00	Nothing to report.	
"	4.3.19	21.00	Nothing to report.	
"	7.3.19	21.00	Seven men sent for demobilisation [illegible]	
"	8.3.19	21.00	Six men & 1 Lt. transferred [illegible] 2 men of this unit [illegible] 2 men additional [illegible] who are [illegible] to be sent [illegible]	
"	9.3.19	21.00.	Nothing to report.	C.P.
"	10.3.19	21.00.	Orders for return of C [illegible] ordnance equipment received, also orders from Bde re [illegible] transport at Caudas rail head	C.P.

A7092). Wt. W12839/M1297 750,000. 1/17. D. D. & L., Ltd. Forms/C2118/14.

Instructions regarding War Diaries and Intelligence Summaries are contained in F. S. Regs., Part II. and the Staff Manual respectively. Title pages will be prepared in manuscript.

WAR DIARY
or
~~INTELLIGENCE SUMMARY.~~
(Erase heading not required.)

Army Form C. 2118.

Place	Date	Hour	Summary of Events and Information	Remarks and references to Appendices
NOEUX	Week 11/3/19 – 18/3/19	–	Nothing to report.	[illegible initials]
"	18–24/3/19	–	All waggons except four have now been sent to park at CANDAS. 19. D.H.Q. has now ceased to function and Divisional remnants are being administered by 58. Bde.	[illegible initials]
VILLERS L'HÔPITAL	25/3/19	–	Unit moved to VILLERS L'HÔPITAL and was accommodated in the 56 F.A. camp.	[illegible initials]
"	26/3/19	–	All C Section equipment has now been handed in and all equipment and stores surplus to [illegible]. Equipment has been got rid of. Lt. Col. C.T. Edmunds is now acting as S.M.O. 58 Bde. Rate of demobilization is still very slow – only two men per week being sent. The unit is now not keeping any sick.	[illegible initials]
"	27–28/3/19	–	Nothing to report.	[illegible initials]
"	29/3/19	–	Orders received that the cadre strength will only include one Med. Officer. All officers other than the C.O. and Q.M. are therefore struck off the strength from today and transferred to the RAMC strength of the DOULLENS area.	
"	30–31/3/19	–	Two RASC (H.T.) and one RASC (M.T.) were demobilized yesterday.	

[illegible signature]
Lieut. Col. RAMC
Commanding 57 Fd. Amb.

NO DIARY
FOR APRIL
1919

VR 47

Cased

War Diary

of 57 Field Ambulance.

From 1-5-19 to 21-5-19

Volume 47.

Completed

Instructions regarding War Diaries and Intelligence Summaries are contained in F. S. Regs., Part II. and the Staff Manual respectively. Title pages will be prepared in manuscript.

WAR DIARY
or
INTELLIGENCE SUMMARY.

(Erase heading not required.)

Army Form C. 2118.

Place	Date	Hour	Summary of Events and Information	Remarks and references to Appendices
Villers Hope	1.5.19		One demobilisation vacancy allotted to under Corps C.C. on 4.5.19.	CW
	2.5.19		Notice received that Field Ambulance cadre will be reduced to 2 off & 46 O.R.	CW
	3.5.19		Nothing to report	CW
	5.5.19		Orders received that F.A. cadre further reduced to 1 off & 46 OR the officer in question being to [illegible]	CW
	6-8/5/19		Nothing to report.	CW
	9.5.19		Orders received that remainder of F.A. cadre will be 10 Rank & 4 A.S.C. M.T.	CW

A7092). Wt. W12839/M1297 750,000. 1/17. D. D & L., Ltd. Forms/C2118/14.

Army Form C. 2118.

Instructions regarding War Diaries and Intelligence Summaries are contained in F. S. Regs., Part II. and the Staff Manual respectively. Title pages will be prepared in manuscript.

WAR DIARY
or
INTELLIGENCE SUMMARY.
(Erase heading not required.)

Place	Date	Hour	Summary of Events and Information	Remarks and references to Appendices
[illegible] Hosp.	10.5.19		Endeavouring to arrange for the demobilisation of 4 A.S.C. M.T. Orders received for embarking at [illegible] on 14.5.19.	CR
"	11.5.19 12.5.19		Nothing to report.	CR
"	14.5.19		Handed command of 57 Field Ambulance over to Lieut T. Armitage. Under instructions received from Corps Demob: Officer for A.S.C. the 4 A.S.C. remained surplus to cadre will be taken home with the unit 4 OR RAMC being left behind for demobilisation on 16.5.19. Took over command from Lt Col C T Edmunds D.S.O.	CR T.A.
	15.5.19		Arrived Le Havre at 8.30 a.m. & proceeded to dispatch camp	T.A.
	16th to 20.5.19		Nothing to report	T.A.
	21.5.19		Embarked for England.	

T Armitage Lt RAMC
oc Cadre 57th Field Amb.

www.ingramcontent.com/pod-product-compliance
Lightning Source LLC
Chambersburg PA
CBHW081425300426
44108CB00016BA/2302